Lecture Notes in Computer Science   12521

More information about this subseries at http://www.springer.com/series/7407

Marco Aiello · Athman Bouguettaya ·
Damian Andrew Tamburri ·
Willem-Jan van den Heuvel (Eds.)

Next-Gen Digital Services

A Retrospective and Roadmap
for Service Computing of the Future

Essays Dedicated to Michael Papazoglou
on the Occasion of His 65th Birthday
and His Retirement

 Springer

Editors
Marco Aiello ⓘ
University of Stuttgart
Stuttgart, Germany

Athman Bouguettaya
The University of Sydney
Camperdown, NSW, Australia

Damian Andrew Tamburri ⓘ
Eindhoven University of Technology
's Hertogenbosch, The Netherlands

Willem-Jan van den Heuvel
Tilburg University
's Hertogenbosch, The Netherlands

ISSN 0302-9743   ISSN 1611-3349   (electronic)
Lecture Notes in Computer Science
ISBN 978-3-030-73202-8   ISBN 978-3-030-73203-5   (eBook)
https://doi.org/10.1007/978-3-030-73203-5

LNCS Sublibrary: SL1 – Theoretical Computer Science and General Issues

The next generation of software services computing; transversal domains are supported with incrementally-defined abstractions towards value, with the service construct as the underlying enabler for all layers.

This Springer imprint is published by the registered company Springer Nature Switzerland AG
The registered company address is: Gewerbestrasse 11, 6330 Cham, Switzerland

Preface

Our generation has witnessed a radical shift in computing: the move from computation being a commodity to it becoming a utility, an on-demand, scale-free, always-available service. If fifty years ago the focus was on building and programming the most impressive piece of hardware and equipment, today we talk about digital services being ubiquitously available, even in connection to the everyday things that we interact with. It is not about the impressive computation the laptops or mobile phones in our hands can do, but what actual problems we can solve while interacting with potentially hundreds—if not more—of remote services.

Shifts like this happen—most often unplanned—as the direct result of a common effort of research and development, as a result of striving to solve current and future societal needs. A small project of organizing data of a European physics research center can turn into a technology like the Web that disrupts basic societal interactions. Most often it is not the intention of an individual to change the world, but simply the idea of inventing something new, useful, and possibly fun. These are pioneers that are willing to explore new territories, possibly taking undetermined risks, but all for the possibility to achieve major success or fail in the process. These are people with highly developed senses that breath the innovation to come and are ahead of the game, people who can visualize the possible future and describe it before it happens. Mike Papazoglou has been and is one such visionary and expert, someone who saw how the combination of advances in middleware technology, software engineering techniques, and the emergence of the Web would change forever the way in which we built information systems and, most importantly, would change how organizations work and people are supported. The links and ramifications of the concepts and theories that Mike defined or inspired do not stop here.

Mike was born on December 2nd, 1953 in Cairo to Greek parents, Pandelis and Despina (Varvounis) Papazoglou. Soon the family moved back to Greece. For his higher education, Mike decided to go to the United Kingdom and Scotland in particular. He obtained a Bachelor of Science in Electronics with honours from the University of Dundee, a Master of Science in Computer Science from the University of Edinburgh, and a Doctor of Philosophy (PhD) in Electronic Engineering and Computer Systems from the University of Dundee in 1982 with a thesis entitled "The Parallel SIMULA Machine".

After his education he returned once again to Greece and accepted his first post as a Research Associate at the Nuclear Research Center of Athens (Demokritos), where he stayed from 1979 to 1981. That year he moved as a senior lecturer to the University of Patras, where he remained until 1984. During that period he participated in the GRASPIN ESPRIT I project, funded with 7.5 million ECU, the European currency of the time, which set the foundations for the EURO introduced a few years later. The project aimed at the implementation of a software engineering environment supporting the development of non-sequential and distributed software systems. The consortium was led by the German Gesellschaft für Mathematik und Datenverarbeitung (GMD), now part of the Fraunhofer Gesellschaft.

The collaboration with GMD was so rewarding that he left Patras and joined the GMD in St. Augustin in 1984 as a project leader at the National German Research Institute of Computer Science, GMD. Here, he became interested in database technology and published his first book on relational database management in 1989. Not only did this book pursue a specific systems programming approach, he and a younger colleague also developed a running system that implemented all the novel concepts and methods taught in this book. During his period in Germany, he was also a visiting professor in the Department of Informatics at the University of Koblenz from 1988 to 1989.

The next move would prove to be a long one. In 1989 Mike moved to Australia to join the Australian National University in Canberra as associate professor. Just two years later, in 1991, Mike moved to the Queensland University of Technology (QUT), Brisbane, Australia as Head of the School of Information Systems and full professor. The next year at the IFIP WG2.6 Database Semantics Conference on Interoperable Database Systems (DS-5), held in Lorne, Australia he met a freshly graduated Athman Bougettaya and invited him to join his research group. Henceforth started a great and long professional and personal relationship between the two. Mike was the perfect mentor, spending a lot of time and effort guiding the young scientist through the process of being an effective and successful academic. They were quite successful at attracting major grants. Mike was instrumental in broadening Athman's horizon in the area of databases, encouraging him to explore the use of emerging middleware architectures such as CORBA as a vehicle to address challenges to interoperating autonomous and heterogeneous databases. Passionate and thorough as he is, he founded a new International Journal of Cooperative Information Systems in 1992 whose Editor-in-Chief he has since been.

After Athman moved to the USA to take up a position at Virginia Tech, the collaboration continued especially exploring new models for interoperating databases, which led to the definition of the emerging area of e-services (a precursor to service computing). Their first paper in the area of services dates back to 2000, presented at the International Workshop on Technologies for E-Services. Little did they know that that area would result in a highly successful research community. There is no doubt that Mike was the single most important factor in starting and sustaining the area of service computing!

The next challenge brought him to Tilburg University, The Netherlands, where he took a Chair in Computer Science in May 1996, and also became Director of the INFOLAB. With his unbridled energy, Mike built up an energetic team around the joint objective of supporting the design and development of IT tools able to access, synthesize, and reason about large volumes of distributed information. Under the guidance of Mike, the INFOLAB would quickly grow out to a research institute with international stature, and a visibility way beyond the Netherlands. He initiated many EU and national research projects around that time, including the prestigious ESPIRIT projects: TREVI on NLP and AI avant-la-lettre for the purpose of European ontology-centric news filtering and enrichment, and MEMO on interoperability issues in electronic commerce marketplaces. Together with Bernd Krämer, he acquired one of the first international collaboration projects between the EU and the Australian Research Council on Information Systems Interoperability, which led to one of the first anthologies on the topic. In addition Mike continued to be very active editing and authoring several seminal works such as "Cooperative Information Systems" that he co-edited with Gunter Schlageter, and, "Advances in Object-Oriented Data Modeling" co-edited with Stefano Spaccapietra and Zahir Tari in 2000.

In 2002, Mike started a long-lasting collaboration with the University of Trento, in Northern Italy. The goal was to support the foundation of a Service-Oriented Computing research unit. Marco Aiello, Vincenzo D'Andrea, and Maurizio Marchese were recruited to this unit. Soon it became clear that results in Service-Oriented Computing were unconventional and that it was hard to define an audience for them. Information Systems, Software Engineering, and Distributed Computing venues could not place them, or at least not entirely, as the subject was so multidisciplinary, so well-varied that conventional communities would not be able to nourish research results into thriving.

It was then that Mike understood the importance of giving a shelter to the sprouting community of service computing and decided to start a new series of conferences, The International Conference on Services Computing, or ICSOC for short. The first edition was held in Trento in the winter of 2003. It has now reached its 18th edition and it is considered the premier venue for all Service-Computing related research results. Since its birth it has seen the number of related and similar events grow very fast, as a further indication that a new community was born. To increase leverage of this quickly emerging discipline, at the same time he initiated a new subline of Springer's Lecture Notes in Computer Science entitled Service Science.

Even while being exceedingly busy shaping this conference and driving the SOC research community at large, Mike continued to author books next to his purely academic book undertakings, including a popular book on the technical and organizational foundations of E-Business, published by Wiley in 2006 and co-authored with Piet Ribbers. He also authored a seminal reference "bible" on the principles and technologies underpinning Web services that was originally published in 2007, with a second edition appearing in 2012 from Prentice Hall.

If this were not enough for the extremely energetic and creative scholar that Mike is, he was instrumental in setting up the EU's FP-7 flagships Network of Excellence on Software Services and Systems, named S-CUBE (2008–2012). For five years he acted as the scientific mastermind building bridges between scientific disciplines that—until then—operated in sheer isolation, such as grid computing, service composition, and business process management. S-CUBE turned out to be the birthplace of many new EU project initiatives, including COMPAS (on service compliance; 2008–2012), 4CAaaST (on PaaS cloud of the future; 2010–2013), SAPIENSA (on service enabled of legacy applications; 2009–2012), and H2020 projects DOSSIERCloud (on DevOps for distributed systems development; 2016–2018), and more recently DESTINI (on smart data processing and systems of deep insight; 2019–2022).

Proceeding in the direction of promoting the thriving software services research community, fuelled behind ICSOC as the flagship event, Mike continued his innovation mission, culminating with a major hand in initiating JADS—the Jheronimus Academy of Data Science in s-Hertogenbosch, The Netherlands—as a joint institute of excellence for Data Sciences and Data-Driven Services Entrepreneurship captained by

Tilburg University and Eindhoven University of Technology. Mike played the role of the pioneer, advising in the management and scientific shaping of the nascent institute together with his pupil from Tilburg University, Willem-Jan van den Heuvel. All in all, key people in Mike's path like Willem-Jan are continuously progressing in pursuing Mike's mission. Willem-Jan currently governs the largest lab in the institute, namely, the Jheronimus Academy Data and Engineering (JADE) Lab together with younger pupils of both Mike and Willem-Jan's like Damian A. Tamburri, who continue the mission of previous institutes captained by Mike such as the European Research Institute on Service Sciences (ERISS).

During such a diverse, successful, global career, Mike has had the opportunity to collaborate, inspire, and mentor many researchers. Many of them have enthusiastically accepted the invitation to contribute to the present volume, which exists to celebrate the achievements of Mike Papazoglou over an incredible career on the Occasion of his 65th birthday and his retirement. The volume broadly focuses on digital services and their next generation. It is organized in five parts: History, Service Engineering, Services and Humans, IoT, and Data & Services.

The history part of the volume contains two chapters highlighting the evolution from component-oriented software development practices to service-orientation, and a short history on service composition. In the first chapter (Chapter 1), Giuseppe De Giacomo, Maurizio Lenzerini, Francesco Leotta, and Massimo Mecella from the University of Rome La Sapienza retrace the evolution of components in software design. From the early days of component-based software architectures till the present days of micro service-based ones, passing through the changes brought about by a pervasive Internet and Web, and all the consequences these have had for middleware and information systems. The second historical chapter (Chapter 2) of this volume is dedicated to the issue of dynamic service composition, which is, most likely, the most interesting and problematic opportunity offered by Service-Oriented Systems. The idea is that if services are available programmatically, then one can write software to invoke them on demand. Alexander Lazovik, Eirini Kaldeli, and Michel Medema first recall the history of (Web) service composition and then provide details of their approach based on AI Planning that has been developed through the years.

The second part of the book, which is also the largest, is devoted to various aspects of Service Engineering, covering architectures, designs, frameworks, patterns, and requirements. The first chapter of this part (Chapter 3), by Vasilios Andrikopoulos and Patricia Lago, is dedicated to software architecting and it argues for the need for approaches that include software sustainability. Here, sustainability refers to the societal and environmental aspects of services. The chapter includes a proposal specified for cloud models, including a framework for managing sustainability indicators for services. In the second chapter on Service Engineering (Chapter 4), Andreas Andreou and Andreas Christoforou consider the problem of migrating existing software and functionalities to the service paradigm. The first step is to decompose monolithic systems into components in order to obtain a Service-Oriented architecture out of the original system. To this end, fuzzy techniques are employed. The second step consists of providing techniques for automatic service composition. The third chapter of this module (Chapter 5) is a contribution by Frank Leymann and Johanna Barzen, focusing on a vision of an all-encompassing tool, the pattern atlas, that supports building complex systems based on pattern languages. The analogy to cartography motivates the name of the tool. The fourth chapter (Chapter 6), by Khalid Belhajjame and Daniela Grigori, focuses on the reuse of service-based workflows. Service-based workflows are implemented by operations that are provided by services. More specifically, two key operations that cater for workflow reuse, namely search and preservation, are addressed. The fifth chapter in the second part of the volume (Chapter 7) has been authored by Amal Elgammal and Bernd Krämer, and introduces and explores a novel reference architecture for personalized prevention and patient management through a smart healthcare platform that is not only agile, robust, reliable, secured, and scalable, but also allows integration of data of all sorts and sizes along pre-existing standards. The sixth and last chapter of this module (Chapter 8), by John Mylopoulos, Daniel Amyot, Luigi Logrippo, Alireza Parvizimosaed, and Sepehr Sharifi, overviews the social requirements models of services. In particular, the focus is on the concept of social dependencies as a mechanism to capture social modeling as found in business processes and legal contract modeling. Of particular interest is the use of such social dependencies as commitments, obligations, and powers.

Services and Humans constitutes the third part of the volume. At the end of the day, Service-Oriented Computing is not really about software services; instead, it is about the humans for whom they have been conceived. This module is composed of five chapters that place emphasis on human-related challenges, including cognitive aspects, context-awareness, as well as how to deliver the new generation of IT service engineers and managers. The first chapter in this module (Chapter 9), by Sergio Laso, Javier Berrocal, Jose Garcia-Alonso, Carlos Canal, and Juan M. Murillo, focuses on humans as service providers in service computing. In particular, human microservices are proposed as a mechanism and architecture to model humans as service providers. New human-in-the-loop challenges are described as they relate to service computing. The next chapter (Chapter 10), by Moshe Chai Barukh, Shayan Zamanirad, Marcos Baez, Amin Beheshti, Boualem Benatallah, Fabio Casati, Lina Yao, Quan Z. Sheng, and Francesco Schiliro, focuses on the use of cognitive augmentation in processes. This is a relatively new and promising area of business process management. The idea is to add layers of cognitive augmentation that combine advances in machine-automation, crowdsourcing and adaptation, and reasoning to address the emerging requirements of highly changeable environments. Moreover, this visionary chapter illustrates future challenges with real-world use cases, and suggests a roadmap for future research that revolves around a well-structured framework for cognitive augmentation. The following chapter (Chapter 11) then continues with a contribution from Michael Sheng, Jian Yu, Wei Emma Zhang, Shuang Wang, Xiaoping Li, and Boualem Benatallah. This chapter revolves around the ContextServ project, which aims to deliver a platform for model-driven development of context-aware services, based on a UML-based modeling language and able to construct smart applications that integrate and ingest data from IoT devices. The chapter not only describes the global setup and architectural approach of the platform, but also surveys representative research efforts in the literature. The fifth and final chapter of this part (Chapter 12) is from Esperanza Marcos, María Valeria De Castro, and Juan Manuel Vara, presenting an analysis of the knowledge and skills that IT service engineers should attain to set up and manage innovation, design, and construction of new services in the sphere of IT, along with their effective management in organizational settings. This analysis revolves around the pioneering degree in Software Services Management and Engineering (SSME) that is delivered at the Rey Juan Carlos University (URJC) in Madrid, whose objective is the specific and integral training of service professionals.

The fourth part of the book addresses the relation of the Internet of Things (IoT) with services. Emerging topics address how conventional software services can be blended with edge computing, deal with semantic "skimpiness" of typical IoT data, and how their security can be leveraged through technologies such as homomorphic encryption. The first chapter (Chapter 13) entitled "Towards IoT Processes on the Edge", written by Schahram Dustdar and Ilir Murturi, sets out to overview and discuss research issues that are at the intersection of the domains of business processes engineering and edge computing. The chapter argues that distributing processing data closer to the end-users through edge devices holds the potential to address several operational and business challenges. Zakaria Maamar, Noura Faci, and Fadwa Inaya provide the next contributed book chapter (Chapter 14), which deals with issues about and the next steps to servitize the Internet-of-Things. In particular, the authors propose an OWL-based ontological framework (OWL-T) as a solution to the no-semantics shortcoming from which many IoT solutions suffer, alluding to the fact that the data stemming from these devices are generally (close to) meaningless, and thus hard to integrate. A research roadmap for a full-fledged servitization framework is suggested. The next chapter contribution (Chapter 15) is from Lara Kallab, Richard Chbeir, and Michael Mrissa. In this chapter, they address the challenging problem of how to effectively select Web Of Things (WoT) types of objects as RESTful services, in an environment that is increasingly populated with services with the same functionalities, and where resource qualities such as availability are getting more and more brittle and shaky, and thus more unpredictable. Here, the concept of Quality of Resource (QoR) may come to the rescue. In particular, in this chapter, a QoR-driven resource selection approach is proposed that considers QoR constraints and Inputs/Outputs matching of related resources, as well as resource availability and users' different requirements. The approach is evaluated against existing ones, and experiments are conducted in various environments to better understand its performance. In the final chapter of the fourth part of this book (Chapter 16), Ali Yavari and Dimitrios Georgakopoulos address a critical aspect of IoT-based applications: the security of the IoT data and related applications. The proposed technique entails homomorphic encryption. The chapter not only discusses the main aspects in securing IoT applications and data but also introduces a holistic and lightweight IoT security mechanism that uniquely blends homomorphic encryption and contextualization to prevent risky vulnerabilities stemming from the lack of sufficient data security.

Finally, the fifth part of the book revolves around Data & Services. Services are usually described in terms of their functionality and ability to perform operations, leaving data as a second-class citizen, while in fact many services are data-intensive and their added value is entirely the data. This part discusses some data-intensive services, including services for sentiment analysis, as well as emerging new applications relying on blockchain. Firstly, Jian Yang, Pin Chen, and Yongping Tang (Chapter 17) study how such data value can be combined with services so that it becomes an intangible commodity. They present a design methodology for data product sharing and a platform for service-based data trading. The next chapter (Chapter 18) is from Barbara Pernici, Francesca Ratti, and Gabriele Scalia, and showcases how quality of the data is central to the definition of value in services, based on the need for data management in the natural sciences domain. In particular, this chapter introduces and discusses a general architecture that reaps the benefits of a contract-based and adaptive approach, taking QoS constraints into consideration. The following chapter (Chapter 19), by Ioanna Karageorgou, Panagiotis Liakos, and Alex Delis, introduces and illustrates a Spark-based Twitter sentiment analysis software architecture that receives online streamed live Tweets in Greek and classifies them, contrasting in-memory, queuing approaches. A prototype based on this architecture exploits a Naive-BayesSA-model based and is evaluated on a set of 10K Tweets that were manually classified as either positive or negative. Through experimentation, the effectiveness and efficiency of the prototype is demonstrated and discussed in light of not only system-level but also real-world considerations such as the COVID virus. To close the last part of this volume, Salima Benbernou and Mourad Ouziri present novel work in Chapter 20 regarding the trustworthiness of smart contracts with respect to major consistency issues of current blockchain-enabled applications. They propose a logic-based blockchain system that may ascertain consistency and additionally safety throughout a network of participants bound by smart contracts. Interestingly, they transpose the concept of service selection to Proof-of-Work of cryptocurrency miners.

In conclusion, we thank all the authors of the present volume for their contributions to and support of this festive initiative. We thank Springer for gladly accepting the proposal to publish this book and for editorial support. Many more people have had the fortune to meet and work with Mike Papazoglou, and we hope this book will function as a further stimulus to them and to the next generation of service-scientists, which undoubtedly will benefit from the foundations laid by Mike for the field.

February 2021

Marco Aiello
Athman Bouguettaya
Willem-Jan van den Heuvel
Damian Andrew Tamburri

Contents

Services and the Internet of Things

Data and Services

History

History

From Component-Based Architectures to Microservices: A 25-years-long Journey in Designing and Realizing Service-Based Systems

Giuseppe De Giacomo⬥, Maurizio Lenzerini⬥, Francesco Leotta⬥, and Massimo Mecella⁽✉⁾ ⬥

Dipartimento di Ingegneria Informatica Automatica e Gestionale,
Sapienza Università di Roma, Rome, Italy
{degiacomo,lenzerini,leotta,mecella}@diag.uniroma1.it

Abstract. Distributed information systems and applications are generally described in terms of components and interfaces among them. How these component-based architectures have been designed and implemented evolved over the years, giving rise to the so-called paradigm of Service-Oriented Computing (SOC). In this chapter, we will follow a 25-years-long journey on how design methodologies and supporting technologies influenced one each other, and we discuss how already back in the late 90s the ancestors of the SOC paradigm were there, already paving the way for the technological evolution recently leading to microservice architectures and serverless computing.

Keywords: Components · SOC · Middleware technologies · Microservices · Design methodologies

1 Introduction

Divide et impera[1] describes an approach, relevant to many fields, where, to solve a problem, it is required or advantageous to break or divide what opposes the solution. As an example, in computer science and engineering, it is applied at the level of standalone programs, by organizing codes in functions, classes and libraries, but is also at the basis of how complex business processes, spanning several departments/offices of the same organization and/or different organizations, are implemented by making different parties collaborating on a computer network [1]. Each part is referred to as a *component* and communicates with other components by means of software interfaces.

The first examples of such interfaces were implemented back in 1984, even though request-response protocols were available since late 1960s, using Remote

---

[1] This was originally an Ancient Roman socio-political technique; the motto is attributed to Philippus II of Macedon.

© Springer Nature Switzerland AG 2021
M. Aiello et al. (Eds.): Papazoglou Festschrift, LNCS 12521, pp. 3–15, 2021.
https://doi.org/10.1007/978-3-030-73203-5_1

Procedure Calls (RPCs) [2]. Since then, technologies evolved in order to support more and more distributed, performing and resilient applications, reaching the current peak of modern highly distributed microservice architectures based on cloud infrastructures.

Concurrently, with the increasing complexity of systems, a joint effort from the research community, practitioners and consultants, and industry led to the development of design methodologies and best practices covering the different phases of software development at any granularity, from classes to distributed architectures. The latter are usually described in terms of software components and interfaces and for this reason they were referred to as *component-based architectures*. Design methodologies for component-based architectures date back to the late 90s, but the features of components they currently define is much more powerful than what technologies allowed at that time.

Technologies then evolved into Web-ready (HTTP-based) components, referred to as *Web services*, leading to the emergence of Service-Oriented Computing [3–5].

In this chapter, we discuss how the potentials of that notion of component can be unleashed only nowadays, when effective technologies for distribution and replication are available, and how the modern concept of microservice was already anticipated by those design methodologies.

2   Design of Component-Based Architectures

The concept behind a component-based architecture is simple: a big application is split into autonomous entities, i.e., components potentially realizing on a distributed scale what classes are in object-oriented programming. As such, components share with classes features, e.g., encapsulation, identity and unification of data and functionalities, standard interfaces, and final goals, i.e., reuse and transparency. However, the different scale at which these principles are applied requires a specific design methodology.

Design of component-based architectures has its roots in the design of object-oriented software. After all, and for the sake of simplicity, components can be considered as classes distributed on a network. A basis for object-oriented design already looking ahead to components is provided by the Catalysis approach [6], where a design methodology is proposed based on the Unified Modeling Language – UML. UML diagrams are used to represent precise specifications of use cases where each operation is described in terms of pre- and post-conditions expressed in Object Constraint Language - OCL.

Later, the authors of [7] extend Catalysis with the emerging concept of component technologies, such as Enterprise Java Beans. The methodology is intended to identify components and their interfaces by a rigorous strategy starting from a business process model describing the domain of interest. The analysis of the business process model produces *(i)* a business concept model and an actor model, both described in terms of UML class diagrams with stereotypes, *(ii)* a use case diagram, with a single use-case for each triggering event in the process model, where triggering events are obtained by looking at which concepts and associations of the business concept model can change, *(iii)* a set of use case descriptions, and *(iv)* a set of quality-of-service requirements for the system.

The next step is to identify interfaces, which are divided into two types: system interfaces and business interfaces. A system interface is associated in particular to each use case identified in the previous step, and this interface contains an operation for each of the tasks of the use case, which is responsibility of the computing system. Business interfaces are obtained from the business concept model identifying core types, i.e., those classes that have an independent existence, not having mandatory associations except with categorizing types. For each of these core types, a business interface is defined, whose methods allow to manipulate instances of the core types and associations to other types in the business concept model. Other interfaces are then provided as input to the design methodology, such as those of pre-existing software systems.

Notably, business interfaces are very similar to *concepts* in conceptual modeling approaches which, in the same period, were investigated in the information systems field. Again, in the same period, the knowledge representation community was starting to investigate formal approaches and possibly automated reasoning for conceptual modeling, through the use of Description Logics - DLs [8]. Further, a bit later, Domain Driven Design [9] – DDD, was proposed as a way to structure systems, and notably *entities* are not dissimilar from concepts and business objects. DDD is considered the starting point of the microservice approach (which we will consider later in the chapter).

Back to [7], after the definitions of interfaces, a single component specification is created for all of the system interfaces and several business components will be defined for each of the core types, each containing the single interface defined for that specific core type. System components will use business components to perform complex tasks, whereas business components perform very basic tasks, thus being very close to the concept of microservice. As business components are derived by UML classes, they also implicitly define the corresponding *information model*, which is an important part of a microservice architecture.

At this point, an initial component-based architecture is available, showing the basic interaction between components. This architecture is then enriched by specifying each operation with pre- and post-conditions.

3 Evolving Technologies

In this section, we briefly outline an historical evolution of technologies used to implement component-based architectures and then services. Technologies and design methodologies evolved somewhat independently, with the former often developed by practitioners [10], playing chase one each other. In particular, as it will be discussed in Sect. 5, the concept of component emerged more and more clearly in recent technologies than in older ones.

3.1   RPC/RMI

Initially, technologies emerged that allowed to abstract the same kind of interaction developers where used to employ in single application programming languages between software modules and classes. They hide to the developer all the challenges related to network communication, providing an experience similar to simply calling a programming language library.

The first example of such technologies is represented by Remote Procedure Calls – RPCs. If request–response protocols date back to the late 1960s, at the very beginning of networking, theoretical proposals of RPCs date to the 1970s, but first commercial implementation only appearing in 1984 [2]. With RPC, in order for a client program to call a servant program, the developer must import a stub library, which takes charge of communication related issues such as marshalling and umarshalling of data. The stub can be automatically generated from a textual description of the interface expressed through an Interface Definition Language – IDL. A seminal implementation of RPCs is represented by Sun's RPC (also known as Open Network Computing – ONC, and based on the C programming language). RPCs have also been adapted to object oriented languages, referred to as Remote Method Invocation – RMI. Java RMI, for example, has been introduced in 1997 with Version 1.1 of Java.

In component-based architectures, which started to require different companies to integrate their functionalities, RPCs found obstacles, as binary protocols involved in the communications were not Web-friendly (i.e., created issues in being filtered by Web firewalls). This was not a big issue when integration was between branches of the same organization, and specific firewall rules could be applied. Nevertheless, as soon as integration started involving different organizations/enterprises, this became a limiting factor.

Currently, gRPC[2], initially developed at Google in 2015, is an open source RPC system that uses HTTP/2 for transport, Protocol Buffers[3] as the interface description language, and generates cross-platform client and servant bindings for many languages. The most common usage scenarios include connecting services in microservice architectures and connecting mobile devices and browser clients to back-end services.

3.2   DCE, Object Brokers and Application Servers

RPCs are technologies that can be used to connect components. The support to component architectures anyway is not limited to the simple communication task. Deployment and usage of components may require additional functionalities that are historically provided by software modules referred to as middleware. An initial example of this category of software, which marks the passage from two-tier to three-tier systems, is represented by Distributed Communication

---

[2] J. Kolhe, S. Kuchibhotlag: RPC Intro, KubeCon + CloudNativeCon 2018, Seattle, USA, December 11–13, 2018, https://www.youtube.com/watch?v=OZ_Qmklc4zE.

[3] Cf. https://developers.google.com/protocol-buffers.

Environment [11] – DCE, which is dated back late 1992/early 1993. The DCE runtime environment supported infrastructural functionalities such as directory, time, thread management and distributed file system, which can be still recognized in modern middleware.

DCE is grounded in RPCs. While object oriented programming aroused, the concept of object seemed more fitting than calls to procedures: object brokers appeared on the landscape, being the first and most famous specification the Common Object Request Broker Architecture – CORBA [12]. Differently from DCE, which also enforces a standard implementation, CORBA only consisted of a specification that was then implemented by different vendors (e.g., Iona's Orbix), thus facilitating its adoption. First CORBA specification dates back to 1991, but widespread adoption started only in 1996, further contributing to the low success of DCE. The most significant competitor in the market of object brokers was represented by Microsoft Distributed Component Object Model – DCOM [13], and its descendant COM+ [14], both extensions to the distributed scenario of the single machine component model adopted on Microsoft Windows.

Both CORBA ad DCOM provide additional functionalities to RMI-based interactions, which resemble and extend those provided by DCE, with a stronger support, for example, to transaction management.

The above technologies easily support a single organization, but show limitations in a multi-organization context. This is the reason why, starting from the early 2000s, the employment of object brokers faded in favour of products having Web technologies and HTTP as main communication and access channel, thus allowing an easier inter-organization integration. These are usually referred to as *application servers* [15]. Most used application servers are based on Java 2 Enterprise Edition – J2EE, or on Microsoft .NET. In J2EE application servers, components are realized as Enterprise Java Beans – EJBs.

In an application server, a component is a software module running inside a container, which provides system-level features, e.g. security, transactions, etc. But in order to have this, components should adhere to a contract with the container: it provides features to the components, which in turn must be developed according to a specific structure (i.e., realizes specific interfaces expected by the container). A developer is therefore in charge of two aspects: to realize the methods required by the *component model* and to realize the specific logic of the application.

CGI/Server Pages and Javascript. Integral part of an application server is the support for the presentation layer, and in particular for dynamically generated Web pages. Common Gateway Interface - CGI, introduced back in 1993, represented the first way for a Web server to return dynamic content. The term gateway is employed to denote an application, serving the calling one, which allows to access the data of another back-end system (e.g., a database/DBMS). Upon the reception of an external call, the Web server executes an instance of the gateway, which is in charge of gathering information from the back-end system (e.g., through a database query), packing it into an HTML page, and returning it back to the Web server, which in turn sends the response back to the client.

Performance issues intrinsic in CGIs, and related to spawning of a new process for each request, have been solved by including gateways as part of the Web server with technologies such as servlets (introduced in 1997), or with the employment of server page technologies, which embed programming language code inside the HTML pages, such as Active Server Pages – ASP, Java Server Pages – JSP, PHP pages, and ASP.NET pages.

CGIs and related subsequent technologies are mainly intended to provide the presentation layers for final users, to be presented directly in a Web browser. In this case, clients are said to be "thin", because they are only responsible for user interaction and visualization of results. Thought still popular, these kinds of technologies have become less and less frequently employed, while client side technologies such as JavaScript has become more and more employed for the presentation layer. In this scenario, remote systems provide functionalities (as discussed in Sect. 3.5 as REST services), and the Javascript code embedded in the HTML page on the client directly executes the entire presentation logic. Clients are, in this case, said to be "fat".

3.3 Asynchronous Integration

Asynchronous integration between components has been always possible since RPCs, which defined both synchronous and asynchronous interactions between clients and servants. In case of long tasks or busy servants, it is better for the client to continue its job waiting for a completion notification from the servant. The servant enqueues requests from the clients and processes them whenever resources are available. A similar need arises when the client needs no answer to a specific request.

Asynchronous interaction is usually supported by Message Oriented Middleware – MOM. MOMs, which are sometimes integrated as part of more complete solution (e.g., CORBA specified its own messaging system), usually provide two kinds of interaction modes: queueing and publish/subscribe. In publish/subscribe systems, the MOM exposes a set of topics where clients can publish messages, that are then broadcasted to topic subscribers following specific authorization rules. This way it is possible to implement different communication schemas such as one-to-many or many-to-many.

MOMs started to widespread in the mid 90s. Historically, among the most widespread technologies, Java Messaging Service – JMS, should be mentioned. Nowadays they represent a very relevant technology, especially in the field of Big Data ingestion including Internet-of-Things (IoT) applications (cf. AMQP, MQTT, RabbitMQ, Kafka).

3.4 Web (SOAP) Services

As already discussed, modern middleware are intended to support integration not only in an intra-organization scenario, but also in an inter-organization one.

Communications among different organizations through the Internet can be limited by the presence on the network path of firewalls filtering certain protocols. As a consequence, in the early 2000s, the idea was to replace protocols typical of objects brokers, directly using TCP as a transport protocol, with textual protocols using HTTP as a transport protocol. The very pragmatic advantage was that most firewalls allow HTTP traffic to pass through. The basic idea was to bind the different functionalities of a component to a specific HTTP URL. Each component, referred to as *Web service*, contains a set of methods that can be called using standard HTTP methods (e.g., GET, POST). The first example of this protocol was Simple Object Access Protocol – SOAP, dating back to 2000, even though the first version recommended by W3C is the 1.2, published in 2003. This started the era of Web services and Service-Oriented Computing [3–5].

In SOAP, the HTTP request/response body issued to/returned from a specific URL contains an XML envelope consisting of an header and a body. The header contains information about the issued methods and other aspects related to security and encoding. The body contains the actual information exchanged between the two parties. Description and specifications of SOAP services is performed through Web Service Definition Language - WSDL (an IDL for Web services). The specifications that were subsequently built on top of SOAP were wide, covering several different aspects needed for application integration.

Using SOAP for inter-organization integration does not prevent intra-organization integration to be performed at the object broker level. For example J2EE application server still allow to use EJBs for intra-organization, allowing to wrap them as SOAP services for inter-organization integration. Nonetheless, practice became more and more to employ SOAP also for intra-organization integration.

3.5 REST Services

SOAP services model the access to a component as a set of high-level functionalities, that can be even very complex. Concurrently (early 2000) to this vision, a different one more focused on resources was developed in [16] under the name of REpresentational State Transfer – REST. The REST approach to services is based on the following considerations:

- operations performed on components can be decomposed in simple CRUD (Create, Read, Update, Delete) operations on resources (e.g., chapters in a book of a book catalogue). The advantage is that it is very immediate to map a resource and CRUD operations to HTTP requests, by making URLs mimicking the hierarchical relationships between resources (e.g., chapters contained in the book with ID 1 can be mapped to the URL books/1/chapters) and HTTP actions to CRUD operations;
- basic operations on a resource can be considered inherently stateless, with no need to maintain sessions, which can be implemented at HTTP level.

The previous considerations make the development of REST services much simpler than SOAP ones. Despite the concurrent conception of the SOAP and

REST approach, the supports from vendors and the employment of services mostly for integration, made during the 2000s SOAP services more popular than REST ones. In the current decade, instead, the explosion of the service economy, the widespread adoption of mobile apps and the seamless integration of REST services with HTTP, which made it perfectly suitable for calling a service from a Web browser, led developers to prefer REST services where the HTTP body contains information expressed in JavaScript Object Notation – JSON, which is easily manipulated by JavaScript engines in Web browsers (see Sect. 3.2 when discussing client-side technologies).

Nowadays, choosing between using SOAP or REST services is still an active source of debate [17], but the growth of cloud and serverless computing is pushing more and more REST services, with SOAP services residually employed for niche business-to-business integration.

3.6 Virtualization, Serverless and Microservices

In the last years, different technology and business trends drove the evolution of development technologies for component-based architectures.

An increasing trend in companies is to deploy developed services and components on servers not directly owned by them, preferring to deploy on remote machines managed by cloud providers (e.g., Amazon, Google, Microsoft), which offer advanced guarantees such as disaster recovery and maintenance. These servers are most of the time virtualized on physical machines owned by cloud providers. Virtualization allows to easily backup and replicate copies of machines for redundancy and load balancing. The extreme evolution of *virtualization* is *containerization*, which allows to very quickly instantiate new containers, each one generally hosting a single component, to accommodate scalability requirements. *Serverless computing* [18] hides server usage from developers and runs code on-demand automatically scaled and billed only for the time the code is running; if the code corresponds to a pure functional component (Function-as-a-Service: the unit of computation is a function that is executed in response to triggers such as events or HTTP requests), the abstraction seen by the developer perfectly correspond to the deployment.

The current evolution of the digital economy is such that the load of services is no longer predictable. In fact, the number of users that need to call services continuously change, making serverless computing a need for organizations, helping them to efficiently use allocated resources on cloud providers, in turn reducing the costs.

The replication of services is a delicate task, as these services may share and distribute also needed resources, in particular data. Keeping a distributed database is a complex task, made even more complex by distributed transactions. This aspect led, on the one hand, to the increasing employment of NoSQL databases that simplify horizontal distribution (sharding) and replication, and, on the other hand, to the development of very fine-grained services performing almost atomic operations on (very few) resources. These services are referred to as *microservices* and perfectly fit with the concepts behind REST services (even though in principle a microservice can be implemented with a different set of technologies). If more complex operations must be performed, involving transactions and sessions for example, they are implemented by other (micro-)services at an higher level (coordinating or aggregating them). The development of microservices is nowadays supported by means of specific frameworks such as Spring (Java), .NET core and NodeJS. Microservices developed with these technologies can be easily deployed and managed using DevOps [19] and exploiting cloud/serverless computing.

4   Design of Service-Oriented Architectures

As seen in the previous sections, Service-Oriented Architectures emerged as a style of software design where functionalities are provided to client components by servant application components, through a communication protocol over a network. The service is therefore a discrete unit of functionalities that can be accessed remotely and acted upon and updated independently. The service has some properties [3,5]:

1. it logically represents a business activity with a specified outcome;
2. it is self-contained;
3. it is a black box for its consumers, meaning the consumer does not have to be aware of the service's inner workings; and
4. it may consist of other underlying services.

Notably, (i) property 1 implies the development of "coarse-grained" services as opposed to microservices, (ii) properties 2 and 3 are shared with component-based design, and (iii) property 4 implies that different services can be used in conjunction to provide the functionality of a large software application, thus giving rise to the attention to composition and orchestration of Web services.

When the focus of the research community and practitioners switched from component-based architectures to Service-Oriented Architectures, whereas the design methods proposed in [7] still remain valid, the interest starts converging on how to specify at design-time the single service interface (system interface in particular as defined in Sect. 2) and the interactions among them.

For what concerns the first aspect, the proposed approaches focus on the specification of a service as a UML state-transition model, thus highlighting the conversational/stateful nature of SOAP Web services [20,21]. An attempt to systematize all of these approaches, starting from the identification of components, to specification of interfaces has been proposed for SOAs in 2008 by Catalysis Conversation Analysis [22].

In addition to UML diagrams, also BPMN diagrams are employed as input for the design process, as they document the process to be partially or fully automated through services/components. The introduction of BPMN, and the attention to business processes, is a distinctive feature of SOA as it allows to better model interactions, which is the second aspect mentioned above, between parties and, as a consequence, services. These services can belong to the very same organization or to a different organization. When a formal specification of single services is available, service composition [23], aiming at formal checking, or at automatically composing services aiming at a specific formal goal, is possible.

In automatic composition of services [24], a formal specification of the goal service to be composed is given as an input to a composer, which creates the new service starting from available ones. In [25–27], for example, a goal service is described as a guarded automaton to be synthesized combining the automatons of the single services. Here the idea was to have a repository of Web services, each with a formal specification, that could be composed in order to provide a more complex service. Automatic service composition has a theoretical background in model checking and a technological justification in the presence of discovery services in the SOAP specification and in the emerging trends of semantic Web services [28,29].

Services obtained through automatic service composition are added themselves to the service repository, making them available to be composed with other services. Unfortunately, so far the availability of such repositories of formal and semantically searchable definitions of Web services has remained quite low, thus limiting the chances to apply service composition.

5   Discussing Technologies and Methods

Technologies and design methodologies has evolved together over years, with the former influencing the latter and viceversa. Initial technologies available for interfaces between components, namely RPCs, reflect a client/server design approach, where servers were monolithic entities encapsulating presentation, application (a.k.a. business) and resource layers [15]. With the increasing complexity of servers, functionalities of the different layers have been distributed on several different machines in two or three physical-tier architectures. Distribution was initially mainly intended as intra-organization leading to the development of object brokers. Design methodologies followed the very same path with the introduction of component identification and specification methods instead of the classical client/server interaction. An architecture had to be compliant with respect to a specific component model (e.g., EJB, COM+, .NET), and ultimately was designed with a goal in mind: the application logic reuse, i.e., the possibility to employ an already available component in a new context. Initially, HTTP-based technologies such as SOAP and, later REST, wrapped component interfaces over HTTP, reflecting the underlying component models.

If the above considerations seem to be in favour of a balanced progression of technologies and design methods, the definition of component introduced in the early 2000s is much more advanced that the technologies available at that time.

The design method proposed in [7] introduces the concept of system and business components, with the latter basically acting as wrappers for the operations allowed on the underneath information model. In this sense, functionalities exposed by business components already support the separation between business layer and resource layer, which is typical of modern architectures. Additionally, these functionalities are very fine-grained thus resembling modern microservices. As in those methods the concept of multiple component instances was already in place, it can be argued that design methodologies were, in this case, far beyond technologies available right then.

Modern microservice-based architectures are of course not only the result of design methods, but also of a different and more dynamic software life cycle based on continuous integration/deployment/delivery and DevOps.

Additionally, microservices are nowadays employed not only as a mean to perform CRUD operations on the underneath information (model). Instead, they are also an active part of big data processing pipelines in kappa, lambda and delta architectures [30].

A difference between component-based architectures and modern microservice-based ones is anyway that microservice frameworks are more intended for the infrastracture/communication-level reuse than for reuse of the application logic. Component models had an heavy footprint to support application reuse, in terms of both development effort and deployment infrastructure. Modern microservices are instead very lightweight (e.g., based on Plain Old Java Objects – POJO) and no longer based on component models. This is due to the modern awareness that due to fast changes in technologies and requirements, reuse of application logic is only possible at a very small scale (e.g., software libraries), whereas it is very important to reuse the infrastructure and the communication functionalities.

6 Concluding Remarks

If, on the one hand, as discussed in the previous section, microservices represent business interfaces described in the early 2000s by design methodologies, on the other hand, their development in the last years has been fast and wild, leaving in some cases part of the design process uncovered.

As an example, the resource layer of microservices is often represented by NoSQL databases, such as document based ones, which are very suitable for replication and sharding, but whose design methodologies are still somewhat weak with respect to those available with relational databases.

Additionally, microservices are usually implemented as REST services. REST is much lighter than SOA, and employed technologies are not anymore based on component models. If WSDL is a rich formalism, which has been, for example, a trigger for an extensive research on semantic Web services and composition techniques, Open API, which is the most widely employed definition approach for REST services, lacks of support for many advanced features such as searchability, support for composition, etc., thus making the development of similar techniques harder. And whereas those approaches failed in the past, probably due to the too large ambition (the entire Web as domain of interest), nowadays services are employed in basically all sectors and maybe limiting to domain-specific scenarios can demonstrate their potential. As a result, component-based architectures and SOC must nowadays be re-thinked, factoring aspects that are still valid and framing them in a world of lightweight frameworks, fast development/integration/deployment, sudden changes in requirements and needs for self-adaptability. For what concerns SOC, in particular, authors in [31] identified, in addition to design and service composition, other two emerging research challenges, i.e., crowdsourcing-based reputation, and the Internet of Things (IoT).

A promising approach may reside in automatic synthesis of programs based on specification. This is now feasible thanks to the employment of artificial intelligence applied to UML and BPMN specifications [32,33]. This approach will be investigated, for example, in the ERC project WhiteMech (n. 834228), which targets the three scenarios of smart manufacturing, smart spaces and business processes.

References

1. Dumas, M., La Rosa, M., Mendling, J., Reijers, H.A.: Fundamentals of Business Process Management, 2nd edn. Springer, Heidelberg (2018). https://doi.org/10.1007/978-3-662-56509-4
2. Birrell, A.D., Nelson, B.J.: Implementing remote procedure calls. ACM Trans. Comput. Syst. (TOCS) **2**(1), 39–59 (1984)
3. Papazoglou, M.P., Georgakopoulos, D.: Service-oriented computing. Commun. ACM **46**(10), 25–28 (2003)
4. Papazoglou, M.P., Van Den Heuvel, W.-J.: Service-Oriented Architectures: approaches, technologies and research issues. VLDB J. **16**(3), 389–415 (2007)
5. Papazoglou, M.: Web Services: Principles and Technology. Pearson Education, London (2008)
6. D'souza, D.F., Wills, A.C.: Objects, Components, and Frameworks with UML: the Catalysis Approach. Addison-Wesley, Boston (1998)
7. Cheesman, J., Daniels, J.: UML Components. Addison-Wesley, Boston (2001)
8. Calvanese, D., Lenzerini, M., Nardi, D.: Description logics for conceptual data modeling. In: Chomicki J., Saake G. (eds.) Logics for Databases and Information Systems. The Springer International Series in Engineering and Computer Science, vol. 436, pp. 229–263. Springer, Boston (1998). https://doi.org/10.1007/978-1-4615-5643-5_8
9. Evans, E.: Domain-Driven Design: Tackling Complexity in the Heart of Software. Addison-Wesley, Boston (2004)
10. Aiello, M.: The Web Was Done by Amateurs. Springer, Cham (2018). https://doi.org/10.1007/978-3-319-90008-7
11. Houston, P.J.: Introduction to DCE and Encina. Whitepaper, Transarc Corp (1996)
12. Vinoski, S.: CORBA: integrating diverse applications within distributed heterogeneous environments. IEEE Commun. Mag. **35**(2), 46–55 (1997)
13. Sessions, R.: COM and DCOM: Microsoft's Vision for Distributed Objects. Wiley, New York (1997)
14. Platt, D.S.: Understanding COM+. Microsoft Press, Redmond (1999)
15. Alonso, G., Casati, F., Kuno, H.A., Machiraju, V.: Web Services. Concepts, Architectures and Applications. Springer, Heidelberg (2004). https://doi.org/10.1007/978-3-662-10876-5

16. Fielding, R.T., Taylor, R.N.: Principled design of the modern web architecture. ACM Trans. Internet Technol. **2**(2), 115–150 (2002)

17. Pautasso, C., Zimmermann, O., Leymann, F.: Restful Web services vs. "big" Web services: making the right architectural decision. In: Proceedings of 17th WWW, pp. 805–814 (2008)

18. Castro, P., Ishakian, V., Muthusamy, V., Slominski, A.: The rise of serverless computing. Commun. ACM **62**(12), 44–54 (2019)

19. Bass, L.J., Weber, I.M., Zhu, L.: DevOps - A Software Architect's Perspective. SEI Series in Software Engineering. Addison-Wesley, Boston (2015)

20. Baïna, K., Benatallah, B., Casati, F., Toumani, F.: Model-driven Web service development. In: Persson, A., Stirna, J. (eds.) CAiSE 2004. LNCS, vol. 3084, pp. 290–306. Springer, Heidelberg (2004). https://doi.org/10.1007/978-3-540-25975-6_22

21. Skogan, D., Grønmo, R., Solheim, I.: Web service composition in UML. In: Proceedings of the EDOC 2004, pp. 47–57. IEEE (2004)

22. Graham, I.: Requirements Modelling and Specification for Service-Oriented Architecture. Wiley, New York (2008)

23. Milanovic, N., Malek, M.: Current solutions for Web service composition. IEEE Internet Comput. **8**(6), 51–59 (2004)

24. Lemos, A.L., Daniel, F., Benatallah, B.: Web service composition: a survey of techniques and tools. ACM Comput. Surv. (CSUR) **48**(3), 1–41 (2015)

25. Berardi, D., Calvanese, D., De Giacomo, G., Lenzerini, M., Mecella, M.: Automatic composition of E-services that export their behavior. In: Orlowska, M.E., Weerawarana, S., Papazoglou, M.P., Yang, J. (eds.) ICSOC 2003. LNCS, vol. 2910, pp. 43–58. Springer, Heidelberg (2003). https://doi.org/10.1007/978-3-540-24593-3_4

26. Berardi, D., Calvanese, D., De Giacomo, G., Hull, R., Mecella, M.: Automatic composition of transition-based semantic Web services with messaging. In: Proceedings of the 31st VLDB, VLDB, pp. 613–624 (2005)

27. Calvanese, D., De Giacomo, G., Lenzerini, M., Mecella, M., Patrizi, F.: Automatic service composition and synthesis: the Roman model. IEEE Data Eng. Bull. **31**(3), 18–22 (2008)

28. McIlraith, S.A., Son, T.C., Zeng, H.: Semantic Web services. IEEE Intell. Syst. **16**(2), 46–53 (2001)

29. Fensel, D., Bussler, C.: The Web service modeling framework WSMF. Electron. Commer. Res. Appl. **1**(2), 113–137 (2002)

30. Ryzko, D.: Modern Big Data Architectures: A Multi-agent Systems Perspective. Wiley, New York (2020)

31. Bouguettaya, A., et al.: A service computing manifesto: the next 10 years. Commun. ACM **60**(4), 64–72 (2017)

32. De Giacomo, G., Oriol, X., Estañol, M., Teniente, E.: Linking data and BPMN processes to achieve executable models. In: Dubois, E., Pohl, K. (eds.) CAiSE 2017. LNCS, vol. 10253, pp. 612–628. Springer, Cham (2017). https://doi.org/10.1007/978-3-319-59536-8_38

33. Oriol, X., De Giacomo, G., Estañol, M., Teniente, E.: Automatic business process model extension to repair constraint violations. In: Yangui, S., Bouassida Rodriguez, I., Drira, K., Tari, Z. (eds.) ICSOC 2019. LNCS, vol. 11895, pp. 102–118. Springer, Cham (2019). https://doi.org/10.1007/978-3-030-33702-5_9

Automated Service Composition Using AI Planning and Beyond

Michel Medema[1]([envelope]) [ORCID], Eirini Kaldeli[2], and Alexander Lazovik[1] [ORCID]

[1] University of Groningen, Groningen, Netherlands
{m.medema,a.lazovik}@rug.nl
[2] National Technical University of Athens, Athens, Greece
ekaldeli@image.ece.ntua.gr

Abstract. Automated Service Composition is one of the "grand challenges" in the area of Service-Oriented Computing. Mike Papazoglou was not only one of the first researchers who identified the importance of the problem, but was also one of the first proposers of formulating it as an AI planning problem. Unfortunately, classical planning algorithms were not sufficient and a number of extensions were needed, e.g., to support extended (rich) goal languages to capture the user intentions, to plan under uncertainty caused by the non-deterministic nature of services; issues that where formulated (and, partially addressed) by Mike, being one of his key contributions to the service community.

In this chapter, we look at the development of the original vision of automated service composition as AI planning, going from planning with extended (rich) goals, further developing into composition under uncertainty, extending it to other domains (and reformulating the service composition as composition of sensors and actuators), and then showing possible alternative techniques for highly scalable service composition at the expense of the richness of the domain representation.

Keywords: Automated service composition · AI planning · Constraint satisfaction · Internet of Things

1 Introduction

Service-Oriented Architectures (SOA) are a modern approach for developing software, where individual, loosely-coupled software components (called services) are accessed via platform-independent APIs [1]. The developed application is then defined by its services and a separate wiring logic for combining them [10]. Often such logic is also defined in a platform-independent language, such as BPEL or BPMN [26]. The process code is typically written in the same way as traditional software–by manually typing code. However, considering the high-level nature of the process languages, such abstractions are good candidates for

This work has been partially sponsored by EU H2020 FIRST project, Grant No. 734599, FIRST: vF Interoperation suppoRting buSiness innovaTion.

M. Aiello et al. (Eds.): Papazoglou Festschrift, LNCS 12521, pp. 16–32, 2021.
https://doi.org/10.1007/978-3-030-73203-5_2

a computer-aided composition, where users define "important" properties of the desired composition, and the rest–actual process code generation–can be done in an automated way. Mike Papazoglou was one of the pioneers in emphasising the importance of automated service composition [28] and AI Planning [2,27] being one of the possible solutions for realisation of the idea in practice.

Several approaches inspired by work in the AI planning community have been proposed in order to move towards compositions characterised by a higher degree of automation and adaptability to different user needs and changing environmental conditions, e.g., [6,24,29,31]. Planning has been described as the process of "choosing and organising actions by anticipating their expected outcomes", with the aim to achieve some well-defined goal [15]. Certain analogies with the problem of service composition can be drawn: the functionalities offered by services can be modelled as *actions*, with preconditions/inputs and effects/outputs, and the goal reflects the request of the user.

In this chapter, we provide an overview of one of the research lines that originated from automated service composition. First, we look at automated planing for extended goals under uncertainty [19], then we apply it to the domain of smart homes [20] and smart offices [14], and, finally, extend the underlying methods of constraint satisfaction to exploit the nature of the problem structure typical for automated service composition in the domain of large scale smart environments. The methods and techniques have also transformed over the years. Initially, services and their operations are uniform and represented as actions in the AI planning problem. To model uncertainty, some service operations are modelled as non-deterministic actions, with unknown outcome. To represent active domain exploration, some services are defined as "knowledge-gathering", which are then used to collect the information about the world state. The "knowledge gathering" and "planning" are then executed repeatedly, leading to the interleaving of planning and execution. In the domain of smart homes and smart offices, a clear distinctions is made between knowledge gathering (sensors) and actions altering the world (actuators). The values of sensors can be read at any time and do not require a separate planning phase. For domains where dependencies between services are not as important, the service composition can be simplified, and planning can concentrate on identifying a small set of actions based on changes in the environment that are then all applied simultaneously during execution. While simplifying the service composition reduces the richness of the domain description language, it allows for automated service composition in large scale domains consisting of many thousands of services (which is typical for smart building and smart city applications).

The rest of the chapter is organised as follows. Section 2 discusses the use of planning for automated service composition. Section 3 presents an approach to automated service composition with extended goals and uncertainty based on encoding a planning problem as a constraint satisfaction problem. An example application of automated service composition in a smart home is provided in Sect. 4. In Sect. 5, we show a different approach to automated service composition, where the services are explicitly modelled as either sensors or actuators, and relations between different services are defined by the constraint rules. Finally, the conclusions are drawn in Sect. 6.

2 Planning for Automated Service Composition

2.1 Expressing User Goals

There are several ways in which the goal can be formulated, and different goal languages vary in the expressivity they support and the flexibility they allow with respect to the possible sequences of actions that can lead to the desired outcome. Different approaches have been adopted in this respect: some build on goal specifications that express in a declarative way the objective to be achieved (e.g. [29,30]) and others prescribe some form of a procedural template, either in the form of Hierarchical Task Network methods, e.g., [3], as a Golog program, e.g., [31], or as a target state automaton, e.g., [8]. The main shortcoming of the latter line of work is that by dictating the possible connections between the Web service operations, they restrict the applicability of the domain to only some predefined set of anticipated user behaviours. Unlike these approaches, a declarative goal specifies *what* has to be achieved and leaves it to the automated planner to compute the how. Such a domain-independent approach fits well with the loosely-coupled nature of services that can be combined in many different ways to serve a variety of objectives. The idea is to maintain a generic and modular repository that comprises a number of atomic service operations, from booking flights to arranging appointments with a doctor, and leave it to the planner to automatically generate the composition which satisfies the desired goal and abides to certain constraints that ensure the prevention of undesirable situations. At the same time, the goal language should be expressive enough to capture complex goals that go beyond the mere statement of properties that should hold in the final state, being able to support conditions over state traversals, maintainability properties, and distinguishing between the desire to observe the environment and the desire to change it. What is needed is a rich declarative language for expressing extended goals, without requiring from the user to be aware of the particularities and underlying inter-dependencies of the available services.

2.2 Dealing with Uncertainty

Service environments are characterised by a high degree of uncertainty in multiple levels. Firstly, there is uncertainty about the initial state, i.e., certain variables may be unknown and certain services have to be invoked in order to get to know their value. In fact, marketplaces consisting of services publicly available on the Web are usually dominated by services that are data sources [31], which in a planning context are modelled as sensing operators (also referred to as knowledge-gathering or observational operators). A successful plan may be conditioned on the outcomes of such actions, e.g., the user may want to go ahead with buying a book from amazon.com if it costs less than a maximum price. In a domain-independent setting, the planning agent is required to plan for sensing; the planner should be able to identify which knowledge it lacks for satisfying the goal, and reason about how to find it. The planner should also proactively take care of the data flow entailed by a service composition, i.e., the way in which values returned by observation actions are used by subsequent actions. For example, a user may want to mail a parcel to someone whose address he does not already know. The plan should thus first consult a white pages service, and then give the order for posting by passing the right address value to the respective input parameter. For data intensive service domains, determining the parameters of an action can be just as difficult as determining which actions belong to the plan.

Besides the uncertainty due to the different possible outputs of sensing actions, non-determinism about the results of an action's execution may also stem from *runtime* contingencies. Service environments are unpredictable and a service invocation may behave in unexpected ways: it may return a failure, not respond at all, or even act in a way different from the one prescribed by its description. To add to the volatility of service environments, the activity of exogenous agents may also change the dynamics of the domain in unintentional ways. For example, considering a smart home environment and a partially executed composition which involves the steering of a hoover, if an external actor puts an obstacle in the hoover's way in the middle of execution, the composition may fail unless decisions about how to move are revised. Moreover, in many service environments, dynamicity also applies to the availability of information and services; e.g., the services offered by a mobile phone may appear and disappear depending on the location of the phone. Thus, the problem of uncertainty is directly related to the interaction between planning and execution. With a few notable exceptions [3,7,22], context dynamicity has largely been overlooked by existing planning approaches to WSC.

3   The RuGPlanner

The RuGPlanner [19] has been proposed as a solution to address the special requirements put forward by service domains and has been used in different domains, including Web services [18], the environment of a smart home [9,20,21], and for the dynamic repair of business processes [4,5]. The RuGPlanner's underlying approach is based on translating the domain and the goal into a Constraint Satisfaction Problem (CSP) and applying a state of the art constraint solver to compute a solution-plan. Planning as CSP fits well with many aspects that are of particular concern for service domains. CSP formalisms are expressive, since constraints in the context of a multi-valued encoding allow us to naturally go beyond logical formulas, and use arithmetic formulas in preconditions and effects without sacrificing efficiency. Describing the world in terms of variables which may range over a domain of possible values is particularly convenient for representing "under-defined" states: the range of the allowed values depends on the current knowledge of the agent and is narrowed down by the application of action effects. With such an encoding, states at which variables are not restricted to a specific value, represent sets of states, thus naturally encompassing uncertainty. Moreover, such an encoding is well suited to most standard Web service description languages, such as WSDL[1], which are based on state variables rather than predicates; complex goals can also be expressed in the form of constraints. Finally, plans can include parallel actions, which are particularly useful at execution time.

To deal with uncertainty and the possible mismatch between offline planning and actual execution results, our proposal relies on continual planning: upcoming plan steps anticipated offline can be revised as execution proceeds in the face of inconsistencies that stem either from the newly sensed information, erroneous service behaviour or the actions of exogenous agents. We describe this alternating sequence of offline planning and online execution as orchestration, a well-known concept in the Service-Oriented Computing community which denotes how the execution of a composition is managed. In a service infrastructure, the orchestration engine is a central coordinator which interacts with the component Web services in accordance with the composite process specifications. We reserve a similar role for an orchestration component that interacts with the environment, informs the planner about the data it has collected, and decides when to switch from planning to execution and vice versa. Depending on the situation, re-using parts of the existing plan may speed up the process of plan revision. Moreover, a non-blocking strategy is adopted with respect to waiting for the response of sensing actions, so that the framework can go on with the planning and execution of actions that do not depend on the expected response. Continual planning can be nicely incorporated into CSPs. In fact, dynamic constraint solving allows for the efficient addition and removal of constraints. This enables the planner to constantly incorporate new facts about the environment or remove obsolete ones, check for possible inconsistencies, and react accordingly.

In general, under conditions of uncertainty about the initial state, the search space is no longer the set of states of the domain, but its power set. The planner can resort to sensing operations to acquire all the knowledge it misses and which is necessary to fulfil a goal. Sensing operations return exactly one outcome amongst a (possibly very large) set of deterministic choices. In that respect, a plan computed online represents a traversal between sets of states rather than complete descriptions of states, and has only the potential to achieve the goal, if there is some state sequence that could arise from the plan's execution and satisfies the goal. Such a plan is usually referred to as weak [11]. Finding such a context-dependent plan is a much simpler task than computing a strong contingent plan with conditional branches which would satisfy the goal in all possible state sequences that could arise from observational effects. Postponing the computation of alternative contingent branches until more information is acquired from the environment is a more feasible approach for Web service scenarios that involve many numeric variables and output-to-input mappings, and being optimistic is likely to pay off. Thus, all sources of non-determinism, where the actual behaviour of actions at execution time contradicts the expected effects as modelled in the planning domain or external agents alter the world in unanticipated ways, are left to be treated by interleaving planning with execution and performing continual planning.

---

[1] www.w3.org/TR/wsdl.

3.1 Representing the Planning Domain and Encoding it as a Constraint Satisfaction Problem

To deal with incomplete knowledge and sensing, the planning domain description is enriched with a knowledge-level representation to model observational actions (sensing effects). Conditional effects are also provided. Moreover, the planning formalism accommodates for numeric functions and effects beyond mere assignments, such as increase/decrease. Another characteristic of the planning schema is that input arguments to actions may range over numeric-valued domains just as all other variables. Since the planning problem is translated into a CSP, the supported variable domains (integer, real, lower and upper bounds) depend on the underlying constraint solver that is used. The planning domain accommodated by the RuGPlanner is described briefly in Definition 1 (for the complete consistent definition see [19]).

Definition 1 (Planning Domain). *A Planning Domain is a tuple* $\mathcal{PD} = \langle Var, Par, Act \rangle$, *where:*

- *Var is a set of variables ranging over a finite domain.*
- *Par is a set of variables that play the role of input parameters to members of Act ranging over a finite domain.*
- *A is the set of actions. An action* $a \in Act$ *is a quadruple* $a = (id(a),\ in(a), precond(a), effects(a))$, *where:*
    - *id(a) is a unique identifier*
    - *in(a) $\subset$ Par are the input parameters of a*
    - *precond(a) is a propositional formula over Var $\cup$ Par*
    - *effects(a) is a conjunction of effects. An effect may refer to assigning to a variable some value or some other variable; increasing or decreasing a variable by some constant; sensing a variable, i.e. observing its current (unknown) value; an "invalidate" effect that states that a variable becomes unknown; or a conditional effect that is applied at the next state only if a proposition holds at the current state.*

Following a common practice in many planning approaches, we consider a *bounded* planning problem, i.e., we restrict our target to finding a plan of length at most k for an a priori given integer k. In the following, we explain how the service domain is encoded into a CSP, for some given integer k. The process is similar to the one described in [16] (alternative encodings based on the planning graph are proposed in [13]). Considering a planning domain $\mathcal{PD}$, the aim is to encode it into a $CSP = \langle X, \mathcal{D}, \mathcal{C} \rangle$, where X is a finite set of variables, $\mathcal{D}$ is the set of finite domains of the variables in X, and $\mathcal{C}$ a finite set of constraints, i.e. propositions that restrict the allowable values of variables in X. First, the variables X are derived as follows: for each variable $x \in V \cup Par$ ranging over D^x, and for each $0 \leq i \leq k$, we define a CSP variable $x[i]$ in CSP with domain D^x. Actions are also represented as variables: for each action $a \in Act$ and for each $0 \leq i \leq k-1$ a boolean variable $a[i]$ is defined. This way the computed plan can include parallel actions, a fact that may save time at execution. After deriving the CSP state variables X, the actions' preconditions and effects are also encoded into constraints as described in [19]. On top of the domain description, restrictions referring to the initial state are expressed in the form of a conjunction of propositions. A strong requirement that all variables involved in the preconditions should be known is also added as part of the precondition constraints, to ensure that the preconditions hold for all possible assignments to variables consistent with their allowed domain at a given state. Frame axiom constraints are also generated, which guarantee that variables cannot change between subsequent states, unless some action that affects them takes place.

The set of constraints that comprise CSP are further extended by additional constraints that constitute the goal (see Sect. 3.2), yielding the planning problem in the form of a CSP that is passed to a standard constraint solver. It should be noted that due to the handling of the sensing effects, which allows the offline solver to assume the existence of "convenient" values for unknown variables, the planner generates an optimistic plan. This means that the offline plan anticipates that all knowledge-gathering actions return information that is in accordance with the user's requirements, and all actions are executed successfully. During execution this optimistic initial plan may be revised, as described in Sect. 3.3.

3.2 Goal Language

Until now, we have described the representation and encoding into a CSP of the planning domain and the initial state. In the following, we present the syntax and semantics of the goal, and show how this can be translated into a set of constraints which together with the constraints formulating the planning domain and initial state constitute the final CSP which is passed to the constraint solver.

The goal language supported by the RuGPlanner equips the user with potent constructs for expressing complex goals, beyond the mere statement of properties that should hold in the final state. Conditions over state traversals, maintainability properties, and distinguishing between the wish to observe the environment and the wish to change it are some of the features this language supports. These aspects are expressed in a declarative way, so that the user does not have to know about the operational details of the available operations and how they can be combined. The basic goal operators have been first presented in [17], while many constructs of its formalisation resemble the syntax presented in [23].

Goal Syntax. The goal syntax is defined as follows:

$$goal \qquad\qquad\quad ::= \quad \bigwedge_i (\textit{condition-goal}_i \mid \textit{condition\_or\_not-goal}_i$$
$$\mid \textit{subgoal}_i)$$

$condition$-$goal$	::=	$(subgoal)$ `under_condition` $goal$
$condition\_or\_not$-$goal$	::=	$(subgoal)$ `under_condition_or_not` $goal$
$subgoal$	::=	`final` $(props)$ |
		`achieve`$(props)$ |
		`achieve-maint` $(props)$ |
		`all_states` $(props)$ |
		`find_out-maint` $(props)$ |
		`find_out` $(props)$

where $props$ is a propositional formula as the $precond(a)$ defined in Definition 1, with $var, var_1, \ldots, var_n \in (Var \cup Par)$. All variables and parameters not specified in the goal (or the initial state constraints) are assumed to be undefined (i.e., their respective knowledge-level variables are set to false).

The `final` subgoal is satisfied if $props$ holds at the last state, while `achieve` requires that $props$ should be true at *some* state over the state traversal. The `maint` annotation adds the requirement that once the respective propositions become true at some state, they should remain true in all subsequent states until the final one. `all_states` imposes that $props$ should be true at all states, and is usually applied on input parameters whose values are set by the user. The `find_out` type of subgoals enforces a hands-off requirement on the variables the respective propositions involve, i.e., the planner tries to satisfy the propositions at some state without allowing any world-altering effect on these variables before that state. `find_out-maint` ensures that the involved variables should remain intact at all states of the plan. For instance, the goal `find_out`($account\_balance > 100$) will be satisfied if the sensed value of the variable $account\_balance$ is greater than 100, without allowing any action to alter the value of the variable before the sensing action. On the other hand, if the goal is `achieve`($account\_balance > 100$), the planner will do everything possible in order to fulfil the proposition, e.g., it might invoke a pay_in action that increases the $account\_balance$ by some amount.

Subgoals can be further on combined through the condition goal constructs, which impose some conditions that should be assured before the fulfilment of the subsequent subgoal. $subgoal_0$ `under_condition` $goal_1$ is satisfied if $subgoal_0$ is satisfied for the first time at some state s and $goal_i$ is satisfied in the state sequence preceding s. `under_condition` thus imposes a before-then relation between goals over the state traversal, and is particularly useful in cases where the user would like to go ahead with altering some variable, only if its sensed value satisfies some property beforehand. `under_condition_or_not` allows the expression of what can be seen as some kind of soft requirements: $subgoal_0$ `under_condition_or_not` $goal_1$ will also be fulfilled if $goal_1$ is not satisfiable; if it is, however, then $subgoal_0$ has to be as well. It should be mentioned that the `under_condition_or_not` structure works as intended only if the variables involved in $goal_1$ are known at planning time. The formal semantics of the goal language is provided in [19].

Example Goals. The following presents three simple example goals to demonstrate the use of some basic constructs supported by the goal language:

Goal 1
achieve-maint($bookedConcert = TRUE$) under_condition
  (find_out-maint($temperature > 0$))

Goal 2
achieve-maint($bookedHotel = TRUE$) $\wedge$ (
achieve-maint($bookedConcert = TRUE$)
  under_condition_or_not (find_out-maint($temperature > 0$)))

Goal 3
$\bigwedge_i$achieve($robotLocation = room_i$)

Goal 1 is accomplished if s is the first state at which $bookedConcert = TRUE$ is satisfied, and find_out-maint($temperature > 0$) is satisfied in the state sequence preceding s (in this example, the maintainability requirement imposed by SPSVERBc15SPSVERBc3 is in practice redundant because there is no way to change the weather). If $temperature < 0$, then Goal 1 fails. On the other hand, Goal 2 ensures that $bookedConcert = TRUE$ will be satisfied if the temperature is not below zero, while if it is, then only $bookedHotel = TRUE$ will be looked after. Goal 3 expresses that a robot should visit *all* rooms in a house, leaving the order of visits to be computed by the planner depending on the structure of the house.

3.3 Orchestration: Interweaving Plan Synthesis with Execution

The suitability of the RuGPlanner for dynamic service environments lies in the idea of delaying the computation of alternative plans until these plans are called for by the new information acquired during execution. Continual planning is performed, so that the upcoming plan steps anticipated offline can be revised as execution progresses, in face of inconsistencies that arise either from the newly acquired information, from services' inconsistent behaviours or from the actions of exogenous agents that interfere with the plan. In such a setting, the goal is considered to have been accomplished, if all individual actions in this sequence of updated plans are successfully executed. We call the process that starts from an initial plan and moves on by interweaving action invocations with plan revisions an *orchestration*. Orchestration is performed by applying gradual modifications to the CSP instance which models the planning domain, the goal and the constantly changing contextual state. The modifications correspond to the incorporation of new facts about the state of the world or the removal of obsolete ones, to refinements of the sequence of actions included in the already computed plan, or to useful information about the behaviour of services that is collected by inspecting how they operate. The orchestration algorithm is characterised by the following traits:

- It exploits the high degree of parallelism in the plan, by performing concurrent invocations and handling the responses in a non-blocking way. Since the execution time of some service operations may be very long, the orchestrator is able to continue planning and proceed to the execution of subsequent actions if this is allowed by the domain and goal restrictions, while waiting for the response of a service invocation.
- It provides the means to recover from failure responses and timeouts. Other arbitrary service outcomes that contradict its expected behaviour can also be tolerated under the assumption of a consistent and timely publish-subscribe mechanism.
- It can cope with possible discrepancies due to the activity of exogenous agents, which may act in parallel with the plan execution and interfere with it.
- It seeks to keep a balance between the effort spent in computing a new plan from scratch and in refining an existing one.
- It takes care of the data flow by instantiating numeric-valued input parameters to the actually sensed output parameters. This is performed through plan refinement, by considering the history of known facts in the form of constraints and the goal requirements.

More information about the orchestration algorithm used by the RuGPlanner can be found in [19].

4 Application: Automated Service Composition in a Smart Home

Pervasive computing environments such as our future homes are the prototypical example of a dynamic, complex system where Service-Oriented Computing techniques will play an important role. Ubiquitous computing technologies can be used to assist people to accomplish their desired tasks, increase their safety and feeling of comfort, and enhance the level of independence of people with functional disabilities by enabling them to access and control their household devices. This vision of homes which exhibit a high degree of intelligence brings a number of fresh challenges, including support for interoperation, dynamic discovery, sensing of the current execution context, and dynamic coordination of the several smart artefacts. A Service-Oriented Architecture, where smart components are exposed as services, can contribute towards addressing these challenges, and fits naturally in dynamic environments, where the location, connectivity, and availability of a large number of autonomous and heterogeneous objects constantly change during the home's life cycle.

To satisfy the wishes of the user and guarantee their comfort and safety, the house has to be able to exhibit quite complex functionalities rather than just triggering some single service or a predesigned sequence of fixed services. A trivial operation such as turning on a light in a corridor can be achieved with a switch or a passive infrared sensor. However, the coordination of the home so as to effectively deal with a gas leak detection is far more demanding, especially when considering the many possible contextual states the house and the user can be in, each of which may require several possible handlings to achieve the same ultimate safety goal. Moreover, developing rigid solutions that are tailored to a specific home instance and user needs is not an efficient approach, given the considerable effort that is required to adapt them for new customers.

In order for smart homes to exhibit a genuinely intelligent behaviour, the ability to compute compositions of individual devices automatically and dynamically is paramount. In this context, the application of appropriate AI planning techniques can address challenges put forward by dynamic domestic settings, offering a high degree of customisability to different home instances and user needs and being able to perform complex reasoning about contextual information rather than relying on hardwired sets of service instances. The application of the RuGPlanner in smart home environments [9,20,21,32] has been particularly promising, being able to effectively address challenges related to dealing with numeric values, extended goals, and dynamicity considering an evolving set of elements typical of the Internet of Things.

4.1 A Motivating Example

Let us consider a home inhabitant who is a disabled person who can move around on an electric wheel-chair, while a nurse pays a visit for some hours every day. A location component keeps track of the location of the users to the level of some predefined areas. Let us see how a home equipped with a service composition architecture that makes use of the RuGPlanner would behave.

At 8 pm the waking-up goal prescribed by the user is automatically triggered: the alarm clock rings, the curtains in the bedroom are opened, the lights may be turned on depending on the amount of daylight detected by a natural light sensor, and the motorised bed is elevated. After taking a shower, the user wants to move to the sitting room and watch some TV. Such a goal dictates that the TV is set to the user's channel of preference, the lights are adjusted depending on the indication of the natural light sensor, and the curtains are also shut accordingly. The air-conditioner is turned on if the temperature sensor in the living room indicates that the temperature is too high, while the necessary doors are opened to facilitate the user moving to the sitting room. At noon, the user goes to the kitchen to prepare something to eat. While being there, the smoke detector in the kitchen identifies a potentially dangerous smoke leak—but fortunately not due to fire. As a result, a predefined home goal for dealing with this situation is automatically triggered: after having ensured that the user has safely moved out of the kitchen (let's say to the adjacent sitting room), the door leading to the kitchen is closed to isolate the smoke in a single room. The ventilator is turned on and the kitchen window is also opened, so that the foul air is expelled, while an alarm notification appears on the TV screen. While waiting in the sitting room, the user wants to move back to the kitchen, but only after having been assured that the environment there is safe, and the smoke has been eliminated. This wish implies resorting to sensing to identify the current situation in the kitchen. Let's assume that after some time the smoke is eliminated, causing the alarm on the TV and the ventilator to automatically turn off.

Later in the afternoon, while the user is taking a bath, and the nurse has gone out for some shopping, a fall is identified by the fall detector attached to him, and an emergency goal is automatically triggered: the health centre is notified and an informative message is sent to the nurse's mobile phone, while the robot is moved to the bathroom in case the user wants to ask for some additional assistance. Given that the fall has not caused any serious trouble, the nurse finds the user lying in his bed reading a book, and after some time he decides that it's time for going to sleep. He thus issues a goal that prepares the bedroom conditions for sleeping, which involves setting the alarm clock to some preferred wake-up time, lowering the motorised bed position, turning off the lights, and closing the curtains.

The aforementioned scenarios assume that no contingencies occur during execution, and that all service invocations complete successfully. What if, however, a service is out of order, and responds with a failure or if a timeout occurs? In such cases, the system will first try to reinvoke the erroneous service, and if again a failure or timeout is observed, it will perform replanning. Let us assume, for example, that, when executing the plan that prepares the living room for watching TV, the automatic turning on operation of the TV service responds with a failure. Assuming that the robot assistant is also endowed with the capability of turning on the TV by manually pressing the button on the device, the composition engine will compute an alternative plan which involves moving the robot in front of the TV so that it can switch it on.

5   Service Composition for Large-Scale Domains

Smart environments such as smart buildings and, at a larger scale, smart cities combine a set of services, primarily consisting of sensors and actuators, to enable automatic control of various processes within the environment with the goal of maintaining a certain desired state of the environment while respecting the preferences of individual users. The highly dynamic nature of these types of problems requires powerful reasoning capabilities, making planning, represented as a constraint satisfaction problem, particularly suitable for modelling them. A representation of the environment consists of uncontrollable variables, whose values cannot be controlled directly but can only be observed through the continuous stream of data provided by the sensors, and variables whose state can be controlled directly, which correspond to the actuators. The values of the controllable variables are determined based on the current state of the environment and the rules governing the environment, thereby performing certain actions within the environment, which may influence the state of the uncontrollable variables, to reach or maintain the desired state. The order in which actions are performed is, unlike many traditional planning problems, often of less importance, because most of the actions do not directly depend on other actions but rather on the state of the environment.

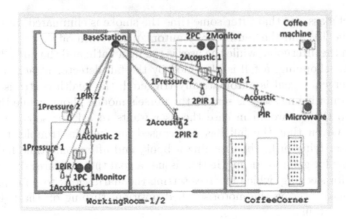

Fig. 1. The deployment of a small-scale smart building system in the Bernoulliborg of the University of Groningen.

Building automation systems are a typical example of smart environments. Sensors installed in the building provide information about the current state of the environment, including the light level and temperature in different parts of the building and occupancy information. Using this information, the system controls processes within the building such as lighting, heating and ventilation as well as individual workstations and appliances. The aim of the system is to provide the occupants of the building with a comfortable place to work by satisfying the preferences of the occupants, such as the desired temperature in a room, while, for example, minimising the energy consumption of the building. Energy savings can be realised by switching off appliances when they are no longer in use or lighting when no occupancy is detected. Integration with a smart grid may additionally allow the building to reduce the overall operational cost by buying energy at times that the prices are lower. The GreenMind project, which presents an architecture and case study of a smart building system, exemplifies the realisation of a small-scale smart building system deployed across several offices [25]. The deployment, shown in Fig. 1, consists of various sensors and actuators to control the power consumption of workstations and other appliances based on the presence of occupants to minimise the energy consumption of the building. As demonstrated by this project, such smart building systems can save a substantial amount of energy, even at a small scale.

The exponential complexity of constraints satisfaction problems makes creating planning problems for large-scale domains such as these difficult because it is not possible to find a solution to the problem in a reasonable amount of time. A reduction of the complexity can be achieved by transforming the constraints into a different representation in which a function of some sensors implies a state of the actuators that must be satisfied [12]. This representation uses the fact that the values of variables corresponding to sensors cannot be changed directly, and introduces a notion of activeness for the constraints. Constraints that are inactive for a particular state of the environment can be removed from the problem, reducing both the computational complexity and, more importantly, the dependencies between different parts of the problem.

Some large-scale domains also have an inherently localised structure. For a smart building, for example, the rooms of the building may serve as a natural boundary for many of the constraints, causing the preferences of any particular occupant to be mostly confined to their office or workspace within the building. As a result, these constraints form small clusters, or islands, of more densely connected constraints, with only some constraints crossing the boundary of such an island. This structure can be made an explicit part of the problem by reformulating the problem as a CSP consisting of sparsely interconnected islands of constraints, where islands correspond to the parts of the problem that are more densely connected and bridges represent the sparse dependencies between them.

Definition 2. *Let $\mathcal{P} = \langle \mathcal{I}, \mathcal{B} \rangle$ be a CSP consisting of a set of islands $\mathcal{I}$ and a set of bridges $\mathcal{B}$. The set of islands $\mathcal{I} = \{I_1, \ldots, I_n\}$ consists of independent CSPs $I_i \in \mathcal{I} = (X_i, D_i, C_i)$. Islands are completely independent, meaning that $I_i, I_j \in I, i \neq j : X_i \cap X_j = \emptyset \wedge C_i \cap C_j = \emptyset$. The bridges $\mathcal{B} \subseteq \{B_{ij} \mid i,j \in \{1, \ldots, n\} \wedge i \neq j\}$ connect islands together, where a single bridge $B_{ij} \in \mathcal{B} = (S_{B_{ij}}, r_{B_{ij}})$ is a constraint between two islands $I_i, I_j \in I$ with $S_{B_{ij}} \subseteq X_i \cup X_j$.*

For a problem of this type, inactive constraints have the potential to partition the problem into several independent subproblems: when some of the constraints corresponding to the bridges become inactive, the dependencies between the islands are removed, resulting in one or more independent subproblems. For each of these problems, a solution can be constructed independently, which can ultimately be combined into a single solution to the complete problem. Previous solutions can also be reused when the state of the environment changes. If a part of the problem remains independent despite the changes in the environment, its solution remains unchanged, making it unnecessary to repeat the search process. The parts of the problem that are affected by the changes in the environment may have to be adjusted, but, as for the complete problem, the previous solution can be used as a starting point for the search, potentially reducing the search time considerably.

6 Conclusion

In this chapter we looked at one of the research directions which originated from a joint work of one of the authors of the paper and Mike Papazoglou. The goal of this chapter was to show how a vision of Mike and the idea of automated service composition has developed over the years, how it has been adjusted and applied to different domains, and how it is still actively developed.

In this work, we first looked into the problem of automated service composition, specifically a composition of services according to a rich (extended) goal language. Traditional planning approaches assume a simple propositional formula representing a set of goal states. With the extended goals you can define more complex properties of the desired plan: order of actions, properties that need to be maintained in all visited states, etc. In practical applications you may not know all the information in advance, for example, the customer may define the shipment address only after he selected and confirmed the products he plans to buy. To model such incomplete information, a new method of interleaving planning and execution was developed, with uncertainty being explicitly modelled via knowledge-gathering actions.

When applied to a domain of Internet of Things, and specifically to smart homes and smart offices, additional assumptions have been made: instead of uniform services, the domain is described via explicit sensors and actuators explicitly representing the state of the domain and active world-altering actions. Unfortunately, solving planning problems for such domains is very difficult due to the computational complexity of the planning algorithms and typical sizes of the domains. Luckily, the structure of the domains allows for a reduction of the complexity, as many world state changes do not necessarily influence the whole domain: often local state changes would imply local planning and actuation. Constraints that are inactive for a particular state of the environment can then be removed from the problem, reducing both the computational complexity and, more importantly, the dependencies between different parts of the problem.

References

1. Aiello, M.: The Web Was Done by Amateurs: A Reflection on One of the Largest Collective Systems Ever Engineered, 1st edn. Springer, Cham (2018). https://doi.org/10.1007/978-3-319-90008-7
2. Aiello, M., et al.: A request language for web-services based on planning and constraint satisfaction. In: Buchmann, A., Fiege, L., Casati, F., Hsu, M.-C., Shan, M.-C. (eds.) TES 2002. LNCS, vol. 2444, pp. 76–85. Springer, Heidelberg (2002). https://doi.org/10.1007/3-540-46121-3_10
3. Au, T.-C., Kuter, U., Nau, D.: Web service composition with volatile information. In: Gil, Y., Motta, E., Benjamins, V.R., Musen, M.A. (eds.) ISWC 2005. LNCS, vol. 3729, pp. 52–66. Springer, Heidelberg (2005). https://doi.org/10.1007/11574620_7
4. van Beest, N., Kaldeli, E., Bulanov, P., Wortmann, J., Lazovik, A.: Automatic detection of business process interference. In: 1st International Workshop on Knowledge-Intensive Business Processes (KIBP), 13th International Conference on Principles of Knowledge Representation and Reasoning (KR) (2012)
5. van Beest, N., Kaldeli, E., Bulanov, P., Wortmann, J., Lazovik, A.: Automated runtime repair of business processes. Inf. Syst. **39**, 45–79 (2014)
6. Berardi, D., Cheikh, F., De Giacomo, G., Patrizi, F.: Automatic service composition via simulation. Int. J. Found. Comput. Sci. **19**(2), 429–451 (2008)
7. Bertoli, P., Kazhamiakin, R., Paolucci, M., Pistore, M., Raik, H., Wagner, M.: Continuous orchestration of web services via planning. In: Proceedings of the 19th International Conference on Automated Planning and Scheduling (ICAPS), AAAI (2009)
8. Bertoli, P., Pistore, M., Traverso, P.: Automated composition of web services via planning in asynchronous domains. Artif. Intell. **174**, 316–361 (2010)

9. Caruso, M., Ciccio, C.D., Iacomussi, E., Kaldeli, E., Lazovik, A., Mecella, M.: Service ecologies for home/building automation. In: Proceedings of the 10th IFAC Symposium on Robot Control (2012)
10. Casati, F., Sayal, M., Shan, M.-C.: Developing E-services for composing E-services. In: Dittrich, K.R., Geppert, A., Norrie, M.C. (eds.) CAiSE 2001. LNCS, vol. 2068, pp. 171–186. Springer, Heidelberg (2001). https://doi.org/10.1007/3-540-45341-5_12
11. Cimatti, A., Pistore, M., Roveri, M., Traverso, P.: Weak, strong, and strong cyclic planning via symbolic model checking. Artif. Intell. **147**(1–2), 35–84 (2003)
12. Degeler, V., Lazovik, A.: Dynamic constraint satisfaction with space reduction in smart environments. Int. J. Artif. Intell. Tools **23**(06), 1460027 (2014). https://doi.org/10.1142/S0218213014600276
13. Do, M.B., Kambhampati, S.: Planning as constraint satisfaction: solving the planning-graph by compiling it into CSP. Artif. Intell. **132**, 151–182 (2001)
14. Georgievski, I., Nguyen, T.A., Aiello, M.: Combining activity recognition and AI planning for energy-saving offices. In: 2013 IEEE 10th International Conference on Ubiquitous Intelligence and Computing and 2013 IEEE 10th International Conference on Autonomic and Trusted Computing, pp. 238–245 (2013)
15. Ghallab, M., Laruelle, H.: Representation and control in IxTeT, a temporal planner. In: Proceedings of the 2nd International Conference on Artificial Intelligence Planning Systems, pp. 61–67 (1994)
16. Ghallab, M., Nau, D., Traverso, P.: Automated Planning: Theory and Practice. Morgan Kaufmann, Amsterdam (2004)
17. Kaldeli, E., Lazovik, A., Aiello, M.: Extended goals for composing services. In: Proceedings of the 19th International Conference on Automated Planning and Scheduling (ICAPS 2009). AAAI Press (2009)
18. Kaldeli, E., Lazovik, A., Aiello, M.: Continual planning with sensing for web service composition. In: Proceedings of the 25th AAAI Conference on Artificial Intelligence. AAAI Press (2011)
19. Kaldeli, E., Lazovik, A., Aiello, M.: Domain-independent planning for services in uncertain and dynamic environments. Artif. Intell. **236**, 30–64 (2016)
20. Kaldeli, E., Warriach, E., Lazovik, A., Aiello, M.: Coordinating the Web of services for a smart home. ACM Trans. Web **7**(2), 10 (2013)
21. Kaldeli, E., Warriach, E.U., Bresser, J., Lazovik, A., Aiello, M.: Interoperation, composition and simulation of services at home. In: Maglio, P.P., Weske, M., Yang, J., Fantinato, M. (eds.) ICSOC 2010. LNCS, vol. 6470, pp. 167–181. Springer, Heidelberg (2010). https://doi.org/10.1007/978-3-642-17358-5_12
22. Klusch, M., Renner, K.U.: Fast dynamic re-planning of composite OWL-S services. In: Proceedings of the IEEE/WIC/ACM International Conference on Intelligent Agent Technology (IAT) - Workshops, pp. 134–137 (2006)
23. Lazovik, A., Aiello, M., Gennari, R.: Encoding requests to web service compositions as constraints. In: van Beek, P. (ed.) CP 2005. LNCS, vol. 3709, pp. 782–786. Springer, Heidelberg (2005). https://doi.org/10.1007/11564751_64
24. Lin, N., Kuter, U., Sirin, E.: Web service composition with user preferences. In: Bechhofer, S., Hauswirth, M., Hoffmann, J., Koubarakis, M. (eds.) ESWC 2008. LNCS, vol. 5021, pp. 629–643. Springer, Heidelberg (2008). https://doi.org/10.1007/978-3-540-68234-9_46
25. Nizamic, F., Nguyen, T.A., Lazovik, A., Aiello, M.: GreenMind - an architecture and realization for energy smart buildings. In: Proceedings of the 2014 Conference ICT for Sustainability, pp. 20–29. Atlantis Press, August 2014. https://doi.org/10.2991/ict4s-14.2014.3

26. Ouvans, C., Dumas, M., ter Hofstede, A., van der Aalst, W.: From BPMN process models to BPEL web services. In: International Conference on Web Services, pp. 285–292 (2006)
27. Papazoglou, M.P., Aiello, M., Pistore, M., Yang, J.: Planning for requests against web services. IEEE Data Eng. Bull. **25**(4), 41–46 (2002). http://sites.computer.org/debull/A02DEC-CD.pdf
28. Papazoglou, M.P., Traverso, P., Dustdar, S., Leymann, F., Krämer, B.J.: Service-oriented computing: a research roadmap. In: Curbera, F., Krämer, B.J., Papazoglou, M.P. (eds.) Service Oriented Computing (SOC). Dagstuhl Seminar Proceedings, vol. 05462, 15–18 November 2005. Internationales Begegnungs- und Forschungszentrum für Informatik (IBFI), Schloss Dagstuhl, Germany (2005). http://drops.dagstuhl.de/opus/volltexte/2006/524
29. Peer, J.: A POP-based replanning agent for automatic web service composition. In: Gómez-Pérez, A., Euzenat, J. (eds.) ESWC 2005. LNCS, vol. 3532, pp. 47–61. Springer, Heidelberg (2005). https://doi.org/10.1007/11431053_4
30. Sheshagiri, M., DesJardins, M., Finin, T.: A planner for composing services described in DAML-S. In: Proceedings of the 13th ICAPS Workshop on Planning for Web Services (2003)
31. Sohrabi, S., Baier, J.A., McIlraith, S.A.: Preferred explanations: theory and generation via planning. In: Proceedings of the 25th AAAI Conference on Artificial Intelligence (2011)
32. Warriach, E.U., Kaldeli, E., Bresser, J., Lazovik, A., Aiello, M.: A tool for integrating pervasive services and simulating their composition. In: Maglio, P.P., Weske, M., Yang, J., Fantinato, M. (eds.) ICSOC 2010. LNCS, vol. 6470, pp. 726–727. Springer, Heidelberg (2010). https://doi.org/10.1007/978-3-642-17358-5_74

Service Engineering

Software Sustainability in the Age of Everything as a Service

Vasilios Andrikopoulos[1]([⊠]) [iD] and Patricia Lago[2,3] [iD]

[1] University of Groningen, Groningen, The Netherlands
v.andrikopoulos@rug.nl
[2] Vrije Universiteit Amsterdam, Amsterdam, The Netherlands
p.lago@vu.nl
[3] Chalmers University of Technology, Gothenburg, Sweden

Abstract. The need for acknowledging and managing sustainability as an essential quality of software systems has been steadily increasing over the past few years, in part as a reaction to the implications of "software eating the world". Especially the widespread adoption of the Everything as a Service (*aaS) model of delivering software and (virtualized) hardware through cloud computing has put two sustainability dimensions upfront and center. On the one hand, services must be sustainable on a technical level by ensuring continuity of operations for both providers and consumers despite, or even better, while taking into account their evolution. On the other hand, the prosuming of services must also be financially sustainable for the involved stakeholders.

In this work, we discuss the need for a software architecting approach that encompasses in a holistic manner the other two dimensions of software sustainability as well, namely the social and environmental aspects of services. We highlight relevant works and identify key challenges still to be addressed in the context of software systems operating across different models for cloud delivery and deployment. We then present our vision for an architecting framework that allows system stakeholders to work in tandem towards improving a set of sustainability indicators specifically tailored for the *aaS model.

Keywords: Software sustainability · *aaS · Cloud computing · Software architecture · Vision

1 Introduction

The last decades have generated an increasing awareness of the need for a more sustainable world that is at the same time increasingly being run by software systems [13]. Sustainability can be defined under two lenses as discussed in [16]: that of *sustainable use* of a system with regard to a function over a time horizon, and that of *sustainable development* that meets current needs without compromising the ability of future generations to do the same. Computing in general, and software in particular has the potential to enable sustainability across the societal

© Springer Nature Switzerland AG 2021
M. Aiello et al. (Eds.): Papazoglou Festschrift, LNCS 12521, pp. 35–47, 2021.
https://doi.org/10.1007/978-3-030-73203-5_3

spectrum by reducing the impact of production and consumption through digitalization, presuming its own footprint is brought under control. In the recent years, sustainability has been acknowledged as an essential software quality across four dimensions [23]: a *technical* one related to the ability of a software system to evolve and remain used in the long term, an *economic* one concerning the preservation and creation of capital and value, a *social* dimension focusing on the continuity of communities using the system, and an *environmental* one aiming to minimize the impact of the system on natural resources. The ubiquity of software, with the world proverbially eaten up by software day by day[1], makes this concept even more important, and nowhere more than in the *Everything as a Service (*aaS)* model as enabled by the extended Service-Oriented Architecture (SOA) paradigm [29]. This is because in that model, service owners and providers have a responsibility to not only their own stakeholders, with respect to generating sufficient profits to justify the existence of services, but also to the consumers of their services so as not to disrupt their operations [28]. Online services act as the backbone of online communities supporting their communication (e.g. Slack and similar) and collaborative work (e.g. GitHub). There are, however, increasing concerns about the environmental footprint of the software industry, especially with respect to the energy consumption of large data centers such as those realizing the public cloud these services rely upon [15,18].

As a consequence, the state of the art on sustainable software engineering has been evolving significantly in the last couple of decades, starting with a focus on 'green' software, i.e. focusing on the environmental dimension, but expanding also to the other ones. A recent survey of sustainable software research based on the 5Ws formula (why, when, who, where, and what) [3], shows that this is a very active and collaborative area of research, with a good level of maturity. Despite the efforts from various research communities, however, there is still a lot of ground to be covered with respect to establishing and exploiting the relation between software architecture and sustainability as a software quality [30], and especially for software services. This gap is even wider when cloud computing as the de facto computing model through which services are delivered to their consumers is brought in the picture. In spite of early efforts in that area, e.g. [9], consequent works have focused almost exclusively on improving the efficiency of cloud data centers with respect to energy consumption and/or CO_2 emissions, i.e. on the environmental dimension of sustainability. Moreover, very little evidence exists on the true software-driven optimizations applied in the data center industry beyond, for instance, the adoption of renewable energy resources or smart techniques for cooling and hardware-level efficiencies [5,18]. This creates the urgent need for an approach encompassing all dimensions in architecting sustainable systems in the *aaS model.

To this aim, we present our vision for an architecting framework focusing on *software systems running either on public clouds or on private/public hybrid cloud deployments*, potentially but not necessarily as *multi- or federated cloud solutions*, offering their functionality *as services* to their users. We scope our

---

[1] As famously noted by Marc Andreessen in his 2011 Wall Street Journal interview.

proposal to such systems because they are becoming the standard model for delivering software to its users in practice. The intended audience for our proposal, and therefore the primary stakeholders to be involved in this framework, are mainly system and solution architects as the potential adopters of our proposed approach. Ultimately, however, all providers and consumers of services are in scope. The objective of this work is therefore *to provide architects with guidance in designing, maintaining and evaluating sustainable systems in the scope of interest across all dimensions of sustainability.*

2   Related Works

In the following, we discuss the state of the art on sustainability in the context of service orientation and cloud computing, since these two fields provide the backdrop for our proposal.

Service Oriented Computing

Early works on sustainability in SOA focused on energy awareness of service-based applications (SBAs) and energy efficiency of services and service providers, that is, on the environmental aspect. Mello Ferreira et al. [25] for example define an energy efficiency metric specifically for services, which aggregates energy consumption with execution time. This metric allows them to treat the problem of implementing SBAs as compositions of services as an optimization problem of the tradeoff between performance and energy consumption. Lago and Jansen [22], on the other hand, discuss the role of software services in making enterprises greener, i.e., more environmentally sustainable. The proposed approach is focused on the creation of awareness across three problem areas: processes, services, and people. A portfolio of green software services for enterprises accessible through the Web that define the environmental strategies to be implemented and the metrics to be used for their evaluation, is envisioned for this purpose. In [8], Dustdar et al. analyze the case for delivering software services that are sustainable across all aspects of the term. The key proposition of this work is the creation of a marketplace of such services which is founded on business models promoting the collaboration of stakeholders towards delivering such services.

Cloud Computing

One of the earliest and most comprehensive works on sustainability for cloud computing was produced by the OPTIMIS EU project. In that context, Ferrer et al. [9] identified *dependable sociability* as one of the major challenges of cloud computing, a concept which encompasses explicitly economic and environmental sustainability, but also incorporates strong elements of social and technical sustainability through its trust and risk aspects. However, this sustainability is to be enabled by means of a service lifecycle management toolkit which focuses on cloud service and infrastructure optimization. As such, architecting of software systems is effectively restricted to the models supported by the toolkit. A lock-in dependence on the toolkit is also inadvertently created by the reliance on it. A similar, CO_2-emission optimizing approach is offered by the ECO$_2$Clouds project [31] across federated cloud solutions, which also includes an application controller that is responsible for redeploying application components across providers in order to minimize carbon emissions.

Branching out from the 2012 work on Green Cloud Architecture by Garg and Buyya [11], a series of works have examined the environmental impact of cloud data centers and aimed to reduce their energy footprint. SMICloud by Garg et al. [12], for example, folds in the concepts developed in [11] for the ranking of cloud service providers. In the recent survey by Gill and Buyya [14] on sustainable cloud computing there are more than a dozen surveys on the subject from the last decade mentioned as related work. The primary focus of these secondary studies, and by definition also of the primary studies they survey, is on optimizing the energy consumption as the means for minimizing the financial and environmental footprint for operating as cloud service providers. Even when other dimensions of sustainability are discussed, as for example in [15], the foreseen benefits are all effectively derived from energy saving and reclaiming techniques on the provider side. However, as discussed by Hilty and Aebischer [16], focusing on energy efficiency in systems where energy costs are a major component, like data centers, creates a high risk of *rebound effect*, i.e. improved energy consumption resulting into more or larger data centers consuming more electricity as a net sum. The continuous growth in the number of cloud data centers belonging to the major cloud providers actually points to this rebound effect in practice during at least the last decade.

Pahl et al. [26] frame the continuous evolution and adaptation of cloud-based software systems in a context of technical and economic sustainability. The proposed approach is building on the use of self-adaptation control loops across cloud delivery models as the means for ensuring the continuity of operations. The biggest difference of that approach with the ones presented above is that it clearly focuses on software systems as consumers of cloud services, instead of taking the service provider perspective.

Outside of "sustainability in cloud computing", Domdouzis [6] discusses cloud computing as an *enabler of sustainability* across social, environmental and economic dimensions. Cloud computing is hailed as a significant factor for achieving sustainability by means of promoting academic research, facilitating business development, and strengthening business competition. A similar multi-dimensional perspective is shared by GeSI (Global enabling Sustainability Initiative): in a recent webinar on "The Cloud as an Enabler of Innovation and Sustainability"[2] (see also [13]), CEO Luis Neves argued that any company (incl. data center leadership) should be driven by sustainability to become more

---

[2] 6 Oct. 2020.

profitable, and that transparency, accountability, trustability are key drivers to remain on the market.

3 Challenges

Architecting sustainable systems in general is acknowledged to be one of the grand challenges in modern software engineering, as discussed by Venters et al. [30]. The need for a more comprehensive view which (i) integrates the various dimensions while taking into consideration their relations and potential trade-offs, and (ii) enables further investigation into the relations of other software qualities and metrics, is also discussed by Condori-Fernandez et al. [4] and Lago et al. [24]. Beyond these general issues with sustainability in software architecture, however, there are additional concerns that rise due to infrastructure, platforms, and software being offered and used as a service, both on and off premises. For starters, *the inherent diffusion of responsibility boundaries in pro-suming relations creates a series of challenges*:

1. Acting as a provider puts the onus of responsibility on the service itself to be sustainable over time; however when services are consumed as part of the implementation of said service then there are obvious external dependencies that are in principle outside of the control of the service stakeholders.
2. There is in many cases a tension between the responsibility to the stake-holders/owner of the service in terms of sufficient revenue generation as the justification for the continued existence of the service, and the responsibilities to the wider society and the environment.

In order to deliver loose coupling [27], service orientation relies on the architecting principles of information hiding and encapsulation behind opaque interfaces. As a result, *services are intentionally offered as black boxes*, with little to no visibility of how they are implemented or operated. This inadvertently leads to a reliance on self-labeling (if at all) of the sustainability and other quality of service metrics by the service providers. It can be easily seen how this model can and has been abused by service providers, sometimes unintentionally so. Furthermore, while *private clouds are for all practical purposes white boxes* and can for example be instrumented to monitor their environmental impact in terms of energy consumption and heat generation, *public clouds are essentially black boxes*. If architecting of systems has to rely on information exposed by the provider, then there has to be a way to verify the provider claim in a controlled manner, even if this is under strict experimental conditions. An objective, standardized and auditable labeling mechanism instead is therefore required for this purpose. Architecting approaches for software systems that operate in this environment have therefore to acknowledge and fulfill the following requirements:

REQ1 The approach must concern itself with how all dimensions of sustainability (economic, technical, social, and environmental) are affected by the system under consideration.

REQ2 The approach must take into account that services are both used for the
design, implementation, and operation of the system (i.e. consumed),
and delivered to the users of the system (i.e. provided).

REQ3 The approach must acknowledge the fact there is limited to no visibility
into the workings of consumed services.

4   A Sustainability-Aware Architecting Framework: Vision and Future Work

Now that (i) practitioners start feeling the urgency to address sustainability
concerns in their business, and (ii) the business models entailing networks of
multiple stakeholders gain traction, a key challenge is to define clear and quantifiable responsibilities and accountability toward (shared) sustainability goals.
In practice, this requires the introduction of a reference architecture, and common standards and metrics. Such architecting tools will allow practitioners to
analyze, design, evaluate, and maintain software systems in collaboration with
the rest of the system stakeholders, both internal and external to their organization. However, as discussed in the previous sections, while we have some knowledge on how to architect systems for sustainability in general, we still have major
challenges to overcome in developing cloud-based systems that rely on services
on multiple levels and expose their functionality as services in a sustainable manner. As an evolutionary step towards this goal, we propose a sustainability-aware
framework which allows existing and to-be developed architecting methods and
techniques to interact with each other towards addressing these challenges. The
underlying idea is to put first the focus on raising awareness on how architecting
decisions affect system sustainability, and to reuse known best practices, before
looking into further empirical evidence on what works best for improving it.

Grounded in SoSA [20], the proposed framework aims to help software architects to address the challenges described in the previous section, taking into
account the need for operating in a hybrid (multi-)cloud deployment model. As
summarized in Fig. 1, it consists of:

- a set of *stakeholders* with distinct roles and responsibilities, and
- a set of *sustainability indicators*, one per dimension, that we perceive as existing in a positive feedback loop relation with each other.

Different stakeholders are involved in different aspects of sustainability, with the
exception of system architects that act as the natural hub of decision making and
consider all dimensions. Not shown in the figure are the architecting decisions
taken over time by the system architects in consultation with the other involved
stakeholders. These are to be reflected and documented following an appropriate
approach for this purpose as it will be discussed below. In the following we
present the components of this framework.

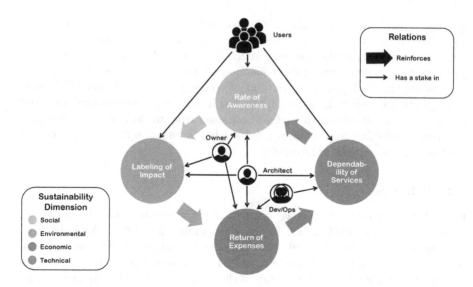

Fig. 1. A high-level view of the sustainability-aware architecting framework: stakeholders, sustainability dimensions and indicators, and their relations (Color figure online)

4.1 Stakeholders

The main stakeholder roles under consideration as summarized by Fig. 1 are:

Owner. The owners of the system to be architected, usually but not necessarily software-intensive enterprises; system owners are also expected to act as the service providers for the involved services.

Users. The sets of users relying on the functionalities delivered by the system; system users are acting as service consumers, and they might be in the same or different organization as the system Owner.

Dev/Ops. These are the developers, operators, and/or DevOps personnel responsible for the realization and running of the system services.

Architect. The software architect (or architects) involved in the requirement analysis, design and evaluation of the system.

Architects are to use architectural decision maps as per [21] to elucidate and communicate the effect of design decisions to the other stakeholders with respect to each dimension, balance concerns across the different dimensions, and exploit the relation of the different aspects as a positive feedback loop to be leveraged to deliver sustainability. As such, they take into consideration and are interested in improving all sustainability indicators discussed below. Owners also have potentially a stake in all indicators, however, the technical aspect of the system is actually relevant to them only if it has implications for the other dimensions, e.g. it results into a loss of revenue. For this purpose, this relation, from the Owner to the technical sustainability indicator is omitted from the figure. Similarly, Users are primarily interested in the continuity of the provided services and the impact that consuming them has on the environment, since it affects them indirectly, and as such they are not involved in decisions related to the economic sustainability of the system. Finally, the technical personnel is involved in principle only in two aspects: its economic one, in terms of e.g. service selection for hosting the deployed software, and of course its technical one. While it is tempting to have all stakeholders interested in all aspects of sustainability, and in some specific situations this might be indeed true, we feel that this mapping between aspects and responsibilities reflects better the stakeholder dynamics for the majority of systems of interest.

4.2   Indicators

Each of the four dimensions is associated in the framework with a *sustainability indicator* serving a dual function, in a manner similar to Hilty and Aebischer [16]: as a *metric* to provide insight into the current state and potential impact of architecting decisions to the stakeholders, and as a *goal* to optimize the architecture in order to reinforce the sustainability of the system. In the following, we discuss the associated indicator per dimension, and identify the research objectives and foreseen outcomes that we aim to address in the future. We start the discussion from the bottom of Fig. 1 and continue counter-clockwise.

Economic Dimension: The economic sustainability of a system in our framework is indicated by its *Return of Expenses* (RoE), that is, the degree of efficiency in consuming cloud resources (services like VM, storage, network etc.) with respect to the generated revenue by the system. Cloud computing was popularized on the basis of capital to operation expenses transfer [2]. RoE is meant to show how successful this transfer actually is, taking into account that despite the utility billing model of cloud services, it is fairly common for cloud-based software to generate *waste*. Waste here refers to the over–provisioning of computational resources within each billing cycle, e.g. VMs with low utilization or even idling for long periods relative to the billing unit. This waste can be generated for multiple and potentially overlapping reasons: over–estimation of the foreseen load for the provided services resulting into selection of over–sized configurations of cloud services during provisioning, absence of an appropriate scaling policy or sufficient guidance in the creation of such policy for the consumed cloud services, an inefficient assumption of underlying infrastructure as "always on" instead of on demand, typically as a result of a lift and shift migratory strategy (Type III migration in the taxonomy of [2]), and/or the inability of the scaling mechanisms put into place to compensate for quickly fluctuating load in an effective manner.

In any case, for software deployed on a public cloud provider the generated waste has a very real monetary impact on the monthly utilization bill which becomes obvious, in the literal sense of the word, to the system stakeholders. The annual practitioner surveys on the State of the Cloud conducted by Rightscale (currently under the Flexera banner) are, for example, showing a consistent waste of around 30% year after year. This is clearly an unacceptable level of resources misuse that needs to be addressed on a systemic level. What's more, addressing inefficiencies in the RoE creates also a positive effect on the technical dimension: the freed up financial resources due to lower expenses can be used instead for improving software quality, and especially "longevity" of the system throughout its evolution over time (red arrow in Fig. 1).

The main objective of the framework with respect to the financial sustainability of systems can therefore be summarized as:

> How to maximize *Return of Expenses* by minimizing the *wasting* of cloud resources in order to shift the *reclaimed revenue* towards improving the overall *software quality* of the system, and its *dependability* in particular?

Technical Dimension: The technical sustainability aspect of the framework is concerned with the particular characteristics of software quality that can benefit from the additional resources generated by its financial aspect, and more specifically, with the *Dependability of Services* that the system exposes to its users (Fig. 1). Dependability as a software quality refers to *the ability of services to deliver their functionality to their consumers in depth of time* [1]. It incorporates both operational attributes like availability, reliability, and scalability, and architectural ones like adaptability. The objective is therefore to allow system architects to develop the mechanisms required to answer the question:

> How to ensure the *continuous evolution* of a system within the confines prescribed by the desired *quality of service* levels to be offered, and the need to improve *the overall quality* of the system and specifically the *Dependability of its Services*?

In principle, the need for continuous evolution of software systems is dictated by the need to address changes across their operating environment: both internal (shifting of priorities and product focus) and external (technological and market changes). The dual nature of services that act as both providers and consumers creates additional complications that need to be taken into consideration:

1. When acting as *providers* of services, systems need to evolve their exposed APIs/service endpoints in a manner which preserves their compatibility with their clients in terms of both functional and non-functional expectations [28].
2. When acting as service *consumers*, and especially of cloud services, the overall quality of service offered by software systems very much depends on the quality of consumed services [2].

Social Dimension: Achieving higher dependability through continuous and controlled evolution empowered by more efficient use of financial resources leads naturally to an increased life expectancy of the offered services, and potentially a much heavier dependence on these services by their consumers (i.e. the Users in Fig. 1). In turn, this leads to the need for more awareness of the sustainability of the system across stakeholders in order to enable the communities of consumers in the long term. A proactive and constructive way of managing this need is by allowing sustainability-affecting decisions to become directly visible to the relevant stakeholders (owners and users). Achieving this effect in the most direct manner entails involving them actively in the decision making loop, or at the very least communicating to them the foreseen impact of e.g. changes to the architecture of the system. By these means, the level of awareness of the various stakeholders in decision making can be used as an indicator of social sustainability:

How to increase the *Rate of Awareness* across the involved system stakeholders as the means for engaging them in the effort to increase sustainability?

Existing approaches such as [7] have already identified methods for involving stakeholders during the analysis phase of architecting. However, our proposal is to expand their participation throughout the architecting life cycle.

Environmental Dimension: The longer life expectancy of offered services and prolonged consumption by engaged user groups creates inadvertently a larger environmental footprint. For the purposes of the framework, this footprint is primarily defined in terms of the energy consumed for operating and cooling the servers hosting the services, or the CO_2 emitted in the atmosphere as a by-product of converting fossil fuels into energy for this purpose. However, we know that eventually we will have to expand our work to also include second and third order effects to the environment through e.g. the consumption of raw material to build the equipment for the data centers hosting the servers, and the impact of the proliferation of services to the lifestyle of their users. Going back to the first order effects for now, being able to assess and label the system footprint in an objective and transparent manner is crucial for diagnosing inefficiencies in it, resulting to the following objective:

How to assign the appropriate *Labeling of Impact* to the environment created through the continuous operation of the offered services?

Ideally, the impact label of an offered service would be something as easy to communicate as the energy ranking of commercial devices, allowing for easy comparison between them by the users, and resulting in raising awareness across the board [10]. However, achieving this goal is far from trivial. First of all, the energy consumption of even simple systems is sensitive to small architecting changes, and extensive benchmarking and monitoring might be required in order to establish the actual footprint of the system [19]. Second, there is still a lack of appropriate methodological aspect and shared benchmarking data sets and tools for this purpose, as highlighted in [17]. Finally, as we discussed in the previous section, while the services owned by an organization can be the subject of both experimental measurement during development and monitoring in production, services consumed e.g. leased virtual machines in the cloud, are effectively opaque to such procedures. Using the published specifications of such services to establish an approximate model of their energy consumption, for example, could be an interesting approach in bypassing this opaqueness. However, further work is required in this direction.

Closing now the feedback loop of the indicators back to the economic dimension, it needs to be pointed out that better environmental labels, both in sense of their accuracy, and in terms of indicating low impact to the environment by the labeled system, have a potential positive effect on the economic dimension (green arrow in Fig. 1). The reasoning behind this is fairly straightforward: energy costs money; better, more reliable labels mean eventually less expenses through better service selection (from the perspective of the users) and less costs for operating data centers (for the system owner, provided they do not fall in the trap of the rebound effect [16]). It is therefore our proposition that it is possible, at least on conceptual level, to use these indicators to create a self-sustaining system which delivers sustainability in turn to its stakeholders across all dimensions. Realizing and assessing the efficacy of this vision lays ahead of us.

5 Conclusions

Prior works have already highlighted the relation between software architecture and sustainable development. When considering, however, software systems consuming cloud services while being offered as services on their own, the majority of existing approaches focuses primarily on the environmental aspect of the systems. As a reaction to this, we proposed our vision for an architecting framework defined along the lines of involved stakeholders and indicators that are used to govern the architecting process. Such indicators are to be used as the means for both improving the architecture of a system in terms of sustainability, and for communicating sustainability-affecting decisions to stakeholders. If implemented correctly, they allow architects to create a positive feedback loop which delivers sustainability across multiple dimensions. Putting this framework into practice, however, requires addressing a number of complex research questions in our immediate future.

References

1. Quality reference model for SBA. Technical report, S-Cube consortium (2008). https://s-cube-network.eu/results/deliverables/wp-jra-1.3/Reference_Model_for_SBA.pdf
2. Andrikopoulos, V., Binz, T., Leymann, F., Strauch, S.: How to adapt applications for the cloud environment. Computing 95(6), 493–535 (2013). https://doi.org/10.1007/s00607-012-0248-2
3. Calero, C., et al.: 5Ws of green and sustainable software. Tsinghua Sci. Technol. 25(3), 401–414 (2020)
4. Condori-Fernandez, N., Lago, P., Luaces, M.R., Places, Á.S.: An action research for improving the sustainability assessment framework instruments. Sustain. Sci. Pract. Policy 12(4), 1682 (2020)
5. DDCA: State of the Dutch Data Centers 2020: go digital, act sustainable. Technical report, Dutch Data Center Association, June 2020
6. Domdouzis, K.: Sustainable cloud computing. In: Green Information Technology: A Sustainable Approach, pp. 95–110. Elsevier Inc., March 2015

7. Duboc, L., et al.: Do we really know what we are building? Raising awareness of potential sustainability effects of software systems in requirements engineering. In: International Conference on Requirements Engineering, pp. 6–16. IEEE, September 2019

8. Dustdar, S., et al.: Green software services: from requirements to business models. In: Proceedings of the 2nd International Workshop on Green and Sustainable Software (GREENS 2013), pp. 1–7. IEEE Computer Society (2013)

9. Ferrer, A.J., et al.: OPTIMIS: a holistic approach to cloud service provisioning. Future Gener. Comput. Syst. **28**(1), 66–77 (2012)

10. Fonseca, A., Kazman, R., Lago, P.: A manifesto for energy-aware software. IEEE Softw. **36**(6), 79–82 (2019)

11. Garg, S.K., Buyya, R.: Green cloud computing and environmental sustainability. In: Harnessing Green IT, pp. 315–339. Wiley, September 2012

12. Garg, S.K., Versteeg, S., Buyya, R.: A framework for ranking of cloud computing services. Future Gener. Comput. Syst. **29**(4), 1012–1023 (2013)

13. GeSI: digital with purpose: delivering a SMARTer 2030. Technical report, GeSI (2019)

14. Gill, S.S., Buyya, R.: A taxonomy and future directions for sustainable cloud computing: 360 degree view. ACM Comput. Surv. **51**(5), 1–33 (2018)

15. Gill, S.S., et al.: Holistic resource management for sustainable and reliable cloud computing: an innovative solution to global challenge. J. Syst. Softw. **155**, 104–129 (2019)

16. Hilty, L.M., Aebischer, B.: ICT for sustainability: an emerging research field. In: Hilty, L.M., Aebischer, B. (eds.) ICT Innovations for Sustainability. AISC, vol. 310, pp. 3–36. Springer, Cham (2015). https://doi.org/10.1007/978-3-319-09228-7_1

17. Hindle, A.: Green software engineering: the curse of methodology. In: International Conference on Software Analysis, Evolution, and Reengineering (SANER), pp. 46–55. IEEE, May 2016

18. Jones, N.: How to stop data centres from gobbling up the world's electricity. Nature **561**(7722), 163–166 (2018)

19. Kazman, R., Haziyev, S., Yakuba, A., Tamburri, D.A.: Managing energy consumption as an architectural quality attribute. IEEE Softw. **35**(5), 102–107 (2018)

20. Lago, P.: SoSA: A Software Sustainability Assessment Method. European Computer Science Summit, October 2016. https://goo.gl/HuY6tf

21. Lago, P.: Architecture design decision maps for software sustainability. In: Proceedings of the 2019 IEEE/ACM 41st International Conference on Software Engineering: Software Engineering in Society, ICSE-SEIS 2019, pp. 61–64. IEEE, May 2019

22. Lago, P., Jansen, T.: Creating environmental awareness in service oriented software engineering. In: Maximilien, E.M., Rossi, G., Yuan, S.-T., Ludwig, H., Fantinato, M. (eds.) ICSOC 2010. LNCS, vol. 6568, pp. 181–186. Springer, Heidelberg (2011). https://doi.org/10.1007/978-3-642-19394-1_19

23. Lago, P., Koçak, S.A., Crnkovic, I., Penzenstadler, B.: Framing sustainability as a property of software quality. Commun. ACM **58**(10), 70–78 (2015)

24. Lago, P., et al.: Designing for sustainability: lessons learned from four industrial projects. In: Kamilaris, A., Wohlgemuth, V., Karatzas, K., Athanasiadis, I.N. (eds.) Advances and New Trends in Environmental Informatics. PI, pp. 3–18. Springer, Cham (2021). https://doi.org/10.1007/978-3-030-61969-5_1

25. Mello Ferreira, A., Kritikos, K., Pernici, B.: Energy-aware design of service-based applications. In: Baresi, L., Chi, C.-H., Suzuki, J. (eds.) ICSOC/ServiceWave - 2009. LNCS, vol. 5900, pp. 99–114. Springer, Heidelberg (2009). https://doi.org/10.1007/978-3-642-10383-4_7

26. Pahl, C., Jamshidi, P., Weyns, D.: Cloud architecture continuity: change models and change rules for sustainable cloud software architectures. J. Softw. Evol. Process **29**(2), e1849 (2017)

27. Papazoglou, M.P.: Web Services: Principles and Technology. Pearson Education, Harlow (2008)

28. Papazoglou, M.P., Andrikopoulos, V., Benbernou, S.: Managing evolving services. IEEE Softw. **28**(3), 49–55 (2011)

29. Papazoglou, M.P., Van Den Heuvel, W.J.: Service oriented architectures: approaches, technologies and research issues. VLDB J. **16**(3), 389–415 (2007). https://doi.org/10.1007/s00778-007-0044-3

30. Venters, C.C., et al.: Software sustainability: research and practice from a software architecture viewpoint. J. Syst. Softw. **138**, 174–188 (2018)

31. Wajid, U., et al.: On achieving energy efficiency and reducing CO_2 footprint in cloud computing. IEEE Trans. Cloud Comput. **4**(2), 138–151 (2016)

On the Migration to and Synthesis of (Micro-)services: The Use of Intelligent Techniques

Andreas S. Andreou$^{(\boxtimes)}$ and Andreas Christoforou

Cyprus University of Technology, 3036 Limassol, Cyprus
andreas.andreou@cut.ac.cy

Abstract. This chapter investigates the use of Computational Intelligence (CI) to tackle two challenges in the area of services. The first is involved with providing efficient decision support for migrating from monolithic to service-oriented software, while the latter addresses automatic service composition, which is a special form of service migration. Migration to service-oriented architecture (SOA) is influenced by a number of different and intertwined factors. These factors are identified through literature review and expert consultation. Different CI models, such as Fuzzy Influence Diagrams and Fuzzy Cognitive Maps, are employed to organize the factors and study their behavior. Various simulations are conducted that enable decision makers to execute what-if scenarios and take informed decisions as to whether to migrate or not to SOA, as well as to study the decisive factors contributing in favor or against this migration. Service synthesis is a tedious task considering on one hand the plethora of available services and on the other their different, often conflicting characteristics. Automation of this task is therefore a critical issue which deserves attention. In this context, the challenge of automatic service synthesis is addressed through specific methods and techniques based on Evolutionary Computation to achieve such automation to the best possible extent.

Keywords: Microservices · Migration · Synthesis · Automation · Decision-support

1 Introduction

Microservices architecture is conceived nowadays as the most prominent approach for the development of cloud-native applications, which are essentially suites of small and autonomous services that are easy to understand, deploy and scale. Following the new software engineering trends, Microservices architecture is tightly connected to the DevOps approach [2], which inherits its basic principles from agile methodologies and describes best practices to support the software development and operation processes. As microservices architecture is gaining popularity in software development, the research community has turned

© Springer Nature Switzerland AG 2021
M. Aiello et al. (Eds.): Papazoglou Festschrift, LNCS 12521, pp. 48–66, 2021.
https://doi.org/10.1007/978-3-030-73203-5_4

its attention to related challenges [12], such as the decomposition of a monolithic system into a set of independent services, followed by synthesis of selected microservices to substitute their functionality. Microservice synthesis relies on locating and combining small functional service components the characteristics of which match those of the decomposed system and put them in a proper order so as to meet the requirements of the initial monolithic system. Despite the hype for microservices, there is still lack of consensus on the adequate conditions to adopt and benefit from this new paradigm [30]. Most systems rely on design principles and infrastructure that do not permit to fully exploit the benefits of microservices, while adapting to this environment is a tedious task [2], since such systems are highly complex, not well documented and involve multiple characteristics that are easy to grasp or differentiate. Therefore, the identification and analysis of the characteristics forming a legacy or monolithic system is very important for both the stakeholders and the users. Particularly, an approach to assist the process of isolating the important functional characteristics and identifying suitable substitutes in the form of microservices is practically very useful. This approach should take into consideration not only the satisfaction of separate functional goals each time, but also the behavior (e.g. performance, security, usability, etc.) of the system, or large parts of it, as inseparable entities.

(Micro)Service composition requires locating the available services, defining the candidate (suitable) ones and finally select those that, when combined, lead to the closest matching of the functional and non-functional requirements of the system. Automation is critical here as it actually supports the DevOps process, the latter relying primarily on the fact that service composition comprises many critical tasks that may be automated apart from software building, like communication, coordination, monitoring, problem-solving, deployment etc.

This chapter focuses on two challenges in services migration and synthesis: The first revolves around the migration from monolithic to service-oriented software and examines the use of efficient decision support tools to assist this process. The second one may be considered as an extension of the first and calls for suggesting ways to automate service composition, a special form of service migration.

The above challenges are addressed under the prism of methods, techniques and tools from the area of Computational Intelligence (CI) [11,19]. Migration to Service-Oriented Architecture (SOA), on one hand, is influenced by a various intertwined or even conflicting factors. These factors are first identified through literature review and expert consultation and then different CI models, such as Fuzzy Influence Diagrams (FID) and Multi-Layer Fuzzy Cognitive Maps (MLFCM), are employed to organise them and study their behavior. Various simulations are conducted which enable decision makers to execute what-if scenarios and take informed decisions as to whether to migrate or not to SOA, as well as to study the decisive factors contributing in favor or against this migration. Service synthesis, on the other hand, is a complicated task considering the fact that there is a plethora of available services with substantial diversity in their characteristics, which does not always guarantee smooth integration and similar levels of performance between the individual services and the integrated part. Automating this task is therefore a critical issue that is also addressed in this chapter through Multi-Objective Genetic Algorithms (MOGA) [25]. We should note here that decomposition is conceived in this work as a step already taken and that it has been successfully concluded.

The rest of the chapter is organised as follows: Sect. 2 provides a brief literature overview in the area of interest, focusing mostly on decomposition aspects, automation of services synthesis and CI models or techniques utilised to tackle the challenges described earlier. Section 3 describes the development and application of FID and MLFCM models to the problem of migrating monoliths to microservices architecture, providing also a brief sketch of the relevant technical background and a small discussion of their differences. Section 4 investigates the problem of automating the process for integrating microservices using MOGA. Finally, Sect. 5 draws the concluding remarks and suggests future research steps.

2   Literature Overview

Contrary to the high interest that microservices architecture is gaining during the last years from both industry and academia, very few research papers deal with the factors that influence the decision to adopt this approach. Balalaie et al. [1] document the steps for the microservification of an on-premise Software-as-a-Service (SaaS) platform, highlighting the complexity of the migration task and at the same time identifying the main drivers for adopting microservices. The authors in [28] performed a survey among industry practitioners who adopted microservices, to analyse the motivations, as well as the pros and cons, of migrating from monolithic to microservice architectures. Aiming to identify intentions and strategies for the migration and the associated challenges that companies face, the authors in [14] conducted 16 in-depth interviews with software professionals based in Germany from 10 different companies. An evidence-based decision support framework was proposed in [27] based on a set of metrics that companies can use to decide whether to migrate to Microservices or not. Similarly, an empirical study was performed in [10] to collect the best practices towards microservice architecture migration. One may argue that no work has been identified to propose an intelligent method for decision support on Microservices migration.

The conventional decomposition problem, in terms of identification of individual services or components, has already been addressed by literature, mainly with the use of clustering techniques. Close to the topic this chapter addresses, even fewer research works deal with the monolithic system decomposition considering at the same time the selection of microservices that could replace fully or partially the integrated functionality. Baresi et al. [3] propose a clustering-like approach to support the identification of microservices and the specifications of the extracted artefacts during either the design phase of a new system or while the re-architecting of an existing system. A step-wise technique to identify microservices on monolithic systems is proposed in [21] in which the authors deliver an approach based on a dependency graph among three distinct parts of an application, client, server and database. The authors in [24] introduced a model for identifying microservices from a monolithic system utilising coupling strategies incorporated in a graph-based clustering algorithm. Another research work [27] proposed a decomposition framework to decompose monolithic systems into microservices, which mainly relies on the investigation and the removal of possible microservices anti-patterns. To tackle the challenge in migrating a monolith to microservices architecture, a three-phased data-flow driver mechanism was proposed by [18].

There is a plethora of research works that deal with service composition, which is recognised as a multi-objective, NP-hard problem [15] and subsequently, this imposes the use of search-based meta-heuristic techniques to deliver near-optimal solutions in an acceptable time. A systematic literature review was conducted in [18] and provided a classification of the existing relevant approaches, as well as described the open problems and the future research directions. Inter-service dependencies and conflicts are one of the open issues that this chapter aims to address.

3   Decision Support for Migration from Monolithic Software Systems to Microservices Architecture

3.1   Fuzzy Influence Diagrams

A simple ID is a directed acyclic graph with three types of nodes and three types of arcs between nodes. The first is called *Decision* node, it is drawn as a rectangle and corresponds to some decision to be made. *Chance* or *Uncertainty* node is the second type, which is drawn as an oval and represents an uncertainty to be modeled. The third one is the *Value* node, which is drawn as a hexagon (or octagon) or diamond, and calculates all possible combinations received from factors in the modeling environment that act as parent nodes. A *Functional* arc ends at a *Value* node and represents the contribution of the node at its tail to the calculated value. The second type of arc is the *Conditional*, which ends at a chance node and indicates that the uncertainty at its head is probabilistically related to the node (oval) at its tail. Finally, an *Informational* arc ends at a *Decision* node and indicates that the decision at its head is made according to the outcome of the node at its tail, which is known beforehand. The nodes of a system under modeling and the weighted arrows connecting these nodes are set to specific values based on the knowledge and beliefs of experts. The input and output values of a node in an ID are represented by probabilities. A common technique for evaluating and solving an ID is based on the Bayesian Theorem [26]. Initially, the possible values of each frontier node are defined, as well as the probability of occurrence of any value. The same procedure is followed iteratively for the direct descendant nodes considering all possible combinations of values of their direct ancestors that yield their own value and then defining the probability of occurrence for each such value. This procedure is terminated when the value node is reached, the latter calculating all possible combinations received.

Fuzzy Influence Diagrams (FID) were firstly proposed by [23] in an attempt to combine the features of IDs and the flexibility of Fuzzy Logic (FL). The FID architecture is the same as that of a generic ID in terms of structure, except that it employs fuzzy reasoning instead of probabilities. Each of the nodes considered as the outer elements of the FID, that is, they receive directly the values from the environment, is associated with a fuzzificator F which converts the node's input values to fuzzy values via its membership function [23]. Then, for each of the children nodes there is a fuzzy set G_i which represents the way the current node influences the given child node and its membership function is selected from a set of sigmoid and bell-shaped (Gaussian) functions. In cases of multiple parents m, the influence of each parent node on a certain child is weighted by the set of the m scalars (weights) using a technique called *hedges*. The output to the $i_t h$ child node is produced by the combination of F and G_i using Scalable Monotonic Chaining [16]. After initialization, the model is run and the values of the direct children nodes are calculated sequentially using the scalable monotonic chaining approach mentioned above.

The development of the proposed model was based on the findings of [7]. This work identified the key factors and drivers that influence the decision of migrating to microservices following a systematic process consisting of literature review and experts feedback. Minor changes were made to these factors as these emerged from a new round of literature review. Specifically, the concept *Business Complexity* was removed since it was found to have a weak presence and influence on the model, while a new concept *Data Migration* was added. The final list of factors is depicted graphically in the FID of Fig. 1.

The relationships between the nodes and the construction of the F- and G-type fuzzy sets, were defined using again the fuzzified values gathered by experts. For all nodes in the diagram, a common F-type graph shape was selected, which represents best these fuzzy sets. The sigmoid equation has been chosen to represent the G-Type fuzzy set for all nodes in the model. The range of the G-type fuzzy set is between -0.5 and $+0.5$, with $\lambda = 5$. The proposed representation is a two-level structure with all factors expressed as frontier nodes in the diagram. Groups of those factors influence intermediary nodes, which, in turn, influence the unique node.

The FID was validated in terms of expected performance under the execution of two scenarios. More specifically, two synthetic (hypothetical but realistic) scenarios were created representing the so-called "extreme cases", that is, a certain situation where everything would be in favor of Microservices migration (positive scenario) and another one where the opposite would hold (negative scenario). The target was to assess the verdict of the evaluation node of the model under known situations and check whether the outputs indicated that the model behaves correctly. After execution the model was led to the value of 0.72 for the positive scenario and to the value of 0.28 for the negative scenario. This performance is considered successful.

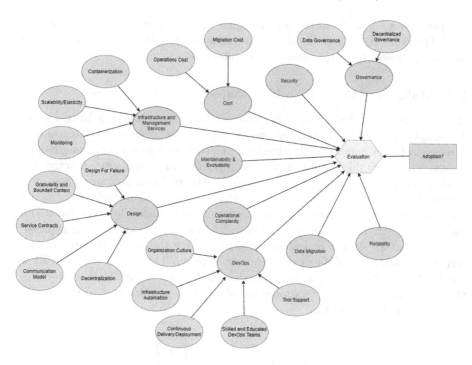

Fig. 1. FID model for the migration of a monolith to microservices architecture.

As mentioned above, one of the most significant benefits of the models based on FID, is their ability to perform simulation analysis based on what-if scenarios making them an efficient tool in the hands of decision-makers. The interactive capabilities provided, enable the study of the effects of changing various parameters (factors) of the problem under investigation, such as the identification of the source of undesired situations. In such a case, the decision-maker will be able to identify which factors are responsible for a particular outcome. This simulation process provides essential information to decision-makers to understand the behaviour of the model in its entirety, as well as the exposure of each node. This information will essentially guide users to perform possible actions.

A series of what-if scenario experiments were conducted so as to identify whether the top three nodes, according to their weight of influence on the final decision, are able to invert the decision for the negative scenario. The values of the concepts, *Governance*, *Maintainability & Evolvability* and *DevOps*, were inverted to a high positive value along with their child concepts. The execution of the FID resulted the value of 0.62, which may be considered as a significant improvement. It is easy for one to conclude that the three top nodes, as a group, have a significant impact over the final decision. Therefore, a decision-maker may focus on these nodes, as well as their feeders, and study their behavior, or even work towards changing this behavior in order to improve the environment for taking a specific decision (e.g. increase the level of tools support that feeds the DevOps node so as to increase its value and make migration more attractive). Overall, FID may be considered a useful tool to guide decision-making for migrating monoliths to microservices architecture.

3.2 Multi-layer Fuzzy Cognitive Maps

An FCM is a directed graph with nodes representing concepts in a domain and weighted edges describing the various causal relationships that exist among these concepts. A numeric activation level of a concept denotes the strength of its presence in the problem domain. The map is initialised with a set of activation levels that represent a particular scenario in the problem domain. Then, it is executed on a series of discrete steps in which the activation levels of the nodes are iteratively updated based on the causation relationship between them and the previous activation value using a transfer function (in our case the sigmoid, see Eq. 1 and 2). At the end of the execution cycle the map either reaches an equilibrium state, or exhibits cyclic/chaotic behavior. The former two cases allow one to develop simulation scenarios and make inference. The main outcome of the execution is the final activation value of the concept of interest (central node) for that particular scenario.

$$A_i^{t+1} = f\left(\sum_{j=1, i\neq j}^{n} w_{ji} A_j^t + A_i^t \right) \tag{1}$$

where

$$f(x) = \frac{1}{1 + e^{-\lambda x}} \tag{2}$$

In case the problem under study is highly complicated and some of the concepts in a typical FCM model are composed of other (sub)concepts that influence their activation levels, a Multi-Layer Fuzzy Cognitive Map (MLFCM) may be formed to handle the complexity introduced by the multifaceted concepts [22] (see Fig. 2a). A MLFCM is basically a hierarchical tree structure, with the topmost level (root) including the most abstract or composite concepts, while the lower branches add more details by decomposing concepts of the immediate higher layer. In this way, several "local" sub-FCMs are formed. The advantage of this structure is the creation of small and more easily manageable models (sub-FCMs), which co-work supporting the main, high level FCM, and at the same time it provides the level of detail required for fully capturing the dynamics of the problem under study. The calculation of the concept activation levels follows a depth-first way in each iterative step.

The development of the proposed model was based also upon the work conducted in [7] incorporating the changes described in the previous section. The identified concepts were organized in a two-layer MLFCM, see Table 1. The construction of the updated version of the model was completed with the definition of the causal relationships by a group of experts where needed after performing the aforementioned changes. The visual representation of the model is shown in Fig. 2a.

Table 1. Concepts that influence the decision for the migration of a monolith to microservices architecture.

FCM	Concepts	Central concept	Layer
1	C1, C2, C3, C4, C5, C6, C7, C8, C9, C10, C28	C28	1
2	C1, C11, C12	C1	2
3	C2, C13, C14, C15	C2	2
4	C8, C16, C17	C8	2
5	C9, C18, C19, C20, C21, C22	C9	2
6	C10, C23, C24, C25, C26, C27	C10	2

A series of steps were applied in an attempt to investigate the model's behaviour following the step-wise process introduced in [6]. This process consists of the static and dynamic analyses, where the first allows one to examine the model's properties before its execution, while the second enables the extraction of additional observations regarding the model's behaviour during execution.

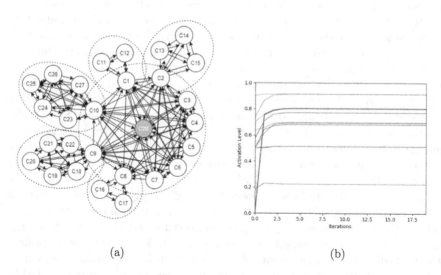

(a)   (b)

Fig. 2. (a) A multi-layer FCM model for the migration of a monolith to microservices architecture, (b) An indicative what-if scenario run for studying the relationship between Cost and Security (the central concept with the bold blue line) (Color figure online)

Static analysis uses notions of Graph Theory to deliver measurements such as: complexity of the graph (in terms of density, depth and breadth); strength of each node (weight and number of its incoming and outgoing edges); and, tendency of cycles in the graph (positive cycles amplify any initial activation value and vice-versa). These measurements may reveal the strongest or weakest concepts in terms of importance and the level of each sub-FCM influences the main FCM in the upper level.

Applying the static analysis and observing the results, it is easy to conclude that this is a high-density model of significant complexity. The tendency of the model is not clear since the main FCM has a higher number of negative cycles than positive, with the rest of the sub-FCMs presenting higher numbers of positive cycles than negative. This unclear result suggests a more extensive study to form a better understanding of the model. The concepts *Infrastructure and Management Services*, *Maintainability & Evolvability*, and *Reliability*, appear to be the three strongest concepts of the main FCM. This finding is a strong indication and calls for further investigation of the behaviour of these concepts individually, in pairs or as a group. Especially for the two first concepts, the study can be broken-down to the corresponding decomposed sub-FCM in order to understand which concepts in the lower layers affect the final value of each of them, and to what extent.

Dynamic analysis includes mainly targeted executions in an attempt to allow the assessment of the model's behaviour through simulations under manually configured what-if scenarios. The execution of the two extreme scenarios, positive and negative, is the first step of the dynamic analysis, which also may be considered as a validation execution. For the positive scenario, the initial activation levels were selected in such a way so as to drive the model to an extremely positive outcome. Inversely, for the negative scenario, the initial activation levels were selected in favour of the negative outcome. The result of this validation step was successful, that is, the model behaved as expected: By applying the extreme scenarios, the model managed to converge to stable values after a small number of iterations (below 10) and matched the desired outcome. Specifically, the execution of the positive scenario led the final activation level of the central concept to the value of 0.95, while the execution of the negative scenario to 0.05.

The successful performance of the model over the two extreme scenarios enabled the design and execution of what-if scenarios the findings of which could confirm, extend and complement those of the static analysis. At first, a series of executions were designed targeting at confirming the results of the static analysis. Through these executions, the concept Infrastructure and Management Services was confirmed as the strongest node of the model. This finding was obtained by setting all concepts to a mean value of 0.5 as initial activation level, except for the concept under investigation or interest. The execution was repeated by changing the value of the concept of interest and observing the effect it had on the final value of the central concept. The list of the concepts investigated was ranked according to the effect (range) of the change caused by each of them on the final value of the central concept, thus producing a robust indication for its strength. Indicatively, we note that the change caused in the final value of the model by the strongest node was 0.12, in contrast to 0.01 by the weakest.

Further simulations were conducted aiming to study the sub-FCM that interact and feed the concept Infrastructure and Management Services, which was identified as the most influential one. These executions targeted to identify the importance and contribution of concept Scalability/Elasticity to the upper layer and subsequently to the final outcome of the model.

A common concern amongst decision-makers that are dealing with Microservices migration is the conflicting relationship between *Cost* and *Security*. A series of dedicated what-if scenarios were designed and executed to study this relationship and the model's behaviour concerning these concepts (see Fig. 2b). Working in the same way as described above, a mean value was set to all initial values of all concepts, while for each execution the initial activation values for the concepts under study were varied accordingly, one each time. The results obtained confirmed the conflicting relation between these two concepts, as well as the level of impact each of them has to the outcome of the model: Strengthening security aspects increases cost, and therefore makes it less attractive to migrate to microservices, while lowering security expectations also lowers cost and this finally promotes migration. This short demonstration example proves the practical value of the model to decision-makers as it allows them to define the hypothetical (what-if) scenarios and study their outcome via simulation, something which is extremely valuable when trying to understand what should be changed in the environment under modelling so that the desired outcome is reached.

4   Automatic Microservices Synthesis

Decomposing a monolith to its distinctive functional parts is the first step towards its migration to a microservices-oriented solution. This problem is not new though, there are various papers in the relevant literature that address the decomposition of software systems into smaller functional parts such as modules, components, functions or even and standalone services mainly by means of clustering techniques upon design artifacts [4] or source code [20]. As the authors indicate in [5], the boundaries between software modules defined by these approaches were too flexible or vague, and allowed software to evolve into "big balls of mud". Microservices are somehow relieving this problem as their use defines better the physical boundaries of functionality. However, the identification of the right microservices should aim primarily on securing the accurate replication of the system's functionality, but at the same time, as Baresi et al. note, on partitioning the system to facilitate easy maintenance [3], something which will also define how the system will be able to evolve and scale.

As previously mentioned, this chapter does not examine decomposition of the monolith under migration; it considers this task as being successfully completed and therefore starts directly investigating the automatic synthesis of the proper microservices. The process followed here adopts the basic principles proposed in [8] which are adapted and refined to reflect the characteristics of the monolithic software, while at the same time accommodating the differences and peculiarities of the Microservices environment. The framework in [8] essentially recommends expressing the set of functional specifications derived from the decomposition of the monolith in a formalised syntax using EBNF. This formalism is then converted to a dedicated ontology which is used as the basis for suggesting candidate solutions, i.e. combinations of microservices, as these are evolved by dedicated MOGAs, matching the required functionality and taking into consideration various constraints.

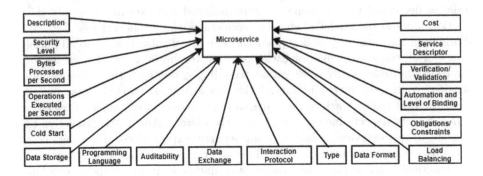

Fig. 3. Microservice ontology.

Different methods are proposed in literature for description processing, such as simple string [13], signature matching [31] and behavioural matching [32]. The approach followed here is a hybrid form combining string and behavioural matching. More specifically, a dedicated parser is implemented that recognises certain parts in a profile (functional, non-functional and other properties) which is translated into an ontology instance (either of a monolith function or of a microservice). The parser first verifies that the profile is expressed in the proper context and semantics using the ANTLR framework[1] and then proceeds with building the ontology tree of instances according to the recognised parts. Parsing and transformation essentially build the ontology tree instances that describe the monolith under decomposition and the available microservices (see Fig. 3). The next step is to match properties between ontology items. The tree instance of the functionality under migration is projected on top of any other candidate microservice assessing the level of requirements fulfilment in two phases: The first phase checks that all required functions (the monolith's part to be replaced) are satisfied by the available microservices; therefore, we treat these as functional constraints. In this case the list of services sought (decomposed part) must be at least a subset of the services offered (candidate microservices). The second phase is executed once all functional constraints are satisfied and calculates the level of suitability of each candidate microservice.

The matching process works as follows: Firstly, we assume that the discrete functionality offered by a monolith and the associated non-functional aspects (performance indicators) are already expressed in ontological form. Then the ontology tree is traversed in a depth-first-search manner until the leaves are reached, that is, the details of the functions/methods (e.g. interfaces, arguments, conditions, etc.) the monolith is made of. Then the algorithm climbs

---

[1] https://www.antlr.org/.

up the ontology structure until it reaches the definition of the function/method to which this detailed information refers. This way the functional parts of interest in the monolith's ontology instance are isolated creating a form of meta-ontology. The non-functional properties are then visited on the ontology tree top-down using a string-matching approach, where we differentiate between two cases: (i) The overall performance indicator(s), which describe how the monolith's functionality behaves as one entity of integrated functions. This will be used during the synthesis part of the matching algorithm to guide the process of recommending microservices for integration taking into consideration how their combination should behave as a whole, any incompatibilities in terms of interfacing, timing (synchronous/asynchronous), its type (SOAP, REST), etc.; (ii) Method-specific indicators, that constrain the way a certain function (method) delivers its functionality as a single unit. This piece of information will be used by the matching algorithm when assessing the suitability of a microservice as it is considered a mandatory requirement. As soon as all meta-ontology parts (i.e. methods) are isolated, the proposed matching algorithm is invoked. Considering a single function (method) from the derived decomposition, we aim to match it with a candidate microservice that resides in the pool of available microservices. For simplicity purposes, let the instance of the source (monolith) function for microservice substitution be denoted as M_{sk} ($k = 1..M$, where M is the number of decomposed monolith functions), which is considered as the profiled microservice sought after decomposition (from now on we will refer to this as the 'source microservice'). At the other end, the profile of all of the available microservices is also parsed and ontology instances are created, let these be M_{ti} ($i = 1..N$, where N is the number of available microservices). Due to the fact that there is a form of heterogeneity between microservice attributes that concern their data types, a combination of metrics is used in order to assess the matching score of each target microservice instance Ti while taking into account the aforementioned heterogeneity.

The ontology profile has three distinct data types, namely *binary*, *numerical* and *string*. Therefore, a different metric function is used for each data type. For the binary data type, the similarity function score is given by the following formula:

$$S_{bin} = \frac{1}{N} \sum_{i=1}^{N} b_{st,i} \tag{3}$$

where,

$$b_{st,i} = \begin{cases} 0, & \textit{if binary attribute } i \textit{ required in } M_s \textit{ is not satisfied in } M_t \\ 1, & \textit{if binary attribute } i \textit{ required in } M_s \textit{ is satisfied in } M_t \end{cases}$$

$$\tag{4}$$

and M_s and M_t are the source and target microservice ontology instances respectively.

Respectively, the score between any two sets of numerical attributes is given by:

$$S_{num} = \frac{1}{N} \sum_{i=1}^{N} \{max_{st,i}, min_{st,1}\} \tag{5}$$

where, $max_{st,i}$ is the formula for attribute i to be maximized between source and target ontology instances given by:

$$max_{st,i} = 1 - \frac{n_{s,i} - n_{t,i}}{max(n_{s,i}, n_{t,i})} \tag{6}$$

and $min_{st,i}$ is the formula for attribute i to be minimized between source and target ontology instances given by:

$$min_{st,i} = 1 + \frac{n_{s,i} - n_{t,i}}{max(n_{s,i}, n_{t,i})} \tag{7}$$

Since some attribute values can be maximized or minimized, we use the correct formula for attribute value similarity calculation each time. For example, the attribute bytes processed per second is maximized because it has to score higher if the value offered is higher than the desired one. On the contrary, the attribute cost has to be minimized due to the exact opposite reason. Cost similarity value has to score higher if the offered value is less than the desired one.

Lastly, the score between any two sets of string attributes s_s and s_t is given by the mean of the Jaccard similarity coefficient:

$$S_{str} = \overline{(J(S_s, S_t))} \tag{8}$$

where (S_s, S_t) is the Jaccard similarity coefficient between source and target string sets respectively, and is calculated as:

$$J(S_s, S_t) = \frac{|S_s \cap S_t|}{|S_s \cup S_t|} = \frac{|S_s \cap S_t|}{|S_s| + |S_t| - |S_s \cap S_t|} \tag{9}$$

where $|S_s|$ is the number of terms contained in string S_s, $|S_t|$ is the number of terms contained in string S_t, and $|S_s \cap S_t|$ is the number of shared terms between strings S_s and S_t respectively.

Using the equations above we can now describe the procedural flow of the matching algorithm. The algorithm consists of two sequential phases:

Phase 1: All attributes of the source microservice, which are considered as mandatory, must map one-on-one to the attributes of the target microservice. This means that, by traversing all of the available target microservices, each attribute of the source microservice is verified to exist in the target microservice. Otherwise, the target microservice is discarded and it is removed from the pool of candidate microservices. Therefore, after Phase 1 concludes, the pool of candidate target microservices has been reformed to include only those target microservices that in general match the mandatory requirements of the source microservice; the level of suitability of the microservices in this pool may vary depending on secondary, desired features or properties they may possess, the respective values of which are subsequently assessed in Phase 2 by the score functions previously described. As previously mentioned, Phase 1 is supported by a variation of the GMO algorithm [17] which was developed to parse every pair of the compared microservice ontologies (source and target) and defines their structural similarity.

Phase 2: The similarity between a source microservice and a specific target microservice in the pool of candidate microservices formed by Phase 1 is assessed through the relevant score functions depending on their data type. The algorithm calculates the mean of binary, numerical and string score of the pair and produces a similarity value. This is repeated for every pair of source and target microservice in the pool, and the final outcome is a ranked matching score:

$$S_{tot} = \overline{(S_{bin} + S_{num} + S_{str})} \tag{10}$$

The experimental process employed two MOGAS to deliver a near-optimal synthesis of candidate microservices considering the required functionality defined by the decomposition of the monolith. Our case study involves the functional parts of an inventory system and are dedicated for invoice updating containing five different functions: *Update Invoice Items, Update Invoice Headers, Update Corresponded Posting, Update Debtor's Balance* and *Print Invoice.* These functions are all sequentially dependent (in the order listed), that is, every function depends on its previous one and starts as soon as its predecessor has concluded.

A pool of 2000 synthetic microservices profiles were randomly constructed ensuring that a minimum number of 100 microservices match the requirements of each functional part. This intuitively means that we make sure that every decomposed part has at least 100 candidate microservices in the pool that matched and satisfy the mandatory requirements, but with unknown suitability score. We validated the scores computed by the matching process by varying certain attribute values of the functional parts that derive from the monolith and repeating the process. We observed that when varying the attribute values, that is, changing the requirements, the matching algorithm correctly yielded different scores and proper rankings among the candidate microservices as expected.

Two MOGAS were selected to solve the multi-objective optimisation problem, which will also be used to compare their performance and effectiveness: The Non-dominated Sorting Genetic Algorithm II (NSGA-II) [9] and the Strength Pareto Evolutionary Algorithm 2 (SPEA2) [33]. The selection of these two specific algorithms was made due to their wide acceptance and use, but most importantly their good performance in such kind of applications which was proven in our case too after a quick verification with preliminary runs. The multi-objective optimisation environment was accordingly adjusted and configured based on the problem under study: The two objectives formed were the minimisation of the microservice cost and the execution time (performance) respectively. We assume that the two are competing in the sense that the higher the performance the more expensive the microservice. The set of decision variables was constructed by five vectors each corresponding to a decomposed function and yielding values related to the selected candidate microservice that delivers the same functionality. Two constraints were also set, one for each objective, both denoting an upper value for the objectives (cost, time) that cannot be tampered. The experimental implementation of the algorithms was performed using Platypus[2], a Python-based multi-objective optimisation algorithms library. The results are provided in Table 2 (sample of the best five ranked microservices) and consist of the id of the best five microservices for each functional part, along with their matched score in descending order.

A total number of 807 unique microservices have fulfilled the mandatory requirements and were selected to be included in the candidate microservices pool as follows: 323 microservices were included in *Print Invoice* function's list, 144 in *Update Invoice* function's list, 126 microservices in *Update Invoice* Headers function's list, 135 microservices in *Update Debtors Balance* function's list, and, finally, 79 microservices are included in *Update Posting* function's list.

The proposed algorithm performed successfully discarding all candidate microservices that failed to satisfy even one mandatory requirement. By choosing and comparing arbitrarily microservices from the same list of candidates we then confirmed the correct assessment of the microservices by the matching algorithm as this is reflected in the calculated suitability scores, as well as the correctness of their prioritisation. The aforementioned results were subsequently used for the assessment of the microservices synthesis. The number of possible solutions (PS) in this case is calculated by Eq. 11 to be over three (3) trillions.

$$|PS| = \prod_{i=1}^{N} x_i \tag{11}$$

N in Eq. 11 corresponds to the number of decomposed functions and X_i is the number of recommended microservices for function i.

Each MOGA was run 100 times for 500000 Fitness Evaluations (FE) resulting in the generation of 100 Pareto fronts. By combining these Pareto fronts, a near-optimal Pareto front was produced for each algorithm (see Fig. 4). By inspecting the Pareto fronts one may observe that the two MOGAs delivered similar solutions. Furthermore, if we focus on the microservices combinations which corresponded to the optimal solutions, we may note that microservices with high individual suitability scores are missing from the proposed optimal solutions and respectively microservices belonging to the optimal solutions sets have relatively low suitability scores compared to others. This finding is perfectly reasonable as this experiment was focused on optimising cost and performance, while the suitability score is the collection of other parameters as well. Therefore, the recommended solutions that will drive the synthesis of microservices

---

[2] https://platypus.readthedocs.io.

will always depend on the aspects that designers need to optimise each time. The performance of the two MOGAs was assessed and compared with the use of the Hypervolume (HV) [34] and the Inverted Generational Distance (IGD) [29] quality indicators. The HV value for both algorithms was identical and equal to 0.0254. The IGD value for the NSGA-II was 0.6211 and for SPEA2 0.6350. The results of the two indicators suggest a similar performance with no clear distinction between the two algorithms used. Two statistical tests were used to determine if there is any statistical difference between the algorithms. Both the Wilcoxon signed-rank test and the Mann-Whitney U test suggested that there is no statistical difference ($p < 0.05$) between the HV and IGD results of the two algorithms. Therefore, the two MOGAs are equally suitable to offer a sound basis to guide the automation of microservices synthesis.

Table 2. Scoring results of components' functional parts with dependencies.

Print invoice	Update invoice items	Update invoice headers	Update debtors balance	Update posting
800 (0.65)	104 (0.50)	329 (0.63)	740 (0.61)	421 (0.90)
1455 (0.60)	1506 (0.49)	1612 (0.60)	692 (0.59)	545 (0.89)
1995 (0.58)	65 (0.48)	312 (0.55)	706 (0.58)	499 (0.89)
1079 (0.57)	101 (0.47)	273 (0.53)	611 (0.55)	524 (0.88)
1137 (0.57)	82 (0.47)	231 (0.52)	1506 (0.54)	1480 (0.87)

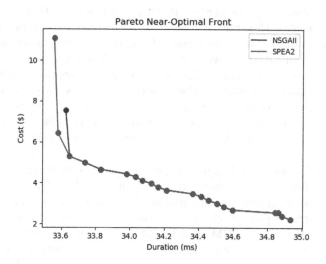

Fig. 4. Near-optimal Pareto fronts

5   Conclusions

This chapter addressed two challenges in the area of service migration. The first one was involved with supporting migration from monolithic to microservices architecture, while the latter dealt with automatic service composition. Both challenges were tackled using models and techniques from the area of Computational Intelligence (CI).

Migration from monolithic software to microservices was approached with two different CI models, namely Fuzzy Influence Diagrams (FID) and Multi-Layer Fuzzy Cognitive Maps (MLFCM). As migration is influenced by a number of different and intertwined factors, initially these factors were identified through literature review and expert consultation, and then they were used to produce FID and MLFCM models that represented the environment of the corresponding decision. The models were successfully validated against known "extreme" scenarios (fully positive or negative towards the decision). Each of the two models was then executed with various what-if scenarios, which allow decision makers to execute simulations and take informed decisions whether to migrate or not to SOA, as well as to study the decisive factors contributing in favor or against this migration. The two models are in general easy to comprehend and use, while their effectiveness and practical usefulness was demonstrated through the experimentation phase. This phase also revealed that the MLFCM are by nature more detailed and offer the ability to investigate the factors that contribute most to the formation of the final result at a finer level of granularity compared to FIDs.

Automatic services synthesis is a difficult task to tackle as there is a plethora of available services with various characteristics which are often conflicting when integrating services together. This chapter focused on the case of automating the migration of a monolithic software to services architecture. A novel matching algorithm was proposed which utilizes an ontological schema, the latter being used to express the functionality of the monolith and the available microservices. Two Multi-objective Genetic Algorithms (MOGAs) were employed to evolve near-optimal solutions which satisfy the required functionality and some non-functional constraints, with the results indicating that both achieved good performance.

The use of CI models and techniques are proven very useful in tackling complex problems like the ones described in this chapter. New CI approaches are continuously produced focusing on handling this complexity and delivering solutions in this area. Future work in the context of this chapter could include revisiting the FID and MLFCM models and adding new and/or more detailed factors that affect the decision to migrate to services architecture. The strength of these models is of course their ability to perform simulations. Therefore, this aspect could be further exploited using various conflicting factors to investigate how they can be handled to avoid problematic situations, like security concerns. Finally, there is still ground to be covered before we reach to solutions that offer full automation of services synthesis. This chapter paved the way of automating the process of selecting the most suitable microservices, both at the entity level and at the integration. Future steps may include automating the actual binding of these microservices and their evaluation at run-time considering the satisfaction of constraints on the Service Level Agreements (SLAs).

References

1. Balalaie, A., Heydarnoori, A., Jamshidi, P.: Migrating to cloud-native architectures using microservices: an experience report. In: Celesti, A., Leitner, P. (eds.) ESOCC Workshops 2015. CCIS, vol. 567, pp. 201–215. Springer, Cham (2016). https://doi.org/10.1007/978-3-319-33313-7_15
2. Balalaie, A., Heydarnoori, A., Jamshidi, P.: Microservices architecture enables DevOps: migration to a cloud-native architecture. IEEE Softw. **33**(3), 42–52 (2016)
3. Baresi, L., Garriga, M., De Renzis, A.: Microservices identification through interface analysis. In: De Paoli, F., Schulte, S., Broch Johnsen, E. (eds.) ESOCC 2017. LNCS, vol. 10465, pp. 19–33. Springer, Cham (2017). https://doi.org/10.1007/978-3-319-67262-5_2
4. Browning, T.R.: Applying the design structure matrix to system decomposition and integration problems: a review and new directions. IEEE Trans. Eng. Manag. **48**(3), 292–306 (2001)
5. Chen, L.: Continuous delivery: overcoming adoption challenges. J. Syst. Softw. **128**, 72–86 (2017)
6. Christoforou, A., Andreou, A.S.: A framework for static and dynamic analysis of multi-layer fuzzy cognitive maps. Neurocomputing **232**, 133–145 (2017)
7. Christoforou, A., Garriga, M., Andreou, A.S., Baresi, L.: Supporting the decision of migrating to microservices through multi-layer fuzzy cognitive maps. In: Maximilien, M., Vallecillo, A., Wang, J., Oriol, M. (eds.) ICSOC 2017. LNCS, vol. 10601, pp. 471–480. Springer, Cham (2017). https://doi.org/10.1007/978-3-319-69035-3_34
8. Christoforou, A., Odysseos, L., Andreou, A.: Migration of software components to microservices: matching and synthesis. In: Proceedings of the 14th International Conference on Evaluation of Novel Approaches to Software Engineering, pp. 134–146. SCITEPRESS-Science and Technology Publications, Lda (2019)
9. Deb, K., Pratap, A., Agarwal, S., Meyarivan, T.: A fast and elitist multiobjective genetic algorithm: NSGA-II. IEEE Trans. Evol. Comput. **6**(2), 182–197 (2002)
10. Di Francesco, P., Lago, P., Malavolta, I.: Migrating towards microservice architectures: an industrial survey. In: 2018 IEEE International Conference on Software Architecture (ICSA). IEEE (2018). 29-2909
11. Engelbrecht, A.P.: Computational Intelligence: An Introduction. Wiley, Hoboken (2007)
12. Esposito, C., Castiglione, A., Choo, K.K.R.: Challenges in delivering software in the cloud as microservices. IEEE Cloud Comput. **3**(5), 10–14 (2016)
13. Frappier, M., Matwin, S., Mili, A.: Software metrics for predicting maintainability. Software metrics study: technical memorandum **2** (1994)
14. Fritzsch, J., Bogner, J., Wagner, S., Zimmermann, A.: Microservices migration in industry: intentions, strategies, and challenges. In: 2019 IEEE International Conference on Software Maintenance and Evolution (ICSME), pp. 481–490. IEEE (2019)
15. Gabrel, V., Manouvrier, M., Murat, C.: Web services composition: complexity and models. Discrete Appl. Math. **196**, 100–114 (2015)

16. Howard, R.A., Matheson, J.E.: The principles and applications of decision analysis, pp. 719–762. Strategic Decisions Group, Palo Alto (1984)
17. Hu, W., Jian, N., Qu, Y., Wang, Y.: GMO: a graph matching for ontologies. In: Proceedings of K-CAP Workshop on Integrating Ontologies, pp. 41–48 (2005)
18. Jatoth, C., Gangadharan, G., Buyya, R.: Computational intelligence based QoS-aware web service composition: a systematic literature review. IEEE Trans. Serv. Comput. **10**(3), 475–492 (2015)
19. Konar, A.: Computational Intelligence: Principles Techniques and Applications. Springer, Heidelberg (2005). https://doi.org/10.1007/b138935
20. Kuhn, A., Ducasse, S., Gírba, T.: Semantic clustering: identifying topics in source code. Inf. Softw. Technol. **49**(3), 230–243 (2007)
21. Levcovitz, A., Terra, R., Valente, M.T.: Towards a technique for extracting microservices from monolithic enterprise systems. arXiv preprint arXiv:1605.03175 (2016)
22. Mateou, N.H., Andreou, A.S.: Tree-structured multi-layer fuzzy cognitive maps for modelling large scale, complex problems. In: International Conference on Computational Intelligence for Modelling, Control and Automation and International Conference on Intelligent Agents, Web Technologies and Internet Commerce (CIMCA-IAWTIC 2006), vol. 2, pp. 131–139. IEEE (2005)
23. Mateou, N.H., Hadjiprokopis, A., Andreou, A.S.: Fuzzy influence diagrams: an alternative approach to decision making under uncertainty. In: International Conference on Computational Intelligence for Modelling, Control and Automation and International Conference on Intelligent Agents, Web Technologies and Internet Commerce (CIMCA-IAWTIC 2006), vol. 1, pp. 58–64. IEEE (2005)
24. Mazlami, G., Cito, J., Leitner, P.: Extraction of microservices from monolithic software architectures. In: 2017 IEEE International Conference on Web Services (ICWS), pp. 524–531. IEEE (2017)
25. Murata, T., Ishibuchi, H.: MOGA: multi-objective genetic algorithms. In: IEEE International Conference on Evolutionary Computation, vol. 1, pp. 289–294 (1995)
26. Shachter, R.D.: Evaluating influence diagrams. Oper. Res. **34**(6), 871–882 (1986)
27. Taibi, D., Auer, F., Lenarduzzi, V., Felderer, M.: From monolithic systems to microservices: an assessment framework. arXiv preprint arXiv:1909.08933 (2019)
28. Taibi, D., Lenarduzzi, V., Pahl, C.: Processes, motivations, and issues for migrating to microservices architectures: an empirical investigation. IEEE Cloud Comput. **4**(5), 22–32 (2017)
29. Van Veldhuizen, D.A., Lamont, G.B.: Multiobjective evolutionary algorithms: analyzing the state-of-the-art. Evol. Comput. **8**(2), 125–147 (2000)
30. Wootton, B.: Microservices: a definition of this new architectural term (2014). http://highscalability.com/blog/2014/4/8/microservices-not-a-free-lunch.html
31. Zaremski, A.M., Wing, J.M.: Signature matching: a tool for using software libraries. ACM Trans. Softw. Eng. Methodol. (TOSEM) **4**(2), 146–170 (1995)
32. Zaremski, A.M., Wing, J.M.: Specification matching of software components. ACM Trans. Softw. Eng. Methodol. (TOSEM) **6**(4), 333–369 (1997)
33. Zitzler, E., Laumanns, M., Thiele, L.: SPEA2: improving the strength Pareto evolutionary algorithm. TIK-report **103** (2001)
34. Zitzler, E., Thiele, L.: Multiobjective evolutionary algorithms: a comparative case study and the strength Pareto approach. IEEE Trans. Evol. Comput. **3**(4), 257–271 (1999)

Pattern Atlas

Frank Leymann$^{(\boxtimes)}$ ⓘ and Johanna Barzen ⓘ

IAAS, University of Stuttgart, Universitätsstr. 38, 70569 Stuttgart, Germany
`{frank.leymann,johanna.barzen}@iaas.uni-stuttgart.de`

Abstract. Pattern languages are well-established in the software architecture community. Many different aspects of creating a software architecture are addressed by such languages. Thus, several pattern languages have to be considered when building a particular architecture. But these pattern languages are isolated, i.e. it is hard to determine the relevant patterns to be applied from the different pattern languages. Moreover, the sum of patterns from different languages may be huge, i.e. restriction to relevant patterns is desirable. In this contribution we envision an encompassing tool, the pattern atlas, that supports building complex systems based on pattern languages. The analogy to cartography motivates the name of the tool.

Keywords: Pattern languages · Software architecture · Cartography · Manifolds

1 Principles of Pattern Languages

Pattern languages have their origin in architecting houses and urban planning [1]. In the meantime it is used in a whole spectrum of fields reaching from information technology (e.g. [5, 11–14, 16, 18]) to the humanities (e.g. [2–4]). In this section we will sketch the basics behind pattern languages and their principle use.

1.1 The Notion of a Pattern Language

A *pattern* is a proven solution of a recurring problem. "Proven" means that the outlined solution has been successfully applied several times, and the situation in which the solution has been applied was not always the same but showed some variance. This indicates that the corresponding problem occurred more than once (and will occur in future again), i.e. it is "recurring". If it would not be recurring, the effort to document the solution would not be worth spending.

The presented "solution" is generic in the sense that it captures the essence of each of the working solutions in the corresponding contexts but no specific details of the working solution at all. I.e. a pattern is in fact derived by abstraction from the working solutions ($\sigma_1,..., \sigma_n$ in Fig. 1) [10, 16]. Because a pattern's solution is generic it can be applied in new, unforeseen situations. Vice versa, instead of forgetting the working solutions a pattern has been derived from, a pattern may refer to these working solutions, and even future implementations of the abstract solution of the pattern (called "concretizations"

© Springer Nature Switzerland AG 2021
M. Aiello et al. (Eds.): Papazoglou Festschrift, LNCS 12521, pp. 67–76, 2021.
https://doi.org/10.1007/978-3-030-73203-5_5

in Fig. 1) may also be associated [6]. This way, a pattern becomes a source of reuse of working solutions freeing users to implement the abstract solution over and over again.

Often, when facing a certain problem, other problems will occur too. This situation is captured by directed links that point from a pattern to the related other patterns. These links may have various semantics like that the problem of the target pattern often appears jointly with the problem of the source pattern or the solution of the target pattern excludes the solution of the source pattern, respectively. $\Lambda 1$ and $\Lambda 2$ in Fig. 1 indicate such links between patterns. Together, patterns form a weighted directed graph the nodes of which are patterns, the edges of which are these links, and the weights are the semantics of the links [7]. Such a graph is referred to as a *pattern language.*

The term "language" indicates the generative nature of a pattern language: by navigating from one pattern to another a corresponding sequence of generic solutions is generated, and these solutions are applied to solve a composite, more complex problem. Such a sequence is referred to as a *solution path* [25].

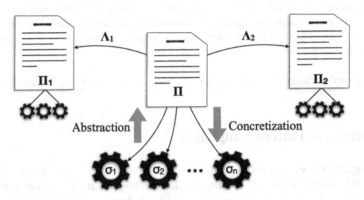

Fig. 1. A pattern as an abstraction of working solutions, and related to other patterns.

1.2 Using Multiple Pattern Languages

A pattern language is specific for a certain domain, e.g. it addresses solutions of integration problems, cloud computing problems etc. In general, a complex system requires to solve many problems from multiple domains: for example, components have to be realized as microservices, these services must be integrated, they have to be secured, their robustness must be guaranteed - and each problem domain is addressed by a separate pattern language.

In order to solve such complex multi-domain problems, a user will have to navigate across pattern languages. For this purpose, *links* between pattern languages are needed (dashed arrows in Fig. 2) [7]. But the authors of individual pattern languages are most often only concerned with links within pattern languages, e.g. simply because they can't consider a whole plethora of other pattern languages. A further complication is that pattern languages are often published as books, i.e. links across books can't be established, they can't be foreseen because the collection of pattern languages evolve over time. Thus, links between pattern languages have to be realized as separate artifacts.

This is why our existing approach to pattern languages (PatternPedia - see Sect. 2.1) publishes pattern languages as online resources (sometimes in addition to published books) like [20–22]. Patterns are realized as marked-up documents (e.g. HTML documents), and links between pattern documents are URLs (e.g. hyperlinks). These links are not embedded in the pattern documents but external to the documents: they are directed, pointing from a source document to a target document.

Especially, a link can originate from a document in one pattern language and target a document in another pattern language: this way, cross pattern language links can be established, and they can be established at a later point in time, e.g. when a new pattern language appears.

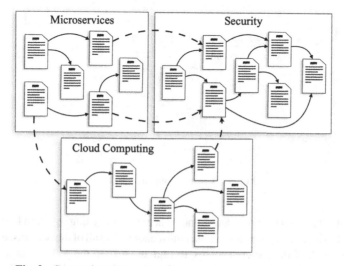

Fig. 2. Connecting pattern languages to solve composite problems.

Also, a cross pattern language link may have the semantics that the target pattern concretizes the solution sketched by the source pattern. For example, a cloud computing pattern describes when and how an elastic load balancer is used, and links may point to patterns that show how this is realized in Amazon Web Services or Azure. Thus, a concretization of a pattern is not necessarily an executable, but may be another, refining pattern.

If concretizations are executables, they may be used for automatically building working *solutions* of a composite problem [9]. When deriving a solution path by navigating through a pattern language and selecting working solutions of each of the patterns along this path, proper annotations associated with working solutions help to derive a working solution of the composite problem represented by the solution path [8].

A pattern language might be quite comprehensive, and if multiple pattern languages have to be consulted, the body of knowledge to consider can easily become hardly comprehensible. In such a situation, a pattern language *view* is quite useful [24]: it consists of a subset of relevant patterns from the pattern languages to be considered together with the relevant links within the pattern languages or across pattern languages (see Fig. 3). Such a view is created by a specialist understanding the collection of relevant pattern languages and its applicability to solve cross-domain problems. To a user, such a view appears like a single pattern language. The view V in Fig. 3, for example, appears to be a pattern language to create secure microservices in a cloud environment.

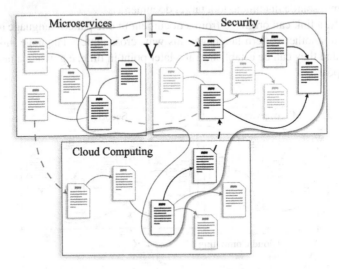

Fig. 3. A pattern language view.

Finally, it is far from trivial to determine "where to start" using a pattern language (be it a view or a basic pattern language). A user must understand all of the patterns, especially the problems each of the patterns solves, to find an *entry* to the pattern language [17], i.e. a first pattern where navigation through the pattern language begins and a solution path is created. By applying the solution path, some of the problems are solved, other remain. Based on the remaining problems another entry is determined and so on.

2 Pattern Atlas

A tool that supports the creation of software architectures based on patterns has to cope with concepts like pattern languages, links, solutions, views, entries (and several more that we did not discuss). In this section we show by analogy how these concepts relate, and this analogy motivates the name of the tool.

2.1 PatternPedia

For more than a decade we built a tool called PatternPedia that supports several of the concepts above, and various pattern languages have been represented in PatternPedia [10]. The existing tool has been described in several publications, and it served as the basis for a couple of projects.

Also, repositories for working solutions (which are often domain specific, i.e. which cannot be generalized) have been created for some domains. Patterns from these domains point to corresponding working solutions. Concepts and tools to (semi-)automatically derive patterns from working solutions by means of data analytics have also been prototypically implemented.

Based on this experience it became clear that a new architecture and corresponding implementation for a general pattern repository (which encompasses solution repositories) is due: the *pattern atlas*. This name is justified because the realization of this new platform is steered by the analogy of an atlas that turned out to be helpful in decisions about the platform's functionality.

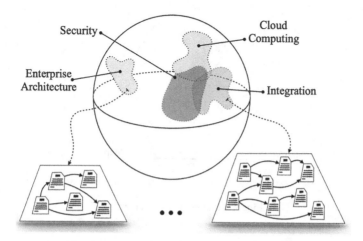

Fig. 4. Pattern languages as maps of IT domains.

2.2 Maps and Atlas: Covering IT with Pattern Languages

Information technology is a huge sphere, too huge to be able to present the knowledge about it as a whole with high precision. It is like the surface of earth, which needs a large collection of maps, i.e. an atlas, that represent information of various kinds to comprehend this surface.

Figure 4 depicts the sphere of information technology as - well - a sphere, a mathematical sphere, i.e. as the surface of a ball in 3-dimensional space. The different domains of information technology are indicated by grey-shaded areas on this sphere. Examples of such domains are the domain of enterprise architecture that has been covered by a pattern language in [12], the domain of cloud computing in [11], the domain of microservices by [18], or enterprise application integration in [13]. In our analogy to earth, the grey-shaded areas are like geographic regions, e.g. countries, and the pattern languages correspond to maps of these regions. In cartography, a collection of maps that covers a certain part of earth is an atlas, and in analogy we call a collection of pattern languages covering a certain part of information technology a pattern atlas.

2.3 Glueing Maps Together: Links Between Pattern Languages

In cartography, maps are flat representations of areas on earth, the latter of which are always curved (which becomes important a bit later). Differential geometry [19] considers the sphere, i.e. the surface of earth, as a 2-dimensional manifold and generalizes the notion of an atlas by emphasizing the functions that transform an area of the manifold into its flat image: an atlas is a set of pairs $\{(U_i, f_i)\}$, called charts, where $f_i: U_i \rightarrow V_i \subseteq \mathbb{R}^2$ is a "structure preserving" function. Then, $f_i(U_i) = V_i$ is what is known as a map in cartography. For $U_i \cap U_j \neq \varnothing$ the so-called transition function $f_j \circ f_i^{-1}$ determines how the maps V_i and V_j are glued together (see Fig. 5).

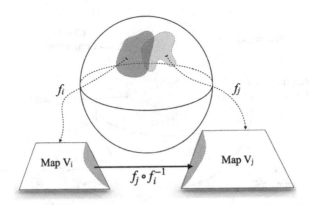

Fig. 5. Glueing maps together.

In our analogy, these transition functions are represented as links between pattern languages. The links define how various patterns of the affected pattern languages relate, i.e. how these pattern languages are glued together into a consistent map of the combined domain of information technology. For example, by establishing links between the microservice pattern language and the cloud computing pattern language a pattern language for microservices in the cloud is created.

2.4 Special Representations of Maps: Views of Pattern Languages

An atlas in cartography supports various special representations of one and the same geographic region: special maps depict transport routes (e.g. highways or railroads), ecological zones (e.g. tropics, subtropics, deserts), mountain structures and so on. Such representations are created by omitting details that are not relevant for the aspect of interest. These omissions allow to focus on specific aspects without having to understand or consider all the details of a geographic region.

The pattern atlas supports such omission to increase focus by means of views. A view is defined by selecting a subset of patterns and links of a given pattern language (or collection of linked pattern languages) to ease comprehension and to focus on certain aspects. For example, restricting the cloud computing patterns of [11] to the data related patterns eases the use of the pattern language for users that need to cope with data management in the cloud; or restricting the combined enterprise integration pattern language and security pattern language to corresponding communication-related patterns in both languages immediately supports users concerned with secured communication between applications.

2.5 Index for Finding Entities in Maps: Entries in Pattern Languages

When working with an atlas an index is used to efficiently find details within a geographic region like a certain city, a certain mountain, or a certain lake. Such an index is mainly a list of names of entities on earth and references to maps that contain their representations, as well as references to detailed positions within these maps. Finding a proper pattern to start solving a complex problem is far from being trivial, i.e. an analogy to an index is needed.

The concept of an entry point [17] corresponds to such an index, but due to the nature of patterns more sophistication is needed: an entry point is the starting pattern of a solution path solving a (probably composite) problem (note, that a solution path may consist of a single pattern only). It is determined based on the context of the overall architectural problem to be solved. A context is described by means of facts. "Negative facts" represent the problems to be solved. Since each pattern solves a problem, applying a pattern removes negatives facts, i.e. it turns them into "positive facts". The goal is to turn as many as possible negative facts into positive facts. Our proposed algorithms in [17] determines all possible solution paths addressing negative facts in the current situation, selects the solution path that will turn most negative facts into positive facts, and offers its start pattern as entry point to the pattern language. This assumes that the pattern language is extended by such facts, which is currently rarely the case.

Another approach to entry points that has been realized in PatternPedia is based on tags associated with patterns, or enabling full-text search on pattern documents: this way individual patterns can be determined that might help solving a problem. But this does not guarantee the determined pattern is the begin of a solution path that solved a maximum number of problems.

2.6 Concrete Renderings of Maps: Working Solutions

A map is a flat representation of a region on earth (see Sect. 2.3). Ideally, the map should faithfully render the region. Here, faithful means that geometric properties like angles, areas, distances etc. of the region on earth are preserved, i.e. are (proportionally) the same on the map as in the region. But according the famous Theorema Egregium by C.F. Gauss, any such flat rendering inherently results in distortions: i.e. a faithful rendering of a region on earth is impossible.

Important applications like navigation require maps that preserve at least one of the geometric properties of the region on earth. Luckily, this can be achieved. For example, equi-area projections preserve areas (e.g. Lambert's cylindrical projection). Azimuthal equidistant projections preserve distances (e.g. Postel's projection). Gnomonic projections preserve shorter routes. While such projections preserve one geometric property, they distort the others: e.g. if areas are preserved, the shape of the areas is changed.

These concrete renderings of a map (i.e. such projections) serve specific needs like determining routes on sea, determining the distances between locations etc. While a map itself renders a region "as good as possible", it is not a proper solution to such specific problems. But the projections are "working solutions": a given map can be associated with a set of corresponding projections allowing to determine the shortest route between two locations on sea, to determine the area of a shape on the map etc. In this sense, maps are abstract while projections are concrete.

Similarly, the pattern atlas supports to associate concrete solutions (aka working solutions) with patterns. This way, the abstract solution sketched in the pattern document is made concrete. For example, if a pattern sketches how to use a message queue, concrete solutions specify how this is done in Amazon's SQS or IBM's MQSeries.

Table 1. Mapping concepts from patterns and cartography.

Patterns	Cartography
Pattern languages	Maps of geographic regions
Links	Arrangements of maps
Views	Special representations of regions
Solutions	Concrete renderings of a map
Entries	Index

Table 1 shows how the discussed features and concepts from cartography correspond to the discussed features and concepts from pattern languages.

3   Conclusion

We reminded the main concepts and entities from pattern languages, especially in their practical use in building software architectures. Extensions like views, entries, and working solutions have been summarized. Our prototypical support of pattern language-based design of software architectures named PatternPedia needs to be revamped after a decade of incremental development. The paradigm that guides us in this new implementation stems from cartography, which motivates the name of the new tool: Pattern Atlas. We have shown by analogy how the concepts and features of an atlas correspond to the concepts and features of the Pattern Atlas. The pattern atlas will be partially implemented in the project PlanQK, a platform to support quantum machine learning [23].

Acknowledgements. We are grateful to our colleagues Uwe Breitenbücher, Michael Falkenthal, Manuela Weigold and Karoline Wild for the discussions about the evolution of PatternPedia towards the Pattern Atlas.

References

1. Alexander, C., Ishikawa, S., Silverstein, M.: A Pattern Language: Towns, Buildings, Construction. Oxford University Press, New York (1977)
2. Barzen, J., Leymann, F.: Costume languages as pattern languages. In: Proceedings of Pursuit of Pattern Languages for Societal Change - Preparatory Workshop (2014)
3. Barzen, J., Leymann, F.: Patterns as formulas: patterns in the digital humanities. In: Proceedings of the Ninth International Conferences on Pervasive Patterns and Applications (PATTERNS) (2017)
4. Barzen, J., Breitenbücher, U., Eusterbrock, L., Falkenthal, M., Hentschel, F., Leymann, F.: The vision for MUSE4Music. Applying the MUSE method in musicology. Comput. Sci. Res. Dev. **32**(3–4), 329–330 (2016). https://doi.org/10.1007/s00450-016-0340-5. In: Hermann Engesser (Hrsg) Advancements of Service Computing: Proceedings of SummerSoC 2016. Springer, Heidelberg
5. Buschmann, F., Henney, K., Schmidt, D.C.: Pattern-Oriented Software Architecture: On Patterns and Pattern Languages. Wiley, Hoboken (2007)
6. Falkenthal, M., Barzen, J., Breitenbücher, U., Fehling, Ch., Leymann, F.: From pattern languages to solution implementations. In: Proceedings of the Sixth International Conferences on Pervasive Patterns and Applications (PATTERNS 2014) (2014)
7. Falkenthal, M., Breitenbücher, U., Leymann, F.: The nature of pattern languages. In: Pursuit of Pattern Languages for Societal Change (2018)
8. Falkenthal, M., Barzen, J., Breitenbücher, U., Leymann, F.: On the algebraic properties of concrete solution aggregation. In: Software-Intensive Cyber-Physical Systems (SICS) (2019)
9. Falkenthal, M., Leymann, F.: Easing pattern application by means of solution languages. In: Proceedings of the Ninth International Conference on Pervasive Patterns and Applications (PATTERNS) (2017)
10. Fehling, Ch., Barzen, J., Falkenthal, M., Leymann, F.: PatternPedia - collaborative pattern identification and authoring. In: Proceedings of Pursuit of Pattern Languages for Societal Change - Preparatory Workshop (2014)
11. Fehling, Ch., Leymann, F., Retter, R., Schupeck, W., Arbitter, P.: Cloud Computing Patterns. Springer, Vienna (2014). https://doi.org/10.1007/978-3-7091-1568-8
12. Fowler, M.: Patters of Enterprise Application Architecture. Addison-Wesley, Boston (2003)
13. Hohpe, G., Woolf, B.: Enterprise Integration Patterns: Designing, Building, and Deploying Messaging Systems. Addison-Wesley, Boston (2004)
14. Leymann, F.: Towards a pattern language for quantum algorithms. In: Feld, S., Linnhoff-Popien, C. (eds.) QTOP 2019. LNCS, vol. 11413, pp. 218–230. Springer, Cham (2019). https://doi.org/10.1007/978-3-030-14082-3_19
15. Nygard, M.T.: Release IT, 2nd edn. The Pragmatic Bookshelf (2018)
16. Reiners, R.: An evolving pattern library for collaborative project documentation. Dissertation, RWTH Aachen (2013)
17. Reinfurt, L., Falkenthal, M., Leymann, F.: Where to begin - on pattern language entry points. In: Software-Intensive Cyber-Physical Systems (SICS) (2019)
18. Richardson, Ch.: Microservices Patterns. Manning Publications (2018)
19. Spivac, M.: Comprehensive Introduction to Differential Geometry. Publish or Perish, Inc. (1999)
20. Website Cloud Computing Patterns. https://www.cloudcomputingpatterns.org/. Accessed 2 Oct 2020
21. Website EAI Patterns. https://www.enterpriseintegrationpatterns.com/. Accessed 2 Oct 2020
22. Website Microservices Patterns. https://microservices.io/patterns/microservices.html. Accessed 2 Oct 2020

23. Website PlanQK. https://planqk.de/. Accessed 2 Oct 2020
24. Weigold, M., Barzen, J., Breitenbücher, U., Falkenthal, M., Leymann, F., Wild, K.: Pattern views: concept and tooling for interconnected pattern languages. arXiv preprint arXiv:2003. 09127 (2020)
25. Zdun, U.: Systematic pattern selection using pattern language grammars and design space analysis. Softw. Pract. Exp. **37**, 983–1016 (2007)

On Reuse in Service-Based Workflows

Khalid Belhajjame[✉] and Daniela Grigori

Université Paris-Dauphine PSL, LAMSADE, CNRS UMR 7243, 75016 Paris, France
{khalid.belhajjame,daniela.grigori}@dauphine.fr

Abstract. Workflows have gained momentum in the last two decades, in industry as well as in modern sciences, as a means for modeling and enacting processes. The value of workflow specifications does not end once they are enacted. Indeed, such specifications encapsulate knowledge that documents business processes or scientific experiments, and are, therefore, worth storing and sharing to ultimately be reused or repurposed. We focus, in this paper, on service-based workflows, in which the steps are implemented by operations that are provided by services. In doing so, we examine two problems that are inherent to workflow reuse, namely search and preservation. The first problem deals with the issue of finding workflows, or fragments thereof, that are of interest to the user. The second problem, on the other hand, deals with the volatility of services. It examines solutions that can be used to curate a workflow specification that utilizes a service that is no longer available. As well as examining the above two problems, we close the paper by discussing future issues that need to be addressed in the field.

1 Introduction

Workflows are popular means to specify and implement processes in business and science. For example, they are used in modern science to specify and implement scientific experiments, allowing scientists to better understand the phenomenon or hypothesis they are studying. Designing scientific workflows can be a difficult task, however, as it requires a thorough knowledge of the field as well as knowledge of the services available to implement the steps in the workflow. To overcome this obstacle and facilitate workflow design, many workflow repositories have emerged, such as myExperiment [28], Crowdlabs [21] and Galaxy [14] to share, publish and enable the reuse of workflows.

However, sharing and publishing workflows is not enough to allow their reuse. In recent years, a significant number of workflows have been shared by scientists in several areas on the myExperiment workflow repository. However, their users are experiencing difficulties when exploring and querying the workflows. Indeed, users have yet to go through the published workflows to identify those that are relevant to their needs. The situation is exacerbated by the fact that a significant number of workflows published in these repositories cannot be executed due to the volatility of the services that implement the steps of a workflow.

© Springer Nature Switzerland AG 2021
M. Aiello et al. (Eds.): Papazoglou Festschrift, LNCS 12521, pp. 77–87, 2021.
https://doi.org/10.1007/978-3-030-73203-5_6

Over the past few years, we have developed solutions to improve workflow reuse with the above concerns in mind [8,9,16,16,18]. The solution we have developed can be organized within a framework that contains five inter-connected steps as shown in Fig. 1.

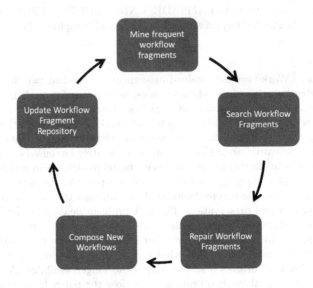

Fig. 1. Five steps for promoting workflow reuse.

The first component is used to extract frequent workflow fragments from existing workflow repositories. The reason for this is that frequent workflow fragments are likely to be reused in the construction of new workflows. The second component is used to search for workflows or fragments of them in order to design a new workflow. The third component is used to repair workflow fragments that can no longer be executed due to the volatility of their underlying services. The fourth component is used to compose a new workflow taking into account existing workflows that were previously retrieved by the user. The last step is then used to enrich the repository with workflow fragments with the newly specified workflow. The remainder of this paper focuses and presents each of the first steps of the framework before closing the paper with a discussion highlighting the outstanding issues.

2   Mining Frequent Workflow Fragments

The literature on business and scientific workflows is rich in proposals that seek to exploit existing workflows. Existing work on the exploitation of workflows has mainly focused on deriving a workflow specification (usually in the form of a Petri net) from workflow execution logs. Very few proposals have focused on mining knowledge from workflow specifications. [29] extracts action patterns from repositories, that capture chunks of actions on business objects often appearing together in business processes. Our work is related to Diamantini's proposal [12] who applied the method of hierarchical clustering of graphs in order to extract common workflow fragments. We focus on fragments rather than entire workflows, as there are more (realistic) possibilities for reuse at the fragment level than at the level of the entire workflow. In other words, the chances that the user will find a workflow that suits his needs are slim. On the other hand, the chances that it will find workflows containing one or more fragments that can contribute to its workflow are greater.

Given a workflow repository, we would like to exploit frequent workflow fragments, i.e. fragments that are used in several workflows. These fragments are likely to implement tasks that can be reused in newly specified workflows. Workflow extraction raises the following questions.

- How to manage the heterogeneity of labels used by different users to model their workflow activities within the repository? Different designers use different labels to name the activities that make up their workflow. We need a way to homogenize the labels before extracting the workflows so that we don't miss relevant (false negative) fragments.
- Which graphical representation is best suited for formatting workflows to extract frequent fragments? We argue that the effectiveness and efficiency of the extraction algorithm used to retrieve frequent fragments depends on the representation used to encode the workflow specifications.

Homogenizing Activity Labels. To be able to extract frequent workflow fragments, we first need to identify common activities. This assumes that activities implementing the same functionality must have the same names. Some workflow modeling tools (see for example Signavio[1]) manage a dictionary and allow reusing dictionary entries via a search or via the auto-completion function (when the user starts typing an activity label, the system suggests similar activity labels from the dictionary). If the models in the repository come from different tools and use different naming conventions, a pre-processing step can be applied to homogenize the activity labels using a [27] dictionary. To facilitate this step, we rely on existing techniques such as [20]. These techniques are capable of recognizing label styles and automatically refactoring labels with quality problems. These labels are transformed into a word-object label by deriving actions and business objects from activity labels. Verb-object style labels contain an action that is followed by a business object, such as *Create Invoice* and *Validate Order*. The advantages of this style of labeling have been highlighted by several practical studies and modeling guidelines. Synonyms are also discussed in this step. They are recognized using the WordNet lexical database and are replaced by a common term.

Workflow Representation. To extract frequent patterns, we make use of an existing graph extraction algorithm, SUBDUE [19]. SUBDUE is a heuristic based

---

[1] www.signavio.com.

algorithm that uses measure-theoretic information to find important sub-graphs. To use SUBDUE, however, we first need to transform the workflow specification into a graph format. To this end, we have studied a number of possible representations, including those proposed in the state of the art, see [12], and proposed one that improves the execution time, the memory space required, and also the meaning of the extracted models. In fact, we have showed (see [9]) that the representation model is of major importance.

The new representation model for workflows that we suggested is compact, in the sense that it contains a small number of nodes, yet complete since it can be used to uncover the original BPMN specification of the original workflow. Using such a model, the nodes represent activities. Control operators in the workflow are not encoded using nodes. Instead, the edge connecting two activity nodes are labeled to indicate the kind of the control operator(s) connecting them. Compared with existing representation models, the results of an experimental evaluation that we conducted showed that this representation model is the most effective and efficient when it comes to mining frequent workflow graphs [9].

3   Searching Workflow Fragments

To facilitate the reuse of workflow fragments, two scenarios for their retrieval can be identified. In the first scenario, user describes the functionality of the fragment that could complete his specification using keywords (or, alternatively, using a dedicated visual query language as in [2]). In the second scenario, the specification of a workflow fragment is already available and user would like to find similar ones in the repository. In the following we present solutions for these two cases.

3.1   Keywords-Based Search of Workflow Fragments

To obtain a workflow fragment that can be used to complete an initial workflow, user issues a query that characterizes the desired workflow fragment. The query consists of a set of keywords $\{kw_1, \ldots, kw_n\}$ characterizing the functionality that the fragment must implement. The user selects the terms of his own choice. In other words, we do not impose any vocabulary for the specification of keywords.

To identify the fragments in the repository that are relevant to the specified keywords, we adopt the widely used technique of TF/IDF (frequency term/inverted document) measurement. It should be mentioned here that the workflow fragments in the repository are indexed by the activity labels obtained after the workflow homogenization (see the previous section). We refer to such an index as IDX. Direct application of TF/IDF based on the set of keywords provided by the user is likely to miss some fragments. Indeed, the designer provides keywords of his choice; a given keyword may not be present in the repository, whereas one of its synonyms could be present. To solve this problem, we adopt the following method which complements the traditional TF/IDF with a semantic enrichment phase. More precisely, from a set of keywords provided by the user $\{kw_1, \ldots, kw_n\}$, for each keyword kw_i we retrieve its synonyms, which we refer to as $syn(kw_i)$ from an existing thesaurus, for example, Wordnet [30] or a domain-specific specialized thesaurus if we are dealing with workflows coming from a specific domain. The IDX index is searched to identify if there is a term in $syn(kw_i) \cup \{kw_i\}$ that appears. If there is, then the term in the index is used to represent kw_i in the vector that will be used to compare the query with the vectors representing the workflow fragments in the repository.

Once the vector representing the user query is constructed and the TF/IDFs of its associated terms are computed, it is compared to the vectors representing the workflow fragments in the repository using the cosine similarity [3]. The set of fragments retrieved in the previous step, which we call candidate fragments, is then examined by the user, who will be able to choose the fragment that meets best his/her needs.

3.2   Similarity-Based Search of Workflow Fragments

A second scenario for reusing fragments is the situation when the user has already a workflow fragment specification and he would like to find in the repository all similar specifications [16]. He may be looking for all the variants of his model or for a correct version when his fragment contains an error [15].

Using graphs as a representation formalism for both user model and workflow models, the above searching problem turns into a graph searching and matching problem. We want to compare the process graph representing user requirements with the target graphs in the repository. The matching process can be formulated as a search for graph or subgraph isomorphism. However, it is possible that there does not exist a process model such that an exact graph or subgraph isomorphism can be defined. Thus, we are interested in finding workflow models that have similar structures if models that have an identical structure do not exist. The error-correcting graph matching integrates the concept of error correction (or inexact matching) into the matching process. Similar to string edit distance, graph edit operations are defined and the cost of applying these operations on a first graph to render it identical to the second one are evaluated. The graph edit distance is defined as the minimum cost over the possible sequence of such operations. For a process graph-based formalism, specific cost functions have to be defined for the edit operations: cost of modifying activity parameters or changing control flow structures. We have also defined an edit operation that merges two activities and its opposite, decomposing an activity into two activities to deal with different granularity levels of activity modelling. Complex mappings (one-to-many) between activities may appear due to multiple ways of implementing an interaction pattern (for instance BPEL synchronous or asynchronous interaction [16]) or different granularity in implementing a functionality as a single or multiple tasks [13].

In the framework presented in [17] we made use of semantic annotations of process models to propose a fast similarity search technique that returns a ranked list of similar models in the repository. In a second step, a more fine-grained matching method can be applied between the query and one or several matching candidates.

For the first step, that can be considered as a filtering step, we use an abstraction function that represents a process as a finite set of flow dependencies between its activities. Thus, the similarity of two processes is defined based on the similarity of their flow dependencies. To speed up the comparison of the flow dependencies of the query and those of the repository processes, we define indexes built on the flow dependencies and the annotations of input/output parameters of activities of the processes.

For applications requiring a more-precise matching and for which the query response time is not constrained, the user can choose to calculate a more fine-grained similarity measure, based on the graph edit distance. A survey of similarity measures can be found in [4] and an overview of process matching techniques is presented in the corresponding chapter in [5].

Besides control-flow specification, quality constraints and preferences can be specified by the user and taken into account into the searching and matching process (see for example [1]).

4 Repairing Workflow

A problem that frequently hinders the reuse of workflows (and thus their fragments) is the volatility of the services that implements the steps of the workflows. This is not surprising; there is usually no agreement between the service providers who implement the workflow steps and the users who require the providers to supply their services on a continuous basis.

We have shown in a previous study [6] that semantic annotations of web services can be used to identify appropriate substitutes for unavailable service operations, thus allowing the preservation of scientific workflows. More precisely, we have developed an algorithm which, by inputting annotations that semantically describe missing service operations using the concepts of domain ontologies [22,31], identifies available service operations that can play the same role as unavailable ones.

Although the algorithm we have developed is sound, its practical applicability is hampered by the following facts. First, semantic annotations of web services are rare: the number of web services that are annotated is much lower than the growing number of available web services. Consequently, the probability of locating substitution operations using the algorithm described in [6], is low. Second, our experience suggests that a large proportion of existing semantic annotations suffer from inaccuracies: annotators tend to use concepts that are sub-concepts or super-concepts of the concepts that should be used for annotating web service parameters. As a result, a substitute discovered to replace an unavailable operation using such annotations may be unsuitable and, conversely, a suitable substitute may be discarded. Finally, scientific workflows may contain operations that are implemented using mechanisms other than web services, such as local programs or scripts whose annotations are not available.

To address the above issues, we proposed a heuristic to locate substitutes in the absence of semantic annotations of web services. The proposed method uses data links linking the inputs and outputs of service operations in existing workflow specifications to locate operations with parameters that are compatible with the missing operations. In addition, it exploits source data [25] collected from previous workflow runs to ensure that candidate substitutes perform tasks similar to the missing operations.

To illustrate this idea, we will use an example of a real workflow *in silico* that is used to perform a value-added protein identification, in which the results of the protein identification are complemented by additional information on proteins homologous to the identified protein [7]. Figure 2 illustrates the workflow that implements this experiment.

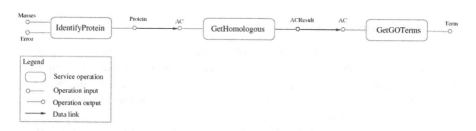

Fig. 2. Value-added protein identification workflow (identified in the text by *protein Identification Wf₁*)

The workflow consists of three operations. The operation *IdentifyProtein* takes as input the peptide masses obtained during the digestion of a protein and an identification error and provides the Uniprot access number of the best match. If a protein is found, the operation *GetHomologous* performs a homology search and returns the list of similar proteins. The homologous protein accessions are then used to feed the execution of the operation *GetGOTerm* to obtain the corresponding term from the gene ontology². Few months after the developement of this workflow, it could no longer be ran. The reason was that *GetHomologous* operation used in the workflow to perform the protein homology search no longer existed, and as such the user was unable to run the workflow. So we had to search for an available web service that performs homology searches and use it instead. This proved to be a lengthy process.

To identify suitable substitute service operations, we defined the notions of parameter compatibility and task compatibility, which we present in the remainder of this section.

4.1 Parameter Compatibility

Consider the existence of the workflow illustrated in Fig. 3. The operation *GetSimilarProteins* of this workflow is linked to both *IdentifyProtein* and *GetGOTerm*

---

² http://www.geneontology.org/.

which are also linked to the unavailable operation *GetHomologous*. If the data links in this workflow are free of discrepancies, then the input and output of the *GetSimilarProtein* are compatible with the output of the *IdentifyProtein* and the input of the *GetGOTerm*, respectively, to the extent that they can be connected within a workflow.

Fig. 3. Value-added pValue-added protein identification workflow (identified in the text by *proteinIdentificationWf₂*)

4.2 Task Compatibility

In addition to compatibility in terms of entries and exits, it must be ensured that the replacement applicant performs a task that is compatible with that of the unavailable operation. This raises the question of *how we can verify that a candidate substitute performs a task that is compatible with that of the unavailable operation in the absence of semantic web service annotations.*

To perform this test, we exploit the following observation. If *GetSimilarProteins* performs a task that is compatible with that of *GetHomologous*, then for the same input, the two operations should in principle provide the same output. An operation is able to replace the operation in terms of task, if for each possible input instance that the operation is able to consume, it provides the same output as the one obtained by invoking the operation. To perform this test, however, we need to call the missing operation! To overcome the above problem, we adopted a solution that uses the logs from past executions of the workflow. These are logs that contain information about past workflow executions. More importantly, they contain intermediate data that was used as input and output by the operations making up a workflow when it was set up. Examples of workflow source logs are Janus [24] and PASOA [23]. Using such provenance information, we are able to identify if the newly identified candidate service operation delivers the same results as the unavailable one, by utilizing the execution of the latter that are stored within provenance logs.

The effectiveness of the above solution has been tested against a small number of real-world workflows (see [10] for more details).

The presented solution verifies parameter and task compatibility of two services. In case when mismatches exist at the level of operations signature (different number or types of parameters), adapters can be semi-automatically generated to ensure service replaceability [11]. The approach is based on a catalogue of mismatch patterns, that contain both formal and informal descriptions of the type of adapter (called adapter template) used to resolve that type of mismatch.

5   Concluding Remarks

In this paper, we have presented a framework of solutions that can be used to promote service-based workflows, or more specifically fragments therof. Although we have been able to demonstrate that the above solutions can be useful, reuse is a difficult problem and the new service-based environments brings new challenges that need to be taken into account to promote reuse.

Indeed, while the reuse of software artifacts is generally a long-standing issue, the open science initiative emphasizes the need to improve the reusability of data-driven workflows. Semantic description is an essential ingredient for finding appropriate artifacts and reusing them. Semantic descriptions of services and workflows, although widely studied, still pose problems that hinder their adoption and use. In particular, support for the definition of domain-specific lightweight descriptions for users unfamiliar with logic, enrichment of descriptions of web services in general and data services in particular (e.g. relationship between input and output parameters (see [26]), tasks/capabilities, prerequisites and domain-specific effects).

Data services as well as entire workflows are increasingly hosted in cloud environments. This raises questions that need to be addressed, such as how to compose a workflow using fragments hosted in different and therefore heterogeneous cloud environments. Services hosted in the cloud typically require accreditation and/or are not free of charge. This raises an optimization issue that has to do with reducing the cost of a new workflow composed from fragments of existing workflows. Another line of research worth studying is to revisit traditional service-based workflows by considering micro-services as a solution that improves their reliability and reusability.

References

1. Abbaci, K., et al.: Selecting and ranking business processes with preferences: an approach based on fuzzy sets. In: Meersman, R., et al. (eds.) OTM 2011. LNCS, vol. 7044, pp. 38–55. Springer, Heidelberg (2011). https://doi.org/10.1007/978-3-642-25109-2_4
2. Awad, A., Sakr, S., Kunze, M., Weske, M.: Design by selection: a reuse-based approach for business process modeling. In: Jeusfeld, M., Delcambre, L., Ling, T.-W. (eds.) ER 2011. LNCS, vol. 6998, pp. 332–345. Springer, Heidelberg (2011). https://doi.org/10.1007/978-3-642-24606-7_25
3. Baeza-Yates, R.A., Ribeiro-Neto, B.A.: Modern Information Retrieval - The Concepts And Technology Behind Search, 2nd edn. Pearson Education Ltd., Harlow (2011)
4. Becker, M., Laue, R.: A comparative survey of business process similarity measures. Comput. Ind. 63(2), 148–167 (2012)
5. Beheshti, S.-M.-R., et al.: Process Analytics. Concepts and Techniques for Querying and Analyzing Process Data. Springer, Cham (2016). https://doi.org/10.1007/978-3-319-25037-3
6. Belhajjame, K.: Semantic replaceability of escience web services. In: eScience, pp. 449–456. IEEE Computer Society (2007)

7. Belhajjame, K., et al.: Proteome data integration: characteristics and challenges. In: UK All Hands Meeting (2005)

8. Belhajjame, K., Goble, C., Soiland-Reyes, S., De Roure, D.: Fostering scientific workflow preservation through discovery of substitute services. In: IEEE 7th International Conference on E-Science, e-Science 2011, Stockholm, Sweden, 5–8 December 2011, pp. 97–104. IEEE (2011)

9. Belhajjame, K., Grigori, D., Harmassi, M., Yahia, M.B.: Keyword-based search of workflow fragments and their composition. Trans. Comput. Collect. Intell. **26**, 67–90 (2017)

10. Belhajjame, K., et al.: Using a suite of ontologies for preserving workflow-centric research objects. J. Web Semant. **32**, 16–42 (2015)

11. Benatallah, B., Casati, F., Grigori, D., Nezhad, H.R.M., Toumani, F.: Developing adapters for web services integration. In: Pastor, O., Falcão e Cunha, J. (eds.) CAiSE 2005. LNCS, vol. 3520, pp. 415–429. Springer, Heidelberg (2005). https://doi.org/10.1007/11431855_29

12. Diamantini, C., Potena, D., Storti, E.: Mining usage patterns from a repository of scientific workflows. In: Proceedings of the ACM Symposium on Applied Computing, SAC 2012, Riva, Trento, Italy, 26–30 March 2012, pp. 152–157. ACM (2012)

13. Gater, A., Grigori, D., Bouzeghoub, M.: Complex mapping discovery for semantic process model alignment. In: iiWAS 2010 - The 12th International Conference on Information Integration and Web-Based Applications and Services, 8–10 November 2010, Paris, France, pp. 317–324 (2010)

14. Giardine, B., et al.: Galaxy: a platform for interactive large-scale genome analysis. Genome Res. **15**, 1451–1455 (2005)

15. Goderis, A., Li, P., Goble, C.: Workflow discovery: the problem, a case study from e-science and a graph-based solution. In: International Conference on Web Services, 2006. ICWS 2006, Chicago, IL, pp. 312–319. IEEE (2006)

16. Grigori, D., Corrales, J.C., Bouzeghoub, M., Gater, A.: Ranking BPEL processes for service discovery. IEEE Trans. Serv. Comput. **3**(3), 178–192 (2010)

17. Grigori, D., Gater, A.: PSearch: a framework for semantic annotated process model search. Serv. Orient. Comput. Appl. **11**(3), 249–264 (2017). https://doi.org/10.1007/s11761-017-0212-2.10.1007/s11761-017-0212-2

18. Harmassi, M., Grigori, D., Belhajjame, K.: Mining workflow repositories for improving fragments reuse. In: Cardoso, J., Guerra, F., Houben, G.-J., Pinto, A.M., Velegrakis, Y. (eds.) IKC 2015. LNCS, vol. 9398, pp. 76–87. Springer, Cham (2015). https://doi.org/10.1007/978-3-319-27932-9_7

19. Jonyer, I., Cook, D.J., Holder, L.B.: Graph-based hierarchical conceptual clustering. J. Mach. Learn. Res. **2**, 19–43 (2001)

20. Leopold, H., Smirnov, S., Mendling, J.: On the refactoring of activity labels in business process models. Inf. Syst. **37**(5), 443–459 (2012)

21. Mates, P., Santos, E., Freire, J., Silva, C.T.: CrowdLabs: social analysis and visualization for the sciences. In: Bayard Cushing, J., French, J., Bowers, S. (eds.) SSDBM 2011. LNCS, vol. 6809, pp. 555–564. Springer, Heidelberg (2011). https://doi.org/10.1007/978-3-642-22351-8_38

22. McIlraith, S.A., Son, T.C., Zeng, H.: Semantic web services. IEEE Intell. Syst. **16**(2), 46–53 (2001)

23. Miles, S., Wong, S.C., Fang, W., Groth, P., Zauner, K.P., Moreau, L.: Provenance-based validation of e-science experiments. J. Web Semant. **5**(1), 28–38 (2007)

24. Missier, P., Paton, N.W., Belhajjame, K.: Fine-grained and efficient lineage querying of collection-based workflow provenance. In: EDBT, pp. 299–310. ACM (2010)

25. Moreau, L.: The foundations for provenance on the web. Found. Trends Web Sci. **2**(2–3), 99–241 (2010)
26. Mouhoub, M.L., Grigori, D., Manouvrier, M.: Towards an automatic enrichment of semantic web services descriptions. In: On the Move to Meaningful Internet Systems. OTM 2017 Conferences - Confederated International Conferences: CoopIS, C&TC, and ODBASE 2017, Rhodes, Greece, 23–27 October 2017, Proceedings, Part I, pp. 681–697 (2017)
27. Peters, N., Weidlich, M.: Automatic generation of glossaries for process modelling support. Enterp. Model. Inf. Syst. Archit. **6**(1), 30–46 (2011)
28. De Roure, D., Goble, C.A., Stevens, R.: The design and realisation of the my$_{experiment}$ virtual research environment for social sharing of workflows. Future Gener. Comput. Syst. **25**(5), 561–567 (2009)
29. Smirnov, S., Weidlich, M., Mendling, J., Weske, M.: Action patterns in business process model repositories. Comput. Ind. **63**(2), 98–111 (2012)
30. Princeton University: Princeton University "about WordNet" (2010)
31. Verma, K., Sheth, A.P.: Semantically annotating a web service. IEEE Internet Comput. **11**(2), 83–85 (2007)

A Reference Architecture for Smart Digital Platform for Personalized Prevention and Patient Management

Amal Elgammal[1,2(✉)] and Bernd J. Krämer[1]

[1] Scientific Academy for Service Technology e.V. (ServTech), Potsdam, Germany
{amal,kraemer}@servtech.info
[2] Faculty of Computers and Artificial Intelligence, Cairo University, Giza, Egypt

Abstract. The maturity of a new generation of information technologies, including the internet of things (IoT), wearables, cloud computing, Artificial Intelligence (AI) and machine learning, has led to the advent of smart domains, such as smart manufacturing, smart logistics, and smart healthcare. Smart healthcare brings unlimited opportunities to solve many of the problems of traditional medical systems, with the ultimate goal of realizing 4P medicine (Predictive, Preventive, Personalized, Participative). However, to realize this ambitious vision in such a highly regulated multi-disciplinary and sensitive domain, a mine of challenges needs to be effectively and efficiently addressed. A smart health digital platform that integrates all relevant (semi-) structured and unstructured health-related data is fundamental. The platform should incorporate a variety of care data, including vital medical information from medical records, current medication, imaging studies, lifestyle, genetic, demographic, psychological & psychosocial and patient-provided health data from exercise or health monitoring applications and medical pathways. These will lead to improving post-operative planning, reduce medical risks and costs, and generate more accurate therapy and increased Quality of Life (QoL) for patients. The main contribution of this article is a reference architecture for a smart digital platform for personalized prevention and patient management that acts as a roadmap for further R&D in this domain.

1 Introduction

Traditional healthcare is being revolutionized as a result of the maturity and synergy of a new generation of information technologies, including IoT, wearables, big data, cloud computing, simulations, AI, and machine learning. The concept "Smart Healthcare" was born out of the concept of "Smart Planet" proposed by IBM in 2009. Smart healthcare is a health service system that uses technology to dynamically access information, connect people, materials, and institutions related to healthcare, and then actively manages and intelligently responds to medical ecosystem needs [1, 2]. Smart healthcare

This research is partially funded by the EC Horizon 2020 project QUALITOP, under contract number H2020 - SC1-DTH-01-2019 – 875171.

opens unlimited opportunities to solve many of the problems of traditional medical systems. This includes: (i) promoting the collaboration between all involved stakeholders, including patients, relatives, doctors, nurses, healthcare providers, healthcare institutions, public health, scientists and policymakers, (ii) improving the monitoring of patient activities outside the traditional care setting – including medication adherence management, chronic disease management support and other interventions – and (iii) reducing costs through improved care coordination and operational improvements founded on the increased visibility of patient activities – reducing unnecessary service utilization, and allocating resources more efficiently.

To realize the real potential of smart healthcare, many challenges are continuously emerging. In particular, smart healthcare lacks macro guidance, which results in poorly planned development goals and ultimately a waste of resources [1]. Furthermore, smart healthcare inherits the problems of Big data 3Vs (Volume, Velocity, and Variety) [2]. In these sensitive and highly regulated domains, the situation is even aggravated by special requirements to data protection, security, and privacy regulations as in GDPR[1]. Particularly, in healthcare, big data challenges are compounded by the fragmentation and dispersion of heterogeneous data among various stakeholders. Besides, for any successful implementation of a smart healthcare system, it should be founded on an agile, robust, reliable, secured, and scalable platform by considering healthcare data standards and information exchange standards. On top of such a platform, various querying, simulations, and data analytics functionalities are enabled and can be adapted to the requirements of the respective stakeholders.

The main contribution of this article is a reference architecture for a smart digital platform for personalized prevention and patient management meeting these requirements. The reference architecture also acts as a roadmap for further R&D activities in this direction and it realizes 4P medicine [3].

The rest of this paper is structured as follows: Sect. 2 analyses related work and identifies the gaps in smart healthcare platforms described in the literature. Based on these findings, Sect. 3 presents the proposed reference architecture for a smart digital platform for personalized prevention and patient management and discusses its main components. Finally, conclusions and future work directions are drawn in Sect. 4.

2 Related Work

Research efforts that specifically focus on smart healthcare platforms/architectures are rare in the scientific literature that are discussed in Sect. 2.1. Other related parallel streams of work addressing specific challenges of individual components of a smart healthcare platform are discussed thereafter in the following sub-sections. They include: (i) big data integration & interoperability techniques, (ii) Domain-Specific Languages (DSL) for data-intensive applications, and (iii) data security and privacy.

2.1 Smart Healthcare Architectures

Prominent work in this direction is reported in [4–7]. The authors in [4] propose an IoT-aware, smart architecture for automatic monitoring and tracking of patients.

---

[1] General Data Protection Regulation: https://gdpr.eu, last access: 03.08.2020.

The architecture integrates with a smart hospital system, which relies on RFID, WSN, and smart mobile gadgets interoperating with each other through a low-power wireless area network. Similarly, the work in [5] builds an IoT-aware architecture for smart healthcare coaching systems that assists families and patients in their daily living activities and hence improving the QoL of patients by allowing them to get the medical care they need at home. Analogously, the study in [6] proposes an IoT network management system architecture that is reliable, effective, well-performing, secure, and profitable for caregivers. Finally, a survey of a 5G-Based smart healthcare network is reported in [7] concluding with a range of challenges and future R&D directions.

The architectures discussed in these papers ignore the challenge of big data variety (big data integration & interoperability) that represents one of the major challenges in big data, especially in the healthcare domain. This lack limits the validity and applicability of the proposed approaches in practice. Furthermore, these approaches offer no solution for managing large scale data processing systems; they neither address data security and privacy nor investigate the role of DSLs for data-intensive applications. The proposed reference architecture described in Sect. 3 considers all these vital points and builds on the concept of modern data architecture as opposed to the traditional concept of data warehouse (cf. Sect.3.2). These concepts form the foundation of employing advanced analytics mechanisms including runtime monitoring, predictive analytics, and simulation for informed clinical decision-making. In addition, they ensure the agility, scalability, security, and privacy of the smart healthcare platform.

2.2 Big Data Integration and Interoperability Techniques

Big data in healthcare refers to electronic health data sets so large and complex that they are difficult to manage with traditional data management tools and methods not only because of their volume but also because of the diversity of data types and the speed at which they must be managed [8]. In healthcare, big data challenges are compounded by the fragmentation and dispersion of data among various stakeholders.

Much of the focus on Big Data integration has been on the problem of processing very large sources, extracting information from multiple, possibly conflicting data sources, and reconciling the values and providing unified access to data residing in multiple, autonomous data sources. The work has mainly focused on isolated aspects of data source management relying on schema mapping and semantic integration of different sources, and its final goal was not reasoning about the content and quality of sources [9–11]. Moreover, most of that work has focused on sources from a specific domain and does not present results for largely heterogeneous sources. Most solutions follow the traditional model in which all data are loaded into a warehouse. This centralized approach is not applicable in the medical domain because hospitals and other stakeholders would never store their patient data in an external data silo.

2.3 Domain-Specific Languages for Data-Intensive Applications

Traditionally, computing models such as MapReduce [12] were proposed to specifically support data-intensive applications. Although such models suited massive-scale data processing, they permit limited application logic complexity [13]. Domain-Specific

Languages (DSLs) can be employed to circumvent such problems. DSLs are usually concise offering a set of pre-defined abstractions to represent concepts from the application domain close to real concepts and terms familiar to the experts in the domain. DSLs can ease the implementation of analytics and machine learning algorithms with the use of high-level abstractions or reusable pieces of code that hide low-level details from lay users letting them focus on the main problem at hand.

Languages like OptiML [14] enable machine-learning algorithms to take advantage of parallelism by bridging the gap between machine learning and heterogeneous big data hardware infrastructure. OptiML is a declarative, statically-typed textual programming language, in which operations support parallel executions (using the MapReduce programming model) on heterogeneous machines. But this language lacks support for a distributed environment or executions in the cloud. ScalOps [15] is another example of a declarative, statically-typed textual DSL, intending to enable machine learning algorithms to run on a cloud computing environment and overcome the lack of iteration limitation of the traditional MapReduce programming model. To date, there is very little use of DSLs in the medical domain, while the reference architecture proposed in this paper will exploit the capabilities of DSLs.

2.4 Data Security and Privacy

Access control [16] mediates every access request to resources and data managed by a system and determines whether the request should be authorized or denied. An access control system can be considered at three different levels of control: access control policy, access control model, and access control mechanism. Access control models have emerged that break the direct relationship between subject/object by introducing new concepts such as tasks, roles, rights, responsibilities, teams, etc.). RBAC Model [17] was the most popular access control model for enforcing access control where the role (job function) is the core of privileges in such a model. Unlike other access control policies, users do not acquire the permissions directly, but they acquire them through the roles they play in the organization. Attribute-Based Access Control (ABAC) [18] overcomes the limitations of RBAC. ABAC is considered more flexible than RBAC because it can easily handle contextual attributes as access control parameters [19, 20] but is more complex from a policy review's perspective.

To address the problem of content-based access control – where queries are defined according to the base tables and, then, are rewritten by the system against the user authorized view –, Oracle has proposed a fine-grained based access control approach, the Virtual Private Database (VPD) [21]. Ensuring data confidentiality in the presence of views is an important element of research. Currently, there are several research efforts devoted to addressing issues related to enforcing access control to view based approaches (i.e., materialized or virtual views). Rosenthal et al. automatically calculate derived permissions on the data warehouse with those of the sources by extending the standard SQL grant/revoke model [22, 23]. This allows automated inference of many permissions for the warehouse to systems with redundant and derived data. Finally, in [24], the authors propose a methodology that allows controlling access to a data integration system.

3 The Reference Architecture

The discussion in the previous section revealed several gaps in the state-of-the-art in realizing the ultimate potential of smart healthcare that mandates the building of smart healthcare networks (SHN). Challenges to achieving the SHN vision include a lack of:

- Common modelling formalisms,
- Configuration and deployment strategies,
- Compliance with data protection and privacy regulations with special attention to GDPR,
- Effective data governance strategies,
- Effective meta-data management,
- Advanced knowledge representation mechanisms enabling dynamic yet controlled collaboration across healthcare systems.

As a foundational component, a smart digital platform should be carefully analysed, designed, and developed to serve the purposes/functionalities/use-cases of respective, usually diverse healthcare stakeholders. Based on the literature analysis and feedback from the medical partners in the context of the EU H2020 project QUALITOP[2], we have iteratively developed and validated reference architecture for a smart digital platform for personalized prevention and patient management. A *reference architecture* describes a software system's fundamental organization, embodied in its modules and their interrelationships. It helps achieve an understanding of specific domains and provides consistency of technology implementation for solving domain-specific applications [25]. We advocate in this article that smart healthcare architectures should be built on technology and healthcare standards, which are largely ignored in related work. The smart digital healthcare reference architecture provides a holistic consolidated view of currently dispersed healthcare data silos, enabling new innovative ecosystems, and capacitating different stakeholders, e.g., patients, clinicians, nurses, family, friends, caregivers, laboratory providers/staff, insurance entities, and public authorities, to use for the continuous monitoring, simulation and analysis of patients. All this will empower proactive health and well-being management and enable 4P medicine [3]: Predictive, Preventive, Personalized, Participative.

Figure 1 presents the medical reference architecture. As shown at the bottom of the figure, data from various sources are collected to provide patient-specific health status and Quality of Life (QoL) measures of patients.

Data can be structured, occurring in the form of electronic medical records, stored and maintained in medical institutions' databases and data warehouses; other data can be semi-structured or unstructured originating from file systems, such as questionnaires regarding lifestyle data, nutrition data, QoL data, and diagnostic imaging datasets.

Privacy and GDPR are specifically addressed and given primary attention in the architecture through the adoption of an edge computing approach and enforcing role-based access. Our edge computing approach requires all computations that could be done

---

[2] Monitoring multidimensional aspects of QUAlity of Life after cancer ImmunoTherapy - an Open smart digital Platform for personalized prevention and patient management: https://h2020qual itop.liris.cnrs.fr/wordpress/index.php/project/.

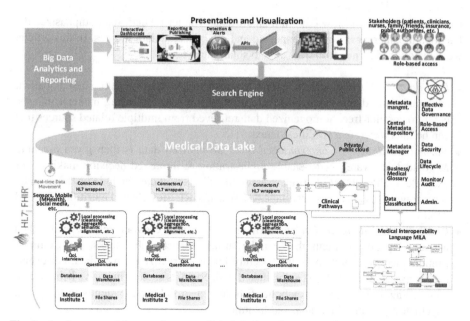

Fig. 1. A reference architecture for smart digital platform for personalized prevention and patient management

locally (without the movement/transfer of data) to be performed at the medical partners' nodes, e.g., cleansing, aggregation, semantic alignment, etc. Only then, anonymized individual or aggregated data will travel to the central data lake for decent querying and advanced analytics. *A data lake* is a centralized repository that allows the storage of all types of structured and unstructured data at any scale. Data can be stored as-is, without having to first structure the data, and run different types of analytics—from dashboards and visualizations to big data processing, real-time analytics, and machine learning to guide better decisions [26]. In the reference architecture presented in Fig. 1, the medical data lake is a virtual layer, which means that transferred data will not be stored in the data lake; only query/analytics results will be maintained in the data lake along with their metadata. The main components of the reference architecture are discussed in detail in the following sub-sections.

3.1 Big Data Management Layer

Due to the sensitivity and strict data protection and privacy regulations of the healthcare domain, such as GDPR, the reference architecture requires that data from different participating medical institutions will still be stored and maintained at respective local nodes (see the bottom of Fig. 1), therefore, as explained earlier in this Section an edge computing approach is adapted. The architecture supports diverse data sources and formats, including structured, semi-structured, and unstructured data, also supporting real-time data streaming from wearable sensors and devices, and runtime data emerging from clinical/medical pathways. Data at the local nodes need to go through several transformation processes to transform raw data into smart data. The term smart data emphasizes the latent value inherent in widely dispersed and unconnected data sources. In this article, we envision the journey from raw data to smart data is:

- *Raw data -> Normalized data*: First we need to convert raw data, such as patient summary data, demographical data, results, and reports including medical images, etc. into conflict-free, homogenized data retrieved from multiple related sources that can be interpreted in a specific context.
- *Normalized data -> Contextualized data*: normalized data is then given meaning & contextual-awareness to enable orchestration & improved decision-making. For example, in the context of "Cancer assessment" relevant data include historical data, screening tests, cancer history, stage, CT scans, MRI, lifestyle and nutrition data, and others
- *Contextualized data -> Orchestrated data*: This step cross-correlates secure data across a specific domain that can be turned to actionable tasks, for example, immunotherapy treatment, at the speed of business, realizing smart data. For example, cancer assessment data can be linked with contexts such as intensive behavioural counselling, treatment of metabolic disorders, also linking a patient's primary and psychiatric care provider data, and treatments.

In the context of the EU H2020 project QUALITOP, a first big data real-life cohort of cancer patients treated with immunotherapy will be created, supporting both prospective and retrospective data coming from five EU countries participating in the project. In prospective studies, individuals are followed over time, and data about them is collected. In retrospective studies, individuals are sampled, and information is collected about their past, through interviews or questionnaires.

To ensure interoperability, enforce standard descriptions, and ensure wide applicability, information exchange standards (message-based and structured document-based) must be supported. In this context, the architecture adopts HL7-FHIR (https://www.hl7. org/fhir/), which is a powerful standard describing resources and an API for exchanging Electronic Health Records (EHRs). Therefore, the architecture integrates a set of HL7 wrappers, adaptors, and connectors that link the data management layer to the medical data lake layer in a loosely coupled manner. This enables the transfer and ingestion of needed on-demand anonymized data to the data lake for processing and advanced querying or analysis.

3.2 Medical Data Lake

The medical data lake represents the heart of the reference architecture. It is an open reservoir for the vast amount of data inherent within healthcare, which can be integrated into an analytics platform to improve decision making. The data lake employs data security and privacy mechanisms to ensure confidentiality and anonymity of data transfer to avoid misinterpretation and inappropriate conclusions by using proper annotation methodologies of the data.

A common misperception is that a data lake is a data warehouse replacement. On the contrary, a data lake is a very useful part of an early-binding data warehouse, a late-binding data warehouse, and a distributed big data processing system, such as Hadoop (https://hadoop.apache.org/). The early- binding mechanism in a data warehouse guarantees that all the data are organized and harmonized before it can be consumed. An early-binding data mechanism is not appropriate for healthcare data as it requires a lot of time to map the data before realizing value. In contrast, when a data lake with a late-binding data mechanism is employed, only the required data are organized, harmonized, and integrated instead of all the data in the data lake. This is called "schema-on-read" or "late binding" because structure and meaning are provided to the data only when the data are read (as users request).

A data lake brings value to healthcare because it stores all the data in a central repository and only maps it as needs arise. The concept of "Map-Reduce" such as in Hadoop systems, when implemented, divides the Big Data integration problem into smaller parts, assigns them to different processing nodes to solve partial tasks, and then accumulates and synthesizes the results on which it applies data-driven analytics and advanced simulation methods. A distributed big data processing system can act as a software framework to handle structured and unstructured data and host analytics mechanisms in a data lake. This approach allows data to be processed faster since the system is working with smaller batches of localized data instead of the contents of the entire warehouse. Therefore, it leads to better and faster means of high-quality response to prevent or timely address the development of new medical conditions and better knowledge for improved patient counselling. Also, it improves the patients' follow-up.

The architecture assumes that the data lake is hosted on the cloud. Given the strict data security and privacy regulations in healthcare, private clouds are recommended.

3.3 Metadata Management

Metadata and efficient metadata management capabilities are mandatory for the success of any data lake implementation, which act to simplify and automate common data management tasks. Metadata ensures that the medical data lake makes the system agile enough to accommodate and scale new types of data. Metadata gives the ability to understand lineage, quality, and lifecycle and provides needed visibility [27, 28]. Metadata is also vital because it enables data governance (cf. Sect. 3.4), the second vital component of any successful data lake implementation. In addition to technical metadata (capturing the form and structure of each data set) and operational metadata (capturing the lineage, quality, profile and provenance of data), business and medical metadata is essential to capture what the data means to stakeholders and to make data easier to find and understand. Harmonization of data digested in the data lake is done through the metadata. Therefore, the metadata management layer of the reference architecture comprises five components: (i) central metadata repository, (ii) metadata manager, and (iii) business/medical glossary that contains definitions agreed upon by stakeholders that ensures that all stakeholders have common understandings and consistently interpret the same data by a set of rules and concepts, (iv) data classification, and (v) the novel Medical Interoperability Language (MiLA), which is a DSL Interoperable Language for health status that is under development in QUALITOP. More specifically, MiLA will:

- Provide appropriate notations, constructs, and a set of operators and offer the expressive power required to integrate a wide variety of medical data sources.
- Provide constructs that make use of high-level abstraction mechanisms that can be used for analytics purposes to improve decision-making.
- Be extensible, pluggable, and parameterizable to avoid problems of current DSLs.

3.4 Effective Data Governance

Effective data governance is the second vital component (in addition to meta-data and meta-data management; cf. Sect. 3.3) for the success of any data lake implementation. Metadata enables data governance that contains the policies and standards for the management, security, quality, and use of data, enforcing data access at the enterprise level [27]. Data lake security ensures that only those users are granted access to the lake, to specific components of the system, or specific portions of the data, who own specific permissions based on the security rules defined for the data lake system [29]. The data governance strategy strictly and reliably secure three components:

- Role-based platform access and privileges: the architecture provides the components to store and process data, and therefore, security for each type or even each component should be defined and enforced. These may rely on federated identity provision, single sign-on, and SSH keys authentication.
- Network Isolation: as described in Sect. 3, the data lake may be hosted on a private cloud to prevent undesired access and protecting the data lake property. However, public clouds are a more doable option, which could be secured through VPNs and firewalls.
- Data Protection: first, data transferred from medical data sources are anonymized, second, anonymized data are encrypted while data transfer, and well as their temporary storage on the data lake for advanced processing and analysis. Once data is processed, it will be permanently deleted from the data lake. Only query and analytics results will be stored on the data lake.

3.5 Search Engine and Big Data Analytics and Reporting

On top of the data lake various search, browse, and analytics capabilities can be devised and implemented using late binding, satisfying the requirements of the various stakeholders. A key aspect of this ubiquitous collection of data is to link them together to reveal elements of the "bigger picture" and use analytics and machine learning techniques to take appropriate actions to solve the problem at hand and build a sound foundation for clinical decision-making. The combination of different sources creates a deeper understanding that leads to decision-making, action-taking, and effective problem-solving in the healthcare domain. The Search Engine allows for substantial performance improvements as well as query capabilities not supported by SQL-based engines, including faceted and text search across many data sets, advanced analytics mechanisms to employ runtime monitoring, predictive analytics, and simulation to extrapolate the course of future events from descriptive data. It is not the aim of this article to provide a review of big data analytics capabilities and use cases in healthcare. Interested readers are referred to [2] for more information about the potential of Analytics.

3.6 Presentation and Visualization

On top of the reference, architecture rests the "Presentation and Visualization" layer that takes inputs from the "Search Engine" and "Big data analytics and reporting" components, and visualize results on customized end-user interactive dashboards, supporting different platforms, e.g., laptops, medium-sized devices, and smartphones. The dashboard provides real-time visibility for clinical decision making using advanced graphic representations of event data, alarms, thresholds, KPI status, drug interactions, patients' vital signs, and performance levels.

4 Conclusions and Future Work

Smart Healthcare brings many promises to the healthcare community in solving the problems of traditional medical systems. The ultimate goal is to realize the concept of 4P medicine (Predictive, Preventive, Personalized, participative). However, to realize this ambitious vision in such a highly regulated multi-disciplinary and sensitive domain, a mine of challenges needs to be effectively and efficiently addressed. Above all, a smart health digital platform that integrates all relevant (semi-) structured and unstructured health-related (big) data is fundamental. The platform should be agile, robust, reliable, secured, and scalable that considers healthcare data standards and information exchange standards. This paper introduces a reference architecture for a smart digital platform for personalized prevention and patient management that meets these requirements and acts as a roadmap for R&D in this direction.

In the context of the EU H2020 project QUALITOP, further R&D efforts will be pursued in parallel and complementary directions to realize the building components of the reference architecture presented in this paper. Following an agile systems development approach, the prototype of an open smart digital platform for personalized prevention and patient management in Europe will be developed. By creating the first big-data real-life cohort of cancer patients treated with immunotherapy, the functional and non-functional requirements of the platform, and subsequently the proposed reference architecture will be iteratively validated and evaluated to ensure the applicability, validity, and efficacy of the proposed architecture and its analytics features.

Acknowledgment. Mike Papazoglou is one of the pioneers in service-oriented computing (SOC) and cloud computing, after having contributed ground-breaking work on database systems. He has strongly influenced the continuously growing SOC community he helped create as a co-founder of the International Conference on Service-Oriented Computing (ICSOC), which will celebrate its 30th anniversary in 2022.

Mike was also instrumental in writing the successful Horizon 2020 proposal QUALITOP whose first results are presented in this paper. Finally, Mike is not only an admirable colleague but also a long-term friend.

Bernd got to know Mike in 1983 during an EU ESPRIT project meeting at the University of Patras. Soon after this meeting, Mike joined GMD - Forschungszentrum Informationstechnik GmbH, a major German research institution for applied mathematics and computer science Bernd was also affiliated with at that time. Amal was a Ph.D. student of Mike who looks back to a fruitful scientific apprenticeship in Mike's lab from 2008 to 2012; He has always been the mentor; role model and continuous supporter and she is honored to have him as an empowering friend since then.

We are deeply honored for the opportunity to contribute to Mike's Festschrift celebrating his 65th birthday and transition to a life with much freestyle and lesser compulsory. We wish him all the best, many more birthdays, and a state of health that does not require him to rely on our smart health platform.

References

1. Tian, S., et al.: Smart healthcare: making medical care more intelligent. Global Health J. 3, 62–65 (2019)
2. Galetsi, P., Katsaliaki, K.: A review of the literature on big data analytics in healthcare. J. Oper. Res. Soc. 71, 1511–1529 (2020)
3. Flores, M., et al.: P4 medicine: how systems medicine will transform the healthcare sector and society. Pers. Med. 10, 565–576 (2013)
4. Catarinucci, L., et al.: An IoT-aware architecture for smart healthcare systems. IEEE Internet Things J. 2, 515–526 (2015)
5. Amato, A., Coronato, A.: An IoT-aware architecture for smart healthcare coaching systems. In: 2017 IEEE 31st AINA, pp. 1027–1034 (2017)
6. Sallabi, F., Shuaib, K.: Internet of things network management system architecture for smart healthcare. In: 2016 6th DICTAP, pp. 165–170 (2016)
7. Ahad, A., et al.: 5G-based smart healthcare network: architecture, taxonomy, challenges and future research directions. IEEE Access 7, 100747–100762 (2019)
8. Frost & Sullivan: Drowning in big data? Reducing information technology complexities and costs for healthcare organizations (2015)
9. Cafarella, M.J., Halevy, A., Khoussainova, N.: Data integration for the relational web. Proc. VLDB Endow. 2, 1090–1101 (2009)
10. Venetis, P., et al.: Recovering semantics of tables on the web. Proc. VLDB Endow. 4, 528–538 (2011)
11. Hassanzadeh, O., et al.: Discovering linkage points over web data. Proc. VLDB Endow. 6, 445–456 (2013)
12. Dean, J., Ghemawat, S.: MapReduce: simplified data processing on large clusters. Commun. ACM 51, 107–113 (2008)
13. Kalavri, V., et al.: m2r2: a framework for results materialization and reuse in high-level dataflow systems for big data. In: 2013 IEEE 16th CSE, pp. 894–901 (2013)
14. Chapelle, O., Li, L.: An empirical evaluation of Thompson sampling. Presented at the Proceedings of the 24th NIPS, Granada, Spain (2011)
15. Xindong, W., et al.: Knowledge engineering with big data. IEEE Intell. Syst. 30, 46–55 (2015)
16. De Capitani di Vimercati, S., Samarati, P., Jajodia, S.: Policies, models, and languages for access control. In: Bhalla, S. (ed.) DNIS 2005. LNCS, vol. 3433, pp. 225–237. Springer, Heidelberg (2005). https://doi.org/10.1007/978-3-540-31970-2_18
17. Ferraiolo, D.F., et al.: Proposed NIST standard for role-based access control. ACM Trans. Inf. Syst. Secur. 4, 224–274 (2001)
18. Wang, L., Wijesekera, D., Jajodia, S.: A logic-based framework for attribute based access control. In: The 2004 ACM, FMSE, USA (2004)
19. Bertino, E., Catania, B., Damiani, M.L., Perlasca, P.: GEO-RBAC: a spatially aware RBAC. In: The 10th SACMAT, Sweden (2005)
20. Rajpoot, Q.M., Jensen, C.D., Krishnan, R.: Integrating Attributes into Role-Based Access Control. Cham, pp. 242–249 (2015)

21. Huey, P.: Using oracle virtual private database to control data access. In: Oracle Database Security Guide, Chapter 7 (2012)
22. Rosenthal, A., Sciore, E.: View security as the basis for data warehouse security. In: 2nd DMDW 2000, Sweden (2000)
23. Rosenthal, A., Sciore, E.: Administering permissions for distributed data: factoring and automated inference. In: IFIP TC11/WG11.3, Canada, pp. 91–104 (2001)
24. Haddad, M., Stevovic, J., Chiasera, A., Velegrakis, Y., Hacid, M.-S.: Access control for data integration in presence of data dependencies. In: Bhowmick, S.S., Dyreson, C.E., Jensen, C.S., Lee, M.L., Muliantara, A., Thalheim, B. (eds.) DASFAA 2014. LNCS, vol. 8422, pp. 203–217. Springer, Cham (2014). https://doi.org/10.1007/978-3-319-05813-9_14
25. Angelov, S., Trienekens, J., Kusters, R.: Software reference architectures - exploring their usage and design in practice. In: Drira, K. (eds.) Software Architecture, pp. 17–24. Springer, Heidelberg (2013). https://doi.org/10.1007/978-3-642-39031-9_2
26. Campbell, C.: Top Five Differences between Data Warehouses and Data Lakes. Blue-Granite.com (2017)
27. Gidley, S.: Tips for managing metadata in a data lake (2017). https://www.oreilly.com/content/tips-for-managing-metadata-in-a-data-lake/
28. Sawadogo, P.N., Scholly, É., Favre, C., Ferey, É., Loudcher, S., Darmont, J.: Metadata systems for data lakes: models and features. In: Welzer, T., et al. (eds.) ADBIS 2019. CCIS, vol. 1064, pp. 440–451. Springer, Cham (2019). https://doi.org/10.1007/978-3-030-30278-8_43
29. Maroto, C.: Data Lake Security: Four Key Areas to Consider When Securing Your Data Lake. https://www.searchtechnologies.com/blog/data-lake-security

Social Requirements Models for Services

John Mylopoulos[1], Daniel Amyot[1(✉)], Luigi Logrippo[1,2],
Alireza Parvizimosaed[1], and Sepehr Sharifi[1]

[1] School of EECS, University of Ottawa, Ottawa, Canada
{jmylopou,damyot,logrippo,aparv007,sshar190}@uottawa.ca
[2] Université du Québec en Outaouais, Gatineau, Canada

Abstract. Social dependance relationships were used in the i^* requirements modelling language to represent dependencies among social actors. We study the evolution of the notion of social dependency into that of commitment in the Azzurra specification language for business processes, and then into the notions of obligation and power in the Symboleo specification language for legal contracts. Our account focuses on the difference in the semantics of these relationships, the language used to talk about them, and how appropriate they are for capturing requirements for services.

Keywords: Requirements model · Social dependency · Service · Business process · Legal contract

1 Introduction

Services are social activities involving a *server* and a *client*, where the client *depends* on the server to deliver the service, be it the sale of an item, the delivery of food, or transportation from home to work. As such, services can be modeled as *social dependencies* in i^* [5], a requirements modeling language founded on the notions of *actor* (agent/role) and *social dependency*.

It turns out that social dependency is a very powerful concept that constitutes the foundation for social modelling and has spawned interesting offspring dependencies that serve as primitives for business process and legal contract modelling. The purpose of this chapter is to discuss the ontological nature and contrast three types of social dependence relationships: social dependencies (i^*), commitments (Azzurra) [4], as well as obligations and powers (Symboleo) [8,10]. These relationships have been studied for over three decades and have involved many collaborators beyond the authors.

2 Social Dependencies (i^*)

As shown in the top model of Fig. 1, in a social dependency the client wants something and the server is able and willing to deliver. However, the force of the

---

This chapter shares much of the narrative with [7], but focuses on modeling requirements for *services* and has been written for a very different audience.

© Springer Nature Switzerland AG 2021
M. Aiello et al. (Eds.): Papazoglou Festschrift, LNCS 12521, pp. 100–108, 2021.
https://doi.org/10.1007/978-3-030-73203-5_8

dependence can vary from weak to strong on either side of the service. Consider a car owner's dependence on a body shop to repair her car: it is usually weak on the car owner's side because there are other body shops that can do the job, and strong on the body shop's side because that's the mission of body shops.

Contrast this with one's dependence on a renowned surgeon for a rare medical operation. This one is strong on the client's side, because there are no substitute servers. The force of the dependence on the server's side is more important, as she is responsible for delivering the service. That force is defined along two dimensions: ability to deliver the service, and degree of commitment to deliver. The dependence on that surgeon is strong on ability and medium on commitment, as surgeons will postpone scheduled operations in case of emergencies.

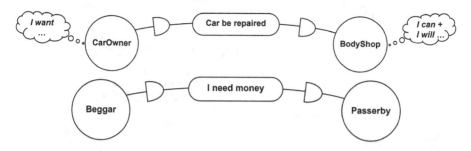

Fig. 1. Examples of social dependence relationships in i^* (adapted from Eric Yu's lectures on i^*)

Now, consider a beggar who depends on passersby to get some money (the service) as Fig. 1 (bottom) shows. This is a social dependency too, and it is weak on both sides: The beggar can switch to another kind of dependency to get money, e.g., work, while the passersby have not even agreed explicitly with the beggar to deliver the service, they are just willing to do it, occasionally. Here, the dependency is established statistically: some passersby give money, and sooner or later this establishes a dependency for the beggar. Note that this dependence does not qualify as a service in the sense that there is no commitment on the part of the server to deliver the service.

i^* does recognize the importance of the *force* of a dependence by allowing three possible levels of force: *critical, committed* and *open* [1]. But, as discussed in the sequel, it turns out that in several areas of research, people have opted for defining specializations of social dependence relationships where the strength of dependence is built into their semantics. Commitments, obligations and powers are three such relationships.

The use of i^* to build requirement models for services goes back to Diana Lau's Masters thesis at the University of Toronto, presented in [6], but also [1] and [9]. All three proposals use the Tropos methodology [3] for deriving agent-oriented implementations from stakeholder requirements.

Figure 2 shows a social dependency model for an online retail service. The service involves several actors (circles), including the retailer, the customer, and the retailer's bank. They each have goals, represented as rounded-corner rectangles, and softgoals (fuzzy goals), represented as clouds: the retailer wants to maximize profits, the customer wants to own products and the bank wants to deliver secure transaction services, among others. There are also dependencies: the retailer depends on a direct supply vendor to ship products to retailer's customers, on the bank to deliver deposit/withdrawal/transfer services, etc.

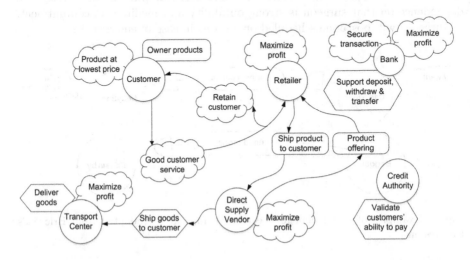

Fig. 2. Social dependency model for an online retail service (adapted from [6])

$i*$ has had many offshoots, including Tropos [3], a methodology for designing agent-oriented software systems, as well as the Goal-oriented Requirement Language (GRL), part of the User Requirements Notation (URN) standard [2].

3   Commitments (Azzurra)

Originating in the area of Multi-Agent Systems [11], *commitments* capture a social dependence where there is an explicit speech act executed "I want X – I commit to fulfill X". This kind of social dependence on a service has substantially more force than the beggar's dependence on passersby. It means that the server intends to deliver, provided that some conditions hold. So, commitments are social dependencies that always arise from intentions, rather than mere practice, and are established through speech acts. More formally, commitments are 4-tuples C(debtor, creditor, antecedent, consequent), where creditor is the client, i.e., the beneficiary of the service, while debtor is the server. Moreover, the commitment is fulfilled when the consequent becomes true, provided that the antecedent is true. Moreover, commitments go through states, such as *created*, *active, suspended, success* and *failure*. Allowable state transitions can be defined by state diagrams, as shown in Fig. 3. Note that commitments constitute a specialization of social dependencies, with better fleshed out semantics, proposed for use in multi-agent systems. They also come with a precise level of force for the debtors/servers who *intend* to fulfill what they are committed to, while the creditors/clients have the *right* to expect that the commitments will be fulfilled. The passersby mentioned earlier have no commitment towards the beggars and, in turn, they have no right to expect anything from them.

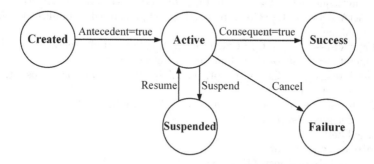

Fig. 3. The lifecycle of a commitment[1]

Azzurra is a conceptual modelling language for business processes. Its main thesis is that business processes, being social artifacts, need to be defined in social terms, rather than system-oriented ones (e.g., Petri nets, BPMN and the like). Accordingly, business processes (aka *protocols*) are defined in terms of roles and commitments, with constraints attached. Azzurra models can be seen as requirements specifications for services, defined in terms of the business processes through which they will be delivered. Moreover, as specifications they describe what a business process is supposed to achieve without getting into the details of how to achieve it.

Table 1 presents an Azzurra protocol for fracture treatment (adopted from [4]). The protocol includes as parameters a hospital number that serves as key for treatment instances, a patient, a specialist; it also includes role parameters, such as a radiologist and a surgeon, as shown.

There are nine commitments for this protocol, each using a $<trigger>$ $\rightarrow$ $<commitment>$ format. The first, C_1, is triggered when the protocol is instantiated, has as roles the specialist (server) and patient (client), it is unconditional (antecedent = true) and is fulfilled when the patient is examined, then diagnosed and then de-hospitalized. The second commitment, C_2, is triggered if there is no need for X-rays and fulfilled when a sling is made for the patient. Protocol refinements constrain the agents that participate in a protocol instance. For example, agents may be constrained on how many concurrent commitments they

---

[1] Figure 3 is actually a simplification of a commitment's lifecycle in Azzurra.

Table 1. An Azzurra protocol for fracture treatment

---

protocol Treatment(**key** hospnr, pt : Patient, sp : Specialist){
   ag-variables: rc : RehabCenter, ra : Radiologist, or : Orthopedist, su : Surgeon,
      nu : Nurse;
   commitments:
    init $\rightarrow$ C_1 : C(sp, pt, $\top$, Examined . Diagnosed . Dehospd) final
    NoXRayNeeded $\rightarrow$ C_2 : C(or, sp, $\top$, SlingMade)
    XRayRequested $\rightarrow$ C_3 : C(ra, sp, $\top$, XRayPerformed)
    XRayRequested $\rightarrow$ C_4 : C*(sp, ra, XRayPerformed, FractAssessed)
    FractAssessed $\rightarrow$ C_5 : C(or, sp, $\top$, ((Fixated$\oplus$Plastered) $\vee$ fulfill(C_6) $\vee$ Sling-
      Made))
    FractAssessed $\rightarrow_{\leq 2h}$ C_6 : C*(su, or, SurgeryRequested, Operated)
    Operated[$\neg$fused] $\rightarrow$ C_7 : C(nu, pt, $\top$, RcChosen(rc))
    RcChosen(rc) $\rightarrow$ C_8 : C(rc, pt, $\top$, fulfil-p(RehabGiven, key=hospnr, pat-
      id=pt, ref-sp=sp))
    MedPrescribed(m) $\rightarrow$ C_9 : C(nu, sp, $\top$, MedApplied(m))
    can-deleg-no-resp(C_3)
    deadline(C_2, 2h)
   protocol refinements:
    role-confl(Radiologist, Orthopedist)
   kb:
    implies(XRayRequested, Diagnosed)
    implies(NoXRayNeeded, Diagnosed)
    implies(MedPrescribed(m), Diagnosed)
    mutExcl(XRayRequested, NoXRayNeeded) }

---

have for a given role, such as a surgeon for treatment protocol instances (max-per-role). Finally, the knowledge base (KB) defines some domain axioms, which can be used to reason about propositions serving as triggers, antecedents or consequents of commitments.

Azzurra supports two types of reasoning for protocols. ENACTPROTOCOL determines how an event updates the state of a protocol instance and of the commitment instances therein. CHECKCOMPLIANCE checks whether an occurred event violates the specification of a protocol instance. This corresponds to identifying commitments that are not created/fulfilled, unexpected commitment operations and protocol constraint violations.

In summary, commitments specialize and improve the formalization of social dependence relationships. They also come with a language richer than i^* for modeling business processes in an outcome-oriented approach. Finally, and most importantly, Azzurra is a more appropriate language than i^* for describing requirements for services, as it commits the server to deliver, and gives the client the right to expect the service.

4   Obligations and Powers (Symboleo)

Obligations are commitments with legal force. The legal force is defined through *powers* that a creditor has towards the debtor of an obligation to cancel or suspend an obligation or another power, or initiate new obligations or powers. The concept of obligation is a specialization of the concept of commitment in that obligations can be created, cancelled, etc. by someone who has the power to do so. In turn, powers constitute a specialization of obligations in that they can include in their antecedent the creation, cancellation, etc. of other powers or obligations.

Obligations and powers constitute the basic elements of *legal contracts*. Legal contracts form the foundation of all commerce world-wide and have been used since time unmemorable. Legal contracts can be thought as process specifications that describe the space of allowable executions that comply with legal terms and conditions. The presence of powers in legal contracts makes them a much more malleable concept than that of business processes in that they can be reshaped with the introduction/cancellation of obligations while contracts are being executed ("performed" in Law).

Symboleo is a formal specification language for legal contracts, intended to serve in formalizing requirements for smart contracts. The latter are software systems, possibly running on blockchain platforms, that partially automate, monitor and control the execution of legal contracts. Symboleo is founded on an ontology that is centered around the notions of *obligation* and *power*, and includes *role* and *party* (the actors playing roles in a contract), *asset, situation* and *event*. Situations occur over time, e.g., the situation of commuting to work. Events, on the other hand, happen instantaneously, e.g., *arrivedAtWork*.

Symboleo adopts many elements from Azzurra. Obligations and powers use the same format as commitments. Their antecedents, consequents, and triggers are expressed in terms of events happening in a certain order and satisfying constraints. For example, for a sale contract the consequent of a delivery obligation may be "Sale item delivered to delivery address by delivery date".

Table 2 presents a Symboleo specification for a contract (adapted from [10]). As shown, a Symboleo specification begins with the description of concepts in the domain. These are defined as classes that specialize concepts in the Symboleo ontology. For example, Goods specializes Asset and has an additional attribute goodsID. Instances of this class include sale items involved in sale transactions. The domain model for a contract is followed by declarations of variables that take as values instances of domain classes. Pre/post-conditions have the same semantics as in program specifications. The core of contract specifications consists of obligations and powers. In our example there are two obligations: the seller must deliver the sale item to the delivery address by the delivery date (O_1), while the buyer must pay on time the sale amount (O_2). The contract also includes one power: if the buyer violates the payment obligation, the seller has the power to terminate the contract (P_1). Note that the creditor of a power may choose to not exercise it.

Table 2. Abbreviated Symboleo specification for a goods sale contract

---

Domain salesD

   Goods **isA** Asset **with** goodsID: Integer;
   ...
   Delivered **isA** Event **with** delAddress: String, delDueDate: Date;

endDomain
Contract salesC(seller: Seller, buyer: Buyer, ID: Integer, amnt: Integer, curr: Currency, delAdd, delDd: String)

   Declarations
     /* *Values of parameters are passed on to the variables defined in the domain*
       model. */
     goods : Goods **with** goodsID := ID;
     ...
     delivered : Delivered **with** delAddress := delAdd, delDueDate := delDd;
   Preconditions
     isOwner(seller, goods) **and not** isOwner(buyer, goods);
   Postconditions
     isOwner(buyer, goods) **and not** isOwner(seller, goods);
   Obligations
     O_1 : O(Seller, Buyer, true, **happensBefore**(delivered, delivered.delDueD));
     O_2 : O(Buyer, Seller, true, **happensBefore**(paid, paid.payDueD));
   Powers
     P_1 : **violates**(O_2, _) → P(Seller, Buyer, true, **terminates**(salesC));
   SurvivingObl
     /* *Some obligations may remain active, e.g., confidentiality obligations.* */
   Constraints
     not(isEqual(buyer, seller));

endContract

Legal contracts can be very complex constructs with many features that go well beyond those of business processes. For instance, some obligations may apply after the successful termination of a contract (and are accordingly called *surviving* obligations). A confidentiality obligation for a sale transaction for 6 months after a contract terminates is an example of such an obligation. A contract may spawn subcontracts that may be established while the contract is executing. For example, when a large project is undertaken in the construction industry, not all the subcontractors with their respective subcontracts might have been identified when the project starts. Symboleo specifications can be validated to ensure that they are consistent with the expectations of the contracting parties by a tool that enacts scenarios and determines the contract's final state. For example, for the scenario "Seller delivers on time, buyer does not pay on time, seller exercises power to terminate", the tool determines that the final state of the contract is 'cancelled'. The scenarios for validation are provided by the contracting parties, along with their anticipated final state of the contract when each scenario is enacted.

All commercial services are defined in terms of legal contracts and they do include both obligations and powers for the contracting parties. But note that not all services need to have associated explicit legal contracts, see for example Government or volunteer services.

5   Conclusions

Social models consisting of actors and social dependencies are useful for capturing requirements for social systems that include software, business processes and services. We trace the evolution of the concept of social dependence to commitments and then to obligations and powers, focusing on changes in semantics, the languages where these relationships inhere, and the application domains, i.e., the types of artifacts we are defining requirements for.

Epilogue

This chapter has been written for the occasion of Mike Papazoglou's retirement celebration, to hopefully happen within 2021[2]. I have known Mike for thirty years as a colleague working on topics of mutual interest, collaborator on international projects, co-author and friend.

Throughout, Mike has been an exemplary researcher not only for his research contributions and their impact, but also for the leadership role he undertook in conceptualizing, shaping and promoting research areas. During the 90s, his passion was with Cooperative Information Systems, an area of research where he founded a conference series and a journal that are still going strong. In the following decade, his allegiance shifted to Web Services and Service-Oriented Computing where he was a key player in framing the area and the research venues that define and serve it.

It is a pleasure to contribute, along with my University of Ottawa colleagues working on smart contracts, a chapter on Service Requirements that spans his interests as well as mine.

John Mylopoulos
Toronto, June 8, 2020

---

[2] Nothing is certain in the days of the pandemic.

References

1. Aiello, M., Giorgini, P.: Applying the Tropos methodology for analysing web services requirements and reasoning about qualities of services. Technical Report DIT-04-034, University of Trento (2004)
2. Amyot, D., Mussbacher, G.: User requirements notation: the first ten years, the next ten years. JSW **6**(5), 747–768 (2011)
3. Bresciani, P., Perini, A., Giorgini, P., Giunchiglia, F., Mylopoulos, J.: Tropos: an agent-oriented software development methodology. Auton. Agents Multi-agent Syst. **8**(3), 203–236 (2004)
4. Dalpiaz, F., Cardoso, E., Canobbio, G., Giorgini, P., Mylopoulos, J.: Social specifications of business processes with Azzurra. In: 9th RCIS, pp. 7–18. IEEE (2015)
5. Eric, S., Giorgini, P., Maiden, N., Mylopoulos, J.: Social Modeling for Requirements Engineering. MIT Press, Cambridge (2011)
6. Lau, D., Mylopoulos, J.: Designing web services with Tropos. In: Proceedings. IEEE International Conference on Web Services, 2004. pp. 306–313. IEEE CS (2004)
7. Mylopoulos, J., Amyot, D., Logrippo, L., Parvizimosaed, A., Sharifi, S.: Social dependence relationships in requirements engineering. In: 13th International iStar Workshop, CEUR-WS 2642, pp. 55–60 (2020)
8. Parvizimosaed, A., Sharifi, S., Amyot, D., Logrippo, L., Mylopoulos, J.: Subcontracting, assignment, and substitution for legal contracts in symboleo. In: Dobbie, G., Frank, U., Kappel, G., Liddle, S.W., Mayr, H.C. (eds.) ER 2020. LNCS, vol. 12400, pp. 271–285. Springer, Cham (2020). https://doi.org/10.1007/978-3-030-62522-1_20
9. Penserini, L., Perini, A., Susi, A., Mylopoulos, J.: From stakeholder needs to service requirements. In: 2006 Service-Oriented Computing: Consequences for Engineering Requirements (SOCCER 2006-RE 2006 Workshop). IEEE CS (2006)
10. Sharifi, S., Parvizimosaed, A., Amyot, D., Logrippo, L., Mylopoulos, J.: Symboleo: A specification language for smart contracts. In: 28th IEEE International Requirements Engineering Conference (RE 2020), pp. 384–389. IEEE CS (2020)
11. Singh, M.P.: An ontology for commitments in multiagent systems. Artif. Intell. Law **7**(1), 97–113 (1999)

Services and Humans

Service Oriented Computing for Humans as Service Providers

Sergio Laso[1], Javier Berrocal[1(✉)], José Garcia-Alonso[1], Carlos Canal[2], and Juan M. Murillo[1]

[1] Universidad de Extremadura, Cáceres, Spain
{slasom,jberolm,jgaralo,juanmamu}@unex.es
[2] ITIS Software, Universidad de Málaga, Málaga, Spain
canal@lcc.uma.es

Abstract. For the past twenty years, Service Oriented Computing has changed the way in which information technology was understood. The approach involves not only technological advances that have influenced the development of Software Engineering, such as Service Oriented Architecture, Web services, Service Choreography, or Microservices. In addition, it has also provided the pillars for the development of Cloud Computing, which has transformed how the business in Information and Communication Technology is developed. In that context, this work focuses on how Service Oriented Computing can also drive the integration of humans in the Internet of Things and Crowd Sensing loops by enabling them to act as service providers. The key to this is the deployment of services on mobile devices, in particular smartphones. The enormous penetration of these devices in today's society, together with the personal nature of the information they handle, open a new horizon for the development of services. Through them individuals are able to make personal information available to others. This paper depicts Human Microservices, an architecture that allows humans to be considered as service providers, and discusses the open challenges in the field that conforms one of the next frontiers for Service Oriented Computing.

Keywords: Service Oriented Computing · Human service providers · Smartphones

1 Introduction

Service Oriented Computing (SOC) [16] has been a driving force behind innovation in computer science for the last decades [19]. From Service Oriented Architectures [21] to Cloud Computing [17], SOC has had a deep impact, both in research and industry.

Additionally to this background, SOC is more active than ever [18], as there is still a lot of challenges to be addressed [8]. Recently, the advances in this area led to the paradigm of Everything as a Service [4], where any component in a system can be handled as a service.

© Springer Nature Switzerland AG 2021
M. Aiello et al. (Eds.): Papazoglou Festschrift, LNCS 12521, pp. 111–122, 2021.
https://doi.org/10.1007/978-3-030-73203-5_9

This situation is complemented by the enormous penetration and the increasing capabilities of smartphones and other smart devices. The constant presence of this kind of devices in everyday life has led to a more direct involvement of humans in SOC. On the one hand, most of the companies and services offered by the so called "collaborative economy" highly depend on service-based applications that need humans to perform some task in the real world [12], such as delivering some food, or driving somewhere. On the other hand, the presence of smart devices around people are producing an amount of information never seen before, allowing to provide new kinds of services related to these people.

Due to their nature, a significant amount of the information gathered by smartphones and other smart devices is personal. There is no doubt of the value that personal information has for the development of context-oriented services. There is also no doubt about the privacy and ethical problems associated with the management of such information. Proposals like People as a Service [11] address this issue by keeping personal information in their owners' devices, giving them back control over their data. However, to take advantage of the information stored in end user devices, there must be a standardised way to offer such information to approved applications.

We will refer to these services—based on smart devices owned by individuals and providing personal information about their owners to approved applications—as Human Microservices. In this paper we present the technological architecture needed to manage and provide them. The ultimate benefit is that humans and their context can be servitized and included in service oriented applications in a completely smart way through their mobile devices.

The rest of the paper is organised as follows. Section 2 presents the motivations and technological foundations behind this work, while Sect. 3 describes the architecture of the proposal and its implementation. Section 4 develops a use case in which we have applied Human Microservices. And finally, Sect. 5 discusses the findings of this work and the conclusions of this paper.

2   Motivations and Technological Foundations

The SOC paradigm uses services to support the development of rapid, low-cost, interoperable, evolvable, and massively distributed applications [18]. During the last few years this paradigm has changed the way in which software is developed, paving the way for the proliferation of smart devices and pervasive and ubiquitous applications [8].

Indeed, the emergence of technological foundations such as Service Oriented Architecture (SOA) [24], and the Semantic Web [5], and the development of standards and recommendations such as OpenAPI [15] and W3C Thing Description [13] has made easier the specification of services, and their deployment. Upon them, Service Composition allows the aggregation of multiple services or microservices for offering higher level services supporting complex tasks or business processes.

The driving goal of these technological advances is to facilitate the flexibility and seamlessly integration of distributed applications, which is also a key issue in IoT applications. Typically, the business process flow of IoT systems depends on the services offered by several smart devices, that may even come from different manufacturers [21]. Consider for instance how the microservices of light bulbs of different trademarks in an office could be composed to be turned on or off depending on the brightness of the environment and the preferences of the employees in the room.

Up to now, the services run by IoT devices have been limited to sensing and changing the state of the environment. More complex tasks (such as storing or computing information), or the orchestration of services were limited to cloud environments, in which research efforts have being invested to address scalability [20] and vendor lock-in problems [14], in order to improve the execution of distributed applications.

Nowadays, the massive deployment of Internet-connected devices has fostered the consumption of services deployed on cloud environments for retrieving, storing or computing the sensed information. However, the specific requirements of IoT applications and the increasing computing capabilities of these devices is changing the way these services are deployed and consumed. Indeed, paradigms such as Edge or Mist Computing are fostering the deployment of microservices on end or near-to-the-end devices. This way, the Quality of Service (i.e., response time, network overload, data traffic, etc.) can be improved [7]. Similarly to cloud-based services, these microservices can be composed for executing complex tasks, and the same technologies for addressing scalability and vendor lock-in problems can be reused to solve some of the issues of these platforms. For instance, by increasing the horizontal deployment of services on the edge layer in order to increase the computational capabilities.

Nevertheless, the nature of IoT devices and the information they handle open new challenges on the services offered and how they are composed. For instance, paradigms such as Human-in-the-loop or User-in-the-loop [22] promote services centred on people and aware of their context [23], mobility or preferences, in order to personalise the behaviour of the environment. Microservices focused on offering human-related information (i.e., the preferences, needs or contextual situation of the users) are needed in order to allow other devices or even third-party entities to consume that information, and to compose services and business flows adapted to the users' needs. These services could be deployed in cloud environment but, as has been discussed before, some stringent requirements may benefit from their deployment near the user [7].

In the next section we present the enabling technologies for such a "close-to-the-user" deployment. First, we introduce a conceptual model, that we have called People as a Service (PeaaS), for storing, computing and providing the user's contextual information within his/her smartphone. Then, we present the current implementation of the model. This implementation is based on Human Microservices, a framework which provides a set of tools for designing, implementing and deploying APIs focused on offering (or storing) contextual information of the users from their mobile devices.

3   Humans as Service Providers

From our point of view, companion devices, more specifically smartphones, can take a much more active role in the integration of humans in the Internet of Things through the use of SOC. During the last few years we have witnessed how these devices have increased their computing and storage capabilities, and the number of built-in sensors in order to gather more information about their owners. Usually, the destination of these data is some storage infrastructure in the cloud. Instead, in order to address the computational requirements of modern service oriented applications, companion devices should be able of capturing, storing and processing information about the users in the device itself, in particular when this information is to be consumed in environments close the user.

3.1   People as a Service

PeaaS is a mobile-centric computing model which proposes using the smartphone's sensors and interactions with other devices in order to gather large amounts of information about the user's context. This information is processed by using the smartphone's computational capabilities in order to infer the virtual profile of the owner. The computed virtual profile is kept in the device and provided by means of services. This allow owners to keep their virtual identity under their own control and, at the same time, the consumers of such services are allowed to get fresh and updated personalised information.

The PeaaS model is based on four principles:

- Mobile devices as interfaces to people. Smartphones are usually Internet-connected. Therefore, they are the interface of humans to the virtual word –they support the virtual links with other people and devices.
- Virtual profiles. Smarthpones have a large number of sensors that collect information about their surroundings. PeaaS allows to compute all this information in order to create and store locally the virtual profile of the owner.
- Virtual profiles as a service. Building a virtual profile of the smartphone's owner is particularly useful if it can be queried by external entities. Virtual profiles are provided as a service to those who might wish to access that information (such as IoT devices or interested enterprises).
- User privacy. PeaaS guarantees that an individual's virtual profile is always exclusively kept in the owner's device. PeaaS allows the users to control and monitor the external entities consuming their information. By means of user-defined privacy rules, PeaaS empowers users to manage their privacy.

Serving virtual profiles allows the integration of humans in the loop by applying SOC together with mobile computing technologies. In addition, PeaaS allows a variety of information to be collected in order to infer higher-level knowledge about the users, such as their mood, the kind of place their current location corresponds to, or the people who are with them. Such analysis requires specific algorithms to process the data and to provide them as part of the virtual profile.

PeaaS first use case consisted in an advertising and a commercial platform called nimBees [2] based on Google Cloud Messaging and Apple Push Notification Service. This implementation had some restrictions due to the limitations of the mobile operating systems and its orientation to the mobile marketing domain. The current implementation of PeaaS is called Human Microservices, and it eases the deployment of microservices on smartphones. In the coming subsections we describe both implementations of the PeaaS model.

3.2 nimBees

NimBees [2] is a smart push notification system with advanced segmentation capabilities based on the user's virtual profile. Figure 1 shows the nimBees architecture compared with the reference architecture of PeaaS.

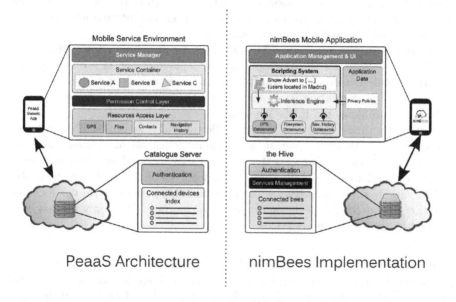

Fig. 1. Architectures of PeaaS and nimBees.

The system consists of a library that can be imported in almost any mobile application. This library allows these applications to receive segmented push notifications (i.e., notifications that are only shown or processed by the smartphones of the users meeting some specific requirements). Once the push notification reaches the smartphone, nimBees checks the owner's virtual profile in order to decide if s/he meets the requirements indicated in the notification. Only in that case, the notification is processed. Otherwise, it is ignored. The whole workflow of push notifications is processed transparently to the mobile applications finally receiving them.

More importantly, nimBees is also in charge of building the virtual profile by getting information from the different sensors of the smartphone and by processing it by means of inference rules [6]. It also allows consulting the virtual profile through push notifications. The richer the profile, the greater the segmentation can be. In addition, every personal datum stays in the owner's device. nimBees has a server-side, but only to manage the connected devices, the nimBees-based applications, and the delivery of the push notifications.

nimBees was a successful commercial implementation exploiting some of the features of PeaaS that allowed us to see its real potential. Thus, more recently we have been working on an implementation applying the SOC technologies and to directly provide the user's profile as a service.

3.3   Human Microservices

Human Microservices are services integrating a human in the loop, and focused on providing very personalised and updated contextual information about this person and his/her context and surroundings.

In order to implement Human Microservices, we have built a framework based on SOC technologies for the development and deployment of APIs on companion devices (mobile devices, smartwatches, etc.) for providing the owner's virtual profile. All the information is obtained at runtime through the device's sensors or from the profile stored in the smartphone.

Differently from nimBees, Human Microservices is not a library to be imported by third-party application developers. Instead, it proposes a set of tools and a development process that can be easily followed by any developer to design and implement the APIs that can be deployed on top of the virtual profile and the device's resources. Please, note that in this paper we will not focus on how the virtual profile or the information is computed, but only on how it is exposed by means of microservices.

Deployment Process. First, a development process has been defined in order to provide a guideline to developers about the different activities that should be performed and their sequencing. This process is based on technologies and standards already used for designing and implementing APIs that will deployed on cloud environments. Figure 2 shows the proposed steps.

– **API Definition.** First, the characteristics of the API are defined through the OpenAPI Specification (OAS) [15] following the same notation as if it were developed for a cloud environment. During the design of the interface, developers must bear in mind that the microservices will provide personal information about one single user. In that sense, the API could be a little different with respect to its design as a cloud microservice.
– **Generate Source Code.** In this step, the source code of the API is generated. Currently, different tools, such as OpenAPI Generator [3] or Guardrail [1], support the generation of source code (mainly the skeleton

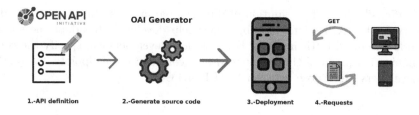

Fig. 2. Process for the development and deployment of Human Microservices.

and the schema of the API) from an OAS design. This scaffolding is based on its deployment on cloud environments. Therefore, as detailed bellow, an extension of the OpenAPI Generator tool has been developed to support the deployment of Human Microservices in smartphones and other companion devices.

– **Deployment.** At this point developers implement the business logic for each endpoint/microservice and configure the communication protocol. As it will be explained bellow, mobile devices present several limitations due to the restrictions imposed by the operating system and the mobile nature of the devices. Therefore, during the API scaffolding asynchronous communication protocols are supported. In this step, these protocols have to be configured, and the API is deployed following the procedure defined by the manufacturer.
– **Service consumption.** Finally, once the API is deployed, any device or third party can invoke the provided Human Microservices to request and consume information about the user, and to adapt the behaviour of the system accordingly.

In the next subsections, the three last steps and the related tools implemented to support them are described in more detail.

API Generator for End Devices - APIGEND. APIGEND is an extension of OpenAPI Generator that allows the generation of APIs that can be deployed on end devices. Currently, we provide support for its scaffolding and deployment on Android-based devices and other devices base on Esp32 Microcontrollers. APIGEND is available to any developer[1].

Figure 3 shows an example of generating an API using APIGEND. As it can be seen, the tool provides a website in which developers have to specify the framework (or the operating system) for which they want to generate the skeleton. Subsequently, In the *parameters* section, they have to indicate the following:

– *"openAPIUrl"*, which is the public URL to the specification of the API with OpenAPI. This specification can be stored in a git repository, a Dropbox folder, or any others web environment.

---

[1] https://openapi-generator-spilab.herokuapp.com.

– *"options"* allows the definition of different parameters that are not mandatory for the API scaffolding, but they help developers to adapt the source
code generated to their needs. For instance, developers can specify the communication protocol they want to use to consume the endpoints. Currently,
developers can choose between MQTT or FCM.

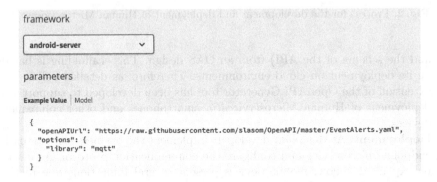

Fig. 3. Parameters to generate an Android API using the MQTT library.

In order to generate the API, the developer must click the *Execute* button
and if there are no errors, a JSON response containing a link for downloading
the generated API is produced.

Deployment. For deploying the API on end devices, the developer first have
to configure the selected communication protocol. For MQTT, she only needs
to indicate the connection parameters for the MQTT broker used to send and
receive the messages consuming the microservices. For FCM, there is a guide
for configuring it either using the Android IDE or manually[2]. Then, the developer has to implement the behaviour of the different endpoints defined (to get
personal information from the stored virtual profile, to access information from
the device's sensors, etc.). Finally, the developed API is deployed following the
procedure recommended by the manufacturer.

Consuming Human Microservices. Due to their mobile nature and to limitations of the operating system, not every companion device supports the provision of services following synchronous communication. As indicated above,
several asynchronous protocols (currently, MQTT and FCM) are supported by
the framework.

For instance, for MQTT the content of the request is defined in JSON. The
different parameters that must be specified are:

---

[2] https://firebase.google.com/docs/cloud-messaging/android/client.

– **Resource**: it indicates the *Tag* associated with the end point to be invoked.
– **Method**: it corresponds to the Id of the endpoint.
– **Sender**: ID or topic of the consumer performing the invocation, used for sending the reply.
– **Params**: parameters associated to the endpoint.

By default, the **MQTT topic** for sending requests to the API is the *title* of the specification without spaces. Listing 1.1 shows an example of an API request.

Human Microservices represent a shift in the role of companion and mobile devices in service oriented applications. It allows them to take full responsibility for storing, processing and exposing users' personal information, having greater control than they currently do, offering updated information, and seamlessly integrating humans in the loop.

4   Case Study

This section presents a case study where Human Microservices are deployed on an Android device and a smartwatch (based on the ESP32 microcontroller). To that end, the development process and the tools described in the Sect. 3.3 have been used.

The case study consists of an API that allows to obtain contextual and health information about people. The API will be deployed on a smartwatch to monitor an elderly person. This same API will be deployed on an Android device, acting as the caregiver's device. The mobile device can obtain information about the elderly person, such as location, body temperature, etc. by invoking the deployed API. In addition, the smartwatch is able to send messages or alerts by invoking the microservice deployed on the mobile device. This case study is fully available on Github[3].

The **first step** is to design and define the API. It is composed of four main microservices. **Get User** allows to obtain personal data stored in the device (such as name, age, etc.). **Get Body-Temperature** provides the body temperature of the elderly person thanks to the sensors of the smartwatch. **Get Location** provides the location through the built-in GPS sensor. Finally **Post Alert** allows to invoke the caregiver's microservices in order to send alerts (e.g., when an elder falls down and cannot get up).

The **second step** is to generate the skeleton of the API for both the Android device and the smartwatch, in this case MQTT is used as the communication protocol.

The **third step** is to deploy the APIs on both devices. On the one hand, it is necessary to configure the MQTT communication protocol for the connection between both devices. On the other hand, the microservices have to be implemented with the behaviour described above.

The **last step** is to invoke the deployed microservices. Listing 1.1 shows an example of invocation of the API developed to obtain the location. The request

---

[3] https://github.com/rurentero/HealthAlerts_M5Stick-C.

is sent to the main topic *'HealthAlerts'* (which is the name of the application) indicating the user id from whom the service consumer wants to get the information. Other topics schemes can be configured, for instance, per endpoint, tag, user, etc.

```
1 {
2     "resource": "Status",
3     "method": "getLocation",
4     "sender": "caregiver293",
5     "params": {}
6 }
7 caregiver.publish('HealthAlerts/user2234',request)
```

Listing 1.1. Content of the request to obtain the location by MQTT.

Thus, using Human Microservices, the elderly person virtual profile is connected to the Internet to be consumed by trusted external entities.

5   Discussion and Conclusions

Current information systems and applications are more focused on the users (e.g., their preferences, their context and their needs). From simple IoT applications [10], such as a smart light-bulb that is automatically turner on or off depending on the luminosity of the environment and the user's preferences, to complex business processes and systems [9], such as a Supply Chain or Smart Manufacturing Systems in which the socio-technical integration is crucial. The integration of people in the Internet is key but, in order to obtain the maximum benefit, this integration should follow standards and mechanisms that already exists.

PeaaS and its implementation Human Microservices allows the definition of APIs and services that can be deployed on companion devices following a specification broadly adopted by the industry. First, this reduces the learning curve, since developers can design the API and generate the source code by using tools already known by them. Secondly, it facilitates the integration of these Human Microservices in the business processes of the information systems because they can be consumed without requiring any knowledge about their implementation in the "server" side (in our case, the companion device).

In addition, the deployment of microservices near the user has positive implications with respect to resource consumption, latency, response times, and privacy. With a client-server model, end devices act as simple clients which constantly collect and send information to a cloud environment. This implies a significant consumption of some of their resources such as battery and data traffic, including heavy use of the network increasing latency and response times. In addition, this architecture can pose a risk to the privacy of users since the information is stored on servers and is beyond their control.

Finally, Human Microservices allows smartphones to change their role from pure consumers of information to also become providers of information. The APIs deployed on companion devices can be consumed by different information systems and third-party entities. For instance, the information gathered by the device's sensors and provided as Human Microservices can be consumed by a smart factory system, a smart city application and by a smart home IoT systems in order to adapt their behaviour to the current context and needs of the user. As future work, we currently work on evaluating the defined process and the related tools developed.

This work is founded on previous work on the Service Oriented Computing and Mobile Computing paradigms. We would like to thank Mike P. Papazoglou for his substantial contributions to these areas and, specially, for inspiring us in the development of the proposal presented in this paper.

Acknowlegments. This work was supported by the projects RTI2018-094591-B-I00, PGC2018-094905-B-I00 (MCI/AEI/FEDER, UE), the RCIS research network (RED2018-102654-T), the 4IE+ Project (0499-4IE-PLUS-4-E) funded by the Interreg V-A España-Portugal (POCTEP) 2014-2020 program, by the project UMA18-FEDERJA-180 (FEDER/Junta de Andalucia), by the Department of Economy and Infrastructure of the Government of Extremadura (GR18112, IB18030), and by the European Regional Development Fund.

References

1. Guardrail. https://github.com/twilio/guardrail
2. nimBees. http://www.nimbees.com
3. Openapi Generator. https://github.com/OpenAPITools/openapi-generator
4. Banerjee, P., et al.: Everything as a service: powering the new information economy. Computer **44**(3), 36–43 (2011)
5. Berners-Lee, T., Hendler, J., Lassila, O.: The semantic web. Sci. Am. **284**(5), 34–43 (2001)
6. Berrocal, J., García-Alonso, J., Murillo, J.M., Canal, C.: Rich contextual information for monitoring the elderly in an early stage of cognitive impairment. Pervasive Mob. Comput. **34**, 106–125 (2017). https://doi.org/10.1016/j.pmcj.2016.05.001
7. Berrocal, J., et al.: Early analysis of resource consumption patterns in mobile applications. Pervasive Mob. Comput. **35**, 32–50 (2017). https://doi.org/10.1016/j.pmcj.2016.06.011. http://www.sciencedirect.com/science/article/pii/S154119216300797
8. Bouguettaya, A., et al.: A service computing manifesto: the next 10 years. Commun. ACM **60**(4), 64–72 (2017)
9. Cimini, C., Pirola, F., Pinto, R., Cavalieri, S.: A human-in-the-loop manufacturing control architecture for the next generation of production systems. J. Manuf. Syst. **54**, 258–271 (2020). https://doi.org/10.1016/j.jmsy.2020.01.002. http://www.sciencedirect.com/science/article/pii/S0278612520300029
10. Flores-Martín, D., Berrocal, J., García-Alonso, J., Murillo, J.M.: Towards a runtime devices adaptation in a multi-device environment based on people's needs. In: IEEE International Conference on Pervasive Computing and Communications Workshops, PerCom Workshops 2019, Kyoto, Japan, 11–15 March 2019, pp. 304–309. IEEE (2019). https://doi.org/10.1109/PERCOMW.2019.8730859

11. Guillen, J., Miranda, J., Berrocal, J., Garcia-Alonso, J., Murillo, J.M., Canal, C.: People as a service: a mobile-centric model for providing collective sociological profiles. IEEE Softw. **31**(2), 48–53 (2013)
12. Huang, K., Yao, J., Zhang, J., Feng, Z.: Human-as-a-service: growth in human service ecosystem. In: 2016 IEEE International Conference on Services Computing (SCC), pp. 90–97. IEEE (2016)
13. Kaebisch, S., Kamiya, T., McCool, M., Charpenay, V.: Web of Things (WoT) thing description. First Public Working Draft W3C (2017)
14. Nguyen, D.K., Lelli, F., Papazoglou, M.P., van den Heuvel, W.: Blueprinting approach in support of cloud computing. Future Internet **4**(1), 322–346 (2012). https://doi.org/10.3390/fi4010322
15. OpenAPI Initiative: The OpenAPI Specification. https://github.com/OAI/OpenAPI-Specification
16. Papazoglou, M.P., Georgakopoulos, D.: Service-oriented computing. Commun. ACM **46**(10), 25–28 (2003)
17. Papazoglou, M.P., van den Heuvel, W.J.: Blueprinting the cloud. IEEE Internet Comput. **15**(6), 74–79 (2011)
18. Papazoglou, M.P., Traverso, P., Dustdar, S., Leymann, F.: Service-oriented computing: state of the art and research challenges. Computer **40**(11), 38–45 (2007)
19. Papazoglou, M.P.: Service-oriented computing: concepts, characteristics and directions. In: Proceedings of the Fourth International Conference on Web Information Systems Engineering, 2003, WISE 2003, pp. 3–12. IEEE (2003)
20. Papazoglou, M.P.: Cloud blueprint: a model-driven approach to configuring federated clouds. In: Abelló, A., Bellatreche, L., Benatallah, B. (eds.) MEDI 2012. LNCS, vol. 7602, pp. 1–1. Springer, Heidelberg (2012). https://doi.org/10.1007/978-3-642-33609-6_1
21. Papazoglou, M.P., Van Den Heuvel, W.J.: Service oriented architectures: approaches, technologies and research issues. VLDB J. **16**(3), 389–415 (2007)
22. Petrov, V., et al.: When IoT keeps people in the loop: a path towards a new global utility. IEEE Commun. Mag. **57**(1), 114–121 (2018)
23. Rosenberger, P., Gerhard, D.: Context-awareness in industrial applications: definition, classification and use case. Procedia CIRP **72**, 1172–1177 (2018)
24. World Wide Web Consortium: Web services architecture (2004). http://www.w3.org/TR/2004/NOTE-ws-arch-20040211/

Cognitive Augmentation in Processes

Moshe Chai Barukh[1(✉)], Shayan Zamanirad[1], Marcos Baez[2], Amin Beheshti[3], Boualem Benatallah[1], Fabio Casati[4], Lina Yao[1], Quan Z. Sheng[3], and Francesco Schiliro[3,5]

[1] University of New South Wales, Sydney, Australia
{mosheb,shayanz,boualem}@cse.unsw.edu.au, lina.yao@unsw.edu.au
[2] Université Claude Bernard Lyon 1, Lyon, France
marcos-antonio.baez-gonzalez@univ-lyon1.fr
[3] Macquarie University, Sydney, Australia
{amin.beheshti,michael.sheng}@mq.edu.au
[4] ServiceNow, Santa Clara, CA, USA
fabio.casati@servicenow.com
[5] Australian Federal Police, Canberra, Australia
francesco.schiliro@hdr.mq.edu.au

Abstract. We present a vision for the next generation of process technology based on cognitive augmentation. Starting from current process technology, we show how by augmenting layers of cognitive intelligence to combine advances in machine-automation, crowdsourcing and more importantly adaptation and reasoning, we can advance support for emerging requirements of highly changing environments. We believe the challenges lie in the synergy between human and machine, in understanding how to orchestrate and combine their contributions. This vision paper sets forth a roadmap for future research by introducing a framework for cognitive augmentation, identifying the relevant research and technologies, and discussing its application amidst real-world use cases.

Keywords: Bots · Cognitive computing · Processes

1 Introduction

Processes are an integral part of everyday life. Often, the most prevalent are those we are least mindful about, yet highly pervasive in everyday tasks (e.g., send an email, schedule a meeting, record notes and gather feedback). Colloquially referred to as "shadow processes", these snippets of the overall process are typically being performed ad-hoc using a variety of cloud-based software tools, while the end process remains hidden [8]. These are highly unstructured processes. On the other extreme, there is an enormous body of work into structured processes. Formally referred to as Business Process Management (BPM), this technology proved monumental in allowing organizations to embrace workflow automation of tasks. However, the challenge in this approach stems for the

© Springer Nature Switzerland AG 2021
M. Aiello et al. (Eds.): Papazoglou Festschrift, LNCS 12521, pp. 123–137, 2021.
https://doi.org/10.1007/978-3-030-73203-5_10

inherent presupposition that processes are well-defined; they thus fail to cater for much needed agility in today's dynamic environments [2].

At present, many have struggled to bridge the gap between highly structured and very unstructured processes – with many solutions ending up closer to either one extreme. We believe the challenges lie in the synergy between human and machine. For some tasks, humans are far more superior than machines, such as in judgement-oriented work. Whereas in other tasks that require consistent iterations, a machine would far outperform human capabilities.

For this reason, we envision the next generation of process capability resembling a humanoid. More broadly termed "cognitive computing", it should be capable of assisting humans in human tasks, while augmenting machine-level capability. It should be capable of thinking, acting as well as learning autonomously akin to the human mind. Our vision is a world where everyday existing work platforms will converse with end-users via digital-assistance services – thus acting to mediate humans and work tools, and between different tools. Underlying all this, we envision a backend powered by several layers of cognitive intelligence, with data as the common factor connecting these disparate work tools.

In this paper, we present a vision that sets sail into this journey. We see this consisting of three main layers: (1) As the foundation, existing process systems, together with apps, tools and services must continue to be used. However we will rely strongly on the "everything-as-a-service" model, whereby such tools, even including sensors and physical monitors will be programmatically accessible. (2) On top of this will be several layers of "cognitive enablement". These layers of intelligence will act in hierarchy where higher layers can be composed (and utilize) lower layers. More so this will include crowdsourcing and methods for continuous learning. (3) Finally, we have a layer of "cognitive delivery", which means a seamless interface for human workers, in the form of bots that offer digital assistance through conversation. Putting it all together, we refer to this idea as "cognitive augmentation".

2   Process Technology Foundations

To project an accurate vision of the future, we must thoroughly understand the past. A fundamental view of a process is the coordination of tasks, data and the communication between tasks and data as well as stakeholders. Beyond this, the remaining technological landscape for processes can be abstracted simply as parameterizations of these three fundamental aspects.

For structured processes, classical business process management systems focused on the process-centric methodology – automating 'tasks' with secondary support for other aspects such as data and communication. Other structured processes systems shifted focus to data, known as artifact-centric systems, such as: structured data repositories, document engineering, artifact governance policing (e.g. IBM Governor [13]), and artifact lifecycle management (e.g. Gelee [4]). From this various synergies emerged. Such as between data and tasks, where the notion of "Business Artifacts (BA)" was introduced to assist in describing the data of business processes. Event-Driven BPM similarly shifted focus offering more powerful control of communication and its synergy with process (sub-)tasks. With an event-driven approach, events produced by the process engine can in turn be prescribed to trigger or influence the execution of another task, and even cross-enterprise business processes.

Many process systems oscillated focus of support between *tasks*, *data* and *communication*, as well as synergies of these – with the goal towards increased flexibility. Ultimately however, it was hard for these approaches to separate between models (or "schemas") and process instances. Even non process-oriented solutions struggled to agree upon accepted rules- or event- processing language.

On the other end of the spectrum, unstructured process support systems are typically present as Web-based SaaS tools, each targeting a specific type of task/s. Such as, communication and collaboration tools, project and task management tools, artifact management as well as visualization and direct-manipulation tools. This approach offered the much needed flexibility. However, multiple different tools are often needed to meet a typical end-to-end solution, resulting in "shadow processes" that are managed manually and difficult to track.

We should now better understand the goal of cognitive augmentation. Until now the mistaken mentality was an automate "everything" approach, and both structured and unstructured processed were incapable of this. The solution rather lies in a part-human part-machine approach - a "humanoid"; it's then about the right type of automation being applied. For structured processes this means empowering human workers by automating the pre- and post- processing steps (e.g., translating natural language into low level commands and vice versa). On the other hand, for unstructured processes this means introducing automation by leveraging existing algorithms and APIs to automate both basic and complex micro-tasks.

In practice today, many enterprises have adopted case-management to draw closer to the reality that most processes are neither fully structured nor fully unstructured, and in fact requires both manual control as well as automation. These types of "semi-structured" processes are devised as a set of repeatable process patterns, yet each specific "case" can take upon its own variation. Case management offers interaction channels between people, services and data sources thus empowering open communication, and moreover Web services are being leveraged for enhanced automation opportunities (e.g., semantic tagging of artifacts to better work with the intensity of data). *ProcessBase* [5] is a unique framework that offers a *hybrid processes* approach to combine from structured to very unstructured processes. In the future, cognitive augmentation would enable autonomic process that ultimately thinks and learns like humans, and with this vision we can move into a reality of model-free processes that are self-descriptive rather than prescriptive.

3 Cognitive Process Augmentation

The next generation of tools are not just about integrating artificial intelligence (AI). It is about augmenting (not reinventing) existing tools, services and process systems (from structured to unstructured) with the rich and already mature advances in data curation [6,7], machine learning as well as crowdsouring, and delivering this to end-users as natural and interactive digital assistance.

Figure 1 proposes a three-faceted framework to realize this vision. We start by leveraging *current process technology*, including structured, unstructured and case management. We analyze this rudimentary layer with respect to: data, tasks and communication capabilities. We then identify what enables *cognitive augmentation*, and this depends on utilizing advances in machine-driven automation, human workers in the crowd and most importantly reasoning and adapting. Cognitive processes must iteratively discover, learn and customize based on accumulated knowledge and experience. Finally, to the end-user cognitive processes means delivering a digital administrative assistant (a "humanoid"). It must support natural language interactions resembling the work practices of humans (providing guidance, advice, recommendation, contextualization and problem solving in decision making). The benefits of cognitive process will felt across the range of information systems, providing in-task assistance from email, groupware, workspaces to enterprise social platforms.

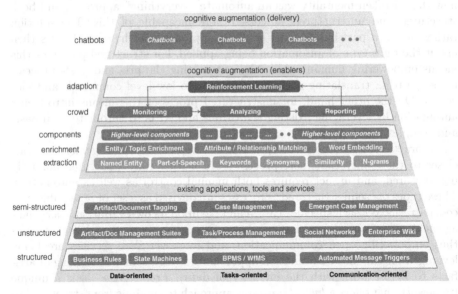

Fig. 1. Framework for cognitive augmentation in processes.

4   Use Cases

Cognitive augmentation in real-world processes would significantly increase the productivity of processes, as well as the ability for enhanced insights and effective decision making. To illustrate this vision, we explore a typical use-case scenario, showing how cognitive capabilities can be enabled and delivered to the process worker. The same would apply to many other real-world scenarios, such as *investigative journalism, systematic literature review* or *activity recognition*.

4.1 Law Enforcement Investigations

Modern police investigations are complex projects that can span for years. As shown in Fig. 2, investigators collect and manage information, as well as ensure evidence collected is relevant, admissible and sufficient to prove offenses at court beyond reasonable doubt. Evidence may be sourced from "witness statements", "forensic reports" and "telephone intercepts". Investigators must not only find content but apply their own cognitive efforts to extract meaning. For example, an investigator may retrieve the passenger manifest for all flights over a given time, and must then search for evidence that their person of interest, with a given passport number, traveled at the time of interest.

The overall process is highly cognitive both with respect to collecting and analyzing information, as well as to inferring interdependencies between data to eventually produce a storyline brief to present in court. Today an enormous amount of relevant data is available, from social media to tracking personal devices (e.g., monitoring a suspect's location and social interaction can provide vital information to a case). Traditional tools are simply inadequate and thus most cognitive tasks are performed manually; this is no doubt tedious, error prone and highly insufficient. In the recent Bali attacks, investigators revealed several perpetrators were left unprosecuted only due to limited manual processing power.

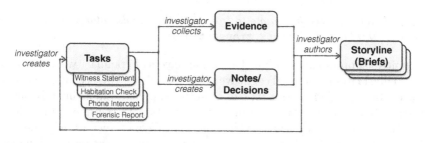

Fig. 2. Law enforcement investigation process.

Cognitive Enablement. With highly knowledge-intensive processes, it becomes paramount to prepare raw information into contextualized knowledge. Raw data is useless to both humans and machines unless processed in the correct order to derive valuable insight. For example, if we were to classify the topic of Tweets, we would first need to apply natural language extraction (e.g. to extract and identify nouns and verbs), before applying a classification algorithm.

As data accumulates during an investigation, it becomes vital to keep track of relevant events and detecting possible offenses from raw evidence logs. The analysis of such text-based logs involves a great deal of qualitative analysis that can be a lengthy process, and cases can even be cut short leaving criminals unprosecuted. Cognitive support can therefore significantly improve productivity:

1. **Offense Detection.** Typically, at the start of an investigation, an allegation statement is composed (e.g., the extract as shown below):

> *"Peterson was found to be in possession of 500 grams of Methamphetamine. It is alleged that Johnson may have sold Peterson the controlled substance discovered."*

Ordinarily, manually sifting through legislation, such as the Criminal Code Act 1995 which codifies thousands of criminal offenses, would be a very exhausting task. We would need to find the right offense (and all the offenses) that match a particular allegation, such as: Sect. 308.1 ("Possessing controlled drugs") and Sect. 400.3 ("Dealing in proceeds of crime").

2. **Event Recognition.** Next, the investigator records all types of evidence, and these logs are later used to prove the elements of an offense. Once again, cognitive support would not only help extract events, but also analyze and attach semantics. Moreover, it could also assist in reconstructing chains of events to simulate how the case developed, the identification of parties involved, understanding of its temporal dynamics, among other aspects. For example, for the sample evidence log show below, we can extract event types such as "phone call", "bank transaction" or "travel movement".

> *"On 23 Feb 2011, Peterson went to Lancaster to meet a person named Johnson in a pub, they watched a football match together until 8.30pm."* (travel movement)

> *"Peterson, used his phone to transfer 6 thousands dollars to Johnson on 23/02/11:20:18."* (bank transaction)

Cognitive support can be applied at various layers of granularity. For example, Fig. 3 illustrates a potential cognitive stack suitable for this scenario – it shows the enablers needed for this type of cognitive support (and ultimately deliver them as end-user digital assistance components). At the fine-grained level, we have various information "extraction" components, such as: named-entity (using lexical analysis); part-of-speech (using synthesis of natural language

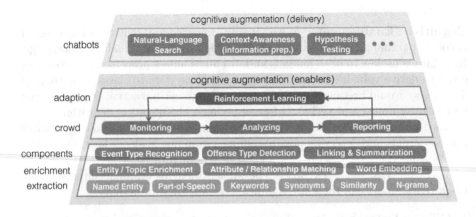

Fig. 3. Cognitive augmentation stack for investigations process.

to identify nouns and verbs); synonyms (using the urban dictionary); and timestamps (using parsers). In the case of event recognition, these rudimentary components assist to lexically deconstruct raw evidence logs.

3. **Linking and Summarization.** We should now appreciate that the underlying objective of the investigative process is to link evidence to elements of the offense (i.e., we try to prove or disprove an offense based on the evidence). This is where an investigator would spend most of his time, sifting through, in many cases, thousands of pieces of evidence and linking them to possible offense violations. Once again cognitive support for this could be used to filter through key facts (such as the events recognized earlier), and for example, using event pattern/templates correlate such sets of events to indicate whether the elements of a particular offense have been committed. For example, to be charged under Sect. 400.3 ("Dealing with proceeds of a crime"), intent to carry out the crime must be established. In some cases, it can done by linking several pieces of evidence to reconstruct the picture.

> *"Section 400.3(1)(b)(ii) the person intends that the money or property will become an instrument of crime"*
> → witness statement #1: phone call
> → witness statement #2: meeting took place
> → bank transaction #1: exchange of monies

Moreover, the key information obtained here (and throughout the investigation) could be auto-summarized and chronologically compiled into a single evidence brief. Effective summarization are vital to present the case in a simple and organized manner in court.

4. **Action Generation.** During the process, investigators may also need to take certain action. For example, approving a search warrant to obtain missing information, or anything else to finalize the case. Once again, cognitive support in the form of summarization (e.g. over existing evidence) can be used to auto-generate tasks and remind/guide investigators about what actions are required.

Cognitive Delivery (Bots). The second part of cognitive augmentation is delivering to end-users a collaboration model that connects people, tools, processes, and automation into a transparent work environment. As mentioned earlier, the key is to balance between humans and machines. In fact, in most work processes, humans require machines as much as machines require humans. We envision conversational bots will achieve this, where end-users can express in a controlled natural language the tasks they want to perform, or provide the requisite feedback, to interact with underlying cognitive services that drive the overall process towards its goal. The following describes two (due to space limitations) types of digital assistance for this scenario:

Fig. 4. Illustration of cognitive depicting the "natural language search" bot in the law enforcement investigations use-case computation.

- **Natural Language Query.** Investigation data can be made available using controlled natural language queries (e.g., search person of interests, documents, artifacts, organization knowledge, people to ask questions, relationship and hypothesis-based search, conversations to construct answerable queries). For example, Fig. 4 shows how a simple question could be asked in natural language. This capability is powered by a number of techniques such as natural language processing, query intend discovery, entity mention discovery, knowledge graphs and deep learning algorithms to perform entity mentions and relationships based indexing over investigations as well external data.

- **Context Awareness and Proactive Information Preparation.** Proactively providing the right information at the right time is a proven technique to improve productivity and reduce information load. Cognitive services in this category capture context (e.g., a task an investigator is working on like a line of inquiry, meeting information) and proactively surface relevant information (e.g., availability status, prepare and recommend information that is relevant to perform a task, advice to correct or complete missing information to increase information quality).

4.2   Systematic Literature Reviews

Systematic Literature Reviews (SLRs) aim at analyzing and synthesizing research evidence by following accepted community guidelines, in response to postulated research questions. They are one of the most important forms of publications in science, and are the basis for evidence-based practices and even government policies. As illustrated in Fig. 5, the SLR process is typically carried out in phases, such as: (i) the definition of a goal and scope of the review (e.g., "studies on the effect of technology-supported interventions to reduce loneliness"); (ii) the output of which are the identification of relevant papers through a search strategy that stems from the research question; papers may also be annotated adding additional semantics and insights; (iii) the screening of these candidate papers – very often thousands of them – based on specified inclusion and exclusion criteria (e.g., "Filter out papers without loneliness as primary outcome"); and then (iii) the analysis of the selected literature and synthesizing summaries based on the findings, along with the discussion of potential biases.

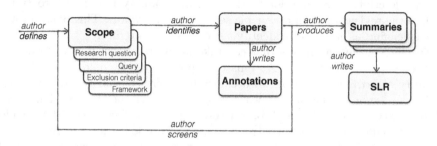

Fig. 5. Systematic Literature Review (SLR) process.

While extremely valuable and of considerable impact, SLRs are very time-consuming, become rapidly outdated and are not easily maintained. The considerable effort required by researchers combined with the acceleration in the research production pace of the scientific community and the lack of adequate tools to support this process makes carrying out an SLR a very challenging endeavor [11]. Indeed, studies have shown that literature reviews might miss from 30% to 50% of relevant papers at the time of publication [9], either due to compromises to make the process manageable or new articles published.

Cognitive Enablement. One of the most labor intensive yet critical phases is the identification of relevant scientific articles [11]. Focusing on this phase alone, we explore how cognitive support can be enabled to deliver a number of assistive components, working together to enable authors in performing a reviews that are unbiased, systematic, inclusive, yet tractable in terms of effort and latency.

This scenario, in particular, exemplifies how cognitive support is enabled using a mesh of automated (i.e., algorithms, services and AI) and crowd-driven techniques. The goal of the crowd in this scenario is both to conduct micro-tasks along the way that require human intuition, as well as providing feedback for ongoing adaptation, such as input to reinforcement algorithms. At the crowd layer, this may be abstracted into the following components that feed into each other but can also be iterated as the authors (and algorithms) gain more insights of the outcomes of each phase: i) search, referring to setting the scope and identifying the relevant papers; ii) annotate, the activity of labeling, filtering out and classifying scientific articles, and iii) synthesize, as the activity of extracting and deriving knowledge in relation to the research question and overall analytical framework of the review.

In the following, we identify some of the relevant cognitive support areas for this scenario:

1. **Query Definition.** Defining the initial query requires capturing the relevant properties of papers, typically by matching keywords found in title, abstract and description. Even prior to this, cognitive ability is required to translate the review scope into a viable set of query keywords. This phase proves challenging as it requires identifying all possible alternative keywords to a specific concept, a process that can take many iterations, involve trade-offs and be prone to error [1]. Automated support for this could be word similarity algorithms (by using word embeddings, either from general language knowledge or by specializing word vectors for a field of science). This word similarity can then be used for keyword expansion. These algorithms could also be enhanced by feeding stronger domain-knowledge, such as from scientific knowledge bases, and low-level data extraction components can be used to extract and curate this knowledge.

2. **Paper Screening.** Even upon refining our query and finding relevant papers, in many cases it is important to filter out papers that are out of scope. This requires a clear definition of the criteria for excluding the papers, namely the exclusion criteria. The selection of primary studies is one of the most difficult tasks in the SLR process, with a direct negative impact on the outcome of the review [11]. Once again automated support could be obtained, for example by using machine-learning classifiers to label papers [10]. An additional benefit of the screening process is that it helps obtain a global view on the body of work in a specific area of research – this also helps further refine the query (e.g., incorporating new keywords) as well as the inclusion and exclusion criteria, and feeds back into the refinement loop of the process.

3. **Recommending Papers.** Recommendation is a useful technique to attenuate the complexities of the overall process, which can complement query-based search strategies [1]. This may be accomplished by leveraging AI approaches based on word similarity, clustering and network analysis to recommend papers and encourage exploring related topics.

Cognitive Delivery. At the end-user level, process workers should be provided with a unified work environment where they express in a controlled natural language the tasks they want to perform and interact with underlying cognitive services to refine their requests and perform desired tasks. In this specific scenario, examples of cognitive capabilities include:

1. **Query Expansion.** The identification of relevant literature can be facilitated by digital assistants that can support authors in scaling search strategies, otherwise unfeasible, using natural language. For example, authors could expand keywords, ask for additional papers from references, or iterate on the search and screening phases to receive query refinement suggestions. To make this possible, the chatbot should orchestrate the combination of crowd and AI support, while providing insights about the impact of each alternative in terms of cost, effort and information retrieval (IR) metrics such as precision and recall.

2. **Multi-Predicate Filtering.** Filtering out non relevant papers is an iterative and time-consuming phase that can greatly benefit from augmentation. Digital assistants offer an appealing interface for assisting authors in for example, understanding of the impact and quality of the different exclusion criteria, and making recommendations for the next iteration of the screening process.

3. **Knowledge Inquiry.** Getting insights on the knowledge residing in the corpus of papers is another very relevant activity where digital assistants can significantly improve productivity and efficiency. For example, elaborating claims and supporting evidence from the literature usually requires authors to go back and forth from writing and preparing summaries to re-reading papers – an activity that requires significant attention and coordination among authors. Digital assistants could allow authors to elaborate queries in natural language to check claims, as well as prepare summaries and insights to inform authors (e.g., summary tables).

Figure 6 summarizes the above in a potential augmentation stack.

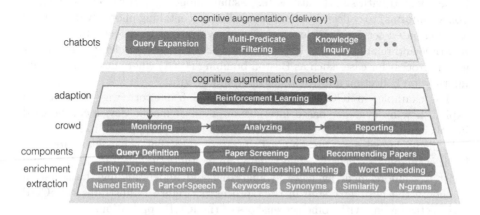

Fig. 6. Cognitive augmentation stack for SLR process.

4.3   Augmentation of IoT-Enabled Processes

Despite the early adoption, IoT based services are still only in their preliminary stages of development, with several unsolved technical challenges stemming from the lack of effective support for complex IoT services management and data analysis processes.

More specifically, a commonly overlooked limitation of current systems is that they do not make federated analytics over IoT services accessible to analysts and decision makers. There is an imperative need to integrate common user productivity services (e.g., spreadsheets applications and tools such as dashboards and collaboration tools) with underlying IoT data capture and management. Analysts often need to access, manipulate and analyze data from various federated IoT and other data services and should be empowered, like data scientists, to also benefit from the power of advanced analytics in analysis and decision making tasks.

The objective of work in this area is to usher increased productivity, effectiveness through greater simplicity, augmented intelligence and automation over IoT and data services. For instance, layering advanced data analysis and digital assistance capabilities on top of IoT, data, crowdsourcing, task management and collaboration services, may bring several advantages to IoT enabled processes (e.g., smart city, policing and health processes). Regarding knowledge-intensive law-enforcement processes, the implementation of information and communications technology has been a success factor for conducting data-driven and knowledge-intensive processes in law enforcement. The focus on making police work more efficient with new technologies is still valid and consists of many trends: extracting and analyzing large repositories of data gathered from various data sources such as open, private, social and IoT data islands. In this context, a knowledge-intensive process (a type of data-driven processes which comprises activities based on acquisition, sharing, storage, and reuse of knowledge) can benefit extensively from IoT. For instance, in law enforcement processes such as police investigation, knowledge workers (e.g., police investigators) can be augmented with smart entities (e.g., smartphones, smartwatches and smart police uniforms) to collect data (e.g., recording voice, taking photos/videos, using location-based services and leveraging sensory systems to detect explosives) in real-time and relate this data to process analysis. This will accelerate the investigation process for cases such as Boston bombing (USA) where fast and accurate information collection and the analysis would be vital.

For example, in iCOP [12], an IoT-enabled framework was presented to explore how an evidence-based interface on a smart mobile device can be used in policing processes to provide a coherent and rigorous approach, to interrogate a "policing knowledge hub": an IoT infrastructure that can collaborate with internet-enabled devices to collect data, understand the events and facts and assist law enforcement agencies in analyzing and understanding the situation to choose the best next step in their processes. Figure 7 illustrates the iCOP architecture along with some screenshots of the iCOP application.

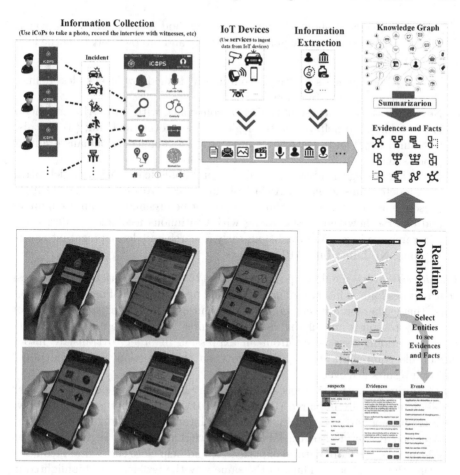

Fig. 7. The iCOP architecture and screenshots [12].

5   Roadmap to the Future

The proposed vision provides an exciting opportunity to the entire community: from research scientists, to engineers and developers, as well as businesses people. This is because we rely on reuse across the spectrum and advocate against the "one-solution-fits-all" or "automate everything" mentality. Until now, many tools often arise strengthening one aspect of improvement (be it data management, control flow or communication) while neglecting the other. Nevertheless, each of these tools carry merit of their own (e.g., an algorithm designed by a research scientist or best practices developed by a business). To put it another way, cognitive augmentation will be about filling in the gaps between these disparate tools, algorithms or services.

Accordingly, we set forth the following roadmap (and identify some of the key challenges) towards the realization of this dream:

Cognitive Enablement should involve a new method of using AI, a "conversational AI" where end-users are able to iteratively and interactively tune the logic needed to achieve their goal.

- We see AI components packaged from highly defined low-level to less defined (blueprint) high-level functions.
- Nevertheless, the purpose of tuning or conversing with these AI components is two-fold: (i) to help define the logic for the process at hand; (ii) but also to train the system to learn the moves with less reliance on humans in future processing.
- Over time, using the above we project a probabilistic execution model rather than a deterministic model. A class of "modelless processes" not requiring to prescribe or implement the whole component beforehand. AI can use humans and observe how they work (along with continuous feedback) to derive the programming logic. We have begun early research and development into auto-mapping NL intent into API calls [14].

Cognitive Delivery should empower end-users to drive the section of the process that requires human intervention. This should be in the form of natural-language bots, that either proactively prompts the end-user to trigger some action; or reactively responds only if the end-user inquires. One of the major challenges is understanding user intent from an expression in order to translate into a executable command. We began to work on this direction with some initial research results achieved.

Cognitive augmentation has also the potential to empower populations, such as blind and visually impaired (BVIP) users. BVIP and other populations have been traditionally challenged by the current interaction paradigm for accessing information and services on the Web. We believe that cognitive augmentation can enable and deliver more natural experiences, and help close the digital inequality affecting the Web today. Thus, in the same way the problems we highlighted in this paper are amplified for vulnerable populations, so the benefits and potential social impact of cognitive augmentation. We have made our first steps in this direction [3] and call on the community to join us.

Putting all the above together, *Cognitive Augmentation* (i.e., AI + chatbots = conversational AI) should be packaged as first-class citizens to existing work tools, in a manner similar to what Service Oriented Architecture (SOA) achieved for Web services.

References

1. Al-Zubidy, A., Carver, J.C.: Identification and prioritization of SLR search tool requirements: an SLR and a survey. Empirical Softw. Eng. **24**(1) (2019)
2. Alotaibi, Y.: Business process modelling challenges and solutions: a literature review. J. Intell. Manuf. **27**(4), 701–723 (2016)
3. Baez, M., Daniel, F., Casati, F.: Conversational web interaction: proposal of a dialog-based natural language interaction paradigm for the web. In: Følstad, A., et al. (eds.) CONVERSATIONS 2019. LNCS, vol. 11970, pp. 94–110. Springer, Cham (2020). https://doi.org/10.1007/978-3-030-39540-7_7

4. Báez, M., et al.: Gelee: cooperative lifecycle management for (composite) artifacts. In: Baresi, L., Chi, C.-H., Suzuki, J. (eds.) ICSOC/ServiceWave-2009. LNCS, vol. 5900, pp. 645–646. Springer, Heidelberg (2009). https://doi.org/10.1007/978-3-642-10383-4_50

5. Barukh, M.C., Benatallah, B.: *ProcessBase*: a hybrid process management platform. In: Franch, X., Ghose, A.K., Lewis, G.A., Bhiri, S. (eds.) ICSOC 2014. LNCS, vol. 8831, pp. 16–31. Springer, Heidelberg (2014). https://doi.org/10.1007/978-3-662-45391-9_2

6. Beheshti, A., Benatallah, B., Sheng, Q.Z., Schiliro, F.: Intelligent knowledge lakes: the age of artificial intelligence and big data. In: U, L.H., Yang, J., Cai, Y., Karlapalem, K., Liu, A., Huang, X. (eds.) WISE 2020. CCIS, vol. 1155, pp. 24–34. Springer, Singapore (2020). https://doi.org/10.1007/978-981-15-3281-8_3

7. Beheshti, A., Benatallah, B., Tabebordbar, A., Motahari-Nezhad, H.R., Barukh, M.C., Nouri, R.: Datasynapse: a social data curation foundry. Distrib. Parallel Databases **37**(3), 351–384 (2019)

8. Cognini, R., Corradini, F., Gnesi, S., Polini, A., Re, B.: Business process flexibility-a systematic literature review with a software systems perspective. Inf. Syst. Front. **20**(2), 343–371 (2018)

9. Créquit, P., Trinquart, L., Yavchitz, A., Ravaud, P.: Wasted research when systematic reviews fail to provide a complete and up-to-date evidence synthesis: the example of lung cancer. BMC Med. **14**(1), 8 (2016)

10. Krivosheev, E., Casati, F., Baez, M., Benatallah, B.: Combining crowd and machines for multi-predicate item screening. In: Proceedings of the ACM on Human-Computer Interaction (CSCW), vol. 2, pp. 1–18 (2018)

11. Palomino, M., Dávila, A., Melendez, K.: Methodologies, methods, techniques and tools used on SLR elaboration: a mapping study. In: Mejia, J., Muñoz, M., Rocha, Á., Peña, A., Pérez-Cisneros, M. (eds.) CIMPS 2018. AISC, vol. 865, pp. 14–30. Springer, Cham (2019). https://doi.org/10.1007/978-3-030-01171-0_2

12. Schiliro, F., et al.: iCOP: IoT-enabled policing processes. In: Liu, X., et al. (eds.) ICSOC 2018. LNCS, vol. 11434, pp. 447–452. Springer, Cham (2019). https://doi.org/10.1007/978-3-030-17642-6_42

13. Yaeli, A., Kofman, A., Dubinsky, Y.: Software development governor: automating governance in software development environments. In: 2009 31st International Conference on Software Engineering-Companion Volume, pp. 413–414. IEEE (2009)

14. Zamanirad, S., Benatallah, B., Barukh, M.C., Casati, F., Rodriguez, C.: Programming bots by synthesizing natural language expressions into API invocations. In: 2017 32nd IEEE/ACM International Conference on Automated Software Engineering (ASE), pp. 832–837. IEEE (2017)

Designing and Building Context-Aware Services: The ContextServ Project

Quan Z. Sheng[1(✉)], Jian Yu[2], Wei Emma Zhang[3], Shuang Wang[1,4],
Xiaoping Li[4], and Boualem Benatallah[5]

[1] Department of Computing, Macquarie University, Sydney, NSW 2109, Australia
`michael.sheng@mq.edu.au`
[2] Department of Computer Science, Auckland University of Technology,
Auckland, New Zealand
[3] School of Computer Science, The University of Adelaide, Adelaide,
SA 5005, Australia
[4] School of Computer Science and Engineering, Southeast University, Nanjing, China
[5] School of Computer Science and Engineering, UNSW, Sydney,
NSW 2052, Australia

Abstract. In the era of Web of Things and services, context-aware services (CASs) are emerging as an important technology for building innovative smart applications. CASs enable the information integration from both the physical and virtual world, which affects the way human live. However, it is still challenging to build CASs, due to lack of context provisioning management approach and lack of generic approach for formalizing the development process. In this paper, we briefly introduce a large research project, ContextServ, which provides a platform for model-driven development of CASs based on a UML-based modelling language. We discuss the literature and also highlight several future research opportunities for context-aware service research and development.

Keywords: Context-aware services · Internet of Things · Model driven development · Modeling language · ContextUML · Adaptive services

1 Introduction

Over the years, the Web has gone through many transformations, from traditional linking and sharing of computers and documents (i.e., "Web of Data") to current connecting of people (i.e., "Web of People"). With the recent advances in radio-frequency identification technology, sensor networks, and Web services, the Web is continuing the transformation and will be slowly evolving into the so-called "Web of Things and Services" [13,27]. Indeed, this future Web will provide an environment where everyday physical objects such as buildings, sidewalks, and commodities are readable, recognizable, addressable, and even controllable using services via the Web. The capability of integrating the information from both the physical world and the virtual one not only affects the way how we

© Springer Nature Switzerland AG 2021
M. Aiello et al. (Eds.): Papazoglou Festschrift, LNCS 12521, pp. 138–152, 2021.
https://doi.org/10.1007/978-3-030-73203-5_11

live, but also creates tremendous new Web-based business opportunities such as support of independent living of elderly persons, intelligent traffic management, efficient supply chains, and improved environmental monitoring [23,27]. Therefore, context awareness, which refers to the capability of an application or a service being aware of its physical environment or situation (i.e., context) and responding proactively and intelligently based on such awareness [1,15,19], has been identified as one of the key challenges and most important trends in computing today and holds the potential to make our daily lives more productive, convenient, and enjoyable.

Nowadays, Web services have become a major technology to implement loosely coupled business processes and perform application integration [24,36]. Through the use of context, a new generation of smart Web services is currently emerging as an important technology for building innovative context-aware applications. We call such category of Web services as context-aware Web services (CASs). CASs are emerging as an important technology to underpin the development of new applications (user centric, highly personalized) on the future ubiquitous Web. A CAS is a service that uses context information to provide relevant information and/or services to users [6,9,19,31]. A CAS can present relevant information or can be executed or adapted automatically, based on available context information.

Although the combination of context awareness and Web services sounds appealing, injecting context into services raises a number of significant challenges, which have not been widely recognized or addressed by the services community [30,31,36]. One reason for this difficulty is that current Web services standards, such as the Web Services Description Language (WSDL), Web Application Description Language (WADL), and the Simple Object Access Protocol (SOAP), are not sufficient for describing and handling context information. CAS developers must implement everything related to context management, including collection, dissemination, and usage of context information, in an ad hoc manner. Another reason is that, CASs are frequently required to be dynamically adaptive in order to cope with constant changes, which means a service being able to change its behavior at runtime in accordance with the contexts. Unfortunately, service-oriented systems built with WS-BPEL (Web Services Business Process Execution Language) are still too rigid. The third reason is, to the best of our knowledge, there is a lack of generic approaches for formalizing the development of CASs. As a consequence, developing and maintaining CASs is a very cumbersome, error-prone, and time consuming activity, especially when these CASs are complex.

In this paper, we will first give an overview of the ContextServ project, which provides a comprehensive platform that supports the full lifecycle of CASs development, including a visual ContextUML editor, a ContextUML to WS-BPEL translator, and a WS-BPEL deployer (see Fig. 1). Another feature of ContextServ is that it supports dynamic adaptation of WS-BPEL based context-aware composite services by weaving context-aware rules into the process. ContextServ exploits a model-driven approach that offers significant design flexibility

by separating the context modeling and context awareness from service components, which eases both development and maintenance of CASs. It also supplies
a set of automated tools for generating and deploying executable implementations of CASs. We will then review the relevant literature and highlight several
future research opportunities for CAS research and development.

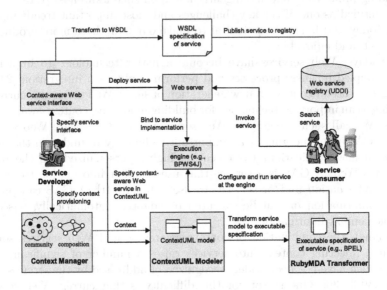

Fig. 1. Architecture of the ContextServ platform

2   The ContextServ Project

ContextServ adopts model-driven development (MDD). The basic idea of MDD
is that by adopting a high-level of abstraction, software systems can be specified in platform independent models (PIMs), which are then semi-automatically
transformed into platform specific models (PSMs) of target executable platforms using some transformation tools. The same PIM can be transformed into
different executable platforms (i.e., multiple PSMs), thus considerably simplifying software development. This section will briefly introduce the ContextUML
language, the RubyMDA transformer, and the adaptive CAS process.

2.1   The ContextUML Language

ContextServ relies on ContextUML [28], a UML-based modeling language that
provides high-level, visual constructs for specifying context-aware Web services.
As shown in Fig. 2, ContextUML metamodel consists of three main parts: the
context modeling metamodel, the *context-awareness modeling metamodel*, and

the *service modeling metamodel*. We will focus on introducing the first two parts since the service modeling metamodel (the left part of Fig. 2) follows the standard service definitions.

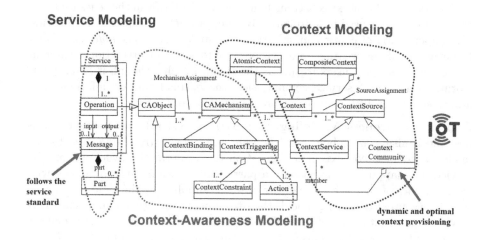

Fig. 2. The ContextUML metamodel in ContextServ

Context Modeling. In ContextUML, a context is further distinguished into two categories that are formalized by *AtomicContext* and *CompositeContext*. Atomic contexts are low-level contexts that do not rely on other contexts and can be provided directly by context sources. In contrast, composite contexts are high-level contexts that may not have direct counterparts on the context provision. A composite context aggregates multiple contexts, either atomic or composite. The concept of composite context can be used to provide a rich modeling vocabulary. ContextUML abstracts two categories of context sources, formalized by the context source subtypes *ContextService* and *ContextServiceCommunity*. A context service is provided by an autonomous organization (i.e., context provider), collecting, refining, and disseminating context information.

To solve the challenges of heterogeneous and dynamic context information, we abstract the concept of context service community, which enables the dynamic provisioning of optimal contexts. A context service community aggregates multiple context services, offering with a unified interface. It is intended as a means to support the dynamic retrieval of context information. A community describes the capabilities of a desired service (e.g., providing user's location) without referring to any actual context service (e.g., WhereAmI service). When the operation of a community is invoked, the community is responsible for selecting the most appropriate context service that will provide the requested context information. Context services can join and leave communities at any time. By abstracting context service community as one of the context sources, we can enable the dynamic context provisioning. In other words, CAS designers do not have to specify which context services are needed for context information retrieval at the design stage. The decision of which specific context service should be selected for the provisioning of a context is postponed until the invocation of CASs.

The quality of context is extremely important for CASs in the sense that context information is used to automatically adapt services or content they provide. The imperfection of context information may make CASs *misguide* their users. For example, if the weather information is outdated, our attractions searching service might suggest users to surf at the Bondi Beach although it is rainy and stormy. Via context service communities, the optimal context information is always selected, which in turn, ensures the quality of CASs.

Context Awareness Modeling. ContextUML abstracts two context awareness mechanisms, namely *context binding* and *context triggering*. The former models automatic contextual configuration (e.g., automatic invocation of Web services by mapping a context onto a particular service input parameter), with the semantics of that the value of the object is supplied by the value of the context. The context triggering models the situation of contextual adaptation where services can be automatically executed or modified based on context information. A context triggering mechanism contains two parts: a set of *context constraints* and a set of *actions*, with the semantics of that the actions must be executed if and only if all the context constraints are evaluated to true.

Context awareness mechanisms are assigned to context-aware objects, modelled as *CAObject*, by the relation *MechanismAssignment*, indicating which objects have what kinds of context awareness mechanisms. CAObject is a base class of all model elements in ContextUML that represent context-aware objects. There are four subtypes of CAObject: *Service, Operation, Message*, and *Part*. It should be noted that the four primitives are directly adopted from WSDL, which enables designers to build CASs on top of the previous implementation of Web services.

2.2   ContextUML Modeler and RubyMDA Transformer

In the ContextServ platform, the ContextUML modeler provides a visual interface for defining context-aware Web services using ContextUML [29]. In particular, we extend ArgoUML[1], an existing UML editing tool, by developing a new diagram type, ContextUML diagram, which implements all the abstract syntax of the ContextUML language.

Services represented in ContextUML diagrams are exported as XMI files for subsequent processing by the RubyMDA transformer, which is responsible for transforming ContextUML diagrams into executable Web services, using Ruby-Gems[2]. The ContextServ platform currently supports WS-BPEL, a de facto standard for specifying executable processes. Once the BPEL specification is

---

[1] http://argouml.tigris.org.
[2] https://rubygems.org/.

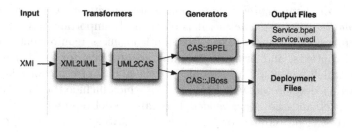

Fig. 3. RubyMDA data flow

generated, the model transformer deploys the BPEL process to an application server and exposes it as a Web service. In the implementation, JBoss Application Server is used since it is open source and includes a BPEL execution engine jBPM-BPEL. RubyMDA is developed based on the model transformation rules. The model transformation rules are mappings from ContextUML stereotypes to BPEL elements.

Figure 3 shows the data flow of RubyMDA model transformer. RubyMDA takes the XMI document as an input which represents the ContextUML diagram. RubyMDA reads the XMI document and constructs the UML model which is a set of data structure representing the components in UML class diagram. After the UML model is constructed, RubyMDA transforms it into CAS model which is a set of data structure representing the CAS described in ContextUML diagram. Finally, RubyMDA generates a BPEL process and WSDL document for a CAS. Moreover, it generates a set of deployment files needed to deploy CAS to a server.

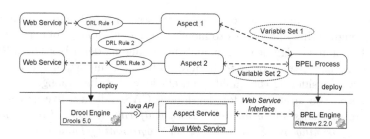

Fig. 4. An anatomy of the adaptive runtime environment

2.3   Adaptive CAS Processes

As stated by Papazoglou in [24], "*services and processes should equip themselves with adaptive service capabilities so that they can continually morph themselves to respond to environmental demands and changes without compromising operational and financial efficiencies*". It is particularly important to CASs to cope with the functional changes raised from both business requirements and environmental contexts, and bringing dynamic adaptability (or agility) to service processes, which means a CAS should have the ability of behavior adaptation.

We further develop MoDAR PIMs [34,35] which include the *base model*, the *variable model*, and the *weave model*. The base model represents the relatively stable processing procedures, or *flow* logic, of a CAS system; while the variable model represents the more volatile *decision* aspect of the business requirements. To make the base model and the variable model semantically inter-operable, we use a minimum set of ontology concepts as the basic elements in defining activity parameters in processes and also in defining rule entities. We also adopt an aspect-oriented approach to integrate the base model and the variable model using a *weave model*. This approach ensures the modularity of the base model and the variable model so that they can evolve independently.

The variable model is automatically transformed into Drools rules, and the weave model is automatically transformed into an abstract BPEL process, where at every *join point*, the invocation to a rule aspect is translated to a special Web service invocation. After the designer manually associates concrete Web services with abstract services in the process to implement their functionalities, the process is automatically transformed into an executable BPEL process. As shown in Fig. 4, the BPEL process and the Drools rules are deployed to their corresponding engines. Dynamic adaptability is achieved in a way that we can freely add/remove/replace business rules defined in the modeling phase and then transform and redeploy them without terminating the execution of the process.

3   Literature Discussions

With the maturing and wide-adopting of Web service technology, research on providing engineering approaches to facilitate the development of context-aware services has gained significant momentum. Using model-driven paradigm to develop CAS has been proven to be a valuable and important strand in this research area considering the quality and efficiency it brings along.

In general, the approaches for developing CASs fall into five categories: i) *Middleware solutions and dedicated service platforms*, ii) *Use of ontologies*, iii) *Rule-based reasoning*, iv) *Source code level programming/Language extensions*, and v) *Message interception* [21]. Each kind of approach has its own pros and cons. For example, the source code level approach can give more freedom to developers to do all kinds of context-aware adaptation, but it does not separate apart the concerns on context-awareness and suffers from a significant maintenance cost. As for the model-driven approach, apart from its advantages, it requires to keep the consistency between high level models and low level executable code at all times, which brings extra complexity.

In this section, we overview the representative research efforts in the literature on model-driven development of context-aware services. Table 1 gives a

Table 1. Summary and comparison of model-driven approaches for context-aware application development

		Ayed 2008	Sindico-Grassi 2009	Prezerakos 2007	Kapitsaki 2009	Hoyos 2013, 2016	Boudaa 2017	ContextServ 2009, 2015
Context modeling	Modeling language (based-Model)	UML	UML (CAMEL)	UML (Contex-tUML*)	UML (Contex-tUML*)	DSL (MLCon-text)	Ontology& UML	UML (Con-textUML)
	Atomic context	+	+	+	+	+	+	+
	Composite context	–	+	+	+	+	+	+
	Context quality	+	–	–	–	+	–	+
	Context sensing	+	–	–	–	+	+	–
Service modeling		–	–	+	+	–	–	+
Context-awareness modeling	Context binding	+	+	+	+	+	+	+
	Context triggering	+	+	+	+	+	+	+
	Behavior adaptation	+	–	–	–	–	+	+
Decoupling business logic and context logic		+	+	+	+	+	+	+
Adaptation time (design-time/run-time)		Design-time	Design-time run-time	Design-time run-time	Design-time run-time	Design-time	Design-time run-time	Design-time run-time
Implementation platform		Unspecified	AspectJ	SOA	SOA	OCP/ JCAF	SOA (FraSCAti)	SOA (BPEL)
Supporting software tools	Graphical modeling environment	-	+	+	–	+	+	+
	Transformation tool	–	–	+	+	+	+	+

detailed summary of some representative related works and comparison from the perspectives of modeling language, MDD techniques, tools and platform.

In [5], Ayed et al. proposed a UML metamodel that supports context-aware adaptation of service design from structural, architectural and behavioral perspectives. The structural adaptation can extend the service object's structure by adding or deleting its methods and attributes. The architectural adaptation can add and delete service objects of an application according to the context. The behavioral adaptation can adapt the behavior of the service object by extending its UML sequence diagram with optional context related sequences. Furthermore, based on the UML metamodel, Ayed ed al. proposed an MDD approach to model context-aware applications independently from the platform, which includes six phases that approach step by step the mechanisms required to acquire context information and perform adaptations.

In [32], Sindico and Grassi proposed CAMEL (Context Awareness ModEling Language) which considers both model-driven development and aspect-oriented design paradigms so that the design of the application core can be decoupled from the design of the adaptation logic. In particular, CAMEL categorizes context into *state-based* which characterizes the current situation of an entity and *event-based* which represents changes in an entity's state. Accordingly, state constraints, which are defined by logical predicates on the value of the attributes of a state-based context, and event constraints, which are defined as patterns of event [7], are used to specify context-aware adaptation feature of the application.

In [17], Hoyos et al. proposed a textual Domain-Specific Language (DSL), namely MLContext, which is specially tailored for modeling context information. It has been implemented by applying MDD techniques to automatically generate software artifacts from context models. The MLContext abstract syntax has been defined as a metamodel, and model-to-text transformations have been written to generate the desired software artifacts (e.g., OCP middleware and JCAF middleware). The concrete syntax has been defined with the EMFText tool, which generates an editor and model injector. Furthermore, in [18], MLContext is extended for modeling quality of context (QoC) and the models can be mapped to code for two frameworks (COSMOS and SAMURA) supporting QoC.

In [25], Prezerakos et al. addressed the decoupling of core service logic from context-related functionality by adopting a model-driven approach based on a modified version of ContextUML [28]. Core service logic and context handling are treated as separate concerns at the model level as well as in the resulting source code. In the design phase, besides class diagrams, UML activity diagrams are used for modeling the core service logic flow in conjunction with MDE (Model-driven Engineering) transformation techniques and AOP (Aspect Oriented Programming). In the coding phase, AOP encapsulates context-dependent behaviors in discrete AspectJ code modules. Context binding information provided in UML models is used to create pointcuts and related advices, as well as to create the binding between them. In [20], Kapitsaki et al. proposed an architecture for the context adaptation of Web applications consisting of Web services and a model-driven methodology for the development of such context-aware composite applications. In the methodology, the Web application functionality is completely separated from the context adaptation at all development phases (analysis, design and implementation). In the modeling level, composite web applications are modeled in UML and the application design is kept, at a great extent, independent from specific platform implementations and flexible enough to allow the introduction of different code specific mappings. Context adaptation is performed on a service interface level to keep client independent. The modeling exploits a number of pre-defined profiles, whereas the target implementation is based on an architecture that performs context adaptation of web services based on interception of Simple Object Access Protocol (SOAP) messages.

In [12], Boudaa et al. proposed an approach taking advantage of combining MDD and AOP to sustain the development of context-aware service-based applications in mobile and ubiquitous environments. Contexts are modeled with a proposed ontology-based context model which is structured on three sub-ontologies:

generic, domain and application ontologies. A UML-based metamodel, called ContextAspect, is proposed to define and specify where and how the context-aware adaptation takes place. The ContextAspect metamodel is composed of three parts: aspect modeling, context modeling and context-awareness modeling. AOM handles the context-awareness logic in ContextAspect models (as variants) to fill context-aware application elements (as variation points) by using weaving techniques at design and run times. At design-time, the weaving enables to produce a wide range of context-aware application models without designing them from the beginning. The run-time weaving consists of weaving necessary reconfiguration into the running application according to the context change, so accomplishing its dynamic adaptation.

To the perspective of modeling language for context-aware application development, we compare ContextUML with the other metamodels from the issues of context modeling, servcie modeling, and context-awareness modeling. It should be noted that, in [20,25], their models are modified versions of ContextUML, so most of the language capabilities of their models equal to ContextUML's and the comparison with them will not discussed below. As we can see from the table, all languages support the modeling of atomic context. For composite context, although CAMEL claims that atomic contexts can be aggregated but no details were given in the paper. In [12], composite context is inferred from low-level contexts using Semantic Web Rule Language (SWRL), and in MLContext, simple references are used to link composite context with their atomic contexts. ContextUML gives a complete approach to composing a composite context from atomic contexts in statechart which is a widely used formalism integrated into UML. ContextUML supports context quality modeling and use context service community to support QoC-based context selection. Although Ayed UML is able to specify the quality attributes of a context, no runtime support was reported in the paper. In [18], MLContext was extended for modeling QoC. However, it does not support QoC-based context selection.

As to service modeling, only ContextUML directly supports the structure of Web services, which is of enormous importance to the development of context-aware Web services. The other languages just use plain UML classes to represent Web services or even without support of Web services.

For context-awareness modeling, all the languages except MLContext support the main features including context binding and context triggering. However, only ContextUML, Ayed UML and ContextAspect model support behavior adaptation, which means a service or process has the ability to change its behavior at runtime in accordance with the changes in the requirements and/or the external environment(contexts). Ayed UML only supports to define behavior adaptation in design-time, and no run-time support is reported in the paper. Both of ContextServ and ContextAspect model support behavior adaptation in design-time and run-time. The mechanism of behavior adaptation in ContextAspect model enables to change alternatively the application behavior by selecting one among several behaviours in accordance with current contextual situation.

Because dynamic adaptation is closely related to the targeting system, we also listed the supported targeting implementation platform of each approach. Different implementation languages or underlying frameworks/platforms and middleware are adopted in each approach. ContextServ and approaches presented in [12,20,25] support the SOA paradigm. After modeling adaptation in ContextUML, it can be transformed and the behavior adaptation will be reflected in standard BPEL that has become a de facto industry standard (widely adopted by major IT service providers including IBM, Oracle, and SAP) to create composite service processes and applications. [12] uses FraSCAti platform as the target platform which supports Service Component Architecture (SCA). Models of MLContext can be transformed to specific context middleware (e.g., OCP and JCAF). CAMEL is still an ongoing work, so only examples on how to transform to ContextJ [16] were described in the paper. As to Ayed UML, no targeting systems are reported in the paper.

For supporting software tools, ContextUML has a comprehensive graphical modeling environment developed on top of ArgoUML and also a full-fledged automatic transformation tool for generating deployable BPEL code. All of CAMEL, MLContext and language in [12] have a graphical modeling environment based on Eclipse EMF[3], but no fully workable transformation tools are reported.

4   Open Research Issues

Although context-aware services have been an active research topic for more than a decade, existing research efforts generally focus more on addressing some specific aspects and lack of a holistic view on the problem [13,24,31]. Moreover, the rapid rise and adoption of new computing paradigms such as the Internet of Things (IoT), Edge Computing also present compounded challenges in CAS development. In this section, we identify several important directions for future research in this area.

Contextual Data Management. Contextual information is a critical integral component of CASs. There is an urgent need for a holistic approach on the life cycle of contextual data management, from data acquisition, contextual data modeling, reasoning, and transformation, to dissemination. IoT is increasingly becoming an important source for rich and real-time contextual information for CASs. However, the diverse, heterogenous, large scale, and unreliable IoT sensors present significant challenges [26,27]. This calls for more research on solutions that can effectively aggregate and distill heterogeneous and large IoT data to obtain contextual data of appropriate quality. Future IoT is expected to be 50 to 100 times bigger than the current Internet. This poses a new set of challenges to discover the right IoT devices at the right time and right place for a particular contextual information offering [4,33]. One technical direction

---

[3] http://www.eclipse.org/modeling/emf/.

towards IoT discovery is to exploit the textual descriptions associated with IoT devices and perform the *natural order ranking* of IoT contents.

Context-Aware Requirements Engineering. ContextUML and the ContextServ platform comprise the design and implementation phases of a software development process. One of the important open research issues remains: How can we inject context-awareness into the initial requirements engineering phase? One line of research on this issue is initiated by Ali et al. [2] where the authors propose a contextual goal modelling framework to derive goal model variants that meet the goals in a given context. Later on, in [3], the framework integrates the detection of both the context specification inconsistencies and goal conflicts resulting from variabilities. Recently, based on the above work, Botangen et al. [11] propose an approach for context-based requirements variability analysis in the goal-oriented requirements modelling where contextual goals and contextual preferences can be defined to specify the relationships of contexts with requirements and preferences. Future research questions include how to optimize the automated conflict detection algorithm and how to deal with evolving contextualization derived from the ever-changing nature of requirements.

Context-Aware Services Recommendation. In the era of information explosion, the number of Web services also increases rapidly, which brings new challenges for users to choose the right Web services among tens of thousands candidates. The research field of context-aware service recommendation aims to recommend services to users based on their contextual information. In [37], a time-aware service recommendation approach that integrates temporal information with content similarity is proposed. In [14], a two-level topic model that combines service content and service social network information is proposed for Web API recommendation. Recently, Botangen et al. [10] propose a geographic-aware collaborative filtering approach for Web services recommendation. Open research questions include how to exploit the recently flourishing deep learning methods in context-aware service recommendation, and how to design a generic ensemble architecture to facilitate the integration of different types of contextual information.

Security and Privacy on Context-Aware Services. Security and privacy are the serious challenges for CASs, which need to be addressed for users to fully embrace the services. Contextual information often is related to sensitive personal data such as activities, transactions, and whereabouts. With embedding sensing being more and more prevalent on personal devices, personal sensing can be used to detect users' physical activities and bring privacy concerns. Building a trusted ecosystem among context-aware services requires appropriate measures on security and privacy between CASs, IoT devices that provide contextual information, and their interactions with service users [8]. Unfortunately, security and privacy are still not adequately addressed by the majority of existing approaches. The Blockchain technology has the potential to address these issues but need to consider several challenges such as resource limitation and low transmission rates of IoT devices. We believe that intensive research and development are needed in order to realize secure and trustworthy context-aware services.

Context-Aware Services in Mobile Edge Computing. With the proliferation of IoT and mobile devices, more and more services are moving towards the network edge, which minimizes the need on data transfers and reduces the latency. Mobile edge computing (MEC) has emerged as a key technology to assist wireless networks with cloud computing like capabilities, offering low-latency and mobility support services directly from the network edge. However, the dynamic and complex environment of MEC makes context-aware and adaptive predicting QoS of services a challenging task. In a recent work by Liu et al. [22], two context-aware QoS prediction schemes are proposed by considering user-related and service-related contextual information and MEC service scheduling scenarios. More research efforts are needed in this important direction.

5   Conclusions

Over the recent years, context-aware services (CASs) are emerging as an important technology for building innovative smart applications. Unfortunately, despite of active research and development, CASs are still difficult to build, due to lack of context provisioning management approach and lack of generic approach for formalizing the development process. In this paper, we have introduced the ContextServ project that focuses on developing a platform for model-driven development of CASs. We also review some representative research efforts on CASs in the literature and identify several open research issues that we wish to stimulate further research in this important area.

Acknowledgments. The ContextServ project has been partially supported by an Australian Research Council (ARC) Discovery Project grant DP0878367. Quan Z. Sheng's research has been also partially supported by an ARC Future Fellowship FT140101247.

References

1. Abowd, G.D., et al.: Context-aware computing. IEEE Pervasive Comput. **1**(3), 22–23 (2002)
2. Ali, R., Dalpiaz, F., Giorgini, P.: A goal-based framework for contextual requirements modeling and analysis. Requirements Eng. **15**(4), 439–458 (2010)
3. Ali, R., Dalpiaz, F., Giorgini, P.: Reasoning with contextual requirements: detecting inconsistency and conflicts. Inf. Softw. Technol. **55**(1), 35–57 (2013)
4. Aljubairy, A., Zhang, W.E., Sheng, Q.Z., Alhazmi, A.: SIoTPredict: a framework for predicting relationships in the social Internet of Things. In: Dustdar, S., Yu, E., Salinesi, C., Rieu, D., Pant, V. (eds.) CAiSE 2020. LNCS, vol. 12127, pp. 101–116. Springer, Cham (2020). https://doi.org/10.1007/978-3-030-49435-3_7
5. Ayed, D., Taconet, C., Bernard, G., Berbers, Y.: CADeComp: Context-aware deployment of component-based applications. J. Netw. Comput. Appl. **31**(3), 224–257 (2008)

6. Badidi, E., Atif, Y., Sheng, Q.Z., Maheswaran, M.: On personalized cloud service provisioning for mobile users using adaptive and context-aware service composition. Computing **101**(4), 291–318 (2019)

7. Benatallah, B., Dumas, M., Fauvet, M.C., Rabhi, F.A., Sheng, Q.Z.: Overview of some patterns for architecting and managing composite web services. ACM SIGecom Exchanges **3**(3), 9–16 (2002)

8. Bertino, E., Choo, K.R., Georgakopoulos, D., Nepal, S.: Internet of Things (IoT): smart and secure service delivery. ACM Trans. Internet Technol. **16**(4), 22:1–22:7 (2016)

9. Botangen, K.A., Yu, J., Han, Y., Sheng, Q.Z., Han, J.: Quantifying the adaptability of workflow-based service compositions. Future Gener. Comput. Syst. **102**, 95–111 (2020)

10. Botangen, K.A., Yu, J., Sheng, Q.Z., Han, Y., Yongchareon, S.: Geographic-aware collaborative filtering for web service recommendation. Expert Syst. Appl. **151**, 113347 (2020)

11. Botangen, K.A., Yu, J., Yeap, W.K., Sheng, Q.Z.: Integrating context to preferences and goals for goal-oriented adaptability of software systems. Comput. J. (2020)

12. Boudaa, B., Hammoudi, S., Mebarki, L.A., Bouguessa, A., Chikh, M.A.: An aspect-oriented model-driven approach for building adaptable context-aware service-based applications. Sci. Comput. Program. **136**, 17–42 (2017)

13. Bouguettaya, A., et al.: A service computing manifesto: the Next 10 years. Commun. ACM **60**(4), 64–72 (2017)

14. Cao, B., Liu, X., Rahman, M.M., Li, B., Liu, J., Tang, M.: Integrated content and network-based service clustering and web APIs recommendation for mashup development. IEEE Trans. Serv. Comput. **13**(1), 99–113 (2017)

15. Dey, A.K., Mankoff, J.: Designing mediation for context-aware applications. ACM Trans. Comput. Hum. Interact. **12**(1), 53–80 (2005)

16. Hirschfeld, R., Costanza, P., Nierstasz, O.: Context-oriented programming. J. Object Technol. **7**(3), 125–151 (2008)

17. Hoyos, J.R., García-Molina, J., Botía, J.A.: A domain-specific language for context modeling in context-aware systems. J. Syst. Softw. **86**(11), 2890–2905 (2013)

18. Hoyos, J.R., García-Molina, J., Botía, J.A., Preuveneers, D.: A model-driven approach for quality of context in pervasive systems. Comput. Electr. Eng. **55**, 39–58 (2016)

19. Julien, C., Roman, G.C.: EgoSpaces: facilitating rapid development of context-aware mobile applications. IEEE Trans. Softw. Eng. **32**(5), 281–298 (2006)

20. Kapitsaki, G.M., Kateros, D.A., Prezerakos, G.N., Venieris, I.S.: Model-driven development of composite context-aware web applications. Inf. Softw. Technol. **51**(8), 1244–1260 (2009)

21. Kapitsaki, G., et al.: Context-aware service engineering: a survey. J. Syst. Softw. **82**(8), 1285–1297 (2009)

22. Liu, Z., Sheng, Q.Z., Xu, X., Chu, D., Zhang, W.E.: Context-aware and adaptive QoS prediction for mobile edge computing services. IEEE Trans. Serv. Comput. 1–1 (2019)

23. Mo, J.P.T., Sheng, Q.Z., Li, X., Zeadally, S.: RFID infrastructure design: a case study of two Australian RFID projects. IEEE Internet Comput. **13**(1), 14–21 (2009)

24. Papazoglou, M.P., Traverso, P., Dustdar, S., Leymann, F.: Service-oriented computing: state of the art and research challenges. Computer **40**(11), 38–45 (2007)

25. Prezerakos, G.N., Tselikas, N., Cortese, G.: Model-driven composition of context-aware web services using ContextUML and aspects. In: Proceeding of the 5th International Conference on Web Services (ICWS 2007), pp. 320–329 (2007)
26. Qin, Y., Sheng, Q.Z., Falkner, N.J.G., Dustdar, S., Wang, H., Vasilakos, A.V.: When things matter: a survey on data-centric Internet of Things. J. Netw. Comput. Appl. **64**, 137–153 (2016)
27. Sheng, M., Qin, Y., Yao, L., Benatallah, B. (eds.): Managing the Web of Things: Linking the Real World to the Web. Morgan Kaufmann, United States (2017)
28. Sheng, Q.Z., Benatallah, B.: ContextUML: a UML-based modeling language for model-driven context-aware web service development. In: Proceeding of the 4th International Conference on Mobile Business (ICMB 2005), Sydney, Australia, pp. 206–212 (2005)
29. Sheng, Q.Z., Pohlenz, S., Yu, J., Wong, H.S., Ngu, A.H., Maamar, Z.: ContextServ: a platform for rapid and flexible development of context-aware web services. In: Proceeding of the 31st International Conference on Software Engineering (ICSE 2009), Vancouver, Canada, pp. 619–622 (2009)
30. Sheng, Q.Z., Qiao, X., Vasilakos, A.V., Szabo, C., Bourne, S., Xu, X.: Web services composition: a decade's overview. Inf. Sci. **280**, 218–238 (2014)
31. Sheng, Q.Z., Yu, J., Dustdar, S. (eds.): Enabling Context-Aware Web Services: Methods, Architectures, and Technologies. CRC Press, United States (2010)
32. Sindico, A., Grassi, V.: Model driven development of context aware software systems. In: International Workshop on Context-Oriented Programming (COP 2009), New York, pp. 7:1–7:5 (2009)
33. Tran, N.K., Sheng, Q.Z., Babar, M.A., Yao, L.: Searching the web of things: state of the art, challenges, and solutions. ACM Comput. Surv. **50**(4), 55:1–55:34 (2017)
34. Yu, J., Han, J., Sheng, Q.Z., Gunarso, S.O.: PerCAS: an approach to enabling dynamic and personalized adaptation for context-aware services. In: Liu, C., Ludwig, H., Toumani, F., Yu, Q. (eds.) ICSOC 2012. LNCS, vol. 7636, pp. 173–190. Springer, Heidelberg (2012). https://doi.org/10.1007/978-3-642-34321-6_12
35. Yu, J., Sheng, Q.Z., Swee, J.K., Han, J., Liu, C., Noor, T.H.: Model-driven development of adaptive web service processes with aspects and rules. J. Comput. Syst. Sci. **81**(3), 533–552 (2015)
36. Yu, Q., Liu, X., Bouguettaya, A., Medjahed, B.: Deploying and managing web services: issues, solutions, and directions. VLDB J. **17**(3), 537–572 (2008)
37. Zhong, Y., Fan, Y., Huang, K., Tan, W., Zhang, J.: Time-aware service recommendation for mashup creation in an evolving service ecosystem. In: 2014 IEEE International Conference on Web Services, pp. 25–32. IEEE (2014)

IT Service Engineering: A New Kind of IT Professional

Esperanza Marcos, Valeria De Castro, and Juan M. Vara[⊠]

Universidad Rey Juan Carlos, 28933 Móstoles (MADRID), Spain
{esperanza.marcos,valeria.decastro,juanmanuel.vara}@urjc.es
http://www.kybele.es

Abstract. In the service world in which we live, businesses and organizations are currently moving away from the traditional product-based business model toward the provision of services. The IT sector is by no means indifferent to this tendency and has for some time been providing services rather than software and/or hardware products. In this context, there is a need to improve the quality and productivity of service organizations through the creation of knowledge related to the concept of service ant the specific training of professionals for this sector. This chapter provides an analysis of the knowledge and skills that an IT Engineer should acquire to adapt to the world of services and presents an answer to these needs.

Keywords: Service science · Service engineering · Higher-education

1 Introduction

If you were to be asked what you have done today before you arrived at work, your reply would probably be something like:

> "I got up I switched on the light, I went to the gym, and after doing sport I had a shower; then I caught the bus and before I got to the office I had a coffee while I read the news on my tablet and answered a few WhatsApp and emails on my mobile phone."

In summary, you have been a service consumer from the beginning of the morning: energy services, leisure services, transport services, IT services, etc., and you will probably continue to be so throughout the day.

Services have invaded our lives and have become the engine of the economy in developed countries and in the sector that generates the greatest employment rate, even in developing countries such as China or India, which are being also the protagonists of an important growth in the tertiary sector [1]. By Service sector we are referring not only to low added-value services that generate relatively little in the way of productivity, but to all services, and particularly those with high added-value that require highly qualified professional: health services, IT services, legal services, etc.

© Springer Nature Switzerland AG 2021
M. Aiello et al. (Eds.): Papazoglou Festschrift, LNCS 12521, pp. 153–164, 2021.
https://doi.org/10.1007/978-3-030-73203-5_12

Traditional industry has also been providing services for some time (i.e., the level to which leasing has been adopted by the car industry). This is known as *servitization* and refers to the process used by organizations to provide services rather than products, or as a complements to them and which obviously includes a change in their business model [2].

These services will be the motor powering the economy in coming decades and the current **information society** will become a **service society**. In this context, the key will be how we use all the information that we are capable of producing to provide the most frequently demanded and highly valued services by the population.

The IT industry must adapt to this economic and social reality in which information technologies play a duel role: supporting the services provided by different sectors (health, tourism, apps, etc.), and producing all the types of services offered by the IT sector (training, consulting, outsourcing, etc.).

This chapter analyzes this need and presents our proposal to deal with it, that takes the shape of a revolutionary degree program. The program is a personal and professional project which Prof. Papazogolou helped to born and raise. We are happy to contribute to this well-deserved tribute to Mike's outstanding career by sharing our project with the community.

2 IT Service Industry

As previously stated, the IT industry has been providing services for some time, either by substituting its provision of products or adding value to their offer of basic products. Here, we are obviously not referring to services-oriented computing [3], but rather to services from the consumer point of view:

- On the one hand, technology evolves very quickly and IT business customers demand the possibility of being able to take advantage of these advances in order to respond to the needs of the changing market. Rather than the traditional acquisition of closed software solutions that currently become obsolete in a short amount of time, the customer therefore opts to contract reconfigurable **software services** that facilitate adaptation to constant changes in the market [4].
- In this respect, the rest of the IT sector is also changing its business model to be able to additionally provide **another type of IT-related services**: services for the citizen in general (Smart Cities, Smart Planet, etc.) [5], and other such as outsourcing, consulting, training, hosting, etc.
- On the other hand, the fall in the price of technology, which has favored the information society to such a great extent and has permitted universal access to it, has led to the emergence of numerous businesses whose business model is based on the provision of **technology-based services**. The majority of these businesses do not even have products to provide, but rather provide access to them, as is the case of Uber or Airbnb [6].

– Finally, we should not forget **traditional IT services**, which are provided by computing and data centers in order to support business and organizational information systems, such as those provided by the IT departments of universities, banks, hospitals, etc. [7].

The challenge for the IT industry in forthcoming decades will therefore be to increase its competitiveness as regards the innovation, design, construction, provision, maintenance, etc., of not only products, as has occurred to date, but rather of services. And the most immediate questions are: How should this change take place? Who should lead it? Do software engineers have the capacity to successfully confront this challenge? Is the education currently provided on Computer and Software Engineering degrees sufficient to train professionals in order to tackle this?

2.1 Service Engineering

Conscious of the importance of services in the global economy, and in the IT sector in particular, IBM launched a new discipline denominated as Service Science Management and Engineering (SSME) [8], an initiative to which many other organizations and business from different spheres have already joined through international organizations and institutes such as the ISSIP[1], the ERISS[2] or the SSRI[3].

SSME or in short, Service Science, is thus emerging as a distinctive field. It was conceived as an interdisciplinary science that emerged from the convergence of, principally, three others: Business and Process, Engineering and Technology and People and Culture. Its object of study is the service, regardless of the sector and whether or not it is supported by technology. Its mission is to discover the underlying logic of complex service systems and to establish a common language and shared frameworks for service innovation.

Holistic Perspective. Various components should be taken into consideration during the construction of a service. Let us, for example, consider a service such as Amazon's book sales. There is, of course, an important *innovative* component when this service is provided the first time; there is obviously a *technological* component that allows the service to be made available to consumers via the Internet; there is also an important *business* and company component to ensure that the service will be profitable; and it is not possible to avoid the perspective related to the concrete *domain* of the service in question (in this case, the book selling); and others, such as aspects of storage and distribution, psychological and sociological aspects that make it possible to identify when a service will be well received by the user and when it will have a social impact, etc.

---

[1] www.issip.org.

[2] https://www.tilburguniversity.edu/research/institutes-and-research-groups/eriss.

[3] www.thesrii.org.

We all know other examples of organizations that provide the same service but have not had the same impact. For example, Google soon became the most frequently used search engine and surpassed others that preceded it, fundamentally because its algorithm provided more relevant results. WhatsApp, meanwhile, became established over other solutions precisely because it was the first App to have these characteristics. Innovation, related to People and Culture dimension, was thus the key to WhatsApp becoming established. Aspects related to the Engineering and Technology dimension was the key to Google success. These examples also serve to provide evidence of the fact that if we tackle the construction of a service from only one of these perspectives, we lose the complete view, and more definitively, we lose the view of the service which is in fact central to the business. A similar mistake would be made if we attempted to tackle the construction of a software product by considering only the data or the interface perspective [9].

Let us similarly suppose that we are admitted into hospital because one of our legs hurts, we have a rash and a rapid heartbeat. Once in hospital, we are visited by an orthopedic surgeon for our leg, a dermatologist for who is only interested in our skin and a cardiologist who takes a look at our heart, and each of them provides us with an independent diagnosis of our illness. It may be that an illness with these three symptoms goes unnoticed. It is therefore necessary for us to see an internist who has an integral view of the person and who can make a diagnosis based on a complete view of him/her. The intention of Service Science is to similarly tackle the problem of services from an integral and holistic perspective.

A New Profile. Software Engineering and Computer Science are the engineering and science that have supported the IT industry as we know it today. The IT Service Industry, which will in our opinion become the IT industry of forthcoming decades, is based on a radically different concept to that of Computer Science and Software Engineering: the concept of service. Regardless of whether it is a technology-based service or an IT service, the key is now the service itself and not the software and/or IT infrastructure that allows the service to be provided. If this new industry is to become competitive then it must be sustained by different principles to those of the traditional IT Industry. It is in this context that Service Science Management and Engineering takes on a fundamental role. We need **Science** to create knowledge related to services; we need specific **Management** processes to guide the way in which service-provider organizations act, since they are generally governed by processes that have been directly imported from traditional industry; and we need **Engineering** in order to conceive, design and construct quality services, applying the knowledge provided by Science in order to create value and management processes with which to operate them once built.

Professionals with a **specific service profile** are therefore required to cover these three areas: Service Scientists, Service Managers and Service Engineers.

Of course, in the IT industry of forthcoming years it will continue to be necessary to build and maintain information systems and conventional applications. We have a consolidated industry that provides us with tools, languages and techniques for this purpose, and we also have perfectly qualified professionals. Nevertheless, as the IT industry is evolving toward a business model based on the provision of services, a new type of professional is required, different than the traditional Software Engineer; from here on s/he will be referred to as an IT Service Engineer.

3   IT Service Engineer: A T-Shaped IT Professional

But, what is a service professional? If we return to the example of Amazon, the service engineer is the person in charge of giving form to the idea of selling books via the Internet. S/he has to have an overall view of the service (the technical aspect, the business aspect, marketing, social impact, etc.) and must seek support from experts in different areas with whom it is necessary to communicate in the same language in order to integrate their work into a single product that is provided in the form of a service. It is, in summary, a person with transversal knowledge and skills like communication, management, leadership, etc.

In order to satisfy these needs, SSME defends the concept of the new professional for the service sector, who must have three types of skills and knowledge:

- **Business**: they must know the target domain of the service (e.g. health, education IT, etc.).
- **Technical**: people who are capable of managing projects, critical thought, systems thinking, can use several languages, among others.
- **Personal**: people with the capacity to work in a team, with communication and negotiation skills, who are capable of leadership, flexibility and adaptation to change, empathy, etc. This block also includes the capacity to understand and adapt to different cultures and religions, which has been determinant in a globalized world.

3.1   Systems Thinking

With regard to professional skills, we wish to stress one that is particularly important for professionals in this sector, which is integrative or *systems thinking* as opposed to traditional thought. A service organization is a system whose parts (financial management, knowledge management, marketing sales, business management etc.) are inter-related with the environment (suppliers' capital, suppliers' technology, change in customer preferences, governmental regulations, global competitors, etc.). A service in itself is similarly a system and, as in the case of all systems, it is important for service professionals to be able to see the wood beyond the trees of which it is composed. Systems thinking is therefore key since it includes a series of cognitive characteristics such as comprehension of the complete system and its environment, the recognition of interconnections among its components and the synergies of the system, etc.

Although systemic vision has always been present in the construction of software systems [10], it is not habitual in many other spheres. In fact, one habitual practice during software development is the decomposition of the problem into sub-problems which are then tackled individually. This is the classical 'divide and you shall defeat' technique. However, a service is a system and one of its parts cannot therefore be viewed in isolation. We might perhaps kill a patient by treating his leg with a medication that affects his heart. In order to avoid this, systems thinking tackles the problem as a whole, examining how the parts fit together and how decisions related to one part affect the others. It is therefore important to promote systems thinking in future service professionals.

3.2   Personal Skills

The aforementioned personal skills that are already considered to be important for any type of professional, are key in the context of services. This is owing to the fact that a service organization is characterized by the *Service Dominant View*, which can be defined as the relationship that the organization establishes and maintains with its customers, acting as co-producers of value [11].

If we consider the education service, what factors make that a class have more or less value? Logically, they are the teacher's training, his/her communication skills and other characteristics of the professional who provides the service. It will also depend on environmental factors, such as the temperature in the classroom, the audio-visual media, etc. But there is also a key factor, which is the receptiveness of the attendants. The class will have more or less value depending on the number of pupils, on their capacity to pay attention, their pro-activity as regards intervening and asking questions, etc. This example could be applied to the provision of any other service. The value of a consulting service depends on the provider (consultant) and consumer (customer) of the service. In the context of software, the possibility of interaction with the consumer of the service in order to adapt it to his/her needs is particularly relevant. In fact, this is one of the reasons why traditional IT companies have adopted service-based business models, in which it is easier to respond to changes in the customer's needs than in the classical turnkey projects.

Service quality is therefore determined by the customer's perception of it [12]. While in traditional industry there are measurable attributes that permit us to objectively determine a product's quality before it is put on sale (for example, a car), a service has better quality when the customer perceives this to be so. In the context of IT the quality of a software product has traditionally been measured on the basis of metrics that are more or less accepted by the community [13]. However, these metrics are not directly applicable to services, signifying that new tools such as SLAs or new IT service management reference frameworks such as ITIL or ISO 2000 have emerged [14].

We can conclude that in a service organization, the **relationship with the customer** is vital. Close long-lasting relationships will be the key to be different from the competition. This will also make it possible to adapt the service to the customer's needs, which is also a determining factor in a service company's success. This is obviously the same despite the sector toward which the service is oriented is and therefore applies also for the IT sector. Personal and emotional skills are therefore fundamental in a service professional, not only as regards work teams, as in any other professional sphere, but also because of the importance of the relationship with the customer.

3.3   T-Shaped Profile

Bearing these characteristics in mind, in SSME a service professional is defined as a *T-shaped professional* [15]. The vertical part of the T refers to the in-depth knowledge that the professional should have as regards at least one discipline and at least one sector, while the horizontal part represents the professional and personal skills that are transversal to any area or sector, among which is the capacity to communicate with other professional profiles.

To continue with the example of Amazon, the Service Engineer must be capable of communicating with the Software Engineer, the book suppliers, the storage and distribution personnel, the marketing department, etc. In other words, s/he must be able to coordinate a multidisciplinary team and have a global business perspective, such that, as stated previously, s/he must have leadership and communication skills, etc.

It is in some respects true that this type of professional already exists in the IT sector. It could be said that this person is generally responsible for managing the IT department of many organizations. This person also conceives, designs and implements the services provided by many IT companies (such as cloud and hosting services, training, outsourcing, etc.) which, although initially provided in an improvised manner, are currently being designed like any other product. However, if we analyze these professionals we realize that they are generally engineers (like Software, Industrial or Telecommunication Engineers) who have not received an ad-hoc education and who have attained their competencies in services on the basis of complementary training (MBA, ITIL certificates, etc.) and a professional trajectory that has allowed them, thanks to their experience in different position and departments, to acquire an integral view of services.

In a service economy this professional profile, which is implicitly present in organizations, must be consolidated into an explicit role in order to increase the quality and productivity of service organizations. Thus it will be determinant to make specific programs and plans available so as to train T-Shaped professionals for the IT sector. The vertical part of the T for these professionals will represent in-depth knowledge of a discipline (IT) and of a sector (e.g. IT for banking), while the personal and professional skills (e.g. communication skills), are represented by the horizontal part of the T.

4   Producing a New Kind of Professional

In the next few years, the challenge will therefore consist of being able to specify both the body of knowledge needed by service professionals, particularly as regards sustaining IT Service Engineering, and providing the mechanisms needed to train this new type of professionals. In order to advance in this direction, several universities mainly in Europe and the US have begun to offer Bachelor's and Master's degree courses with the objective of training service professionals.

Some of these courses are more focused on the area of business, while others focus to a greater degree on training in services for the IT sector. The Rey Juan Carlos University (URJC) has, in contrast, set up a pioneering degree in SSME whose objective is the specific and integral training of service professionals[4].

Besides, three companies that are representative of three different service sectors are participating in the design and implementation of this degree course: IBM (IT Services), EULEN (Facility Services) and Melia International Hotels (Tourism Services). More specifically, IBM and EULEN have made a decisive contribution to the creation of the study plan, which spread out across four academic years and contains material related to computing, business, sociology, psychology, marketing and human resources, among others. Specific content for the training of personal skills such as emotional intelligence, communication skills, leadership and teamwork are included from the first year onward. This first year also includes a subject related to the theory of systems which, together with the systemic approach of other subjects such as Information Systems, boost systems thinking in the student from the outset. Finally, the last year is dedicated to specialization in a specific domain (IT, Tourism, Facilities, etc.) which will lead to graduates with different profiles such as IT Service Engineers, Tourism Service Engineers, Facility Service Engineers, etc.

In addition to the contents, the key to training in SSME lies in the way in which this content is taught. And this qualitative difference is perhaps the main differentiating characteristic with regard to others such as Information Systems or a joint honors degree in Business Management and Software Engineering.

SSME is a transdisciplinary science that has emerged as the result of the convergence of various disciplines; but transdisciplinarity is much more than the mere combination of the knowledge from each of the sciences of which the course is made up as occurs in an interdisciplinary approach. Thus, subjects related to computing (as with the subjects related to other areas, such as business) are not taught as it would be on a software engineering degree course, since the graduates will be Service Engineers, rather than Software Engineers.

They will not therefore be responsible for constructing the software that composes the technological basis of services, but will rather be responsible for the management of multidisciplinary teams in the departments of IT service businesses and organizations, and for the innovation and design of new services. This signifies that although they should have knowledge regarding programming, networks, data management, etc., it will not be necessary for them to obtain it at neither the same level nor by using the same approach as would a programmer or a Software Engineer.

Like a doctor cannot contemplate certain parts of the body independently from the rest of the body, services should be understood globally. A service

---

[4] http://ise.edu.es/.

engineer is like the internist, rather than the orthopedic surgeon, cardiologist or dermatologist in our example. It is not therefore a question of teaching what each part of the system is or how to construct them. The concept of service as a whole is rather the core of the training, allowing the student to acquire a holistic and integral view of it.

4.1   The SSME Degree Project

The study plan of the SSME degree program at URJC is the result of a project that lasted more than three years, as shown in Table 1 below and culminated with the degree being launched in 2014/15.

Table 1. The SSME degree program project.

Objective	Participants	Activities	Outputs
Phase 1: Competences and Subjects selection (Jan'11 - Oct'11)			
• Identify competences and subjects	• 1 SSME Expert from URJC • 3 Experts from IBM-Spain • 1 Expert from EULEN	1. Literature Review on national and international SSME education proposals (*Libro Blanco SSME* [16]) 2. Search for national and international Master programs related to SSME	GP-SSME_V0 (Graduate Program in SSME, V0)
Phase 2: Contents Definition (Nov'11 - Apr'12)			
• Specify the contents for each subject • Refine the subjects set	• Experts from URJC on SSME (3), Service QA. & Mgt. (1), Business Mgt.(3), CS (1) • New Experts from IBM • External Advisers on: marketing, economics, emotional intelligence, soft-skills & team mgt.	3. In-depth analysis of national and international Master programs related to SSME 4. Working group experts debates	GP-SSME_V1
Phase 3: Experts Review (May'12 - Oct'12)			
• Gather experts from different fields feedback	• SSME Experts • External Advisors ⋆ SRII ⋆ ERISS ⋆ ISSIP ⋆ IBM-Almaden Service Research Center	5. GP-SSME_V1 SSME Experts reviews 6. Feedback gathering from ERISS and SRII experts 7. ISSIP & IBM-Almaden joint review. URJC Expert moved to San Jose for 3 months	GP-SSME_V2
Phase 4: ANECA Formal Verification (Nov'12 - Dec'13)			
• Get official approval from ANECA	• SSME Experts • 1 Expert from IBM-Almaden • ANECA Committee	8. ANECA Review Report 9. GP-SSME_V2 review to fit ANECA comments (*5 iterations*)	GP-SSME_V3 (SSME Verified Degree Program)

The initial phase served to outline a very preliminary version of the study plan. As mentioned before, such draft was developed in close collaboration with experts from two representative companies from different service sectors: IBM and EULEN. During this starting step, the key areas that should cover the study plan (somehow discussed in previous sections) were discussed and identified.

Then, a rough plan was structured in order to cover these key areas and ensure the acquisition of the competencies found to be needed by the new kind of professional (GP-SSME_V0).

Contents for each subject were then identified and adjusted until a more mature version of the study plan was obtained (GP-SSME_V1). For this phase to succeed the contributions of the experts from different areas were decisive. Their different expertise played a key role to give the plan its transdisciplinary nature.

The proposal was then submitted to recognised experts from different fields related. The feedback from Mike Papazoglou (ERISS), Jorge Sanz (IBM-Almaden) and Jim Spohrer (IBM) contributed decisively to produce an improved revision of the plan (GP-SSME_V2). All of them have visited us later to meet our students. Likewise, one of our researchers moved to San Jose (CAL.) to work close with the people from the IBM Service Research Center for three months.

Finally, the plan was submitted to ANECA (*Agencia Nacional de Evaluación de la Calidad y Acreditación*), the Spanish governmental agency in charge of the assessment and accreditation of Higher-Education programs. After five rounds of reviews the plan (GP-SSME_V3) got finally approved by the end of 2013. The vision and contributions from stakeholders of every involved area was key also in this phase since the degree program under consideration was radically different from those existing at that time and communicating the idea of transdisciplinarity to the committee was nothing but easy. It was probably the biggest challenge addressed during this project. And it is worth noting that the total number of challenges was significant.

5   Conclusions

We have entered the Service Revolution era – the stage after the Industrial Revolution, which is marked by a strong domination of the service sector in the world economy. All of this will naturally affect society, which will gradually change from being an industrial society to being a service society, with all that this implies. Or it may in fact be the opposite. It is society that is promoting the implementation of services as the hub of the world economy. Whatever the case, the most immediate consequences of social and economic change are determined by the labor market and the change in professional roles. It is necessary to have professionals who have adapted to the new demands, which will undoubtedly be reflected in education and training as regards both content and method.

The IT industry cannot distance itself from this change and must therefore adapt as regards both business models and professionals. More specifically, we argue in favor of the creation of a new role – that of **IT Service Engineer**. This professional will be in charge of the innovation, design and construction of new services in the sphere of IT, along with the management of the IT services of different organizations. S/he will therefore be supported by interdisciplinary teams composed of different profiles depending on the service and the sector toward which the service is oriented (Software Engineers, programmers, DB and Web administrators, human resource managers, doctors, etc.).

Although it is true that there are currently professionals who are already playing this role, the predominant role services have started to play signifies that this profile is becoming increasingly more necessary, and businesses and organizations should therefore consider it explicitly among their professional descriptions, while universities should offer degrees fulfilling the new training requirements required by this profile. We firmly believe the SSME degree program at URJC answers this need.

As of today, the degree is on its 7th year. Two promotions have graduated and employability indicators yield 100%. SSME graduates are playing key roles in companies from different service sectors, consultancy firms and banking being among the most popular employers. Due to its interest for service professionals without a service-oriented background, the on-line program was launched 4 years ago having also a warm reception.

During this time, a relevant number of firms from different service sectors, like MELIA, RENFE, BBVA or IFMA to name a few, have joined the project. Seminars, invited talks and panels are periodically organized (once a month) with professionals from these companies. The events cover different topics: to share the SSME companies' vision with the students; to tell them about the role of SSME graduates in their firms; to describe the experience of young professionals and SSME graduates, etc. Renowned experts that contributed to the project, like Profs. Papazoglou and Sanz have also visited Madrid to talk to SSME students.

In parallel, we have launched different initiatives to contribute to define a body of knowledge for SSME and spread the word. For instance, we drove forward the Spanish Days on Service Science and Engineering (JCIS)[5], now in its 10th edition and we have created a MOOC on Service Engineering MOOC[6], which more than 4000 students have followed so far.

During the next years, we shall be monitoring the results and employability of SSME students and graduates and their feedback. Using such information and the lessons learned since the degree was launched, the program is being revised in close collaboration with our industrial partners [17]. The recent advent of similar programs in different countries, e.g. [18,19], confirm that we were working in the right direction.

To conclude, we would like to show Mike our gratitude for being an extraordinary colleague, a formidable host and a very good friend, who always found the time to meet us and have a good time during so many years in so many places.

Acknowledgements. Our research in service engineering has been founded by the Regional Government of Madrid under the FORTE-CM project (S2018/TCS-4314) and the Spanish Ministry of Business and Economics under the MADRID project (TIN2017-88557-R).

---

[5] https://bit.ly/3d2JtoJ.

[6] https://bit.ly/2Yozx3o.

References

1. World Bank: Employment in services (% of total employment) (modeled ILO estimate) (2020). Accessed 31 May 2020
2. Lightfoot, H., Baines, T., Smart, P.: The servitization of manufacturing: a systematic literature review of interdependent trends. Int. J. Oper. Prod. Manage. **33**(11–12), 1408–1434 (2013)
3. Papazoglou, M.P., Traverso, P., Dustdar, S., Leymann, F.: Service-oriented computing: state of the art and research challenges. Computer **40**(11), 38–45 (2007)
4. Turner, M., Budgen, D., Brereton, P.: Turning software into a service. Computer **36**(10), 38–44 (2003)
5. Zanella, A., Bui, N., Castellani, A., Vangelista, L., Zorzi, M.: Internet of things for smart cities. IEEE Internet of Things J. **1**(1), 22–32 (2014)
6. Heidenreich, S., Handrich, M.: Adoption of technology-based services: the role of customers' willingness to co-create. J. Serv. Manage. (2015)
7. Karimi, J., Somers, T.M., Bhattacherjee, A.: The role of information systems resources in ERP capability building and business process outcomes. J. Manage. Inf. Syst. **24**(2), 221–260 (2007)
8. IBM Research. Services sciences: a new academic discipline? Technical report, Report on the Architecture of On Demand Business Summit, Yorktown Heights, NY (2004)
9. Shaw, M., Garlan, D., et al.: Software Architecture, vol. 101. Prentice Hall Englewood Cliffs, New Jersey (1996)
10. Checkland, P.B.: Information systems and systems thinking: time to unite? Int. J. Inf. Manage. **8**(4), 239–248 (1988)
11. Maglio, P.P., Spohrer, J.: A service science perspective on business model innovation. Ind. Market. Manage. **42**(5), 665–670 (2013)
12. Chang, C.M.: Service Systems Management and Engineering: Creating Strategic Differentiation and Operational Excellence. John Wiley & Sons, Hoboken (2010)
13. Kitchenham, B.A.: Software Metrics: Measurement for Software Process Improvement. Blackwell Publishers Inc., United States (1996)
14. Galup, S.D., Dattero, R., Quan, J.J., Conger, S.: An overview of it service management. Commun. ACM **52**(5), 124–127 (2009)
15. Maglio, P.P., Spohrer, J.: Fundamentals of service science. J. Acad. Market. Sci. **36**(1), 18–20 (2008)
16. Lázaro, P., Galán, L., Suárez, B., Domínguez, A.: La ciencia de los servicios: Un desafío para el sistema universitario español. Programa de Estudios y Análisis del Ministerio de Educación (Ref. Proyecto EA2008-0307) (2008)
17. Marcos, E., De Castro, V., Martín-Peña, M.L., Vara, J.M.: Training new professionals in service engineering: towards a transdisciplinary curriculum for sustainable businesses. Sustain **12**(19), 8289 (2020)
18. Frankfurt University of Applied Sciences: Service engineering bachelor of engineering (2020). Accessed 3 June 2020
19. Nile University: Bachelor of Science in Industrial and Service Engineering and Management ISEM (2020). Accessed 3 June 2020

Services and the Internet of Things

Towards IoT Processes on the Edge

Schahram Dustdar$^{(\boxtimes)}$ and Ilir Murturi

Distributed Systems Group, TU Wien, Vienna, Austria
{dustdar,imurturi}@dsg.tuwien.ac.at

Abstract. Edge computing is a fundamental enabler for the proliferation of the Internet of Things (IoT). Resources, including compute and storage, are increasingly located at the edge of the network and bridge the gap between the cloud and IoT entities. Edge computing enables low-latency, privacy-awareness, and resilient applications. Many of the applications are in fact business process-based and are distributed over edge as well as cloud resources. Edge devices can be used to analyze high-volume IoT data streams for on-premises monitoring and alerting, and at the same time to aggregate and forward these data to other premises or the cloud for long-term storage and analytics. Many operational and business challenges can be solved by running applications on edge resources or on-premises of Edge-Cloud infrastructure. However, the broad range of IoT application requirements concerning latency, QoS, or fault-tolerance, combined with the heterogeneous and dynamic nature of edge networks, make it particularly challenging to develop, configure, deploy, and operate such applications. In this paper, we discuss some of the research issues with span the domains of business processes engineering and edge computing.

Keywords: Edge-Cloud continuum · Distributed processes

1 Introduction

In recent years, the Internet of Things (IoT) has been diffused into the society, and many services are constructed on the top of IoT technologies in various industries such as Industrial Manufacturing, Healthcare, Lifestyle, Automotive, and Smart Building, just to name a few. At the same time, it is well accepted that a centralized architecture does not scale well regarding the enormous number of devices, although the system infrastructure of central computers processing those data have improved by cloud computing technologies. In contrast to a fully distributed and decentralized architecture (e.g., peer-to-peer network), many IoT services need to maintain a partially centralized design to operate the service. Nonetheless, the significant portion of decentralization is often achieved by delegating functions from central servers to edge computing devices [1]. Edge devices are essentially computers close to the edge of the network, hence, closer to the sensors, which create the data streams to be processed later. Edge devices, therefore, can be utilized to process data streams pumped into an IoT system

© Springer Nature Switzerland AG 2021
M. Aiello et al. (Eds.): Papazoglou Festschrift, LNCS 12521, pp. 167–178, 2021.
https://doi.org/10.1007/978-3-030-73203-5_13

by providing analytics capabilities, providing decision functions as to which data has to be forwarded to a cloud infrastructure or not and possibly also providing decisions based on modeled business processes as well as business models.

Another important aspect in the age of the IoT is the heterogeneity of IoT components. Several vendors provide different products not only across different layers but also for the same type of components. Different products may have different operating systems, available support for programming languages, resource constraints, and so on. In contrast to our expectations, each device's functions are hard-coded in most of the current implementations. This causes inflexibility and limited extensibility for future changes. This leads to a plethora of point-to-point solutions being developed based on proprietary protocols. Any change being made to one IoT component leads to many possible changes in many other components thus leading to a situation which resembles the state of software infrastructure in the age of enterprise computing before the emergence of Web services and Service Oriented Architectures and their respective middleware infrastructure such as Enterprise Service Bus (ESB). This insight led us to (re-)design IoT systems into a distributed and decentralized architecture that is scalable not only in numbers but also concerning its heterogeneity as well as its notion of processes being supported.

A similar problem to managing heterogeneous entities with different functionalities in highly distributed yet still partially centralized settings has been addressed by business process management (BPM) for several years. Before the establishment of business process engines (BPE), or workflow engines, processes were directly implemented in information systems. In other words, tasks and their sequences were hard-coded altogether in the source code of the information system. This style of design causes inflexibility and low extensibility against changes demanded from ones in business requirements. As a solution to this problem, BPEs enable overseeing the execution and maintenance of workflows and their enactments with high flexibility and extensibility by integrating different data sources and execution entities spread across IT applications and services.

1.1 Background

A business process consists of a set of related structured events, tasks, decisions, inputs, and outputs. Events happen in the environment and trigger tasks in a business process. Tasks are the smallest units, which can be performed by various entities such as people, machines, or software within the business process. A process may contain decisions based on certain business rules apart from the process itself. Inputs can be physical goods or in-materialistic (such as filling out a form and inputting data) required to complete a business process in question, including information. A process produces outputs, which is the goal of the process, to the environment.

A business process engine (BPE) is a software middleware overseeing the technical instantiations of business processes and their associated activities. A BPE copes with more than one application and services regardless of their layers (e.g., front-end, back-end, or middleware), boundaries (e.g., internal or external services), or vendors. A BPE becomes involved in interlinking and interprocessing between activities by routing and transforming data across different components, rather than executing each activity itself. Those interlinks are automated based on the process specification often given by a business process modeling language, which the BPE supports. Users can change how activities are interlinked by updating the process model.

Among others, BPE's benefits in the context of BPM that are relevant to the rest of this article can be summarized with two aspects: flexibility and monitoring. Since a BPE separates each activity's actual technical execution and its coordination (orchestration), we can change the process specification without changing the technical implementation, thus acquiring flexibility for future changes, which might be referred to as extensibility or agility depending on the context. Monitoring is a fundamental property of BPEs as it allows an understanding of utilized resources and their time as well as involved actors and additional auditing information.

1.2 Distributed Process Execution

Several approaches have been proposed to enable the distributed execution of business processes. Essentially, the BPE engine is replicated among computation entities (i.e., distributed clouds), and process activities are distributed among available entities. Muthusamy et al. [2] presents a Service Level Agreement (SLA) driven approach to BPM for service-oriented applications in environments such as cloud computing platforms. Initially, the proposed approach decomposes a business process into a set of dependent activities. Afterward, each activity is mapped into a set of distributed computation entities (i.e., execution engines) closer to the data sources. The coordination among activities (i.e., communication/messaging) is achieved by emitting and consuming events over the PADRES distributed publish/subscribe platform. The proposed approach aims to minimize the overall communication costs by executing process activities as closely as possible to the data source. A comprehensive survey on the distributed execution of business processes is provided by Wutke [3].

A similar approach can be adopted in the context of Edge-Cloud continuum systems. One the one hand, various mechanisms for resource coordination [4], service deployment [5], controlling elasticity in application [6], IoT system deployment [7], or monitoring [8] can be dynamically placed at the edge. On the other hand, a service deployment mechanism provides functionality to accept requests to deploy an IoT application (i.e., service) comprised of a set of small tasks (i.e., microservices [9]) and distribute them into the Edge-Cloud infrastructure. When placing decision mechanisms at the edge, a challenging aspect is each edge device's resource capabilities. For instance, the service deployment mechanism's main prerequisite is the real-time monitoring of available resources in the infrastructure. Placing both functions on the same edge device is computationally and network demanding; therefore, some functions should be delegated to available edge devices or other computation entities that meet their Quality of Service (QoS). Thereby, distributing functionalities and dynamically place them in the heterogeneous and dynamic edge networks enable relieving complex computations to occur on a single computation entity. The same appears when considering distributing IoT application components over edge resources or on-premises of Edge-Cloud infrastructure.

2   An Overview of Edge-Cloud Continuum

Edge computing is positioned as one important architectural layer in addition to fog and cloud. It can be considered as paramount to systems including (but not limited to) IoT deployments and the cloud, providing data and control facilities to participating IoT devices. Up to now, several comprehensive surveys have been published, describing the edge computing paradigm and its challenges [10, 11]. According to [12], the Edge-Cloud architecture is divided into three layers: the cloud layer, the fog layer, and the edge layer (as illustrated in Fig. 1). A comprehensive description for each layer is given below.

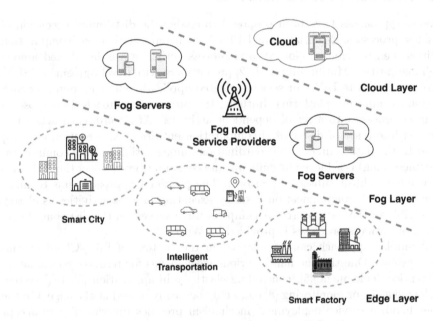

Fig. 1. An overview of Edge-Cloud architecture.

2.1   The Edge Layer

The edge layer is the lowest layer of the architecture, which represents the edge of the network. As can be denoted in Fig. 1, various domains such as smart city,

intelligent transportation, or smart factories can benefit from available computation devices closer to the IoT domain. Essentially, this leads to having various
edge networks formed for different contexts. Generally speaking, edge networks
are highly dynamic, heterogeneous, and resource-constrained environments. Such
environments are composed of a set of low-powered end devices with various computation capabilities (e.g., smartphones, smartwatches, Raspberry Pis, etc.) and
IoT resources (e.g., sensors, actuators, etc.).

Edge devices at this layer provide their computation and storing capabilities
to process the IoT data streams generated by IoT resources. Essentially, these
devices enable processing data streams as close as possible to the data sources
and handling the most substantial network traffic that may occur. Nevertheless,
resource-constrained edge devices do not pose the ability to process vast amounts
of data. Consequently, processing such data on a single edge device may cause
high-latency and poor overall performance. To overcome such challenges introduced by resource-constrained devices, distributing processes become a crucial
aspect. Recent developments suggest adding more computation devices in edge
networks. Concretely, through forming peer-to-peer edge networks, the scope of
resources is extended, and the opportunity to distribute processes among devices
becomes feasible.

Edge-to-edge collaboration, respectively, an *edge network*, provides a seamless
opportunity for placing control mechanisms closer to the end-users, which results
in creating more *autonomous environments* and less dependent on the external
environments (i.e., cloud, or fog). For instance, in a smart home, residents should
be able to control their devices and process data locally without depending on
the cloud resources. However, it is worth noting that even though extending
resource scope through edge-to-edge collaboration provides many benefits, there
are still many complex tasks that cannot be processed at this layer. Thus, in such
situations, the edge devices must forward their processing to the upper layers
(i.e., fog or cloud systems).

2.2   The Fog Layer

The fog layer includes a set of powerful devices in charge of managing, connecting, and enabling sharing resources among different edge networks. This
layer essentially represents the external environment where several fog nodes are
connected, offering computation and storage resources for edge networks and
roaming end-devices in proximity. Similarly, fog devices (e.g., servers and base
stations) are connected, forming fog infrastructure. In contrast to the edge networks, the fog infrastructure tends to be composed of stationary and powerful
devices (typically maintained and provided by Telco operators). Several tasks
can be deployed at this layer, for example, processing data streams, caching,
device management, and privacy protection.

At first glance, one can note that both layers provide similar features. Generally speaking, edge and fog paradigms foresee enabling more computation
resources closer to the end-users and the IoT/sensor domain - at the edge of
the network, respectively. However, the most significant difference between the

two layers is administrative differences and responsibilities. Furthermore, fog nodes (e.g., deployed in base stations) may provide their services for larger geographical areas. For instance, intelligent transportation systems may benefit from connecting and processing vehicle data in fog infrastructure [13].

Even though fog infrastructure provides more powerful devices, long-term data storage is impractical—similarly, processing tasks with heavy computation requirements are infeasible. Thus, in such situations, fog devices must forward their data and heavy computation tasks to the upper layer. Nonetheless, both layers provide low-latency services since the end-devices are closer to the source where the data is produced and consumed.

2.3 The Cloud Layer

The cloud layer provides "unlimited" computational and storage resources. This layer includes cloud servers that are deployed far away from the end devices and the IoT domain. Essentially, the cloud-based servers perform computationally intensive operations received from lower-layers of the architecture. Such environments provide advanced features for both end-users and service providers, such as performance configurations and security controls. Moreover, this computing utility has been seen as a critical component for the development, deployment, and execution of IoT platforms promising to meet the general community's everyday needs.

Despite the numerous resources available, this paradigm faces increasing challenges in meeting new IoT applications' stringent requirements. At present, geographically distributed IoT devices with intensive data generation cannot efficiently utilize resources available in Cloud environments [12]. Transferring intense and large amounts of data to a centralized cloud over Wide Area Networks (WAN) generates latencies and poses risks of service unavailability due to the non-persistent connectivity or eventually scheduled system maintenance. On the other hand, real-time distributed applications require fast response time, high-availability, and increased privacy, which centralized environments such as clouds often fail to fulfill.

3   Use Cases of Edge-Cloud Systems

3.1   Emergency Situations

To motivate our subsequent discussion, we consider emergencies such as natural disasters (e.g., earthquakes, fires, floods) in the city. Emergencies like earthquakes may affect various city zones, which can damage infrastructure, cause injury or loss of life, and trap people under buildings. In such situations, time is valuable, and drones may be used to analyze the entire situation and help rescue teams find and communicate with victims under a collapsed building. In this scenario, we consider multiple connected drones (i.e., form an edge neighborhood) flying over the city's affected areas (i.e., neighborhoods) aiming to provide services for the rescue teams in finding victims under a collapsed building. Each drone (i.e., edge node) is equipped with various computation capabilities and integrated sensors (e.g., radar sensor, infrared cameras, etc.). We consider that drones are multi-purpose devices where the rescue teams may request to deploy various services depending on the emergency. Meanwhile, base stations may provide computational and storage capabilities (i.e., fog nodes) and provide docker charge stations for charging drones. At the same time, cloud capabilities may be used to store data for long terms.

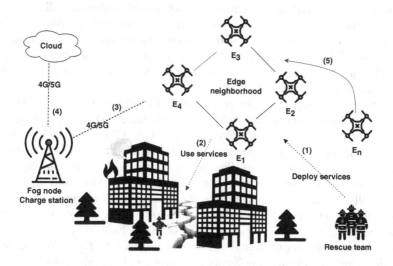

Fig. 2. IoT public safety service.

We assume that a rescue team deploys (1) a public safety IoT service that detects a dangerous zone in the affected area (i.e., discovering cracks, smoke, hazardous gases, etc.) (as illustrated in Fig. 2). Such service aims at assisting rescue teams (2) in finding a safe path and avoiding dangerous zones. The service is dependent on various resources such as multiple infrared cameras, radar sensors, and an electronic nose that are integrated into numerous drones. Since each drone is a potential candidate to run the service, it is evident that each node should be able to automatically discover resources in a decentralized manner and make them available at runtime. In such use case scenarios, we cannot depend on physically static entities to provide their services (3–4). Additionally, the edge neighborhood cannot be built as a centralized edge-system and dependent on particular nodes. This due to the network dynamicity (i.e., drones may join (5) and leave often), connectivity and latency issues, and the master drone may run out of energy or get out of the connection range. As a result, shifting various processes closer to the edge and dynamically place them in the most suitable nodes is crucial. Thus, deploying decentralized decision mechanisms and dynamically placing them makes edge networks *autonomous environments* and less dependent on centralized nodes that are located far away.

3.2   Smart Building Evacuation

The building evacuation is another example that can benefit from enabling the executing of various processes on edge. We consider a smart building, equipped with an infrastructure that supports inhabitants to evacuate the building safely in case of fire. On each floor, several IoT sensors are deployed and connected to servers (e.g., fog nodes) through edge gateways. We consider a goal-driven IoT system (GDS) [7], which is composed of a set of devices with individual functionalities that connect and cooperate temporally to achieve the user goal. For instance, in a smart meeting room, a GDS could be dynamically formed by connecting the motion detection sensor, smart screen, and speakers to achieve the goal (e.g., *safe evacuation*). The motion detection sensor detects the presence of the people. The smart screen displays the location(s) of the fire and possible safe paths for evacuation. Speakers also play a voice message asking people to evacuate the building.

The servers are responsible for dynamically forming and enacting GDSs that facilitate the evacuation of the building. Essentially, each computation entity may become responsible for forming and enacting GDSs seamlessly. Assume that communication between the edge gateways on one floor and the on-premise server is lost, e.g., due to the fire. The edge gateway decides whether to connect to the cloud or collaborate with other edge devices to form and enact GDSs automatically. In case the connection to the cloud can not be established, or due to the high-latency, the edge gateways collaborate to form and enact GDSs at the edge network. Generally speaking, such GDSs include fewer IoT sensors and should require less computational resources compared to those formed by the fog or the cloud. As a result, deploying IoT systems at the edge overcomes many undesired and critical situations.

4   Distributed Processes on the Edge

In the past few years, researchers in edge and fog computing have been mostly focused on proposing multiple techniques for resource allocation problems aiming to minimize various trade-offs such as latency, bandwidth, energy consumption, or maximizing the utilization of resources at the edge. In general, IoT applications and their associated business process models are deployed according to the following models [14]: i) *everything in the cloud*, ii) *everything in the edge*, and iii) *hybrid edge-cloud model*. Essentially, allocation techniques may deploy software components entirely on a single environment (e.g., cloud or edge) [5], or components are deployed and executed in both cloud and edge.

Recent developments within distributed systems have led to emerging commercial cloud-based IoT and cloud/edge integration solutions. Edge computing platforms such as EdgeX Foundry[1], AWS IoT Greengrass[2], or Google IoT Edge[3]

---

[1] https://www.edgexfoundry.org/.

[2] https://aws.amazon.com/greengrass/.

[3] https://cloud.google.com/solutions/iot.

promise to bridge the gap between the IoT and the cloud by providing a flexible runtime for applications running at the edge. However, these systems are extremely limited in their operational capabilities, missing elasticity features, and lack of self-adaptive mechanisms required in dynamic edge and IoT settings.

In general, the proposed solutions assumed that application demands remain static and do not change over time. This implies that hardware resources are reserved more than needed to guarantee application functionality when the workload is increased. However, over-provisioning in resource-constrained edge infrastructures is highly impractical, resource-expensive, and decreases system performance considerably. Furthermore, application developers or end-users cannot specify QoS and elastic requirements of the application, as well as there is no mechanism support to enact them. To fill this gap, we identify challenges and potential solutions that the IoT applications deployed in Edge-Cloud architecture must overcome to fulfill their full potential.

4.1 IoT Application Requirements

Future IoT systems for the described Edge-Cloud continuum architectures need to hide their operational complexity from application developers. In particular, programmers should not have to deal with the heterogeneity of the edge network setting. For instance, developers should be able to express the context in which IoT application components are allowed to run and their requirements (e.g., QoS, elastic requirements, etc.) in a high-level way [15]. In particular, identifying the current and future demands of IoT applications from various areas is decisive for any contemporary IoT system's success. However, this necessitates that the programming model is intuitive for developers but expressive enough to help the execution system perform runtime decisions on (re)scheduling and scaling operations.

To overcome such challenges, as a potential candidate for defining these requirements, we consider a declarative language called *Simple Yet Beautiful Language* (SYBL) [6] and its runtime mechanism for controlling elasticity in applications. SYBL enables the user to specify elastic requirements at different granularities and enables applications to scale in elasticity space (*cost, resources*, and *quality*). In essence, SYBL allows the user to define: i) *monitoring* (i.e., specifying metrics to be monitored), ii) *constraints* (i.e., specifying the limits in which the monitored metrics are allowed to oscillate), iii) *strategies* (i.e., specifying actions to be taken when a constraint is violated), and iv) *priorities* (i.e., specifying constraints priority to be executed first). Furthermore, SYBL provides features such as enabling the user to achieve various trade-offs, such as specifying demands on the relation between cost, resources, and quality. For instance, when the cost is high, the IoT application needs to scale up to achieve higher service quality. Or, the IoT application should scale down in order to optimize the usage and the cost. Nevertheless, an extension to the language, as well as to the runtime mechanism, is required. Moreover, developing novel high-level constraints and enforcement strategies related to the IoT applications and Edge-Cloud architecture is crucial.

4.2   IoT System Deployment and Resilient Application Runtime

As we explore new IoT systems, IoT applications, and the heterogeneous edge networks, distributing system components and application processes among various computation entities becomes increasingly apparent. For instance, an IoT system can comprise a set of dependent software components (i.e., controlling module, scheduler, resource manager, etc.) that can be deployed individually on multiple edge devices. Thus, we analyze and discuss the pros and cons of three main IoT system architectures that enable distributing application tasks among edge devices, such as *centralized*, *distributed*, and *decentralized*.

In the centralized architecture, a single edge device acts as a master device responsible for monitoring and distributing tasks among other available computation entities in the Edge-Cloud continuum. In essence, placing a set of functionalities on a single edge device may be feasible in the context of small and non-dynamic edge networks (e.g., smart homes). As mentioned previously, centralized architecture does not scale easily, while a master edge device may be overwhelmed quickly due to resource limitations. In contrast, the distributed solution treats all edge devices equally in terms of system responsibilities. In an environment without a master device, nodes in proximity are consensually coordinated and distribute processes to some SLA agreement. In practice, distributed solutions may face latency issues when nodes need to find consensus to distribute processes, and the number of nodes in topology is limited. However, regardless of the approach, both solutions may have plenty of advantages in various IoT scenarios.

In the decentralized architecture, the master device functionalities may be placed *statically* (i.e., at design time) or *dynamically* (i.e., with self-adaptive capabilities). However, the dynamic nature of edge networks requires the continuous re-evaluation of placement decisions for such functionalities. Thus, a possible solution is considering election based algorithms. For instance, through initiating an *election* between edge devices, the most suitable node (e.g., in terms of computation power) is elected as a master device. In fact, through exchanging election results, nodes in the network come to the same result independently of each other. Such a solution denotes a very decentralized approach to automatically electing the master device and succeeding over the challenges introduced by mobile devices and possible failures in edge networks. However, to overcome the obstacles with resource-constrained edge devices, further improvements are required. For instance, the master device must delegate various functionalities to other nodes to handle the computation and network overheads.

To overcome such aforementioned challenges, a possible solution is to elect new coordinators (i.e., superpeers [16]) in the system. Each coordinator is responsible for managing a set of nodes in the edge network. As the network size grows, new coordinators are introduced on the system as well. In particular, coordinators provide similar functionalities as the master device. However, the master device becomes a supervising node responsible for managing coordinators, monitoring, and distributing applications among coordinators. For instance, a user can submit a request to the master device for application deployment. The master device examines his/her geographically location and asks the closest coordinators to determine if their group can meet the application requirements. Afterward, the coordinator who fulfills application demands gets the application and distributes it to the group's edge devices. Nevertheless, various scheduling algorithms, communication protocols, self-adaption techniques, and monitoring tools are required to deploy IoT systems in a decentralized manner.

Another important aspect is executing software components on heterogeneous environments (i.e., edge layer, fog layer, or in the cloud layer). To this end, we require a homogeneous runtime platform that follows the *"run once, run anywhere"* model. Thus, to overcome such challenges, as a potential candidate for executing IoT applications, we consider Docker[4] or Java-based OSGi[5]. Nevertheless, an extension is required for the runtime mechanism to monitor the edge device's real-time internal resources (e.g., CPU, memory, storage), network QoS, and application performance (e.g., application responsiveness).

5 Summary and Conclusions

In recent years, processing IoT data streams closer to the end-users and IoT domain has received significant attention from the research community and industry stakeholders. Enabling to process data closer to the end-user can solve several operational and business challenges. Since then, we have seen a rapidly increasing number of available resources in IoT infrastructures. Essentially, resources with computation and storage capabilities (i.e., perceived as *edge devices*) promise to offer various services and enable processing data with low-latency, high-availability and increased privacy. However, with acquainting new IoT scenarios and their stringent requirements (i.e., latency, QoS, dynamicity, or fault-tolerance), deploying IoT systems and processing data on a single edge device becomes impractical. To that end, in this paper, we discussed some of the research issues and the necessity of decentralizing IoT systems and distributing processes among devices at the edge.

Acknowledgment. Research supported by the Research Cluster "Smart Communities and Technologies (Smart CT)" at TU Vienna.

References

1. Shi, W., Dustdar, S.: The promise of edge computing. Computer **49**(5), 78–81 (2016)
2. Muthusamy, V., Jacobsen, H.-A.: BPM in cloud architectures: business process management with SLAs and events. In: Hull, R., Mendling, J., Tai, S. (eds.) BPM 2010. LNCS, vol. 6336, pp. 5–10. Springer, Heidelberg (2010). https://doi.org/10.1007/978-3-642-15618-2_2

---

[4] https://www.docker.com/.
[5] https://www.osgi.org/.

3. Wutke, D.: Eine infrastruktur für die dezentrale ausführung von bpel-prozessen (2010)
4. Tsigkanos, C., Murturi, I., Dustdar, S.: Dependable resource coordination on the edge at runtime. Proc. IEEE **107**(8), 1520–1536 (2019)
5. Avasalcai, C., Dustdar, S.: Latency-aware distributed resource provisioning for deploying IoT applications at the edge of the network. In: Arai, K., Bhatia, R. (eds.) FICC 2019. LNNS, vol. 69, pp. 377–391. Springer, Cham (2020). https://doi.org/10.1007/978-3-030-12388-8_27
6. Copil, G., Moldovan, D., Truong, H.L., Dustdar, S.: SYBL: an extensible language for controlling elasticity in cloud applications. In: 2013 13th IEEE/ACM International Symposium on Cluster, Cloud, and Grid Computing, pp. 112–119. IEEE (2013)
7. Alkhabbas, F., Murturi, I., Spalazzese, R., Davidsson, P., Dustdar, S.: A goal-driven approach for deploying self-adaptive IoT systems. In: IEEE International Conference on Software Architecture (ICSA 2020), pp. 1–11. IEEE (2020)
8. Bajrami, X., Murturi, I.: An efficient approach to monitoring environmental conditions using a wireless sensor network and NodeMCU. e & i Elektrotechnik und Informationstechnik, **135**(3), 294–301 (2018)
9. Bouguettaya, A., et al.: A service computing manifesto: the next 10 years. Commun. ACM **60**(4), 64–72 (2017)
10. Shi, W., Cao, J., Zhang, Q., Li, Y., Lanyu, X.: Edge computing: vision and challenges. IEEE Internet of Things J. **3**(5), 637–646 (2016)
11. Avasalcai, C., Murturi, I., Dustdar, S.: Edge and fog: a survey, use cases, and future challenges. Fog Comput. Theory Pract. 43–65 (2020)
12. Dustdar, S., Avasalcai, C., Murturi, I.: Edge and fog computing: vision and research challenges. In: 2019 IEEE International Conference on Service-Oriented System Engineering (SOSE), pp. 96–9609. IEEE (2019)
13. Hussain, M.M., Alam, M.S., Sufyan Beg, M.M.: Fog computing model for evolving smart transportation applications. Fog Edge Comput. Principles Paradigms **22**(4), 347–372 (2019)
14. Ashouri, M., Davidsson, P., Spalazzese, R.: Cloud, edge, or both? towards decision support for designing IoT applications. In: 2018 Fifth International Conference on Internet of Things: Systems, Management and Security, pp. 155–162. IEEE (2018)
15. Dustdar, S., Guo, Y., Satzger, B., Truong, H.-L.: Principles of elastic processes. IEEE Internet Comput. **15**(5), 66–71 (2011)
16. Jesi, G.P., Montresor, A., Babaoglu, O.: Proximity-aware superpeer overlay topologies. In: Keller, A., Martin-Flatin, J.-P. (eds.) SelfMan 2006. LNCS, vol. 3996, pp. 43–57. Springer, Heidelberg (2006). https://doi.org/10.1007/11767886_4

A Guiding Framework for IoT Servitization

Zakaria Maamar[1]([✉]), Noura Faci[2], and Fadwa Yahya[3]

[1] Zayed University, Dubai, UAE
zakaria.maamar@zu.ac.ae
[2] Université Claude Bernard, Lyon, France
[3] Prince Sattam bin Abdulaziz University, Al-Kharj, Saudi Arabia

Abstract. This paper discusses the necessary steps and mechanisms that would allow servitizing the Internet-of-Things (IoT). Servitization exposes functionalities as services allowing potential users to consume these functionalities regardless of the development technologies. To ensure successful use of IoT functionalities, restrictions that hinder this use are identified and then, addressed from a servitization perspective. These restrictions are referred to as no-semantics, silo, and no-reasoning with focus on the first restriction in this paper. Customer-Facilitator-Provider interaction model is developed in the paper allowing to define who does what in the context of IoT servitization.

Keywords: Internet-of-Things · Restriction · Semantics · Servitization

1 Introduction

The science of services is described as *"a melding of technology with an understanding of business processes and organization [which is] crucial to the economy's next wave"* [4]. IBM is among the pioneers that defined the science of services as the study of service systems that combines organization and human understanding with business and technological understanding to categorize and explain the many types of service systems that exist and interact to co-create value [10]. A plethora of online and offline services complemented by powerful digital communication means like the Internet and social media are helping organizations shape and strengthen their competitiveness posture. According to the Organization for Economic Cooperation and Development (OECD) Forum, services constitute two third of the world's Gross Domestic Product (GDP, https://tinyurl.com/t6kd3ov). The service sector (e.g., logistics and distribution, hospitality, education, and healthcare) represents the largest proportion of the world economy.

Many definitions of the term service exist. A simple definition is any activity that leads to a tangible or intangible effect (e.g., good delivery or improved customer satisfaction), which is the result of a client interaction that creates and captures value. A computational definition according to 3WC is that a service

© Springer Nature Switzerland AG 2021
M. Aiello et al. (Eds.): Papazoglou Festschrift, LNCS 12521, pp. 179–188, 2021.
https://doi.org/10.1007/978-3-030-73203-5_14

is *"a software application identified by a URI, whose interfaces and binding are capable of being defined, described, and discovered by XML artifacts, and supports direct interactions with other software applications using XML-based messages via Internet-based applications"*.

Although servitization has been around for many years [14], it now is the new trend that many organizations are embracing to achieve digital transformation and other benefits like securing additional sources of revenue, provisioning products as services, and packaging expertise as services. To minimize one-time sales operations, organizations would like to extend these operations from different perspectives such as after-sale. Organizations would also like to see customers focus on their core competencies while standing by to offer the necessary support through on-demand and customized services. Many industries are already tapping into servitization like airline (Rolls-Royce selling "power-by-the-hour" instead of selling aero engines), oil & gas, and software (usually referred to as cloud computing). In the Information & Communication Technologies (ICT) community, *aaS is a well-known acronym standing for Everything-as-a-Service [3]. Everything (i.e., thing as a general term) could be software, platform, infrastructure, data, security, etc.

In conjunction with servitization, organizations are also tapping into other trendy ICT such as blockchain, 5G networks, and Internet-of-Things (IoT). IoT is about making things like sensors and actuators "keep-an-eye" on cyber-physical surroundings so, that, contextualized, smart services are provisioned to users and organizations. Gartner reports that 6.4 billion connected things were in use in 2016, up 3% from 2015, and will reach 20.8 billion by 2020[1]. Despite the popularity of IoT, it still suffers from many restrictions that, in the long-run, could undermine this popularity. Among these restrictions, we cite diversity and multiplicity of things' development and communication technologies, users' reluctance and sometimes rejection because of things invading their privacy, limited IoT-platform interoperability, lack of an IoT-oriented software engineering discipline that would guide thing analysis, design, and development, and, finally, passive nature of things that primarily act as data suppliers (with some actuating capabilities). In this paper, we examine how servitization could address some IoT restrictions. For instance, separate things could engage in collaborative scenarios by adopting guidelines that would have been packaged as services (Collaboration-as-a-Service, CaaS). The objective of CaaS is to "tell" things how to collaborate, with whom, where, and when.

Our contributions are, but not limited to, (*i*) shedding light on some IoT restrictions that servitization could address, (*ii*) defining a guiding framework for servitizing IoT, (*iii*) illustrating how IoT servitization could be actionned, and (*iv*) demonstrating the technical doability of the guiding framework. The rest of this paper is organized as follows. Section 2 is a brief overview of the service economy. Section 3 discusses restrictions undermining IoT. Section 4 presents how servitization addresses one particular restriction. Section 5 concludes the paper and presents our ongoing research agenda on IoT servitization.

---

[1] http://www.gartner.com/newsroom/id/3165317.

2   Service Economy in Brief

It is not a secret that the world's economies are shifting from sectors like agriculture and manufacturing to services [15]. The percentage of labor force employed in each sector confirms this shift that is backed with many reasons like automation prevalence, global competition, innovation pressure, and changes in customers' demands and habits. In addition, the boundaries between products and services are blurring while customization and personalization have become important. According to a Delicate 2018 report (https://tinyurl.comy785n684), *"In 2015, services value added accounted for 74% of GDP in high-income countries, up from 69% in 1997. The contribution of services value added to GDP was higher in the United States than among its peer high-income nations. The increase in services share of GDP was even more prominent in low- and middle-income countries, where it jumped to 57% in 2015 from 48% in 1997"*.

ICT continuous advances such as World Wide Web, ubiquitous systems, and IoT allow organizations to export their know how, target new markets, and provide services that are previously available to, only, a limited community of local customers. Service adoption is enabling a wave of innovations that are forcing organizations to review their practices of dealing with all stakeholders. Many organizations are packaging their operations into services and moving these services to the Web for more automation, better efficiency, and global visibility.

3   Restrictions Undermining IoT

As stated in Sect. 1, multiple restrictions are making IoT acceptance by end-users a bit "difficult". According to Wu et al., today's things act like *"awkward stegosaurus: all brawn and no brains"* [17]. Over the past few years, our research findings on IoT, reported in venues like [6, 7], and [13], have shed light on 3 restrictions that we refer to as no-semantics, silo, and no-reasoning. To illustrate the negative impact of these restrictions on blueorganizations that are willing to embrace IoT, let us consider a simple, yet realistic, example that is about a care center for elderly people. Many studies confirm that population ageing is a dominant global demographic trend of the 21st century[2]. Without proper mechanisms, things like smart TV, remote control, and light switches would function independently from each other despite the synergy that exists between them. To offer a seamless watching experience to a group of elderly persons based on their habits, the remote control could instruct the smart TV to switch to the right channel, to adjust the volume, and to set the brightness. In addition, the remote control could request the light switches to dime the light based on the smart TV's brightness level. To allow such a scenario to happen, these things need to exchange details that they could understand, to break down the silos that confine them, and to reason over end-users' profiles.

---

[2] http://www.weforum.org/agenda/2019/10/ageing-economics-population-health.

Known for their passive nature [11], today's things do not or barely engage in collaborative scenarios. This is not in line with the nature of business applications that are distributed and heterogenous calling for the collaboration of all parties. Because of this lack of collaboration, direct interactions between things are somehow inexistent or scarce making the importance of having a common understanding of the content to exchange not a major concern. Unfortunately, this should not be the case. Things should be equipped with capabilities that would let them "understand" what they exchange, should they decide to engage in collaborative scenarios. In the rest of this paper, we only examine, due to lack of space, the no-semantics restriction and how servitization addresses it.

4   Servitization and IoT

This section consists of 3 parts. The first part is an overview of some initiatives that address things' no-semantics restriction with focus on our own initiative, Ontology Web Language for Things (OWL-T, [8]). The second part details how OWL-T is exposed as a service. Finally, the last part implements this exposure.

4.1   Reviewing Some Works

Our literature review identified 4 initiatives that address the no-semantics restriction. These initiatives are presented by Maamar et al. who introduce the Ontology Web Language for Things (OWL-T) [8], Agarwal et al. who develop an ontology for the semantic interoperability between IoT heterogeneous testbeds [1], Li and Jiang who use the Ontology Web Language (OWL) to develop an IoT context ontology [5], and Seydoux et al. who propose IoT-O (O for ontology) to describe devices and their relations and how these devices strongly bind to the cyber-physical surroundings [12]. We discuss in the following the mechanisms of exposing OWL-T as a Service (OWLTaaS).

Figure 1 presents the key concepts of OWL-T that are anchored to Thing. Thing acts as a "parent class" for all forthcoming abstract things that will be semantically specified using OWL-T concepts. We refer to these concepts as *interaction, consumption,* and *operation* dimensions. A dimension encompasses conceptual areas whose benefits depend on how these areas are intended to be used during discovery of and composition of things, for example. Finally, a conceptual area is instantiated with concrete areas that receive values according to the area's intended use.

4.2   Exposing OWL-T as a Service

To expose OWL-T as a service, we identify 3 stakeholders that are provider, consumer, and facilitator. On the one hand, the provider's role is to make all relevant abstract things in a certain application domain, e.g., freight, "inherit" from Thing so they can be specified using OWL-T concepts of dimension, abstract area, and concrete area. At this stage of servitization, abstract things capture an

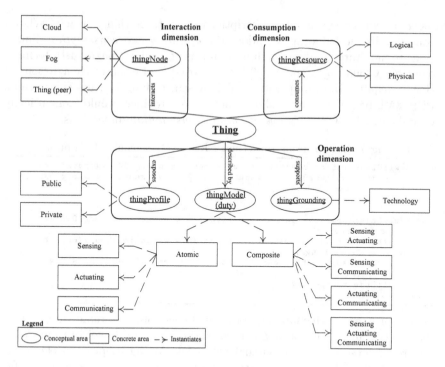

Fig. 1. Representation of OWL-T's key concepts anchored to Thing

application domain's core concepts such as truck, ship, invoice, and goods in the freight domain. On the other hand, the consumer's role is to identify the concrete things that would be relevant for her case-study and to bind these concrete things to the provider's abstract things, should this binding be possible. Finally, the facilitator's role is to implement as-a by allowing the binding of concrete things to abstract things. Additional details about the operations of the provider, consumer, and facilitator are given afterwards.

Figure 2 is a general representation of the concepts that underpin OWLTaaS. Plain (black) lines correspond to provider, dashed (red) lines correspond to consumer, and dotted (blue) lines correspond to facilitator.

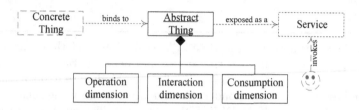

Fig. 2. Representation of OWLTaaS's concepts (Color figure online)

Provider develops the semantic descriptions of abstract things using OWL-T's concepts. In the following, we adopt the *operation* and *consumption* dimensions to illustrate an abstract thing in terms of profile (thingModel), technology (thingGrounding) upon which it is deployed, and resource (thingResource) that it requires during operation. This abstract thing is TruckThing whose RDF/XML-based Listing 1 shows how the provider would semantically describe it using OWL-T's *operation* and *consumption* dimensions.

Listing 1. Excerpt from TruckThing's RDF/XML semantic description

```
1    <owl:Class rdf:about="http://www.semanticweb.org/OWL-T#TruckThing">
2        <rdfs:subClassOf rdf:resource="http://www.semanticweb.org/OWL-T#
           Thing"/>
3    </owl:Class>
4
5    <owl:ObjectProperty rdf:about="http://www.semanticweb.org/OWL-T#
         described_by">
6        <rdfs:domain rdf:resource="http://www.semanticweb.org/OWL-T#
           TruckThing"/>
7        <rdfs:range rdf:resource="http://www.semanticweb.org/OWL-T#
           ThingModel"/>
8    </owl:ObjectProperty>
9    ...
```

Consumer proceeds with mapping concrete things onto electronic things. This mapping ensures that real (e.g., truck) and digital (e.g., invoice) things have electronic presences in the virtual world [2]. Acting as proxies, electronic things are described using a certain specification, as the consumer sees fit, for instance, JSON-based WoT TD [16]. Listing 2 illustrates MyTruckThing's JSON WoT-TD specification.

Listing 2. Excerpt from MyTruckThing's JSON WoT-TD specification

```
1    {"@context": "https://www.w3.org/2019/wot/td/v1",
2    "id": "urn:dev:ops:32473-WoTTruck-1",
3    "title": "MyTruckThing",
4    "securityDefinitions":{
5      "basic_sc": {"scheme": "basic", "in":"header"}},
6    "security": ["basic_sc"],
7    "properties":{
8        "pneumaticStatus" :{
9            "type": "string",
10           "forms": [{"href": "https://mytruck.example.com/status"}]}},
11   "actions":{
12       "drive":{
13           "forms": [{"href": "https://mytruck.example.com/drive"}]}},
14   "events":{
15       ...},
16   }
```

Facilitator becomes active at run-time by exposing abstract things as a service so, that, a consumer invokes the service and hence, initiates the binding of concrete things to abstract things. To allow the binding to happen, the facilitator relies on some correspondence mechanisms between the specification of concrete things (e.g., JSON WoT-TD) and the specification of abstract things in RDF/XML OWL-T. Should the correspondence happen to be incomplete (not all OWL-T details are identified in the specification of concrete things), the facilitator would complete the concrete thing's description with the assistance of consumers by adding the necessary OWL-T's concrete areas to this description. An illustration of this completion is presented in Sect. 4.3.

Prior to discussing OWLTaaS's technical doability, we briefly suggest some Quality-of-Service (QoS) properties that could drive the definition of Service Level Agreement (SLA) in the context of OWLTaaS. For this purpose, end-users correspond to consumers and providers correspond to facilitators.

– *Binding quality* defines how well a facilitator identifies abstract things according to the consumer's case study.
– *Binding time* defines the time that a facilitator would need to make concrete things bind to abstract things.

4.3   Demonstrating OWL-T as a Service

To demonstrate the technical doability of our servitization framework with focus on OWLTaaS, we developed a Java-based distributed system using the IDE NetBeans and Remote Method Invocation (RMI) package to support the interactions between the facilitator, consumer, and provider. From an RMI perspective, the provider and facilitator are deployed on the server side while the consumer is deployed on the client side.

– Provider is a set of Java classes that remotely expose the available abstract things to consumers. These classes provide the necessary methods to invoke remotely by the consumers so, that, they semantically enhance the descriptions of their concrete things. These methods allow among others to search for an abstract thing that could meet a consumer's requirements and to access their semantic description (i.e., OWL-T) in preparation for enhancing the descriptions of consumers' concrete things (i.e., JSON WoT-TD).
– Facilitator also is a set of Java classes allowing to expose abstract things as a service that consumers invoke when initiating the binding of concrete things to abstract things. This binding allows the consumer to select the semantic information that she needs to enhance the description of the current concrete thing based on its characteristics. For instance, pneumaticStatus property of MyTruckThing example could be improved with details related to useLevel as per Listing 3 lines 11–16.
– Consumer provides the consumer (i.e., user) with the necessary user graphical interfaces that support the interactions with both Provider and Facilitator. Figure 3 is an example of user interface to search for abstract things. Furthermore, Consumer includes a JSON parser that collects the content of any JSON WoT-TD specification prior to enhancing this specification with semantic details that the user would have selected.

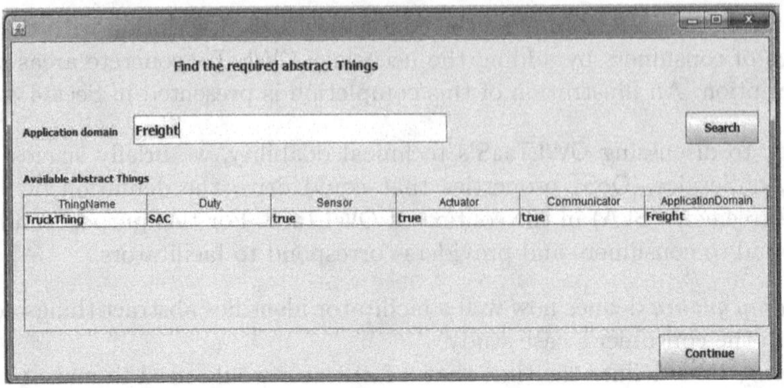

Fig. 3. Search facility for abstract things

Listing 3. Enhanced JSON WoT-TD specification of MyTruckThing

```
1   {"context": "https://www.w3.org/2019/wot/td/v1",
2   "id": "urn:dev:ops:32473-WoTTruck-1",
3   "title": "MyTruckThing",
4   "securityDefinitions":{
5   "basic_sc": {"scheme": "basic", "in":"header"}},
6   "security": ["basic_sc"],
7   "properties":{
8       "pneumaticStatus" :{
9           "type": "string",
10          "forms": [{"href": "https://mytruck.example.com/status"}]
11          properties:{
12          "useLevel" :{
13          "type": " integer",
14          "forms": [{" href ": "https :// mytruck.example.com/useLevel"}]
15          }
16      }
17  }},
18  "actions":{
19      "drive":{
20          "forms": [{"href": "https://mytruck.example.com/drive"}]}},
21  "events":{
22      ...},
23  }
```

5 Conclusion

Over the recent years, we identified many restrictions that are undermining the benefits of IoT. One of these restrictions, which we refer to as no-semantics, is preventing things from exchanging meaningful information and hence, engaging in collaborative sessions. To address the no-semantics restriction, we proposed OWL-T as an ontology for defining things and servitization as a mechanism for exposing this ontology's concepts as services. The result of this exposure is OWL-TaaS. A proof-of-concept of OWL-T and servitization combination is presented in the paper, as well. This combination was made possible thanks to an interaction model that we refer to as provider-facilitator-customer.

Our IoT servitization research-agenda consists of addressing other IoT restrictions, for instance silo and no-reasoning. On the one hand, the silo restriction that impedes things from collaborating could be addressed thanks to our concept of Process-of-Things (PoT) [9]. The servitization framework could be extended to offer PoT-as-a-Service (PoTaaS). On the other hand, the no-reasoning restriction that prevents things from adapting to new situations and learning from past experiences could be addressed thanks to the notion of cognitive things. Our servitization framework could be extended to offer Cognition-as-a-Service (CaaS) helping things to be "smarter". Finally, an additional item in our research agenda is to build a generic (regardless of any initiative) and integrated (including all restrictions) servitization framework so, that, IoT designers can capitalize on it when developing their applications.

References

1. Agarwal, R., et al.: Unified IoT ontology to enable interoperability and federation of testbeds. In: Proceedings of the 3rd IEEE World Forum on Internet of Things (WF-IoT 2016), Reston, VA, USA (2016)
2. Atzori, L., Carboni, D., Iera, A.: Smart things in the social loop: paradigms, technologies, and potentials. Ad Hoc Netw. **18**(16), 121–132 (2013)
3. Duan, Y., Sun, X., Longo, A., Lin, Z., Wan, S.: Sorting terms of "aaS' of everything as a service. Int. J. Netw. Distrib. Comput. **4**(1), 32–44 (2016)
4. Horn, P.: The new discipline of services science. Technical report, Bloomberg (2005). https://www.bloomberg.com/news/articles/2005-01-20/the-new-discipline-of-services-science. Accessed Feb 2020
5. Li, K., Jiang, L.: The research of web services composition based on context in Internet of Things. In: Proceedings of the IEEE International Conference on Computer Science and Automation Engineering (CSAE 2012), Shanghai, China (2012)
6. Maamar, Z., et al.: Towards a Quality-of-Thing based approach for assigning things to federations. Cluster Comput. **23**(3), 1589–1602 (2020). https://doi.org/10.1007/s10586-020-03047-9
7. Maamar, Z., et al.: Cognitive computing meets the Internet of Things. In: Proceedings of the 13th International Conference on Software Technologies (ICSOFT 2018), Porto, Portugal (2018)
8. Maamar, Z., Faci, N., Kajan, E., Asim, M., Qamar, A.: OWL-T for a semantic description of IoT. In: Darmont, J., Novikov, B., Wrembel, R. (eds.) ADBIS 2020. CCIS, vol. 1259, pp. 108–117. Springer, Cham (2020). https://doi.org/10.1007/978-3-030-54623-6_10
9. Maamar, Z., Sellami, M., Faci, N., Ugljanin, E., Sheng, Q.Z.: Storytelling integration of the Internet of Things into business processes. In: Weske, M., Montali, M., Weber, I., vom Brocke, J. (eds.) BPM 2018. LNBIP, vol. 329, pp. 127–142. Springer, Cham (2018). https://doi.org/10.1007/978-3-319-98651-7_8
10. Maglio, P.P., Spohrer, J.: Fundamentals of service science. Acad. Mark. Sci. **36**(4), 18–20 (2008). https://doi.org/10.1007/s11747-007-0058-9
11. Mzahm, A.M., Ahmad, M.S., Tang, A.Y.C.: Agents of Things (AoT): an intelligent operational concept of the Internet of Things (IoT). In: Proceedings of the 13th International Conference on Intellient Systems Design and Applications (ISDA 2013), Bangi, Malaysia (2013)

12. Seydoux, N., Drira, K., Hernandez, N., Monteil, T.: IoT-O, a core-domain IoT ontology to represent connected devices networks. In: Blomqvist, E., Ciancarini, P., Poggi, F., Vitali, F. (eds.) EKAW 2016. LNCS (LNAI), vol. 10024, pp. 561–576. Springer, Cham (2016). https://doi.org/10.1007/978-3-319-49004-5_36
13. Qamar, A., Muhammad, A., Maamar, Z., Baker, T., Saeed, S.: A Quality-of-Things model for assessing the Internet-of-Thing's non-functional properties. Trans. Emerg. Telecommun. Technol. (2019, forthcoming)
14. Vandermerwe, S., Rada, J.: Servitization of business: adding value by adding services. Eur. Manag. J. 6(4), 314–324 (1988)
15. Vargo, S.L., Lusch, R.F.: Service-dominant logic: continuing the evolution. J. Acad. Mark. Sci. 36, 1–10 (2008). https://doi.org/10.1007/s11747-007-0069-6
16. W3C: Web of Things (WoT) thing description. Technical report, W3C (2020)
17. Wu, Q., et al.: Cognitive Internet of Things: a new paradigm beyond connection. IEEE Internet Things J. 1(2), 129–143 (2014)

QoR-Driven Resource Selection for Hybrid Web Environments

Lara Kallab[1]([✉]), Richard Chbeir[2], and Michael Mrissa[3]

[1] Groupe Open, 92300 Levallois Perret, France
`lara.kallab@open-groupe.com`
[2] Univ Pau & Pays Adour, E2S UPPA, LIUPPA, EA3000, 64600 Anglet, France
`richard.chbeir@univ-pau.fr`
[3] InnoRenew CoE, Livade 6, 6310 Izola, Slovenia
`michael.mrissa@innorenew.eu`

Abstract. In the Web of Things (WoT) context, an increasing number of objects provide functions as RESTful services (resources), that can be composed with other existing resources, to create value-added processes (compositions). However, to form a composition, selecting the suitable resources is becoming more challenging, due to: (1) the growing number of resources providing identical functions, which calls for the use of Quality of Resource (QoR) to distinguish between them, and (2) the transient nature of resource availability as a result of objects' sporadic connectivity in the WoT environments. In this chapter, we present a QoR-driven resource selection approach that forms i-compositions (with $i \in \mathbb{N}^*$) offering different implementation alternatives. This is done using a selection strategy adaptor that considers QoR constraints and Inputs/Outputs matching of related resources, as well as resource availability and users' different needs (e.g., optimal compositions having the highest scores, and optimistic compositions having acceptable scores but obtained in more satisfactory delays). Analysis are made to evaluate our resource quality model against existing ones, and experiments are conducted in different environments setups to study the performance of our work.

Keywords: Hybrid web environments · Resource selection · i-compositions

1 Introduction

Nowadays, a plethora of Web environments (Web applications, Web platforms, etc.), publish their functions as RESTful services, i.e., self-contained and self-describing resources that follow the REpresentational State Transfer (REST) architectural style [7]. As the Web has become a major medium of communication, integrating objects (e.g., smart devices) into the Web and taking advantage of its open popular standards (e.g., HTTP), has created an emerging trend: the Web of Things (WoT) [1]. In the WoT, objects are abstracted as RESTful services, which are resources individually identifiable with a Uniform Resource

© Springer Nature Switzerland AG 2021
M. Aiello et al. (Eds.): Papazoglou Festschrift, LNCS 12521, pp. 189–202, 2021.
https://doi.org/10.1007/978-3-030-73203-5_15

Identifier (URI) and provide functions callable using HTTP methods (e.g., GET and POST). A resource is either (i) dynamic, connected to and removed from the Web environment at different instances, or (ii) static, always connected to the environment. In many cases, a single resource is not sufficient to satisfy specific user requests, and often, resources are combined forming a composition that achieves the desired results. To form a composition, selecting the appropriate resources is essential. However, several challenges arise:

1. **Selecting the appropriate resource for a function**: With the growing number of resources realizing the same function, selecting the appropriate one while considering user constraints (if given), is non-trivial for end-users. Therefore, taking into account the Quality of Resource (QoR) attributes used to differentiate resources having identical functions [15], is important to select the suitable resource for a function. The increasing number of candidate resources and their various QoR attributes [8] (e.g., Availability and Cost) require an automatic approach that facilitates the task for end-users, and accelerates the selection process. Also, during selection, considering the matching of the input and output (I/O) parameters of the related resources is essential to generate compositions that fit efficiently users needs.
2. **Forming different composition alternatives**: The selected dynamic resource(s) for a composition may be unavailable for execution. To avoid repeating the selection process to form new suitable composition, providing i-compositions (i ∈ $\mathbb{N}^*$), i.e., a set of compositions having different implementation alternatives, becomes important. These compositions respond to the user request by using, each, a different set of resources. This allows to substitute a composition that misses a resource, by another one consisting of available resources. Furthermore, in some cases, users require compositions having the highest possible scores, others may need compositions having acceptable scores obtained in more satisfactory delays, etc. Thus, forming compositions that are adaptive to different user needs is essential.

In the literature, some works [2,14,16] were based on Quality of Services (QoS) to select the most suitable ones according to user constraints or preferences, without taking into account I/O service matching and service dynamicity. Others [10,13] aimed at finding a sequence of services starting from given inputs and leading to the desired outputs, without considering service matching on the functional level, their QoS, and dynamicity. Also, none of the existing service composition approaches [3,6], forms several types of compositions realizing different user needs (optimal compositions having the highest scores, optimistic compositions having acceptable scores but obtained in more satisfactory delays, etc.).

To address the aforementioned challenges and existing limitations, we present, in this chapter, a QoR-driven resource selection that forms i-compositions (with i ∈ $\mathbb{N}^*$) offering different implementation alternatives for user request. To do so, we define a Selection Strategy Adaptor (SSA) that allows selecting the suitable resources, while considering user QoR constraints and I/O matching of related resources, as well as resource dynamicity and user requested composition type (e.g., optimal compositions having the highest scores, and optimistic compositions having acceptable scores but obtained in more satisfactory delays). Resource selection is automatic, i.e., based on semantic annotations integrated within resource descriptions expressed using Hydra [9] in our work.

The rest of the chapter is organized as follows. Section 2 motivates our work, and describes the main challenges and needs. Section 3 discusses related work and shows the originality of our solution. Section 4 details our resource selection solution. Section 5 compares our defined QoR model against existing works, and evaluates the solution performance. Finally, Sect. 6 concludes the chapter.

2   Motivation, Challenges and Needs

We motivate our work through OpenCEMS[1]: a Web platform that provides solutions for energy data management in connected environments. The platform allows to connect (1) stationary and mobile objects that provide static/dynamic resources, and (2) Web applications exposed as static resources. The resources, described in Hydra, are used for: collecting on-site data, preprocessing collected data, and analyzing data. Many requests occur in OpenCEMS. We consider a building manager that wants to predict the temperature in the conference room A. To satisfy his request, specified by the "ATP" (Air Temperature Prediction) function, it is important to select the appropriate resources realizing his need[2]. However, several challenges arise, as illustrated in Fig. 1:

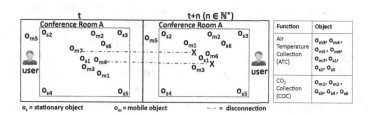

Fig. 1. Challenges illustration in the OpenCEMS platform

1. **Select the appropriate resources to form a suitable composition.** When several resources are identified having the same function required to answer "ATP", as "Air Temperature Collection", selecting the appropriate ones among others is not obvious for end-users, as the building manager. Therefore, QoR plays an essential role to select the suitable resources. For instance, object o_{s1} can be better than others (e.g., o_{m3} and o_{m4}) as it may

---

[1] Connected Environment & Distributed Energy Data Management Solutions: https://opencems.sigappfr.org/.

[2] We assume the resource discovery is already performed based on the required location.

have: (i) full battery capacity denoting a full availability, (ii) continuous connectivity to the environment (since it is static), (iii) cost free when using it, and (iv) high usage rate (it has been invoked many times). Considering these QoR, allows selecting the appropriate resources among other candidates. As many candidate resources can connect to openCEMS with various QoR, resource selection requires an automatic approach to facilitate and accelerate the task for the building manager. Such approach should also consider I/O matching of the linked resources to guarantee efficient composition results. Moreover, in some cases, the building manager may require:

(a) **Prediction results using the most qualified resources.** In this case, the resources to be selected are the ones having the highest values of quality aspects, independently of the selection response time, as the building manager may need to adjust the necessary temperature, in conference room A, for a meeting that will start in the late afternoon.

(b) **Fast but good prediction results.** As the building manager might be feeling very hot in the conference room A, he needs fast prediction results to regulate the temperature. This is done by selecting the first resources realizing his demand without the need to check others. However, and despite requiring fast results, it is important that the selected resources have minimal quality aspects to guarantee good composition results.

(c) **Always available results.** The building manager may need to have results at anytime of his request, i.e., even if dynamic resources are disconnected from the Web platform there are always other resources that can take over. Thus, the resources that will be selected are always connected to the environment (static resources) at both instants t and t+n.

In other particular cases, the building manager may define other needs as: (i) **Trusted results**, generated by only static resources already provided by the OpenCEMS Web platform (e.g., o_{s1}, o_{s2}, and o_{s5}), (ii) **Cost free results**, using resources without any charge, and **Reliable results**, using resources that can be linked in the most proper way (i.e., best I/O matching between the related resources), etc. Thus, it is necessary to consider user needs and constraints, and adapt resource selection accordingly.

2. **Form several composition alternatives**. The selected dynamic resource(s) for a composition may be unavailable during execution. As such, at instant t, 5 mobile objects providing "ATC" are positioned in the conference room A. If o_{m4} provides the appropriate resource among these objects, it will be selected to take part in the composition. However, at t+n, o_{m4} is disconnected, and thus, the composition will miss a resource if the composition execution time is $\geq$ t+n. To avoid repeating resource selection process to form a new suitable solution with available resources, it is important to identify i-compositions during resource selection, with $i \in \mathbb{N}^*$.

To address these challenges and respond to user needs, we propose a QoR-driven resource selection adapted to: (i) different requested composition types (e.g., Optimal, Optimistic, and Optimistic cost-free), and (ii) QoR constraints.

Our solution considers I/O matching between the related resources and resource dynamicity (when it is necessary), to form the required i-compositions.

3   Related Work

3.1   QoS-Based Approaches

In [2], a quality-driven solution for resource selection is presented. The approach uses a set of quality attributes incorporated into each resource description expressed with Hydra, and implements a skyline-based algorithm that reduces the set of candidates for a given task. In [4], a heuristic is proposed to solve QoS-aware Web service composition problem. It uses a backtracking algorithm on the results computed by a Linear Program relaxation, while considering user constraints given to the overall composition. In [14], an approach for a service selection based on both qualitative and quantitative user QoS preference with services trust properties is presented. The solution is applicable in Big Data Web environments consisting of massive migrated services, i.e., business applications, to the cloud. The work in [5] proposes a QoS-aware service composition based on QoS correlations. It produces the optimal composite service, and considers service plans with sequence structure.

Discussion: Although these works consider QoS attributes and user constraints/preferences, they neglect services dynamicity and I/O matching between the linked services. Moreover, they are not adapted to generate different composition types to realize different user needs.

3.2   I/O-Based Approaches

Work [13], presents a graph-based framework for automatic service composition, by focusing on the semantic I/O services matching. It produces a service composition containing the minimum number of services, and multiple compositions can be extracted satisfying user request in terms of I/O. In [10], a formal model is provided for an AI planning-oriented service composition. It precomputes the I/O semantic similarity between services, according to causal links, which are logical dependencies among input and output parameters of different services.

Discussion: Despite computing I/O services semantics, these works do not consider the functional aspect of the related services, nor even the dynamicity of services. Also, QoS attributes and user constraints/preferences are neglected.

3.3   k-Compositions Approaches

A top-k automatic service composition solution is presented in [6]. It adopts the idea of MapReduce, by mapping the top-k service compositions into multiple tasks that can be executed in parallel. The solution considers one quality of service, i.e., Response time, and I/O services similarities to filter the services. In [3], an approach for composing the top-k DaaS (Data as a Service) services is proposed. The top-k compositions are computed based on a fuzzy score, associated for each service and service composition, and fuzzy user preferences expressed in fuzzy terms (e.g., "cheap" for services price).

Discussion: Although these works produce several service compositions, and consider QoS attributes, they are not designed to handle service dynamicity, nor the generation of different composition types answering user needs. Also, only in [6], I/O matching and QoS attributes are used in the same approach.

4   QoR-Driven Resource Selection for i-Compositions

4.1   General Overview

Figure 2 shows the process overview of our resource selection, applicable in hybrid Web environments providing static and/or dynamic resources. The process is used to form i-compositions responding to user request, r, and adapted to user request type. The latter includes one of the following desired compositions types: (i) optimal, denoting compositions having the highest scores, (ii) optimistic, referring to compositions having acceptable scores, i.e., $\geqslant$ a specific computed threshold (see Sect. 4.4), or (iii) hybrid, denoting compositions having acceptable scores but whose dynamic aspect is considered, guaranteeing the existence of a composition at any instant. A composition type can be followed optionally by other subtypes (e.g., trusted, denoting that only static resources can be part of the compositions). As for the user request, r, it is defined formally as:

Definition 1 - $r = (f, P, C)$, where:

- f, is the user requested function, selected from a list of functions, F, provided by the resources connected to the Web environment at the current instant.

  - P, is the set of parameters necessary to execute f, such as the required location (e.g., conference room A). P is mainly used by the resource discovery process, which is out of scope of this chapter, to identify the needed resources.
  - C, is the given user constraints according to which, i-compositions are obtained, and such that $C = Q_c \cup i \cup W \cup d$, with:
    - $Q_c = Q_c^{res} \cup Q_c^f$, refers to the set of constraints given to the resources (Q_c^{res}) and to their provided functions (Q_c^f), with $Q_c^{res} = \bigcup_{i=1}^{n} \{q_i^{res}\}$, and $Q_c^f = \bigcup_{j=1}^{m} \{q_j^f\}$, and where:
      - n is the number of attributes describing a resource, and m the number of attributes describing its provided functions (see Sect. 4.2).
      - $q_i^{res} | q_j^f = [min_{i|j} - max_{i|j}]$, with $min_{i|j}, max_{i|j}$ are respectively the minimum and maximum values given for q_i^{res} and q_j^f.
    - $i \in \mathbb{N}^*$, is the desired number of compositions. By default i=1, and can be only specified for optimal and optimistic compositions. For the hybrid compositions, the number of solutions depends from resource dynamicity aspect of the formed compositions (see Sect. 4.4).

○ $W = \{w_{qor}, w_{io}\}$, are the weights given respectively to the score of the resources and their I/O matching, during compositions score calculation (see Sect. 4.3). $w_{qor}, w_{io} \in R^+$ and are bounded by [0, 1].

○ d, is the degree value rate (in %) of the threshold, T (see Sect. 4.4), that refers to the minimal acceptable score of the i-compositions.

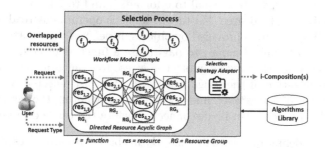

Fig. 2. Overview of the resource selection process

The selection process, illustrated in Fig. 2, is executed when there are several candidate resources for at least one required function necessary to realize user request, r. The required functions for r form a Workflow Model, WM. During the process, the resources realizing an identical function are grouped into the same resource group, RG. Each resource of a RG can be linked to the resources included in the RG related to the next function (as defined in WM), forming a Directed Resource Acyclic Graph, DRAG. In order to satisfy user different requested composition types, we define a Selection Strategy Adaptor (SSA) that adapts to user needs to form the required i-set of resource compositions. Using a graph algorithm, as DFS (Depth First Search), from the algorithms library, SSA can traverse DRAG to compute the I/O matching of the linked eligible resources (whose QoR values respect user constraints defined in Q_c), and produces optimal compositions having the highest scores. SSA allows also to form compositions having acceptable scores, i.e., $\geqslant$ a computed threshold, T (see Sect. 4.4, obtained in more satisfactory delays. Such threshold is computed for the compositions types: optimistic and hybrid.

4.2 Preliminaries

In our work, a resource, res, can be either static, res^s, or dynamic, res^d. It provides a set of functions: $F = \bigcup_{i=1}^{N^*} \{f_i\}$, with: $f_i = (n, I, O, m, Q_f)$ denotes a single function, and where: n refers to f_i name, I denotes the input(s) of f_i, O denotes the output(s) of f_i, m is the HTTP verb used to call f_i, and Q_f is the set of quality attributes related to each function (f_i). $Q_f = \bigcup_{i=1}^{N^*} \{(qf_i : vf_i)\}$, with qf_i is the name of the quality attribute, and $vf_i \in \mathbb{R}^+$. Each resource has also directly related quality attributes: $Q_{res} = \bigcup_{i=1}^{N^*} \{(qres_i : vres_i)\}$, with $qres_i$ is the name of the attribute, and $vres_i \in \mathbb{R}^+$.

In the literature, we find various QoR used to differentiate resources with similar functions [15]. In this chapter, we consider 4 QoR, where some are related to the resource itself, and others related to each of its provided functions:

- **Dynamicity**, is the quality aspect of whether the resource is always available (res^s) or not (res^d). It is equal to 0 for res^s, and to 1 for res^d.
- **Availability**, is the degree (%) to which res is operational/ready for immediate use. For resources provided by objects, it denotes their battery capacity.
- **Cost**, is the amount of money to pay to use a function of res.
- **Usage**, is a value that increments when a resource function is used. To avoid the re-initialization of the usage when a res^d is disconnected, we define for each function of a res^d, a Time To Live value denoting the maximum time during which a res^d can be disconnected before the usage decrements by 1.

Based on res definition, we extended Hydra-based resource description[3], to include the QoR values. QoR are grouped as: (i) maximization attributes, whose values should be maximized (e.g., Availability), and (ii) minimization attributes, whose values should be minimized (e.g., Cost). They are used to compute, for each provided resource function, a global score that is defined as: score(res_f) = $\sum_{i=1}^{N^*} \{vres_i\} + \sum_{i=1}^{N^*} \{vf_i\}$, where $vres_i$ (excepting the "Dynamicity" attribute value) and vf_i are normalized based on the work in [11].

4.3   QoR-Based Resource Graph: Formal Modeling

The functions required for **f** in **r**, define with their dependencies a Workflow Model, WM. Based on the functions order in WM, the overlapped resources are linked, forming a Directed Resource Acyclic Graph, DRAG, that is defined as:

Definition 2 - $DRAG = (RES, Rel, f_{RES}, f_{Rel})$:

- *RES, is the set of the identified and overlapped static/dynamic resources.*
- *Rel, is the set of relations linking the resources together.*
- *f_{RES}, is the function computing the score of each resource function.*
- *f_{Rel}, is the function linking the resources together, and computing their link score based on their I/O similarities.*

The resources providing the same function, form a resource group, RG_f, relative to that function, where: $RG_f = \bigcup_{i=1}^{m} \{res_{(f,i)}\}$, with m is the number of candidate resources realizing function f, and $res_{(f,i)}$ refers to the resource res_i providing f. A resource composition, RC, consists of a set of resources included, each, in a different RG_f, where: RC = $\bigcup_{f=1}^{n} \{res_{(f,i)}\}$, such that n is the number of functions in WM, and $i \in m$, with m denotes the number of resources in the correspondent RG_f. During selection, I/O matching

---

[3] Hydra description example is available online: https://tinyurl.com/tose56k

score between every linked eligible resources is computed, using any similarity measure function between keywords (as Jaccard measure [12]), as follows: $\mathrm{sim}(res_{(f,i)}, res_{(f',j)}) = \sum_{u=1}^{U} \sum_{v=1}^{V} sim(out_u^{res(f,i)}, in_v^{res(f',j)})$, with:

- $res_{f,i}$, $res_{f',j}$, denote resources that belong, respectively, to RG_f and $RG_{f'}$, where f precedes f' in WM.
- out_u, is an output of $res_{f,i}$, and U is the number of $res_{f,i}$ outputs.
- in_v, is an input of $res_{f',j}$, and V is the number of $res_{f',j}$ inputs.

Each RC in DRAG has a score, score(RC), with: **score(RC) = Score(RES) + Score(Rel)**, and where:

- **Score(RES)** = $\sum_{f=1}^{n} score(res_{(f,i)})$, is the scores sum of the involved resources realizing the required WM, with n is the number of WM functions.
- **Score(Rel)** = $\sum sim(res_{(f,i)}, res_{(f',j)})$, is the sum of I/O similarity scores of each 2 eligible linked resources in RC, where: f precedes f' in WM, and $sim(res_{(f,i)}, res_{(f',j)}) \in [0, 1]$.

Score(RES) and Score(Rel) can be multiplied, each, by a weight value defined in **r**, allowing users to assign them a priority for compositions score calculation.

4.4 Selection Strategy Adaptor for i-Compositions

In order to form i-compositions satisfying different user needs, we define the Selection Strategy Adaptor (SSA) that allows the generation of 3 main compositions types: (1) optimal, (2) optimistic, and (3) hybrid (see Sect. 4.1). Each of these composition types can be followed optionally by several composition subtypes, e.g., (i) trusted, refers to compositions having only static resources that are already provided by the Web environment, and (ii) efficient, denotes compositions that include resources with minimal acceptable normalized usage value. As shown in Table 1, the composition subtypes are defined according to either: (i) a minimal QoR attribute value (e.g., Dynamicity for trusted compositions), or (ii) a set of minimal QoR attributes values (Availability, Cost, and Usage for qualified compositions), or (iii) a minimal Score(Rel) (as for reliable compositions), computed based on "l", which is the number of dependencies links between the required functions in WM. However, in addition to these constraints highlighted in red, both optimistic and hybrid composition types should respect other QoR attributes and Score(Rel) values, to ensure having compositions with an acceptable score(RC), and thus, good compositions results. If optimal compositions subtypes are needed (e.g., optimal cost-free), a filtering process is executed before score(RC) calculations. Such filtering is done based on the maximum values of the constraints for which the values are highlighted in red in Table 1, among the resources in DRAG. For example, Optimal Efficient compositions will include resources having Max(Usage), which refers to the maximum value of the Usage attribute among the resources in DRAG.

Table 1. QoR values and Score(Rel) in optimistic and hybrid compositions subtypes

	Dynamicity	Availability	Cost	Usage	Score(Rel)
Trusted	0	$\geqslant 0.5$	$\leqslant 0.25$	$\geqslant 0.5$	$\geqslant (1 \times 0.5)$
Cost-free	0|1	$\geqslant 0.5$	0	$\geqslant 0.5$	$\geqslant (1 \times 0.5)$
Efficient	0|1	$\geqslant 0.5$	$\leqslant 0.25$	$\geqslant 0.75$	$\geqslant (1 \times 0.5)$
Effective	0|1	$\geqslant 0.75$	$\leqslant 0.25$	$\geqslant 0.5$	$\geqslant (1 \times 0.5)$
Qualified	0|1	$\geqslant 0.75$	$\leqslant 0.25$	$\geqslant 0.75$	$\geqslant (1 \times 0.5)$
Reliable	0|1	$\geqslant 0.5$	$\leqslant 0.25$	$\geqslant 0.5$	$\geqslant (1 \times 0.75)$

Based on the given composition type, SSA forms the necessary i-compositions. The i value ($\in \mathbb{N}^*$) can be determined by the user in r, for the 2 main types: optimal and optimistic, where SSA retrieves the i-compositions having the best or acceptable scores respectively. As for hybrid compositions, SSA stops generating the solutions having acceptable scores until having one containing only static resources, guaranteeing the existence of a composition at any instance. If the user defines in r, constraints that do not align with the designated composition subtype constraints, the latter are considered.

When optimistic or hybrid compositions are required, SSA applies several steps:

1. **Compute the minimum score of an acceptable composition.** A composition is considered acceptable, if its score(RC) is $\geqslant$ a specific Threshold, T. When optimistic or hybrid composition types are requested without subtypes, T is defined as: T = $[(n \times Avg(Q_c)) + (l \times 0.5)] \times (d/100)$, where:
   - **n** is the total number of functions in WM.
   - **$Avg(Q_c)$** are the average of the normalized QoR constraints defined in r (excepting the "Dynamicity" attribute). If Q_c are not given, the average of each QoR is calculated using their maximum values among DRAG.
   - l, is the number of the dependencies links between WM functions. We consider that there is, at least, an I/O similarity match (=0.5) between any two linked resources.
   - d, is the composition acceptance degree value (%) given in user request. If subtype compositions are requested, T is computed as: $T_{subtype} = [(n \times Q) + (l \times s)] \times (d/100)$, with Q denotes the minimum values of the attributes as in Table 1 (excepting the "Dynamicity"), and s $\in [0,1]$ is the minimum I/O similarity matching score between any two linked resources. s = 0.75 whenever subtype = reliable, and s = 0.5 for the rest of subtype values.

2. **Compute the score of a composition formed by eligible resources.** To do so, a generator is used to get the possible set of RC without score calculation. During RC generation, the following conditions are performed:
   (i) If a resource in RC is not eligible, it is registered in array, **arr_notEl**, and another possible RC is generated
   (ii) If all the resources of RC are eligible, score(RC) is computed. If score(RC) $\geqslant$ **T**, RC is saved into the suitable compositions array, **arr_suitRC**, if not, another possible RC is generated

While analyzing a RC, if a resource is in **arr_notEl**, another possible RC is generated. If not, conditions (i) and (ii) are tested. If optimistic compositions are required, the generator stops when having i-compositions respecting T. However, if hybrid solutions are needed, the generator stops when having a composition that respects T, and contains only static resources (always available). SSA results are the set of RC included in **arr_suitRC**.

5 Evaluation and Discussion

In this section, we compare our QoR model to existing works, and evaluate our resource selection solution in a simulated environment provided by OpenCEMS. OpenCEMS offers 2 types of operation: real and simulated. As the real environment is currently being developed with a limited number of resources, in this chapter, we evaluated our work in the simulated functioning of OpenCEMS. The evaluation in the real environment will be presented in a dedicated work. In the experiments, we considered the requested composition type is hybrid, to focus on resources dynamicity aspect while forming the compositions. During the tests, conducted on a Linux Debian (64 bits) virtual machine, with 1 dedicated Intel® Core™ i7-46000 CPU @ 2.10 GHz 2.70 GHz processor and 1 GB RAM, we show the response time (in ms) based on an average of 5 sequential executions.

5.1 Comparison with Existing QoS Models

The comparison between our QoR model against the QoS model of existing works [2,4,14], is done independently of the number and type of the QoS used, since our work supports various attributes as long as they are presented in resources descriptions. The work in [2] uses 3 attributes: Performance: [0–10], Availability: [0–100], and Reputation: [0–5]. During selection and based on user constraints, a service is chosen over a candidate service if all of its QoS are equal or better than the other, preventing thus having optimistic/hybrid compositions having acceptable overall QoS. Also, and besides neglecting I/O matching of the linked services, by applying our threshold formula, a service with a high attribute value (Availability = 90) and a very low value for another one (Performance = 2) is selected over a service with acceptable values for both attributes (Availability = 70 and Performance = 6), as QoS are not normalized. In [4], several QoS are used to describe the services as Response Time and Availability. Contrary to our work, user constraints are given to the global composition (e.g., the overall response time should be <50 s) and not to each service, thus, aggregation functions are used for every QoS parameter. Moreover, weights are given to each QoS while computing the composition score. However, in our approach, user constraints are given to each of the involved services, and weights are assigned to (i) the overall services score and (ii) the overall I/O score that is not considered in [4]. In [14], a service has a score based on the sum of weighted utility functions relative to each QoS attribute. Similar to our work, QoS are normalized and user constraints are given to each service. However, the work does not define a global composition score, since the service of a specific task with the highest score is selected. Therefore, and apart of neglecting I/O matching of related services, no optimistic/hybrid solutions with acceptable scores can be formed.

5.2 Resource Selection Performance

For the selection tests, we varied: (1) the number of overlapped resources per function, and (2) the number of functions required in the WM. For these 2 cases, we applied several scenarios: (i) All static resources in DRAG are eligible, (ii) 50% of the static resources in DRAG are eligible, and (iii) all DRAG resources are dynamic and eligible. For (i) and (ii), the first generated possible compositions (without score calculation) include dynamic resources, thus, the selection process continue generating compositions until having one including only static resources with acceptable score. In the best cases, static resources are traversed first, and the selection process responds more rapidly. In the tests, each resource has 2 inputs and 2 outputs, and user constraints are given to: Dynamicity (where static and dynamic resources can be selected), Availability, Cost, and Usage. In the experiments, we assumed that the I/O similarity score between a resource and another related one is ≥ 0.5. In Fig. 3, in which the workflow consists of 3 functions, response time evolves with the growing number of resources.

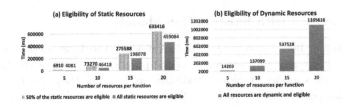

Fig. 3. Response time while varying number of resources

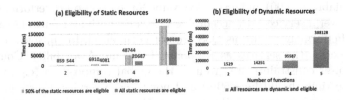

Fig. 4. Response time while varying number of functions

Comparing Fig. 3(a) to (b), response time increments less significantly with the existence of static eligible resources, as the selection process stops when having a composition of static resources. Figure 3(b) represents the worst case scenario, where DRAG contains only dynamic resources that are eligible. Thus, all compositions scores are computed, causing an important response time with the evolution of resources number. Figure 4(a), in which resource number per function is fixed to 5, shows that response time increases with the number of required functions. Similar to the first case, the selection process is faster when there are static eligible resources, as the selection process stops before the generation of the rest of the possible compositions. As for Fig. 4(b), response time evolves significantly, since DRAG contains dynamic eligible resources, thus, all compositions scores are calculated. The results highlight the importance of the existence of static eligible resources in DRAG, as the selection process stops when having a composition including static resources with an acceptable score. When dynamic resources exist, the response time increases, as their dynamicity is considered. The results also show that the increasing number of resources affects more the response time, comparing to the number of functions.

6 Conclusion

This chapter presents a QoR-driven resource selection approach that forms i-compositions ($i \in \mathbb{N}^*$) in Hybrid Web environments connecting static resources (always available), and dynamic resources (connected/disconnected at different instances). To do so, we defined a Selection Strategy Adapter that considers different compositions types (e.g., Optimal and Optimistic) and subtypes (e.g., Cost-free), QoR constraints, as well as resource I/O matching and dynamicity. Analysis are made to compare our QoR model with existing works, and tests are conducted to study our solution in a simulated Web environment offered by OpenCEMS. In the future, we plan to evaluate our work in the OpenCEMS real functioning, while considering subtypes compositions. We also seek to deploy an automatic orchestration to execute the compositions.

References

1. Barnaghi, P., Sheth, A., Henson, C.: From data to actionable knowledge: big data challenges in the web of things [guest editors' introduction]. IEEE Intell. Syst. **28**(6), 6–11 (2013)
2. Basholli, A., Lagkas, T.: Resource request mapping techniques for OFDMA networks. In: Resource Management in Mobile Computing Environments. MOST, vol. 3, pp. 145–163. Springer, Cham (2014). https://doi.org/10.1007/978-3-319-06704-9_7
3. Karim Benouaret et al. Top-k web services compositions: a fuzzy-set-based approach. In: ACM-Symposium on Applied Computing (SAC), pp. 1038–1043 (2011)
4. Berbner, R., et al.: Heuristics for QoS-aware web service composition. In: ICWS 2006, pp. 72–82. IEEE (2006)
5. Deng, S., et al.: Service selection for composition with QoS correlations. IEEE Trans. Serv. Comput. **9**(2), 291–303 (2014)
6. Deng, S., et al.: Top-k automatic service composition: a parallel method for large-scale service sets. IEEE T-ASE **11**(3), 891–905 (2014)

7. Fielding, R.T., Taylor, R.N.: Architectural Styles and the Design of Network-Based Software Architectures, vol. 7. University of California, Irvine (2000)
8. Kaewbanjong, K., Intakosum, S.: QoS attributes of web services: a systematic review and classification. J. Adv. Manage. Sci. **3**(3), 194–202 (2015)
9. Lanthaler, M., Gütl, C.: Hydra: a vocabulary for hypermedia-driven web APIs. In: LDOW, vol. 996 (2013)
10. Lécué, F., Léger, A.: A formal model for semantic web service composition. In: Cruz, I., et al. (eds.) ISWC 2006. LNCS, vol. 4273, pp. 385–398. Springer, Heidelberg (2006). https://doi.org/10.1007/11926078_28
11. Murakami, Y., Lin, D., Ishida, T. (eds.): Services Computing for Language Resources. CT. Springer, Singapore (2018). https://doi.org/10.1007/978-981-10-7793-7
12. Niwattanakul, S., et al.: Using of Jaccard coefficient for keywords similarity. In: Proceedings of IMECS, vol. 1, pp. 380–384 (2013)
13. Rodriguez-Mier, P., et al.: An integrated semantic web service discovery and composition framework. IEEE TSC **9**(4), 537–550 (2015)
14. Wang, H., et al.: Effective bigdata-space service selection over trust and heterogeneous QoS preferences. IEEE TSC **11**(4), 644–657 (2015)
15. Wang, L., et al.: A survey on bio-inspired algorithms for web service composition. In: Proceedings of the 2012 IEEE CSCWD, pp. 569–574. IEEE (2012)
16. Xiaofei, X., et al.: Novel artificial bee colony algorithms for QoS-aware service selection. IEEE Trans. Serv. Comput. **12**(2), 247–261 (2016)

IoTSec: A Lightweight and Holistic IoT Security Based on IoT Data Contextualisation and Homomorphic Encryption

Ali Yavari$^{(\boxtimes)}$(iD) and Dimitrios Georgakopolous(iD)

Internet of Things Lab, Digital Research Innovation Capability Platform, Faculty of Science, Engineering, and Technology, Swinburne University of Technology, Melbourne, Australia
{ayavari,dgeorgakopoulos}@swin.edu.au

Abstract. The Internet of Things incorporates billions of sensors, cameras, RFID and other machines that observe and/or affect the physical world, as well as IoT applications that harvest and analyse IoT data in the cloud, edge computers, and/or the IoT devices themselves. To realise its full potential IoT must ensure the security of the IoT data and related applications that support the IoT-based services and products that are provided to their consumers. Although IoT devices, networks, and computing resources support robust security standards and include related mechanisms that can secure IoT data within the scope of these IoT components, compositions of such point security solutions often fail to ensure the security of IoT data across the IoT ecosystem. In this article we will discuss the main challenges in securing IoT data acquisition, communication, analysis, actuation and illustrate the need for IoT security solutions that are both holistic and lightweight. In addition, we propose a holistic and lightweight IoT security mechanism that via a novel combination of contextualisation with homomorphic encryption prevents harmful outcomes from lack of IoT data security.

Keywords: Internet of Things · Security · Contextualisation · Homomorphic encryption

1 Introduction

The Internet of Things (IoT) combines billions of IoT devices (e.g., sensors, cameras, RFID readers, wearables, etc.) that sense the physical world and send sensor observation data (we refer to as IoT data) to IoT applications that run in the cloud, edge computers, and/or the IoT devices themselves [14].

According to Intel, the number of such connected IoT devices has reached 26.6 billion in 2019, and it is expected to exceed 75 billion by the end of 2025. The unprecedented ability of IoT to observe the physical world and provide

© Springer Nature Switzerland AG 2021
M. Aiello et al. (Eds.): Papazoglou Festschrift, LNCS 12521, pp. 203–217, 2021.
https://doi.org/10.1007/978-3-030-73203-5_16

valuable information allows it to address several grand challenges in our society and support novel IoT services and products that were unachievable before due to lack of appropriate information. Nevertheless, the full potential of IoT is still far from being realised because the IoT data security is hindered by lack of a holistic and lightweight data security solution.

IoT data security is needed because the sensor data that are generated by IoT devices, transported by a variety of networks (e.g., NB IoT, LoRA, BLE, WiFI, Broadband) and analysed by IoT applications running in the cloud or other computers closer to the sensors, may be sensitive and must be kept private and secure. For example, sensitive IoT data that need to be secured include: (1) health-related sensor data, such as vital signs, movements, cardiac echo data, etc., that can be used to determine the health condition of an individual [37], (2) smart parking meter data that can be expose the location of a vehicles and its driver [47] and, (3) smart electricity meter data that can be used to monitor the presence and activities of people at a home or work [51]. lack of protection for such sensitive IoT data can cause serious financial lose, social harm, harm or even death form related criminal activity. To ensure IoT data security and prevent such harmful outcomes from lack of IoT data security we must employee security solutions that are holistic and lightweight.

An IoT security solution is holistic when it incorporates a combination of security techniques that when they are applied to an IoT solution (i.e., the IoT devices, networks, computing resources, and applications that support an end product or service) will result is a recognisably secure IoT solution.

Currently there many existing security standards and related techniques (e.g., [6,24,35]) for defending IoT devices and the data they produce, protecting IoT data on the move (i.e., IoT data transmitted form IoT device to a computer that process them), and securing IoT data in situ (i.e., IoT data collected in the cloud for use by IoT applications. However, IoT is an ecosystem of more than just IoT devices, networks, computers and application where scalability, interoperability and volatility considerably complicate the IoT security solution. Therefore, if the security techniques that are supported by the variety of IoT devices, networks, computers and applications are not considered holistically, it is possible to deliver an insecure IoT solution to the marketplace, even if it meets all of the existing individual security standards [2].

A main research challenge in holistic IoT security is to device context- and risk-based security mechanism that are adaptive to support various IoT applications but also take into account the IoT application constraints so as not to hamper competitiveness in the marketplace.

An IoT security solution is lightweight when it incorporates security techniques that IoT devices can implement and compute with the limited computing resources they have and at the same time meet the constraints (e.g., time bounds) of the IoT applications they support. For example, many IoT devices have modest computing and storage resources that fall short in meeting the resource and storage demand of most of encryption techniques that are current used for general-purpose internet computing.

This paper discusses the main security challenges in IoT data acquisition, communication, storage, and analysis. To address these challenges, it proposes a holistic and lightweight IoT security technique that combines IoT data contextualisation with homomorphic encryption. This novel security technique provides efficient IoT data security by preventing both disclosure and unauthorised access. To encrypt and decrypt IoT data we utilise the homomorphic encryption algorithm we proposed in [18] and for contextualisation we employee the framework we introduced in [29, 45, 48].

The remaining of this article is organised as follows. Section 2 presents an overview of existing lightweight techniques for IoT security. In Sect. 3 include present an overview of holistic techniques for IoT security. Section 4 presents a contextualisation technique that provides both holistic and lightweight IoT security by utilising a combination of contextualisation and homomorphic encryption techniques. Section 6 present a conclusion.

2   Overview of Techniques for Lightweight IoT Security

In this section, we will describe existing lightweight techniques for IoT security.

2.1   Key Agreement Techniques

To secure communication in the IoT, it is important to encrypt the data sent between sensor nodes, gateways and other devices due to the public nature of the internet. Keys for encryption must be agreed upon by communicating nodes [19]. Due to resource constraints, key agreement in IoT is non-trivial. Many key agreement schemes used in general networks, such as Kerberos [26] and RSA [33], may not be suitable for the IoT because it usually has no trusted infrastructure. Pre-distribution of secret keys to all pairs of nodes is not viable due to the large amount of memory used when the network size is large. To overcome this problem, a random key pre-distribution scheme [12] has been proposed, where each sensor node receives a random subset of keys from a large key pool before deployment. Any two nodes can find a common key within their subsets and use it to secure their communication. Without requiring any key pre-distribution, data sensed within the IoT has been used to establish the common secret key. For example, in [40], two sensors, in a Body Sensor Network (BSN), used the common electrocardiogram signals of a patient to establish a secret key.

Roman et al. [34], Du et al. [11] and Camtepe et al. [9] analysed the applicability of several link-layer oriented Key Management System (KMS), which establish keys for sensor nodes within the same Wireless Sensor Network (WSN) using techniques such as linear algebra, combinatorics and algebraic geometry. However, the authors mention that not all mathematically-based KMS protocols can fulfil the IoT context. According to their analysis result, only [11] and [21] might be suitable for some IoT scenarios.

2.2   Identity Protection Techniques

Hu *et al.* [16] proposed an identity-based system that, protects the location information of IoT devices during emergency situations. In this approach, each user communicates with others using Virtual Identity (VID), which does not contain any real information about the user. Under this architecture, users' privacy can be protected well because they only send VID(s) to communicate, and VID is anonymous and unlinkable to users. The location information will finally be sent to the user making a request only after verification of their identity. In the IoT, verifying the identities of 'things' is crucial to preventing unauthorised access to users' private data, and granting access to legitimate users only. Liu *et al.* [22] propose an authentication protocol for IoT systems. Under the proposed protocol, "things" and objects are end nodes, and each node has a unique global address for connecting over the internet. To establish a session key, both secret-key cryptosystem (SKC) and Public Key Cryptography (PKC) have been considered for IoT environments, but they all suffer several problems. For example, SKC requires large amount of memory to store key chains and PKC suffers from high energy consumption. Kalra *et al.* [19] proposed an Elliptic Curve Cryptography (ECC) based key establishment method suitable for IoT environments. Their analysis indicates that the proposed protocol can prevent eavesdropping, man-in-the middle attacks, key control attacks, and replay attacks.

2.3   Attribute-Based Encryption Techniques

As a large amount of sensed data is stored in sensor nodes or databases, it is important to control access to it. ABE [36] was used to control access to sensor data in [31,50]. In traditional public-key cryptography, a message is encrypted for a specific receiver using the receiver's public-key. Identity Based Encryption (IBE) [8] changed the traditional understanding of public-key encryption by allowing the public-key to be an arbitrary string, *e.g.*, the email address of the receiver. ABE goes one step further and defines the identity not atomic but as a set of attributes, *e.g.*, roles, and messages can be encrypted with respect to subsets of attributes (key-policy ABE - KP-ABE) or policies defined over a set of attributes (ciphertext-policy ABE - CP-ABE). The key issue is, that someone should only be able to decrypt a ciphertext if the person holds a key for "matching attributes". User keys are issued by a trusted party. In CP-ABE, a user's private-key is associated with a set of attributes and a ciphertext specifies an access policy over a defined universe of attributes within the system. A user will be able to decrypt a ciphertext, if and only if their attributes satisfy the policy of the respective ciphertext. Policies may be defined over attributes using conjunctions, dis-junctions. For instance, let us assume that the universe of attributes is defined to be {A = General, B = Nurse, C = Doctor, and D = Specialist} and User 1 receives a key to attributes {A,B} while User 2 to attribute {D}. If a ciphertext is encrypted with respect to the policy $(A \wedge C) \vee D$, then User 2 will be able to decrypt, while User 1 will not be able to decrypt. In KP-ABE, an access policy is encoded into the users secret key, *e.g.*, $(A \wedge C) \vee D$, and a ciphertext is computed with respect to a set of attributes, *e.g.*, {A,B}. In this example the user would not be able to decrypt the ciphertext but would for instance be able to decrypt a ciphertext with respect to {A,C}. Based on KP-ABE, Fine-grained Distributed Access Control (FDAC) was proposed for IoT in [50]. FDAC is resistant against user collusion, *i.e.*, cooperation by colluding users will not lead to the disclosure of additional sensor data. Based on CP-ABE, another fine-grained access control scheme for IoT was proposed in [31] which allows AND-based policies only.

2.4   k-Anonymity Techniques

IoT data are valuable for knowledge discovery. Given that the IoT is regarded as the next generation worldwide network that connects every necessary object to facilitate our daily lives, security is a major concern and challenge. Current solutions to this problem include the [4] use k-anonymity techniques to anonymise sensor data before releasing it for analysis. The concept of k-anonymity was first formulated by Latanya Sweeney in [38] as an attempt to solve the following problem: "Given person-specific field-structured data, produce a release of the data with scientific guarantees that the individuals who are the subjects of the data cannot be re-identified while the data remain practically useful." A release of data is said to have the k-anonymity property if the information for each person contained in the release cannot be distinguished from at least $k-1$ individuals whose information also appears in the release. For example, if k = 5 and the potentially identifying variables are age and gender, then a k-anonymised data set has at least five records for each combination of age and gender. The most common implementations of k-anonymity use transformation techniques such as generalisation, global recoding, and suppression.

In summary, in most of the existing sensor networks based IoT security solutions, such as CodeBlue [23], ALARM-NET [42] and MEDiSN [20], the sensitive data collected by sensors and things is sent and stored in a database for users to access and analyse. Although the data is encrypted during the transmission and decrypted in the data server, these solutions have to trust the data server. If the data server is compromised by hackers, all IoT data are disclosed. In the existing biometric-based key agreement protocols, such as [40], the things in BSN establish the cryptographic keys with the common biometric (*e.g.*, EKG). So far, the security of such protocols has not been analysed under any formal security model. It is not clear if there is any security weakness in these protocols. In the existing authenticated broadcast protocols [30], the sensors and things authenticate the broadcast data with the key disclosed by the gateway in next time interval. This causes a delay in the authentication. A sensor has to keep all unauthenticated packets in the buffer. However, an IoT device usually has a limited buffer only. In addition, there is no security for the broadcast messages and no formal security model. In the existing ABE-based access control scheme [31,50], the sensors need to encrypt the sensed data with ABE schemes. The encrypted data can be decrypted only by the user who meets the access control policies. However, ABE schemes [36] usually require high computation and are difficult to be implemented in wireless sensors and things with limited power and computation capabilities. In addition, the sensor data encrypted with ABE schemes cannot be shared for data analysis. In the existing security solution [4], the user's privacy is protected on the basis of the concept of k-anonymity [38] Although the data is made to be indistinguishable from other $k-1$ data in the database, data analysis on such data may not be precise because the data has been changed. In addition, k-anonymity is often vulnerable to the re-identification attacks.

Although most proposed techniques discussed earlier can ensure security, their ability to scale up to support millions of IoT devices and their data has not been validated.

3   Overview of Techniques for Holistic IoT Security

Typical security threats that can compromise IoT applications include eavesdropping, impersonation, modification and data breaches. Moreover, to protect the IoT data of individual IoT devices, e.g. in the case of healthcare applications, it is important to provide security to prevent exposing or compromising of the actual data.

IoT systems and their applications must deal with malicious disclosure and attacks and provide mechanisms that protect sensitive data such as patients' physiological data, energy consumption data from smart meters, and the locations of mobile users. Existing techniques for IoT security are as following.

There are several aspects of the IoT that present security problems, including IoT device communications, constrained resources (e.g., limited battery life), variety (e.g., different types of devices made by multiple manufacturers), and scale (billions of devices) [41]. Among the plethora of recent research solutions [5,15, 24,27,39] for protecting IoT data, some related research (e.g., [15,24,32]) focuses on security and privacy preservation policies while others (e.g., [5,15,27,39]) focus on encryption frameworks for the IoT [28].

The most common access control mechanisms are DAC, LBAC, and RBAC [7]. DAC is discretionary in the sense that the owner of the requested resource controls the access to that resource. Each access request is checked against the specified authorisations. If there exists an authorisation stating that the user can access the resource in a specific mode (read or write), access is granted, otherwise it is denied. LBAC enforces unidirectional information flow via a predefined lattice of security labels that are associated with every resource and user in the system. RBAC determines the access level via the role abstraction, rather than simply by the identity or clearance of the requester. In this model, a role is a semantic construct, which is often a representation of a job in an organisation.

In an IoT setting where both data and access control policies can change rapidly, the above access models cannot deal with such frequent changes. To deal with such changes, another trend in research enriches access polices with contextual information. For instance, several extensions to the basic RBAC model have been proposed to incorporate context variables such as the GRBAC model [10]. GRBAC introduces environmental information such as temperature or location to activate roles based on the value of conditions in the environment where the request was made. A similar context-aware RBAC model has been proposed for health-care applications [17], where the contextual information invokes the relevant access policies for a specific role. A major deficiency of these approaches is that data access is either granted or denied.

In order to provide flexibility for situations where different data granularities are needed, disclosure control methods are advantageous. Existing disclosure control techniques are divided into identity and data disclosure control. Identity-based disclosure techniques, such as k-anonymity and l-diversity or pseudonymity, attempt to detach or replace identifiers from data, whereas the latter techniques protect the data itself. A comprehensive review of identity disclosure control techniques was conducted by Aggarwal and Philip [1].

Common techniques for data disclosure control include generalisation and suppression, data swapping and noise addition. Data generalisation attempts to prevent data linkages for the privacy preservation of published datasets. An example would be replacing an exact date of birth with only the year. Suppression techniques can be viewed as the ultimate form of generalisation since no information is released. Unfortunately, these techniques cause information loss and, also, are not appropriate for real-time applications because of the complexity of the required calculations.

Achieving multi-granular disclosure requires the use of obfuscation techniques. Data obfuscation, in this case, involves generalising or degrading sensitive data to establish the desired level of granularity for disclosure. Existing obfuscation techniques include data randomisation, data anonymisation, random sampling, or data swapping [3]. For instance, Mivule [25] investigated techniques for adding noise to sensitive data, including additive noise, multiplicative noise, logarithmic multiplicative noise and differential privacy, with respect to the statistical preservation of a published dataset.

Security in an IoT setting only at the time of data dissemination may not be effective and the whole data life-cycle needs to be considered to ensure end-to-end security. Although most proposed techniques discussed earlier can ensure security, there is no working IoT system that provides data security across the IoT stack.

4   Holistic and Lightweight IoT Security

In this section we will describe a framework that benefits from contextualisation techniques and homomorphic security algorithm to provide security to IoT applications.

4.1   Contextualisation for Holistic Security in IoT

Holistic security (*i.e.*, end-to-end security) for IoT is an approach which protects the IoT during all it's life cycle from the collection point, communication, processing, and visualisation/actuation. As illustrated in Fig. 1, an IoT application generally has 3 main components.

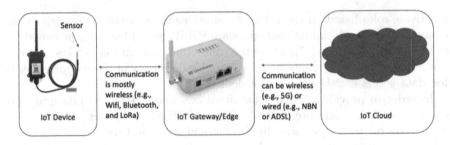

Fig. 1. IoT components.

Most of the IoT applications are not providing holistic security considering that they only secure the cloud environment where the processing and decision making is happening and in some cases the go beyond that to secure the communications between edge and cloud computers.

As discussed earlier, one of the main reasons that IoT applications do not tend to secure IoT devices is the fact that they are very limited in terms of computing, power, and memory resources.

Contextualisation is defined as the processes of contextually filtering, aggregating, and inferring (contextual operations) data using context [45, 46]. Contextualisation of the IoT data is generally a process to reduce the data or increase the value of the data by using context. Contextualisation has been used for security applications before [29, 48]. Contextualisation can be applied on IoT application data to reduce the amount of the data needed to process and has the potential to improve resource consumption (including all memory, computing, and power) in IoT components. This will help IoT devices to initiate the encryption from the IoT devices.

As described in [45], contextualisation operations are contextual filter, contextual aggregate, and contextual infer. In [44], an IoT platform is described that is capable of detecting hydrocarbon in the water monitoring wells in fuel stations. This platform follows the typical structure of IoT application including the 3 components shown in Fig. 1. In this example, the IoT device has a duty-cycle which is (10 min). The IoT device will wake up and sense the hydrocarbon in the water monitoring well and sends the data to the IoT gateway. Next, the IoT Cloud will process the data received from the IoT gateway to check whether there was any hydrocarbon in the water. However, by applying contextual filter, the sensor is aware about the parameters and threshold for existence of hydrocarbon in the water monitoring well and will only send the data when it is possible to have hydrocarbon in the water. This will save a lot of resources by the IoT application particularly in the IoT device.

Please assume an IoT application where the objective is to know the profile of the dairy product such as milk. IoT device in this example will be responsible to collect data related to the protein and fat contents in the milk [43]. Consider that we want to detect if the milk is full-fat or low-fat. An agnostic IoT device (not aware of the context) will constantly sense and monitor the percentage of the fat. Then, this data will be sent to the IoT gateway every 10 min. Next, the IoT gateway will send the data to the IoT Cloud. Finally, the IoT Cloud will process the data and will check/flag if the the milk is full-fat or low-fat. However, if the IoT device is aware about the context of the IoT application. It can only aggregate the amount of the fat in the milk by calculating the average of the percentage of the fat in a few hours and only send the calculated values.

In the examples above it is described that the data generated by the IoT devices can potentially be decreased significantly (*e.g.*, 6 observations per hour to only 1 observation in a day or even months). This can benefit the security algorithms to use the computing, power, memory, and communication resources to improve the IoT security and privacy by providing a holistic security and privacy-preserved IoT environment. Even though, we still do not have enough resource to run any available encryption algorithms in resource-constrained IoT devices. Homomorphic algorithms [13,18] has the potential to be applied to use the resource gained/saved from the contextualisation process to provide holistic security and privacy-preservation to the IoT applications including the IoT devices.

4.2 Homomorphic Security Algorithm

The fundamental concept of homomorphic encryption algorithms is that each data such as x that is collected from an IoT device will be split into several pieces in such a way that $x = x_1 + x_2 + ... + x_n$ while $n > 1$. Homomorphic encryption is a form of encryption that allows mathematical operations on ciphertexts generated from the data (*i.e.*, data pieces) in such a way that each of these data pieces can be encrypted separately. In order to get the the data we will need to summarise the data pieces and decrypt the result. As illustrated in Fig. 2, homomorphic algorithm is a form of encryption which allows specific types of mathematical operations on encrypted data pieces while keeping the data secure [49].

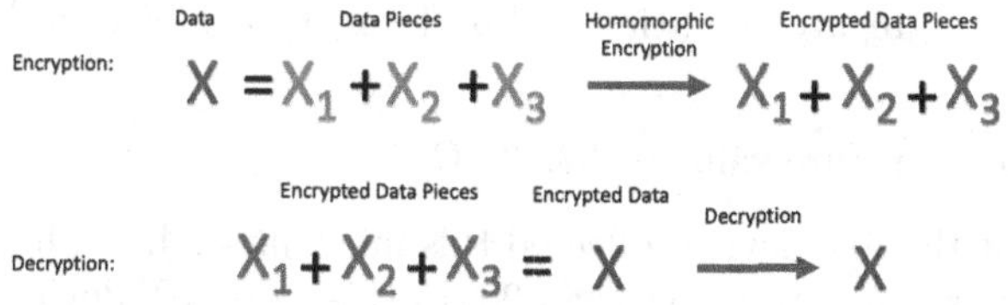

Fig. 2. Homomorphic encryption and decryption.

4.3 Data Ingestion

The fundamental idea behind our security approach is to split the data collected by the IoT devices to smaller data pieces. Then each of these data pieces will be encrypted and sent to the IoT gateway. As mentioned earlier IoT devices are not necessarily capable of performing encryption algorithm on the data duo to limited resources available on IoT devices. However, by splitting the data to smaller pieces the IoT devices will have more time and less memory will be needed to perform the data encryption. Assume an COVID-19 IoT application scenario where the IoT device will monitor individuals' body temperature in an area to see if they are suspicious for Corona virus disease (*i.e.*, COVID-19). The normal human body temperature remains between 36.5 °C to 37 °C, regardless of the external temperature or weather according to the World Health Organisation. Body temperature over 38 °C is classified as a fever. The COVID-19 IoT application is interested to know if any person body temperature is more than 37 °C. Duo to sensor errors and accuracy this IoT application needs more than one observation with a value higher than 37 °C for each person to flag the person with fever.

There is an IoT device which is collecting the temperature data with the following values for one person:

- Person A, temperature value is: 36.432986 °C.
- Person A, temperature value is:: 36.5354 °C.
- Person A, temperature value is: 37.5346 °C.
- Person A, temperature value is: 38.2123 °C.
- Person A, temperature value is: 37.8745 °C.
- Person A, temperature value is: 38.1001 °C.

Contextual filter operation will filter the data as it knows less than a certain temperature is not interested by the IoT application. As a result, we will have the following data left:

- Person A, temperature value is: 37.5346 °C.
- Person A, temperature value is: 38.2123 °C.
- Person A, temperature value is: 37.8745 °C.
- Person A, temperature value is: 38.1001 °C.

Now contextual aggregate operation will perform the aggregation operation and we will have:

- Person A, temperature value is: 37.93 °C.

Assume that the IoT device collected this information has a limited resource that cannot encrypt a data larger than 20. In this case, IoT device will split the data ($x = 37.93$) to smaller pieces ($x_1 = 20$, $x_2 = 17$, $x_3 = 0.9$, $x_4 = 0.03$) in such a way that the summarise of the data pieces is equal to the data. Then, each of these data pieces will be encrypted by the IoT device and will be sent to the IoT gateway and IoT Cloud.

4.4   Conceptual Architecture

In this section we will describe the conceptual architecture of the proposed framework for security and privacy-preservation in IoT. As it is illustrated in Fig. 3, the architecture has three main components including IoT device, IoT gateway, and IoT Cloud. IoT device is responsible to collect the data and contextualise it based on the context data received from the contextualisation server. Then, it will split the data into several pieces and encrypt them as discussed earlier. The data will be sent to the IoT gateway. IoT gateway is aware of the context data so it can validate if the data is contextualised properly. If needed, it can perform contextualisation on the data received from the IoT device. For example, a more complex aggregation that was not possible to do in the IoT device because of resource limitations. As an instance, aggregation of the temperature data collected in a day while the data cannot be stored in the IoT device but gateway can easily accommodate the data).

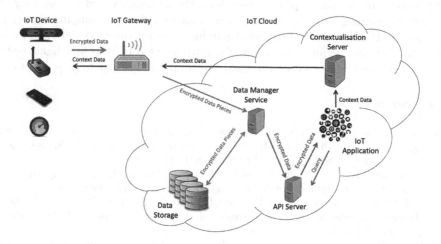

Fig. 3. Conceptual architecture for IoTSec.

Data received from the IoT gateway will be sent to the Data Manager Server (DMS). DMS is responsible for distributing the data pieces in several different data storage. If any of these data storage get compromised the data is still safe unless all the data storage get compromised. IoT application has two main roles in this architecture. It should provide the context information to the contextualisation server so it can be shared with IoT gateways and devices. In addition, IoT application will send the data queries for the CRUD operations to the API server. API server can retrieve the encrypted data - not data pieces as the data pieces are already summed up in Data Manager Server - and provide it to the IoT application.

5 Conclusion

In this paper we focused on the problem of IoT security that is currently preventing IoT to achieve its full potential. We recognised that IoT security is often subject to (1) the security mechanisms provided by heterogeneous IoT devices and limited computing resources they provide to support/compute them, (2) the variety of security protocols provided by low-power (e.g., NB-IoT), 4G, and WiFi networks that connect IoT devices in the internet, and (3) the variety of security mechanism supported by edge and cloud-based computers. Based on these, we identified that (1) the security of IoT applications depends on the specific orchestration of the IoT security mechanisms that are provided in the IoT devices, networks, and computing resources, and (1) the viability of secured IoT applications in the marketplace, depends on the availability and provisioning of enough computing resources at the device, edge and cloud to compute the security actions the IoT applications require to both protect their IoT data and meet their marketplace requirements. Finally, introduced a holistic and lightweight IoT security technique that can be easily customised for many IoT applications.

References

1. Aggarwal, C.C., Philip, S.Y.: A general survey of privacy-preserving data mining models and algorithms. In: Privacy-Preserving Data Mining, pp. 11–52. Springer, Boston (2008). https://doi.org/10.1007/978-0-387-70992-5_2
2. Andrukiewicz, E., Cadzow, S., Górniak, S.: IoT security standards gap analysis. European Union Agency For Network and Information Security (2018)
3. Bakken, D.E., Rarameswaran, R., Blough, D.M., Franz, A.A., Palmer, T.J.: Data obfuscation: anonymity and desensitization of usable data sets. IEEE Secur. Priv. 2(6), 34–41 (2004)
4. Belsis, P., Pantziou, G.: A k-anonymity privacy-preserving approach in wireless medical monitoring environments. Pers. Ubiquit. Comput. 18(1), 61–74 (2014)
5. Bera, A., Kundu, A., De Sarkar, N.R., Mou, D.: Experimental analysis on big data in IoT-based architecture. In: Satapathy, S., Bhateja, V., Joshi, A. (eds.) International Conference on Data Engineering and Communication Technology, pp. 1–9. Springer, Singapore (2017). https://doi.org/10.1007/978-981-10-1678-3_1
6. Bertino, E., Ooi, B.C., Yang, Y., Deng, R.H.: Privacy and ownership preserving of outsourced medical data. In: 21st International Conference on Data Engineering, pp. 521–532. IEEE (2005)
7. Bertino, E., Sandhu, R.: Database security-concepts, approaches, and challenges. IEEE Trans. Dependable Secure Comput. 2(1), 2–19 (2005)
8. Boneh, D., Franklin, M.: Identity-based encryption from the Weil pairing. In: Kilian, J. (ed.) CRYPTO 2001. LNCS, vol. 2139, pp. 213–229. Springer, Heidelberg (2001). https://doi.org/10.1007/3-540-44647-8_13
9. Camtepe, S.A., Yener, B.: Combinatorial design of key distribution mechanisms for wireless sensor networks. In: Computer Security-ESORICS 2004, pp. 293–308 (2004)
10. Covington, M.J., Long, W., Srinivasan, S., Dev, A.K., Ahamad, M., Abowd, G.D.: Securing context-aware applications using environment roles. In: Proceedings of the 6-th ACM Symposium on Access Control Models and Technologies, pp. 10–20. ACM (2001)

11. Du, W., Deng, J., Han, Y.S., Varshney, P.K., Katz, J., Khalili, A.: A pairwise key pre-distribution scheme for wireless sensor networks. In: ACM, pp. 42–51 (2003)
12. Eschenauer, L., Gligor, V.D.: A key-management scheme for distributed sensor networks. In: Proceedings of the 9th ACM Conference on Computer and Communications Security, pp. 41–47. ACM (2002)
13. Gentry, C.: Toward basing fully homomorphic encryption on worst-case hardness. In: Rabin, T. (ed.) CRYPTO 2010. LNCS, vol. 6223, pp. 116–137. Springer, Heidelberg (2010). https://doi.org/10.1007/978-3-642-14623-7_7
14. Georgakopoulos, D., Jayaraman, P.P.: Internet of Things: from internet scale sensing to smart services. Computing **98**(10), 1041–1058 (2016)
15. Hahn, J.: Security and privacy for location services and the internet of things. Libr. Technol. Rep. **53**(1), 23–28 (2017)
16. Hu, C., Zhang, J., Wen, Q.: An identity-based personal location system with protected privacy in IoT. In: 2011 4th IEEE International Conference on Broadband Network and Multimedia Technology (IC-BNMT), pp. 192–195. IEEE (2011)
17. Hu, J., Weaver, A.C.: A dynamic, context-aware security infrastructure for distributed health-care applications. In: Proceedings of the First Workshop on Pervasive Privacy Security, Privacy, and Trust, pp. 1–8. Citeseer (2004)
18. Jayaraman, P.P., Yang, X., Yavari, A., Georgakopoulos, D., Yi, X.: Privacy preserving internet of things: from privacy techniques to a blueprint architecture and efficient implementation. Future Gener. Comput. Syst. (2017)
19. Kalra, S., Sood, S.K.: Secure authentication scheme for IoT and cloud servers. Pervasive Mob. Comput. **24**, 210–223 (2015)
20. Ko, J., et al.: MEDiSN: medical emergency detection in sensor networks. ACM Trans. Embed. Comput. Syst. (TECS) **10**(1), 1–29 (2010)
21. Liu , D., Ning, P.: Establishing pairwise keys in distributed sensor networks. In: Proceedings of the 10th ACM Conference on Computer and Communications Security, CCS 2003, New York, NY, USA, pp. 52–61. ACM (2003)
22. Liu, J., Xiao, Y., Philip Chen, C.L.: Internet of Things' authentication and access control. Int. J. Secur. Netw. **7**(4), 228–241 (2012)
23. Malan, D.J., Fulford-Jones, T., Welsh, M., Moulton, S.: CodeBlue: an ad hoc sensor network infrastructure for emergency medical care. In: International Workshop on Wearable and Implantable Body Sensor Networks (2004)
24. Martucci, L.A., Fischer-Hübner, S., Hartswood, M., Jirotka, M.: Privacy and social values in smart cities. In: Angelakis, V., Tragos, E., Pöhls, H.C., Kapovits, A., Bassi, A. (eds.) Designing, Developing, and Facilitating Smart Cities, pp. 89–107. Springer, Cham (2017). https://doi.org/10.1007/978-3-319-44924-1_6
25. Mivule, K.: Utilizing noise addition for data privacy, an overview. arXiv preprint arXiv:1309.3958 (2013)
26. Neuman, B.C., Ts'o, T.: Kerberos: an authentication service for computer networks. Commun. Mag. **32**(9), 33–38 (1994)
27. Ouaddah, A., Abou Elkalam, A., Ouahman, A.A.: Towards a novel privacy-preserving access control model based on blockchain technology in IoT. In: Europe and MENA Cooperation Advances in Information and Communication Technologies, pp. 523–533. Springer, Cham (2017). https://doi.org/10.1007/978-3-319-46568-5_53
28. Ould-Yahia, Y., Banerjee, S., Bouzefrane, S., Boucheneb, H.: Exploring formal strategy framework for the security in IoT towards e-health context using computational intelligence. In: Bhatt, C., Dey, N., Ashour, A.S. (eds.) Internet of Things and Big Data Technologies for Next Generation Healthcare. SBD, vol. 23, pp. 63–90. Springer, Cham (2017). https://doi.org/10.1007/978-3-319-49736-5_4

29. Panah, A.S., Yavari, A., van Schyndel, R., Georgakopoulos, D., Yi, X.: Context-driven granular disclosure control for internet of things applications. IEEE Trans. Big Data **5**, 408–422 (2017)

30. Perrig, A., Szewczyk, R., Tygar, J.D., Wen, V., Culler, D.E.: SPINS: security protocols for sensor networks. Wirel. Netw. **8**(5), 521–534 (2002)

31. Picazo-Sanchez, P., Tapiador, J.E., Peris-Lopez, P., Suarez-Tangil, G.: Secure publish-subscribe protocols for heterogeneous medical wireless body area networks. Sensors **14**(12), 22619–22642 (2014)

32. Rayes, A., Salam, S.: Internet of Things—From Hype to Reality. Springer, Cham (2017). https://doi.org/10.1007/978-3-319-44860-2

33. Rivest, R.L., Shamir, A., Adleman, L.: A method for obtaining digital signatures and public-key cryptosystems. Commun. ACM **21**(2), 120–126 (1978)

34. Roman, R., Alcaraz, C., Lopez, J., Sklavos, N.: Key management systems for sensor networks in the context of the internet of things. Comput. Electr. Eng. **37**(2), 147–159 (2011)

35. Roman, R., Zhou, J., Lopez, J.: On the features and challenges of security and privacy in distributed internet of things. Comput. Netw. **57**(10), 2266–2279 (2013)

36. Sahai, A., Waters, B.: Fuzzy identity-based encryption. In: Cramer, R. (ed.) EURO-CRYPT 2005. LNCS, vol. 3494, pp. 457–473. Springer, Heidelberg (2005). https://doi.org/10.1007/11426639_27

37. Shah, T., et al.: Remote health care cyber-physical system: quality of service (QoS) challenges and opportunities. IET Cyber Phys. Syst. Theory Appl. **1**(1), 40–48 (2016)

38. Sweeney, L.: k-anonymity: a model for protecting privacy. Int. J. Uncertainty Fuzziness Knowl. Based Syst. **10**(05), 557–570 (2002)

39. Tragos, E., Fragkiadakis, A., Angelakis, V., Pöhls, H.C.: Designing secure IoT architectures for smart city applications. In: Angelakis, V., Tragos, E., Pöhls, H.C., Kapovits, A., Bassi, A. (eds.) Designing, Developing, and Facilitating Smart Cities, pp. 63–87. Springer, Cham (2017). https://doi.org/10.1007/978-3-319-44924-1_5

40. Venkatasubramanian, K.K., Banerjee, A., Gupta, S.K.S., et al.: EKG-based key agreement in body sensor networks. In: INFOCOM Workshops 2008, IEEE, pp. 1–6. IEEE (2008)

41. Weber, R.H.: Internet of things-new security and privacy challenges. Comput. Law Secur. Rev. **26**(1), 23–30 (2010)

42. Wood, A., et al.: ALARM-NET: wireless sensor networks for assisted-living and residential monitoring. University of Virginia Computer Science Department Technical Report, 2:17 (2006)

43. Yavari, A., Georgakopoulos, D., Agrawal, H., Korala, H., Jayaraman, P.P., Milovac, J.K.: Internet of Things milk spectrum profiling for industry 4.0 dairy and milk manufacturing. In: 2020 International Conference on Information Networking (ICOIN), pp. 342–347 (2020)

44. Yavari, A., Georgakopoulos, D., Stoddart, P.R., Shafiei, M.: Internet of Things-based hydrocarbon sensing for real-time environmental monitoring. In: 2019 IEEE 5th World Forum on Internet of Things (WF-IoT), pp. 729–732 (2019)

45. Yavari, A.: Internet of Things data contextualisation for scalable information processing, security, and privacy. Ph.D. thesis, RMIT University (2019)

46. Yavari, A., Jayaraman, P.P., Georgakopoulos, D., Nepal, S.: Contaas: an approach to internet-scale contextualization for developing efficient internet of things applications. In: Proceedings of the 50th Annual Hawaii International Conference on System Sciences. IEEE (2017)

47. Yavari, A., Jayaraman, P.P., Georgakopoulos, D.: Contextualised service delivery in the Internet of Things: parking recommender for smart cities. In: IEEE 3rd World Forum on Internet of Things, pp. 454–459. IEEE (2016)
48. Yavari, A., Panah, A.S., Georgakopoulos, D., Jayaraman, P.P., van Schyndel, R.: Scalable role-based data disclosure control for the Internet of Things. In: 2017 IEEE 37th International Conference on Distributed Computing Systems (ICDCS), pp. 2226–2233. IEEE (2017)
49. Yi, X., Paulet, R., Bertino, E.: Homomorphic encryption. Homomorphic Encryption and Applications. SCS, pp. 27–46. Springer, Cham (2014). https://doi.org/10.1007/978-3-319-12229-8_2
50. Shucheng, Yu., Ren, K., Lou, W.: FDAC: toward fine-grained distributed data access control in wireless sensor networks. IEEE Trans. Parallel Distrib. Syst. **22**(4), 673–686 (2011)
51. Zhang, T., Siebers, P.-O., Aickelin, U.: Modelling electricity consumption in office buildings: an agent based approach. Energy Build. **43**(10), 2882–2892 (2011)

Data and Services

Design Methodology for Service-Based Data Product Sharing and Trading

Jian Yang$^{(\boxtimes)}$, Yongping Tang, and Amin Beheshti

Macquarie University, Sydney, NSW 2190, Australia
{jian.yang,amin.beheshti}@mq.edu.au, yongping.tang@students.mq.edu.au

Abstract. The data economy is inevitably rising while data is becoming the 'new fuel' driving the world economy as discussed in many studies from a number of viewpoints including economics, technology development, digitisation, and data analytic technologies. Although the significance of data trading is recognised as a critical part of data economy, how data should be described, protected, packaged and priced as data product for trading has not been fully explored. In this chapter we present a service-based approach for data resources to data product transformation and mechanism for data product trading.

Keywords: Design methodology · Data as Service · Data product · Data trading · Data economy

1 Introduction

The importance of data is widely recognised, but so far mainly shown in successful data applications internally for systems and organisations through using a variety of enabling technologies. The current practice in data management and governance in many areas and most organisations, however, significantly limits usages and values of data, especially for external applications crossing companies and organisations. There has been no effective measure and solution to systematically deal with the challenges and difficulties facing a common and well-designed practice of data sharing and data exchanges across businesses, companies, organisations and sectors. Effectively unlocking data values and enabling data sharing across businesses, companies and organisations has become the holy grail for data technologies and the data-driven world. The next wave of new data technology development is going to be in the areas related to the emerging concept of **Data Economy** (DE), and its ecosystems.

Data is an important element in service computing since it is accessed and processed by services and exchanged through services. However many enterprises are spending a significant amount of their time analysing data silos that provide some helps to partial business decision rather than worrying about the design principles of their data as products to trade and engage with others to understand a big picture the data can bring. The real value and true function of DE will

© Springer Nature Switzerland AG 2021
M. Aiello et al. (Eds.): Papazoglou Festschrift, LNCS 12521, pp. 221–235, 2021.
https://doi.org/10.1007/978-3-030-73203-5_17

not be realised if no effective method or solution is provided for data providers (producers or owners) to (1) explore the value of their data set, to (2) package their data adequately in various forms for sharing and exchange, and to (3) manage data security and privacy as required.

Simply considering database applications (or software) on top of existing data sets to expose the data, as suggested by the thinking of Software-as Service (SaaS) is not enough to provide reliable, manageable and re-usable data products. There is still a list of open issues that need to be addressed and researched in connection with the design methodologies and engineering principles before data products become the prominent paradigm for DE.

Let us take an example of IoT data with sensors deployed on the street in our Smart City Project (http://smartcity-api.science.mq.edu.au/). There are different vendors of IoT sensors that produce different formats of data in different protocols. Questions arise on how to (1) collect the data without loosing important information and relationship among the data, (2) facilitate different user scenarios, and (3) enable the IoT data sharing and trading to different parties with different interests and purposes. Most common data sensor datasets in this project includes timestamp, interval, humidity, temperature, pedestrian count, longitude, latitude, and coverage. The pedestrian count data can provide valuable input to decision making such as on transportation, merchant location selection, business open hours, etc. The environment temperature data can give us ideas such as where to plant trees and where to place pedestrian path. The humidity and temperature data is important to plants and animals. If these data resources can be properly designed and specified as data products, then their potential values can be further revealed and tested so that they can be traded in the marketplace [3]. We can imagine local council would be interested in purchasing them together with data products such as mobile usage on roads so that the traffic conditions on the roads can be analyzed for better arrangement of social events and road maintenance.

Inspired by Mike's work in [12] on design methodology for web services, in this chapter, we present our preliminary thoughts on a new design methodology for Data-as-Service (DaaS) that puts design focuses on data products, rather than software. Web services and data products share the similar characteristics as both are designed for data sharing and extended data applications. However, the significant differences lie in the design of data product presentations that allow data users or data buyers to explore, to test on different data utilization scenarios, and to potentially combine with other data products for comprehensive data analysis or data fusion.

In the following sections, we first introduce the concept of data products and then will define a data appreciation process that helps data owners and stakeholders analyses their data resources, unleashes the value of data by discovering the inter-relationship between data and potential applications, and makes data be appreciated in terms of knowledge about data, potential values or applications throughout the data lifecycle.

2 Data Product: Types, Design and Development

Data is like crude oil with potential value but often has less or limited economic value in its raw form. Making the distinction between data resources and data products is extremely important to understand what features DE will operate with. Generally speaking, data resources possessed or controlled by an organisation are not ready for trading as products for data marketplaces. From an economic viewpoint or a business perspective, the business winners in DE are those who produce and sell designed and value-added products, rather than those who simply sell data (resources) or poorly designed data products. Thus, simply pushing data resources to data marketplaces without knowing their true or potential values means missing business opportunities and fails in maximising economic or financial benefits for data owners and stakeholders. It may also involve high risks to sell data without good guidance and adequate implementation of data governance, policy and regulations.

Now, it is time to clearly differentiate data resources from data products. Strictly speaking, a data product is a purposely itemised and market-ready data piece, and more importantly plus its descriptions or metadata [7], as an output of certain design efforts made for achieving specific outcomes. Such a differentiation to treat data resources and data products differently is very important as shown later in the discussions on data values analysis and data product design. A set or collection of data resources can be used as a basis to derive or design a variety or collections of data products if different parts or subsets of data resources can be identified with potentials for different applications, or some relevance to data or business of other areas, parties or companies. Therefore, relations between data resources and data products can be very complex, given some specific features of both data resources and data products. The process to effectively derive and design useful data products is thus challenging as data resources often vary, due to high complexity in many aspects, such as structure, storage arrangements, conditions, and regulations or policies. In the following subsections we will look into the data types and the design issues related to data products.

2.1 Data Products

The data product design is focusing on transforming data resources into data products, and providing solutions for data product delivery and subscription for potential buyers and end users. Same data resource can be used to generate different data products for different purposes. The new and increasing demands for data products will be considered and derived from a wide range of data resources, including the following categories (but not limited to):

- **Fact-based** that describes or reflects (or shows) a fact or situation of reality or real things/ objects/situations (such as IoT data, surveillance data, image data, medical data, climate/weather data, personal data, communications, organisational data, customer/personal data, sale/commercial data, transport data, operational data, and so on);

- **Social and opinion data** that is collected to describe social activities/events, interests, activities, opinions and demands of people or communities;
- **Statistic data** that is generated on the basis of fact-based data or social opinion data and is a kind of value-added data products showing trends or describing insights;
- **Intelligence data** (including insight, information and knowledge derived) that is generated (on a basis of other data resources or even data products) and delivered as intelligence services for a various purposes in various areas or sectors; and
- **Data farming** that is purposefully generated through conducting special activities such as simulation and experimentation (including computational, chemical or physical experiments) or internet web crawling (for special purposes of indexing or data curation).

Data resources include not only those already exist and will be continuously acquired in the current practice, but also future new ones to be generated and captured in different manners. Some data resources have been processed towards data products, in particular those as statistic and intelligence information (or services) (such as services and products provided by Bloomberg). Data products differ from data resources, and are special products and different from traditional physical and material products. Data products have their special features that are very different from other products and data resources, in particular in the following aspects:

- Products design, description, and presentation/packaging;
- Special and complex relations between data resources and data products;
- Data product generation or production;
- Use and lifecycle of data products;
- Data product applications and users/buyers;
- Quality assurance;
- Data governance for trading as products;
- Data product delivery, accesses and protection in trading;
- Valuation and accounting; and
- Marketing and trading.

The Data product development is a complex task. This chapter can just present and discuss some insights and a preliminary study. The logical thinking of the data product development and its outcomes, however, may have significant impact to design and applications of the future service computing. We will thus briefly discuss how data products can be created on the basis of data resources and how some service concepts can be embedded and implemented in data product design.

2.2 From Data Resource to Data Product

Depending organizations and their data-related practices, data resources vary in types, formats, volumes, and are under different conditions and statuses in processing, storage, management and governance. Generally speaking, these data resources are mainly used internally and not ready for trading and markets in their existing forms. Relations between data resource and data products are critical to the generation and management of data products, which are based on the following concepts:

- **Data Resource** represents all data sets, structured, unstructured, or raw data from various data sources;
- **Data Resource Specification** is the meta model of data resources, which captures and presents knowledge about data in standardized structures or representations, including how to access;
- Staged **Data Resource Graph** (DRG) presents data resource in a knowledge graph [4–6] under Data Resource Specification;
- **Data Product Specification** is the meta model of data products, which standardise how data products will be presented and delivered for purposes of marketing and trading;
- **Data Rule** is the governance and policy rules directing data product generation and transaction;
- **Data Product Catalog** is the catalogue of data products;
- **Presentation** is the exposure interface or presentations of data products in trading or marketplaces to clients or users.

The data product generation is not about the generation or physical production of a real piece of data, in addition to data resources. Instead, the generation of products, or the transformation of data resources into data products, is about the derivations and conceptual construction of data product specifications on the basis of relevant data resource specifications. The existence of a data product is the presentation of a data product specification and mappings established to specifications of relevant data resources, which jointly determine how data products can be traded and marketed. Thus, the data product development is a knowledge processing task to generate adequate descriptions and presentations of data products ready for trading and markets. As a result of the current data practice, data resource specifications for existing data resources do not exist in most organizations. This makes it hard to effectively generate data product specifications, if without conducting an adequate process of Knowing Your Data (KYD) and capturing important information and knowledge about data.

Data appreciation is a such process to understand data resources and effectively capture and represent knowledge about data in the form of data resources specifications. This implies that, in order to achieve the transformation from data resources to data products, we needs deal with three main tasks: data resource appreciation, data product creation, and data product presentation, as illustrated in Fig. 1. The logical steps of the data appreciation and transformation process can be described as the following:

- First of all, assume data resources, which have been properly collected and stored, exist in real world in different formats. A generic Data Resource Specification schema needs to be designed so that it can be used to describe all forms of data resources;

- Secondly, to capture the core information and knowledge together with the relationships between data and potential applications, we propose to store this core information and knowledge in a Knowledge Graph presented by Data Resource Graph (DRG) [9];
- Thirdly, data resources are conceptually presented in different forms as data products through specially designed enablers and then managed and listed in product catalogues. A data Resource is not yet data products. It is conceptually transformed into adequate presentations of data products for marketing and delivery through an adequate transformation guided by enabling rules and mapping rules used in the data product design process;
- Lastly, a data product is formally established by mapping its attributes, relationships and correspondence from the data product specification to relevant resource specifications. A data product is presented in its specification to potential users and buyers through the presentation in trading and marketplaces.

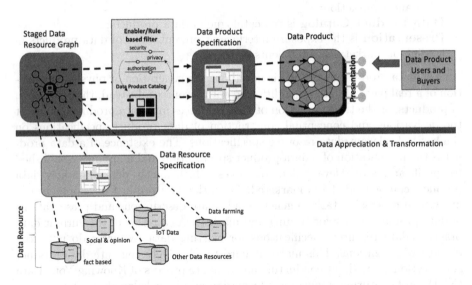

Fig. 1. A logical model from data appreciation to data product generation

2.3   Data Product Catalog

Similar to the role of Service Catalog and Registry (such as UDDI) in the service computing, the data product catalog that is a collection of specifications of data products available plays an important role for marketing and trading. Data products vary. Some products are simple; some may be complicated, depending on types. Different types of data products need to go through different design processes, involving with different levels of complexity in design, generation and presentation of products. Many data products are derived directly from a basis of data resources. But, some may be designed on a combination of data resources and relevant data products. We categorise data products into a data catalogue in terms of complexity in generation and delivery for a data-intensive business or organization or in data marketplaces:

- *primitive data products*, which is a result from the data product design process, generated from data resources of content based data, fact based data, social and opinion data and data farming. Examples of primitive data product include a dataset of tweets in a certain period of time and a specific region, a history of consumer location tracking, or raw data extracted from an IoT sensor on pedestrian counts;
- *statistics data products*, which is a result of the first level ETL processing on fact-based data, social and opinion data;
- *intelligence enhanced data products*, which is processed by specially designed intelligence algorithms for specific purposes. For example, an algorithm is used to calculate and report the relatively busier train station by comparing pedestrian counts. Typically intelligence algorithms are offered to users in combination with primitive data or statistics data;
- *intelligence data products*, which is processed data by certain intelligence algorithms. Taking sensor pedestrian count as example, a geographical distribution of train stations ordered by pedestrian counts is a sample of intelligence data. Intelligence data products are typically generated through processing primitive data and statistics data with intelligence algorithms. Users can choose to either purchase lower forms of data (including primitive data, statistics data and intelligence algorithm) and then do analysis themselves, or purchase the intelligence data to gain insight of data directly at a higher cost;
- *insight data products*, which are provided as recommendations or for decision making to buyers/users with a decision suggestion. For example, a coffee franchise can purchase an insight as the recommendation for location suggestions to open new branches.

Apart from deriving or generating data products directly from data resources, it is also possible to generate the second order or higher order data products on a basis of data products, which will certainly involve a different process and deal with different issues in the product generation. This is because of different relations between different data products in either same or different categories, as shown in Fig. 2.

The diversity of data products requires different approaches and measures for delivery and access. As discussed in later sections, the approaches and measures to deliver and access data products are to be determined in the data product design, and presented as part of the data product specifications. In addition to the collection of data resources, the data product registry in an organization and the data product catalog in data marketplaces can also be viewed as another source or a basis to consider and design data products if adequate approaches and supports are available.

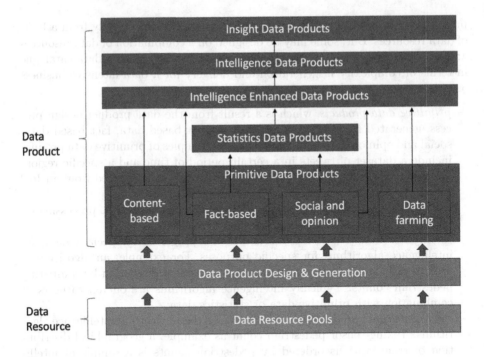

Fig. 2. Data product catalogue

2.4 Data Appreciation Process

The data appreciation is the very first step toward the generation of data products for the data economy and data product marketplaces. The data appreciation process is set to perform two main tasks, illustratively described in Fig. 3, that is, 1) capturing and representation of knowledge about data resources in an adequate fashion; and 2) identifying potential applications of data in relevant areas and possible use scenarios.

The main steps of the appreciation process are briefly explained as below:

1. *Choose or design a schema*, which can not only effective capture data knowledge but also include importing data resource meta-model or data schema as required;
2. *Populate data resource information and knowledge in the schema*, which includes extracting and capturing knowledge on data resource through a guided and specially designed process, and staging data resources for presentation with information on access control and measures;
3. *Construct the Resource Data Graph*, which builds up schematized knowledge graphs based on data resource information and relevant rules, especially relevance to potential applications to certain areas;
4. *Conduct data validation and regulation checking with enabling rules*, to ensure that resources are validated against the enabling rules and policies;

5. *Conduct data quality evaluation*, to ensure the quality of data is evaluated as the preparation for data product transformation under different data product standards. Data quality is considered in multiple aspects, including time relevance and coherence, accuracy, completeness and consistency [8].
6. *Present data resource specifications* into a data resource registry and make them ready for use as a basis for data product design and generation

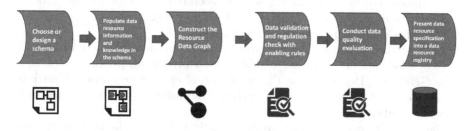

Fig. 3. Data appreciation process

3   Data Product Design Principle

The data products design principles differ in many aspects from those used in the service oriented computing design in [11]. The data product design principles underlying the data design stages described above, however, are suggested to revolve around the well-known software design guidelines: coupling and cohesion. These principles guarantee that data products are self-contained, modular and able to support trading in data product marketplace.

3.1   Coupling Between Resources and Products

It is important that the data appreciation process and the data product design are separate but strongly related. The main task of the data product design is to create a special conceptual data coupling between a given data resource (or a data set) and a candidate data product. The coupling is achieved through generating a data product specification, based on the knowledge about the data resource presented in the resources specification. As mentioned earlier, two different generic schema formats are considered for the generation of the data resource specification and the creation of the data product specification respectively. The mechanisms used in the coupling include:

1. *Representation coupling*: The design of data products should not depend on specific representational or computational details of data resources. The data resource and data product use different meta models (schema formats) with notations of entities, entity attributes and relationships which minimises dependencies on irrelevant representational and computational details. This solves several data product trading options related to marketplace, including:

- Multiple data versions: different versions of a data product may work best in parts of a decision making depending on the client's needs. For example, a consumer behavior data product may provide different levels of detail, e.g., personal financial status details, personal interests, locations, depending on the charging options.
- Multiple data dimensions: different dimensions of data provide different perceptions on data so that client can correlate data with different scenarios. For example, an IoT sensor generated data product may provide pedestrian counts on dimensions of working days, area, and busy hours. Other sample dimensions can be found in [10].

2. *Data privacy coupling*: data product should not depend on sensitive privacy information. There are regulations on processing personal data such as GDPR [1]. Depending on the regulation of specific geographical markets and nature of clients, data product should be easily enabled or disabled with privacy data.

3. *Data security coupling*: data product should not be combined with specific security mechanism.

4. *Data authentication coupling*: data product should not be bound to particular user authentication process and applications. Client can access data through different interfaces, such as DB query, API, etc. Data product should be accessible regardless of the interfaces and authentications layers.

5. *Data transaction coupling*: A provider of a data product should rely only on those efforts necessary to achieve effective data transfer method. For example, one way style of operation where a data product client receives a dataset without having to send an acknowledgement places the lowest possible demands on the data product offering. The presentation of data product does not assume anything about when and how the data product is requested and consumed, or even requires that a notification be sent back indicating completion.

6. *Data media coupling*: A data appreciation process should not tie to specific data resource media. Whether data resource is provided on file, or on air, data collection and processing should not be impacted.

These coupling mechanisms not only increase the accessibility to different levels of data resources and maintain the relevance and coherence between the data resource appreciation and the data product design, but also simplifies data product design and further increases flexibility and usability of data products.

3.2   Data Cohesion

Data Cohesion is about usability and readiness of data products in marketplace. The following guidelines for increasing cohesion are recommended:

1. *Data collection cohesion*: A robust cohesive data collection is facilitated to be able to access multiple data resources, in order to allow all potential sources of data to contribute to the data collection. The collection process in the appreciation stage should be designed in accordance with the data resource specifications.

2. *Data categorisation cohesion*: A cohesive data categorisation effectively connects data resource and data product. Cohesive data products also have quite clean coupling, because their internal data entities and relationships are hardly related to the elements in data resources and other categories of data products.
3. *Data rule cohesion*: Cohesive data rule is embedded into the data insights. Data rule is rooted in how the data resource and data product is structured.
4. *Data product presentation cohesion*: Because of special features of data products, their specifications should be clear and adequate when they are presented to users or buyers. Data product design should generate cohesive data product descriptions and specifications to ensure search-ability, usability and quality of products, in particular for complicated and higher order products. For example, financial market data product is typically presented in clear patterns including color codes, icon shapes, and chart styles so that data buyers can understand the data and make decisions without delay [2].

3.3 Data Product Enabler

The enabler plays critical roles in data product generation and lifecycle. It enables and facilitates the process to transform data resources into data products. The value of data resource is unleashed primarily with the assistance from the enabler that includes a set of elements. There are several examples of the enabler, such as: 1) a registry able to manage data entities or all important data resources and to capture data knowledge; 2) taxonomies and catalogues; 3) rules on data or relationship; 4) AI/ML-powered processes for exploration of potential data application fields; and 5)algorithms for data value analysis and product pricing.

The enabler or its elements work with a number of data knowledge concepts, from knowledge graphs, ontology, taxonomy to semantic reasoning. They work together to make the transformation or the product generation be a knowledge-enabled, heuristic and semi-automatic process. Many interesting and promising knowledge and reasoning related concepts, methods and techniques can be used in designs of these enabling elements.

Therefore, whether the data product design or generation, or transformation from data resources into data products, can be effectively and adequately conducted is largely determined by the availability and supports of these enabling elements. Data product design and generation is a new data professional activity, different data analysis, data processing and data engineering. Due to the special relations between data products and the service computing, the concept of the service-based data product design may also need some special enabling elements for either the data product design process or the later stages of data product trading and delivery.

4 Role of SOC in Data Product Design

4.1 Services Vs. Data Products

Web services and data products share some similar characteristics as both are designed for data accessing. However, the significant differences lie in the purpose and the strategy to deal with interface complexity:

- Purpose: the design purpose of web service is to overcome heterogeneity and hide the implementation details so that the invocation to designed functions or transactions can be carried out, based on the WSDL interface specification. While the design purpose of data products is to package the data set in a specific fashion so that their values can be revealed, explored, and the products can be adequately delivered to clients or users, and data products can be traded externally.
- Interface: the interface in WSDL specifies the functionalities a service provides and how it can be invoked. While the specification for data products will need to cover all the aspects of data products such as schema information, potential applications, usage constraints, legal bindings, etc. Furthermore, we can expect certain mechanisms that will enable exploring more potential applications or values of data sets when they are combined with other data sets.

Along with fast developments in AI, ML and IoT, developers of AI and ML applications (or services) or their users do not have to own or hold data required, as far as they can purchase the related data products available on markets or from any owner or producers. This also means people can design and develop their AI or ML applications based any data resources as far as data owners are willing and ready to open these resources (through providing data products as services). In Open Banking, for example, FinTech companies and developers can design their new services or products as far as they can purchase and access required data products provided by banks who act as product sellers in DE and may share benefits from data product sale with real owners of data, i.e., bank customers.

4.2 Considerations for the Shifting of Service Design

Emerging DE and its ecosystems bring both significant uncertainties and great opportunities for SOC. A new data product-based working paradigm of SOC in future DE ecosystems is illustrated in Fig. 4. There are certain specific considerations in the service design that must pay attentions to what DE-related activities and its ecosystems are, in addition to the general principles of SOC [11]. These considerations include:

- Its fitness to both enterprise data ecosystems and DE ecosystems;
- Association with DE-related activities and methodologies;
- Under guidance of data governance, police and regulations; and
- Delivering specific outcomes and results required by DE practice.

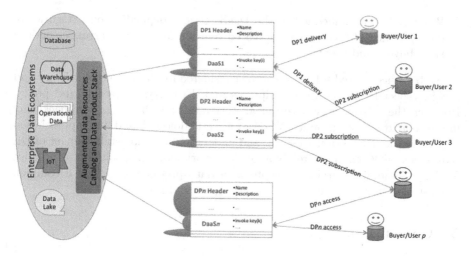

Fig. 4. An illustrative model for E2E data product delivery

4.3 Service Designed as Part of Data Products

Up to this point of discussions, a question for applications of SOC in future DE becomes critical, that is, how services can be designed as part of data products and function as data products are marketed and delivered. As the fundamental concept of DE, data products are the core of design for methodologies, practice and technologies of DE ecosystems. Data product design is a complex task involving high complexity in various data-relevant concepts and knowledge handling about data resources, governance, applications and special delivery requirements for different data products. As illustrated in Fig. 4, a data product is designed as a special knowledge-based and governance-enabled gateway between data resources and data product buyers and users, which includes a number of sections defined in a design schema for data products. One of important sections in the schema is DaaS (Data as a Service) where services are designed to address all technical and governance issues on both sides of the gateway, namely, mappings with access solutions to relevant data resources, and data product delivery arrangements and solutions to buyers and users. While going through the data product design process, main design issues related to both data products and services in DaaS include:

- Which data pieces and fields are included in a data product;
- What regulation/policy and governance rules are applied to these data pieces and fields, and how they can be implemented against data products to be designed;
- How these data pieces and fields can be accessed as required, and packaged (even encrypted) as deliverable products with satisfactions or compliance to relevant governance and regulation conditions; and

– What APIs are embedded in the DaaS section, depending on categories of data products, to work as a key-based solution for delivery arrangements to their buyers and users.

Web services-based solutions can be considered for data product delivery and access, especially in service descriptions and discovery, inspection and policy. However, the existing service technical stack needs a rethinking and repackaging in the context of data product. Without a methodology-based data appreciation process in the data product design, and understanding and establishment of DE ecosystems, SOC cannot directly applied to work alone as a solution or practice for DE. Combining service concepts with data products design is a common interest of SOC community and DE developers and practice.

5   Conclusion

The emerging data economy (DE) brings both challenges and opportunities for existing computing concepts and technologies. In this chapter, we introduce Data Product design as the core concept in DE. The rise of DE and its ecosystems present new contexts for the community to consider and investigate how service concepts and technologies should adopt to new challenges and environment changes for design and implementation of SOC. Data product-based SOC can be considered as a new fashion in design and applications of SOC for DE-related activities and systems, in particular as a universal practice for data sharing and exchanges, or data flows, across organisations.

Acknowledgements. The authors thank Dr Pin Chen for discussions, insights, contributions and support to help the team in the efforts to explore and investigate this complex but promising research area, and to write this chapter.

References

1. General Data Protection Regulation. https://gdpr-info.eu
2. Market Data. https://www.bloomberg.com/professional/product/market-data
3. Agarwal, A., Dahleh, M., Sarkar, T.: A marketplace for data: an algorithmic solution. arXiv:1805.08125v4 [cs. GT], 12 May 2019
4. Beheshti, A., Benatallah, B., Sheng, Q.Z., Schiliro, F.: Intelligent knowledge lakes: The age of artificial intelligence and big data. In: Web Information Systems Engineering - WISE 2019 Workshop, Demo, and Tutorial, Hong Kong and Macau, China, January 19–22, 2020. Communications in Computer and Information Science, vol. 1155, pp. 24–34. Springer (2019)
5. Cimiano, P., Bielefeld, U.: Knowledge graph refinement: a survey of approaches and evaluation methods (2016)
6. Elfaki, A.O., Aljaedi, A., Duan, Y.: Mapping ERD to knowledge graph, May 2018
7. Falkenberg, E.D., Brinkkemper, S.: The meta model hierarchy: a framework for information systems concepts and techniques, pp. 1–30 (1992)
8. Fricker, S.A., Maksimov, Y.V.: Pricing of Data Products in Data Marketplaces

9. Ji, S., Pan, S., Cambria, E., Member, S., Marttinen, P., Yu, P.S.: A survey on knowledge graphs: representation, acquisition and applications, pp. 1–25

10. Juckes, T.I.M.J., Barresi, J.: The subjective-objective dimension in the individual-society connection: a duality perspective (1976)

11. Papazoglou, M., Traverso, P., Dustday, S., Leymann, F.: Service oriented computing: state of art and research challenges. Computers 40(11) (2002)

12. Papazoglou, M., Yang, J.: Design methodology for web services and business processes. International Workshop on Technologies for E-Services (2002)

About the Quality of Data and Services in Natural Sciences

Barbara Pernici[✉][ID], Francesca Ratti[ID], and Gabriele Scalia[ID]

Department of Electronics, Information and Bioengineering, Politecnico di Milano,
Milan, Italy
{barbara.pernici,francesca.ratti,gabriele.scalia}@polimi.it

Abstract. Managing data related to natural sciences poses new and challenging problems as it is impossible to represent reality on a one-to-one scale, and imprecision has to be taken into account, both in data memorization and in its processing. Machine learning has been a key enabler in the context of information extraction from natural sciences data. However, data-driven results are strongly affected by the volume, the sparsity and different types of imprecision in the available sources. Therefore, it becomes pivotal to associate both to data and to data-driven services information about their quality, in order to effectively interpret the results. Different levels of granularity and multiple data modalities captured from the same processes could coexist, due to technological constraints or other intrinsic limiting factors. In addition, different levels of granularity might be also the result of application requirements, and outcomes at multiple levels of precision needs to be provided. Affinities of quality issues in domains such as chemistry, biology, and geoinformatics are discussed in the paper.

Keywords: Data quality · Quality of service · Machine learning

1 Introduction

The online provisioning of services and data has been studied since the early 2000's in terms of ensuring the characteristics of the services being provided. In particular, quality of service (QoS) characteristics and the problem of representing the quality requirements have been studied in detail [29]. In many cases the provided services are a composition of several services and this poses additional challenges to providers, as the service composition has to perform according to agreed QoS levels.

In his research work, Mike Papazoglou has always promoted the idea of focusing on service management at different levels in service-oriented computing [34,35]. Furthermore, he pointed out the importance of an infrastructure support for data and process integration. The service execution environment, its underlying infrastructure and the data provided in service requests have very variable characteristics. For this reason, several approaches have been proposed

© Springer Nature Switzerland AG 2021
M. Aiello et al. (Eds.): Papazoglou Festschrift, LNCS 12521, pp. 236–248, 2021.
https://doi.org/10.1007/978-3-030-73203-5_18

for service management, for providing adaptivity in services and for their compositions in order to guarantee the QoS requirements [32]. Adaptation has been investigated in many papers by Papazoglou towards guaranteeing compliance and QoS with Service Level Agreements (SLA) and contracts, focusing also on the evolution of services (e.g., [2]).

Nowadays, services have become a common infrastructure in many application domains. Nevertheless, the Service Computing manifesto of 2017 [9], advocates that the efforts of researchers have been mainly focused on technological aspects of services, in particular on web services. However, new challenges are posed by emerging technologies. A stronger need of inter-organizational cooperation is growing. The ability of supporting the collection of sensing data from pervasive sensing devices and (re)using data collected by other organizations is required. It is also important to support the human interpretation of the results obtained by services. In a recent Dagstuhl seminar [13] the importance of creating ecosystems for sharing data and providing services in an inter-organizational context was discussed, where the quality of data and services are a key issue.

The goal of this paper is to revisit the research challenges posed by data and services, in the light of requirements emerging in the context of natural sciences and scientific data. In this context, data are characterized by an intrinsic and heterogeneous level of imprecision. In addition, pipelines of data analysis services, which include modeling services, simulation tools and other data-driven services often based on Machine Learning (ML) and Deep Neural Networks (DNN), have added new sources of uncertainties in the process. We will discuss how the service computing principle can be tailored to this context and how imprecision can be managed following QoS principles. Some examples will be derived from chemistry, biology, and geographical spatio-temporal representations.

The paper is structured as follows. In Sect. 2, we go over related work on adaptivity and compliance and on data representation and imprecision. In Sect. 3, we discuss challenges and open problems in representing and managing imprecise data in natural sciences. Finally, in Sect. 4 we discuss how imprecision can be managed within a service computing approach.

2   Related Work

In this section, we briefly examine some of the key papers that put the basis for the discussion about providing services in the natural science domain, with a focus on imprecision in data and services.

One of the key issues is to represent and guarantee data quality. The characteristics of data quality modeling and representation for service computing are described in detail in [29], which compares the many dimensions, models, and methods proposed in the area. As discussed in [7], data and information quality has to be managed from a number of points of view. Some of the main issues are related to the structure of information and the representation of data values.

As mentioned in the introduction, adaptivity is advocated as a key feature in composed services. To the purpose of this paper, we focus mainly on quality issues. In the direction of representing QoS in variable contexts, in [3] the issue of varying soft and hard constraints within a contract is analyzed. In [2] the evolution of services, also due to QoS-level induced service changes, is studied, distinguishing between shallow changes, limited to the single service, and deep changes, that have an impact also on other services and providers.

Since the publication of [33], the semantics of conceptual schemas has taken a key role in database design. Different structures can be defined for the same data domain and a systematic approach is needed to identify objects and their relationships in a schema, as well as similar objects in different schemas. Based on [33], some systematic schema similarity assessment metrics have been defined and further developed in [14]. As natural science data are likely to originate from different heterogeneous sources, similar problems can be encountered in integrating them. As discussed in [13], different data interoperability architectures can be envisioned for data integration, data exchange, data repositories, and collaborative data sharing. The semantic associated to the schemas is a critical issue in data ecosystems [13]. In some cases inconsistencies and incompabilities can not be avoided, thus services are needed to access and manage them.

This requires adequate metadata, but "adequate" has a different meaning when the goal changes [26]. Context-aware data quality management supported by an effective metadata management has been recently discussed in [5]. General challenges related to the management of data and data-driven services in the context of scientific data frameworks have been discussed in [38]. In this context, metadata management has a key role.

Another issue impacting data quality and, as a consequence, the quality of services, is that data can be not only imprecise, but also represented at different levels of granularity. Spatio-temporal data is characterized by an intrinsic imprecision and by (sometimes implicit) relationships. The modeling of spatio-temporal data has been studied in [28], integrating work from temporal database literature and spatial data management. Implicit temporal information which can be extracted from temporal relations between events (e.g., before or after) and temporal indeterminacy are difficult to represent and query in conventional databases [4,11]. Challenges in this directions permeate the analysis of data in natural sciences. The integration of spatial information at different levels of granularity and with a varying accuracy has been recently highlighted as a key issue in various domain, from the integration of single cell biological data [30] to geographical data extracted from social media [25].

3   Representing Imprecise Data and Services

In the following, several open challenges are introduced and discussed. These are characterized by being common to virtually all fields within natural sciences, and derive from data and service quality limitations, in particular related to uncertainty of data and data-driven models. After presenting an overview of the main challenges, relevant directions investigated in recent years are discussed, focusing, in particular, on machine learning-based services. We conclude the section with a discussion on uncertainty of data and services in relation to quality for data-driven applications.

3.1 Overview and Challenges

Some recurrent themes characterizing scientific data are the varying levels of granularity, the highly variable quality of the information available (which includes the uncertainty about and originating from the data) and the high number of dimensions (which includes multiple modalities) captured. In turn, the latter can be highly heterogeneous across data points. These characteristics of the data can stem from the model(s) designed to explain them, be the result of technological limitations and of other trade-offs, or be the consequence of a limited knowledge when interpreting and analyzing the gathered information.

The varying granularity, quality and number of collected features characterize the integration and the analysis of scientific experiments from multiple sources and collected over extended periods of times (for example, in the combustion kinetics domain [38]). In this case, technological limitations constrain the *resolution* and the *confidence* of the collected measurements. On top of this, arbitrary choices on the *aggregation level* at which the collected data are described (for example, in scientific papers or repositories) further increase the variability across all directions. Finally, *ambiguities* related to the experimental description, which can also be promoted by flexible and unstructured formats, can further exacerbate these phenomena.

Trade-offs related to the obtainment of the data are often responsible for the variability of its features, with less accurate methods being more cost and time effective. For example, in an ideal world thermochemical properties for all the relevant chemical species would be obtained experimentally or by using high-quality quantum mechanical calculations. However, the cost and time involved would be unbearable, and several other progressively less accurate but more scalable approaches have been proposed, and are used to build varying quality datasets upon which state-of-the-art ML models are trained [22].

A notable example of varying granularity is the *spatial granularity*, observed across many domains beyond that of geographic information analysis. Even though in theory geographic data can be represented at an arbitrary resolution, in practice their extraction in limited-knowledge contexts drastically hinders the available resolution. This is, for example, the case for locations extracted from social media analysis [25]. Here, the location extraction step usually involves data-driven *disambiguation* or crowd-sourcing based activities, which also introduce a varying accuracy in the results. This means that, for example, the location associated to an image extracted from social media is known only up to a certain administrative level (e.g., city or country) even though its "true" location is, in principle, a point in space. Moreover, the inferred location could be only partially correct, for example being correct up to a certain administrative level. Similar issues are central to many other scientific domains. For example, in biology, recent efforts towards the creation of single-cell resolution atlases of organs (e.g., [16]) have highlighted challenges related to the integration of spatial data with a varying resolution, quality and number of modalities [30]. In this case, variability mainly stems from the existence of different technologies with different trade-offs in terms of resolution, throughput, confidence, etc. This has led to the development of integration services to overcome the limitations of each individual technology, and to enable analyses at multiple resolution scales.

Even though only based on few examples, the above discussion makes evident how many recurrent themes can benefit from the investigation of common solutions.

3.2   Requirements and Application Solutions

The recent focus on the development of data-driven scientific frameworks, atlases and computing pipelines has highlighted a set of specific requirements and architectural needs to support them. While often arising in a specific domain, these requirements are for the majority general, and shared among scientific fields.

Recently, a set of requirements to enhance the capabilities of data-driven scientific frameworks has been discussed in [38]. These include:

- The continuous and semantic *multi-source integration*, with a focus on the heterogeneous quality of the sources and their mutual dependencies.
- The *dynamic acquisition* of new information ("open-world" assumption).
- the *continuous dynamic validation* of stored information as new knowledge and sources are acquired, accounting for data and model uncertainties.

Though not exhaustive, these requirements provide an abstract framework to describe the application solutions recently investigated across domains. In the following, these requirements are generalized, and key application solutions are framed within them.

Multi-source Integration. As previously mentioned, the information conveyed by the different data sources is heterogeneous and can vary largely in terms of resolution, accuracy and coverage. For its importance, integration is a prerequisite in most of the other activities [30]. One additional challenge often faced in this area is the lack of references or ontologies to drive the integration [38]. Instead, little or no prior information is often available, and complementary strengths of the different sources need to be exploited to automatically generate ontologies or achieve integration in the absence of curated references. Focusing on data-driven methods, we can identify several directions.

Different sources can be individually analyzed and their outputs jointly used to overcome the limitations of each individual source. This is often the case when the analysis of one source can enhance the information extraction process from the others (see also *dynamic acquisition*). For example, it has been shown how the integration of spatial proteomics data and protein-protein interaction network data enables the extraction of more information and increases the predictive power [39]. On the same line, extracting geographical information from multiple social media, an iterative triangulation-based approach can overcome the limitations of each individual source in terms of accuracy, volume and available modalities [6].

In many cases, different sources are *fused* and *aligned* in a common shared space. This unsupervised process is particularly challenging in the absence of reference data. Finding common sources of variation in heterogeneous data is key in health research, metabolomics, epigenetics and epidemiology, to name a few [23]. It has been recently shown how, by detecting common sources of variation, single-cell transcriptomic data can be effectively integrated across different conditions, technologies, species, and modalities [12]. Unsupervised deep learning methods have been used to achieve a similar goal [19]. In all cases, the aim is to derive a shared manifold across data features. Even though promising, existing methods are characterized by scalability and flexibility limitations [12,19].

Finally, a class of integration strategies characterizing ML-based services is based on *domain adaptation*. Strategies such as *transfer learning* (transferring the knowledge learned in a source domain to a target domain) and multi-task learning (using multi-task objectives to implicitly learn and exploit a shared latent space) have been recently used to cope with heterogeneous sources in natural sciences domains. Transfer learning techniques are particularly effective in these domains, given the challenges usually faced constructing large-scale well-annotated datasets [40]. Transfer learning has shown promising results in molecular property prediction, integrating small sets of high-accuracy data to larger set of less accurate datasets [22]. Similar strategies have been also used integrating single cell transcriptomics across batches and datasets [42,43].

Dynamic Acquisition. Even though including new samples usually improves the performance of data-driven algorithms (assuming new data has comparable precision), the extent of this effect largely depends on *which* new samples are available. By making an "open-world" assumption, a system accounts for the existence of data samples external to it, which can be queried/produced (with an associate cost) and integrated into the system (e.g., in the training phase). In this setting, the best predicate for querying new information depends, in general, on the already available information, the cost associated to gather the new information and on a background knowledge [38]. The net result of this approach is a virtuous refinement cycle.

This cycle can follow also the time direction. For example, as time passes, new information can be made available and already collected data can drive more accurate queries. This approach has been used, for example, to extract geographical information from social media and to iteratively evaluate the relevance of collected contents to refine the search keywords [6].

In the ML community, the iterative refinement of a model through the acquisition of new training data is named *active learning*. The acquisition of new training samples usually involves time consuming and/or costly operations (e.g., human in the loop), thus the need to optimize new queries. This is often the case in natural sciences, where DNN-based active learning frameworks have been recently proposed to query manual annotations [21] or other more accurate models [31]. An active learning framework often includes the calculation of the *uncertainty* of the model over the predictions, which contributes to the selection of the best new samples to be added.

Continuous Dynamic Validation. In a data-driven framework, data validation is both a prerequisite for further analyses and the result of data integration and cleaning services. These two activities can follow a virtuous cycle.

The validation of input data to ML pipelines is subject of active research and has to be tackled from different perspectives. For example, [10] distinguishes between *single-batch*, where the focus is on highlighting anomalies in a single batch of data, *inter-batch*, to capture significant changes between training and serving data or different batches of training data, and *model testing*, to ensure that there are no assumptions in the training code that are not reflected in the data.

When little or no prior references/ontologies are available, data validation and curation activities can follow integration and acquisition steps. Comparisons across data features and modalities, possibly with additional data gathered through targeted queries, can enable the validation of existing data in the absence of prior ground truth. For example, a transfer learning approach has been used to integrate and correct multiple RNA sequencing batches [43] and to improve the quality of noisy and sparse single-cell transcriptomics data [42]. Cross-comparison of experimental datasets and models extracted from the literature can help discovering inconsistencies [24,38].

The goal of the above discussion is to link general data and service quality management requirements to recent data-driven application solutions explored across domains. The similarities pointed out should drive the research of both general techniques and shared theoretical frameworks. One key feature underlying all the discussed requirements is the management of *uncertainty* in the data and introduced by services. This becomes particularly important when data are inherently noisy and for machine-learning based services. This is discussed in the following.

3.3 Uncertainty of Data and Services

The quality of the data is central to the definition of *value* in services. Indeed, the value obtainable from service orchestration hinges on the quality of the data exchanged among the orchestrated services [1]. Being at the highest level in the computing value chain, the quality of a service is generally affected by the knowledge it relies on, which ultimately depends on the underlying data. This relationship, which usually exists in terms of data exchanged between services, takes a much wider significance for data-driven and, especially, ML-based services. In the latter case, indeed, available data contribute to the definition of functions processing new data (think, for example, of a service based on a trained ML models, which output/quality depends on the underlying dataset and its quality). Therefore, in this context, the relationship between data and service quality needs to be revised [8].

We observe how progresses in the deep learning community have recently led to the development of models that can efficiently compute calibrated uncertainties over their predictions. Notably, approximate Bayesian DNNs have been proposed as principled methods to separately compute the *epistemic uncertainty*, which stems from the model's ignorance about the underlying model (e.g., insufficient training data) and the *aleatoric uncertainty*, which intrinsically characterizes the data (e.g., experimental noise, stochasticity, etc.) [18,27]. The recent spread of these models in fields such as chemistry, biology and medicine [17,37,41] has shown promise in explaining and discerning a model's predictions when trained on noisy, incomplete and heterogeneous data. However, some challenges related to the robustness and the interpretability of the estimated uncertainties still remain [37].

Another peculiar feature of ML-based services is the relationship between data volume and uncertainty in the results. Epistemic uncertainty can be explained away given enough data. For this reason, expanding the dataset, even through the usage of *data augmentation* techniques, can enhance the accuracy of the trained model and, consequently, the quality of the resulting service. In this case, the optimal accuracy consists in the right balance between volume and quality of the underlying dataset (with data augmentation techniques promoting the first while, potentially, hindering the second). Outcomes of ML models can complement and augment experimental datasets (with, in particular, DNN-based models being particularly effective to approximate complex natural phenomena), thus ultimately increasing the quality of resulting data-driven services [15,36].

The above discussion highlights some interdisciplinary research directions which should be investigated in the future:

- How to effectively *transfer* quality dimensions (including uncertainty) back and forth between services and data. Indeed, in this context, data define and refine the services through ML techniques, while, at the same time, datasets are enhanced and extended by other services (e.g., active learning, data cleaning and data augmentation routines).
- How to assess and store the *evolving quality* of the data, distinguishing between "inherent" data quality and other quality indicators progressively introduced by the analysis models, which also take into account the relationship with the (evolving) quality of other data and services.
- How to integrate ML *explainability* techniques [8,20] to data and service quality management routines and orchestration.

4   Managing Imprecision with Services

After the discussion on the origin and the characteristics of imprecision in data and service in the context of natural science at large presented in Sect. 3, in this section we propose a general architecture that highlights how a contract-based and adaptive approach can support the requirements previously discussed.

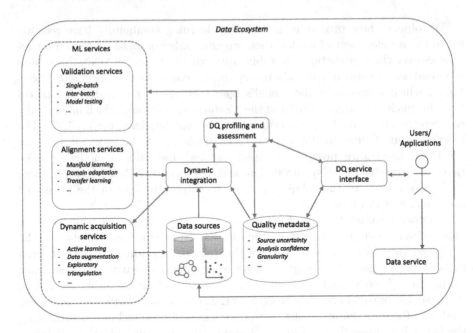

Fig. 1. Schematic architecture of the framework

The proposed architecture in Fig. 1 generalizes the one presented in [38], and contextualizes the machine learning services presented in Sect. 3 within the identified requirements. At the same time, the architecture extends the Data Quality Service Architecture introduced in [5], with metadata management (which, in our discussion, is mainly represented by *uncertainty management*) having a key role.

While the *dynamic integration* component handles the integration of different sources and metadata at the format/schema level, specific *alignment services* handle integration at the conceptual level. All the ML services interact with and enrich the *quality metadata* through the core *DQ profiling and assessment* service. The *dynamic acquisition services* also feed the data sources, thus allowing an iterative process. Other than feeding new data to the framework, the user/application interacts with the system through the *DQ service interface*. Through this, it has access to a complete quality overview.

5   Concluding Remarks

In this paper we discussed how a service computing approach can be tailored to the needs of data management in natural sciences. Focusing on the requirements emerging in this context from data and data-driven services (in particular, ML services), we discussed quality-related challenges and application directions, paying attention in particular on uncertainty management. We proposed a general architecture highlighting the advantages of a contract-based and adaptive approach, taking QoS constraints into consideration.

This work has highlighted several directions which necessitate further investigation. First of all, uncertainty estimation needs to become a central part of scientific data ecosystems. In this respect, investigating how to effectively transfer uncertainty properties back and forth between services and data, taking into account the evolving nature of both, represents an open challenge. On top of this, ML explainability techniques should be integrated to data and service quality management, ideally enriching the DQ service interface presented to the Users/Applications. In addition, if an adaptive approach is pursued, the stability of results should be evaluated, to assess the impact of adaptations in the ecosystem. Finally, as illustrated in [9], data acquisition, integration and validation services, could benefit from crowdsourcing activities. This approach is currently being proposed in the Crowd4SDG project[1], where citizen science is going to be supported by decision making/collaborative platforms and crowdsourcing tools.

Acknowledgements. This work was funded by the European Commission H2020 project Crowd4SDG "Citizen Science for Monitoring Climate Impacts and Achieving Climate Resilience" under project No. 872944. This work expresses the opinions of the authors and not necessarily those of the European Commission. The European Commission is not liable for any use that may be made of the information contained in this work.

References

1. Ameller, D., Illa, X.B., Collell, O., Costal, D., Franch, X., Papazoglou, M.P.: Development of service-oriented architectures using model-driven development: a mapping study. Inf. Softw. Technol. **62**, 42–66 (2015). https://doi.org/10.1016/j.infsof.2015.02.006

2. Andrikopoulos, V., Benbernou, S., Papazoglou, M.P.: On the evolution of services. IEEE Trans. Softw. Eng. **38**(3), 609–628 (2012). https://doi.org/10.1109/TSE.2011.22

3. Andrikopoulos, V., Fugini, M., Papazoglou, M.P., Parkin, M., Pernici, B., Siadat, S.H.: QoS contract formation and evolution. In: Buccafurri, F., Semeraro, G. (eds.) EC-Web 2010. LNBIP, vol. 61, pp. 119–130. Springer, Heidelberg (2010). https://doi.org/10.1007/978-3-642-15208-5_11

4. Anselma, L., Piovesan, L., Terenziani, P.: Dealing with temporal indeterminacy in relational databases: an AI methodology. AI Commun. **32**(3), 207–221 (2019). https://doi.org/10.3233/AIC-190619

5. Ardagna, D., Cappiello, C., Samá, W., Vitali, M.: Context-aware data quality assessment for big data. Future Gener. Comput. Syst. **89**, 548–562 (2018). https://doi.org/10.1016/j.future.2018.07.014

6. Autelitano, A., Pernici, B., Scalia, G.: Spatio-temporal mining of keywords for social media cross-social crawling of emergency events. Geoinformatica **23**(3), 425–447 (2019)

---

[1] http://www.crowd4sdg.eu/.

7. Batini, C., Scannapieco, M.: Data and Information Quality - Dimensions, Principles and Techniques. DSA. Springer, Cham (2016). https://doi.org/10.1007/978-3-319-24106-7

8. Bertossi, L., Geerts, F.: Data quality and explainable AI. J. Data Inf. Qual. (JDIQ) **12**(2), 1–9 (2020)

9. Bouguettaya, A., et al.: A service computing manifesto: the next 10 years. Commun. ACM **60**(4), 64–72 (2017). https://doi.org/10.1145/2983528

10. Breck, E., Polyzotis, N., Roy, S., Whang, S., Zinkevich, M.: Data validation for machine learning. In: Talwalkar, A., Smith, V., Zaharia, M. (eds.) Proceedings of Machine Learning and Systems 2019, MLSys 2019, Stanford, CA, USA, 31 March–2 April 2019 (2019). https://proceedings.mlsys.org/book/267.pdf. mlsys.org

11. Brusoni, V., Console, L., Terenziani, P., Pernici, B.: Qualitative and quantitative temporal constraints and relational databases: theory, architecture, and applications. IEEE Trans. Knowl. Data Eng. **11**(6), 948–968 (1999). https://doi.org/10.1109/69.824613

12. Butler, A., Hoffman, P., Smibert, P., Papalexi, E., Satija, R.: Integrating single-cell transcriptomic data across different conditions, technologies, and species. Nat. Biotechnol. **36**(5), 411–420 (2018). https://doi.org/10.1109/69.824613

13. Cappiello, C., Gal, A., Jarke, M., Rehof, J.: Data ecosystems: sovereign data exchange among organizations (Dagstuhl Seminar 19391). Dagstuhl Rep. **9**(9), 66–134 (2020). https://doi.org/10.4230/DagRep.9.9.66. https://drops.dagstuhl.de/opus/volltexte/2020/11845

14. Castano, S., De Antonellis, V., Fugini, M.G., Pernici, B.: Conceptual schema analysis: techniques and applications. ACM Trans. Database Syst. **23**(3), 286–332 (1998). https://doi.org/10.1145/293910.293150

15. Ching, T., et al.: Opportunities and obstacles for deep learning in biology and medicine. J. Roy. Soc. Interface **15**(141), 20170387 (2018)

16. Consortiu, H., et al.: The human body at cellular resolution: the NIH Human Biomolecular Atlas Program. Nature **574**(7777), 187 (2019)

17. Fauw, J.D., et al.: Clinically applicable deep learning for diagnosis and referral in retinal disease. Nat. Med. **24**(9), 1342–1350 (2018). http://lmb.informatik.uni-freiburg.de/Publications/2018/Ron18

18. Fox, C.R., Ülkümen, G.: Distinguishing Two Dimensions of Uncertainty, vol. 14, chap. 1. Universitetsforlaget Oslo (2011)

19. Gala, R., et al.: A coupled autoencoder approach for multi-modal analysis of cell types. In: Advances in Neural Information Processing Systems, pp. 9267–9276 (2019)

20. Gilpin, L.H., Bau, D., Yuan, B.Z., Bajwa, A., Specter, M., Kagal, L.: Explaining explanations: an overview of interpretability of machine learning. In: 2018 IEEE 5th International Conference on Data Science and Advanced Analytics (DSAA), pp. 80–89. IEEE (2018)

21. Gilyazev, R., Turdakov, D.Y.: Active learning and crowdsourcing: a survey of optimization methods for data labeling. Program. Comput. Softw. **44**(6), 476–491 (2018). https://doi.org/10.1134/S0361768818060142

22. Grambow, C.A., Li, Y.P., Green, W.H.: Accurate thermochemistry with small data sets: a bond additivity correction and transfer learning approach. J. Phys. Chem. A **123**(27), 5826–5835 (2019)

23. Gu, Z., de Schipper, N.C., Van Deun, K.: Variable selection in the regularized simultaneous component analysis method for multi-source data integration. Scientific Rep. **9**(1), 1–21 (2019)

24. Hansen, N., He, X., Griggs, R., Moshammer, K.: Knowledge generation through data research: new validation targets for the refinement of kinetic mechanisms. In: Proceedings of the Combustion Institute (2018)

25. Havas, C., et al.: E2mC: improving emergency management service practice through social media and crowdsourcing analysis in near real time. Sensors **17**(12), 2766 (2017)

26. Jagadish, H.: Big data and science: myths and reality. Big Data Res. **2**(2), 49–52 (2015)

27. Kendall, A., Gal, Y.: What uncertainties do we need in Bayesian deep learning for computer vision? In: Proceedings of the 31st International Conference on Neural Information Processing Systems, NIPS 2017 pp. 5580–5590 (2017). http://dl.acm.org/citation.cfm?id=3295222.3295309

28. Sellis, T.K., et al. (eds.): Spatio-Temporal Databases. LNCS, vol. 2520. Springer, Heidelberg (2003). https://doi.org/10.1007/b83622

29. Kritikos, K., et al.: A survey on service quality description. ACM Comput. Surv. **46**(1), 1:1–1:58 (2013). https://doi.org/10.1145/2522968.2522969

30. Lähnemann, D., et al.: Eleven grand challenges in single-cell data science. Genome Biol. **21**(1), 1–35 (2020). https://doi.org/10.1186/s13059-020-1926-6

31. Li, Y.P., Han, K., Grambow, C.A., Green, W.H.: Self-evolving machine: a continuously improving model for molecular thermochemistry. J. Phys. Chem. A **123**(10), 2142–2152 (2019)

32. Metzger, A., Pohl, K., Papazoglou, M.P., Di Nitto, E., Marconi, A., Karastoyanova, D.: Research challenges on adaptive software and services in the future internet: towards an S-cube research roadmap. In: Metzger, A., Pohl, K., Papazoglou, M.P. (eds.) First International Workshop on European Software Services and Systems Research - Results and Challenges, S-Cube 2012, Zurich, Switzerland, 5 June 2012, pp. 1–7. IEEE (2012). https://doi.org/10.1109/S-Cube.2012.6225501

33. Papazoglou, M.P.: Unraveling the semantics of conceptual schemas. Commun. ACM **38**(9), 80–94 (1995). https://doi.org/10.1145/223248.223275

34. Papazoglou, M.P., Georgakopoulos, D.: Introduction. Commun. ACM **46**(10), 24–28 (2003). https://doi.org/10.1145/944217.944233

35. Papazoglou, M.P., Traverso, P., Dustdar, S., Leymann, F.: Service-oriented computing: state of the art and research challenges. IEEE Comput. **40**(11), 38–45 (2007). https://doi.org/10.1109/MC.2007.400

36. Ratti, F., Scalia, G., Pernici, B., Magarini, M.: A data-driven approach to optimize bounds on the capacity of the molecular channel. In: GLOBECOM 2020 - 2020 IEEE Global Communications Conference, Taipei, Taiwan, pp. 1–7. IEEE (2020). https://doi.org/10.1109/GLOBECOM42002.2020.9322078

37. Scalia, G., Grambow, C.A., Pernici, B., Li, Y.P., Green, W.H.: Evaluating scalable uncertainty estimation methods for deep learning-based molecular property prediction. J. Chem. Inf. Model. **60**(6), 2697–2717 (2020). https://doi.org/10.1021/acs.jcim.9b00975

38. Scalia, G., Pelucchi, M., Stagni, A., Cuoci, A., Faravelli, T., Pernici, B.: Evaluating scalable uncertainty estimation methods for deep learning-based molecular property prediction. Data Sci. **2**(1–2), 245–273 (2019)

39. Squires, S., Ewing, R., Prügel-Bennett, A., Niranjan, M.: A method of integrating spatial proteomics and protein-protein interaction network data. In: Liu, D., Xie, S., Li, Y., Zhao, D., El-Alfy, E.-S.M. (eds.) ICONIP 2017, Part V. LNCS, vol. 10638, pp. 782–790. Springer, Cham (2017). https://doi.org/10.1007/978-3-319-70139-4_79

40. Tan, C., Sun, F., Kong, T., Zhang, W., Yang, C., Liu, C.: A survey on deep transfer learning. In: Kůrková, V., Manolopoulos, Y., Hammer, B., Iliadis, L., Maglogiannis, I. (eds.) ICANN 2018, Part III. LNCS, vol. 11141, pp. 270–279. Springer, Cham (2018). https://doi.org/10.1007/978-3-030-01424-7_27

41. Tomašev, N., et al.: A clinically applicable approach to continuous prediction of future acute kidney injury. Nature **572**(7767), 116–119 (2019). https://doi.org/10.1038/s41586-019-1390-

42. Wang, J., et al.: Data denoising with transfer learning in single-cell transcriptomics. Nat. Methods **16**(9), 875–878 (2019)

43. Wang, T.T., et al.: BERMUDA: a novel deep transfer learning method for single-cell RNA sequencing batch correction reveals hidden high-resolution cellular subtypes. Genome Biol. **20**(1), 1–15 (2019). https://doi.org/10.1186/s13059-019-1764-6

Just-in-Time Sentiment Analysis
for Streamed Data in Greek

Ioanna Karageorgou, Panagiotis Liakos, and Alex Delis(⊠)

University of Athens, 15703 Athens, Greece
{sdi1600057,p.liakos,ad}@di.uoa.gr

Abstract. The growth of social-media platforms has been remarkable in terms of both number of users and volume of content generated. Twitter now reports approximately 166M *daily active* users who generate in excess of 500M tweets. Such volumes pose major challenges when it comes to providing analytics services and sentiment analyses for specific issues. As citizens tend to freely express their sentiments on social platforms, Twitter has inherently become an indispensable source for the public discourse in a wide variety of topics. Carrying out sentiment analysis on a timely manner on streamed tweets is undoubtedly a demanding endeavor. In this paper, we propose a Spark-based Twitter sentiment analysis software architecture that receives online streamed messages and compiles analytics. We outline the main elements of our proposal and discuss how they collectively help address the challenges involved in this big-data processing task. In particular, our framework: *i*) exploits the Spark machine-learning library to classify Greek tweets in a timely-manner, *ii*) manages streamed tweets in synergy with contemporary queuing and in-memory data systems, and *iii*) determines with high accuracy whether a sentiment is expressed by a genuine account. We report on the findings while experimenting with a novel model for sentiment analysis we created for Greek and ascertain the effectiveness of our proposed architecture.

Keywords: Just-in-time sentiment analysis · Handling tweets in Greek · Spark-based big-data architecture

1 Introduction

Twitter is an influential micro-blogging social networking platform whose Web popularity has endured over time and it now stands at the top-5 for both most-accessed portals [8] and social networks worldwide [15]. In the past, the platform has consistently produced breaking international and regional news, worthy announcements, statements, and positions through its snippet-like payload. Subsequently, Twitter's usage has propelled it to not only inform but also to influence public opinion. To this end, key international events appeared early on in Twitter if compared to traditional media outlets. Events that were first reported and extensively covered through the contribution of Twitter's users include the financial crisis of 2008, the Japan earthquake and tsunami, the peak

© Springer Nature Switzerland AG 2021
M. Aiello et al. (Eds.): Papazoglou Festschrift, LNCS 12521, pp. 249–263, 2021.
https://doi.org/10.1007/978-3-030-73203-5_19

of the 2015 refugee crisis, the Ebola outbreak and of course major political events and elections. Along the way, the platform has been extensively used as a forum to express opinions on public affairs and as means to forward items of interest through its *retweeting* feature. In early 2020, Twitter had a worldwide 166 Million of *daily "monetizable"* active users who are its key content contributors [23].

As positions and statements constantly appear on the platform, arguments and counterarguments ensue helping morph opinions on contemporary issues with individuals ultimately making up their mind and taking stands on current affairs. This is of course, the *virtual discourse* appearing daily in the Twitter-sphere. In this regard, it is of paramount importance for both individuals and groups of users to not simply follow this discourse, but also seek to better understand and quantitatively ascertain the impact of these on-going discussions. In this process which has become collectively known as *Sentiment Analysis* (SA), there are a few key factors that have to be considered, namely:

1. *just-in-time* compilation of aggregations of opinions expressed on a specific topic,
2. management of the *voluminous* content generated by potentially large (i.e., tens of thousands or even millions of users) on a particular issue,
3. effective handling of the abbreviated and occasionally mal-formed statements expressed in the textual part of tweets.

A key requirement in successfully addressing the above factors and produce reliable Twitter-SA analyses would be to create data-systems mostly based on contemporary and off-the-shelf software components. Such an system should warrant the effective and timely harnessing of SA-derived information. To this end, a number of application areas could be facilitated by providing insights into business and existing practices, events of imminent global importance, stock market movement, rapid dissemination of emergency information and even infectious disease and outbreaks management and coordination of response-teams [26].

In this paper, we investigate the Greek Twitter-sphere while considering streamed live tweets as they arrive from the platform's API. Our main objective is to propose a software architecture that is flexible, efficient, and presents features that both enable the timely processing of SA-analyses and addresses our 3 above-mentioned *must-have* factors. To attain our objective, we initially create a *Naive-Bayes* model for the Greek language based on 10K tweets we have collected using the platform's API. The messages are cleansed of visual and unnecessary content, get "normalized", and receive due pre-processing for stemming. We then manually annotate and label every tweet in this dataset of 10K as either positive or negative [13]. We then propose a software architecture to help in the just-in-time handling of streamed tweets. Our architecture is primarily based on the integration of Spark with the RabbitMQ queuing system and Redis in-memory database. Spark is a contemporary data-engine that offers not only flexibility and fast cluster-based computing but also an assortment of specialized-operations including interactive algorithms, queries and streaming [2]. RabbitMQ and Redis components serve as our buffering means in the processing of incoming tweets. Our aggregate infrastructure can handle multiple analysis through its various classes of topics that can be introduced in the queuing and storage mechanisms exploiting the versatile computations offered in the form of pipelines on `DataFrames`. Last but not least in `Twitter`, the operation of botnets is invariably a major concern for they can potentially distort the nature of discussions in contested topics in rather unexpected ways [22]. We introduce a genuine-user detection mechanism based on a ML-service that can identify in real-time bots and so, our analyses of streamed tweets can render reliable assessments.

We carry a comprehensive evaluation using a number of test datasets while experimenting with our prototype. In this, we assess both the effectiveness and efficiency of our proposed architecture and its underlying design choices in having Greek-tweets being classified as they are streamed in. The contributions of our paper are:

1. we develop a *Naive-Bayes*-based model for Greek based on a large dataset whose items we labeled as either positive or negative tweets,
2. we design and develop a software architecture that is capable of carrying out just-in-time tweet-fetching and classification, and lastly,
3. the system design choices as far as its machine-learning (ML) algorithms are concerned lead to highly accurate results that are produced within short periods of processing.

A number of efforts have been reported regarding the Greek tweet-sphere and are related to our work. In [11], an approach to derive sentiments using the lexicon in [25] is discussed and the polarity of these sentiments is derived using hashtags. An effort to enrich the above lexicon with synonyms is discussed in [7] while relying on unsupervised ML-techniques; the latter do not work well with snippets of informal languages present in tweets. [14] presents a SA approach for micro-blog streaming based on `Storm` where pre-processing occurs and the behavior of different classifiers is examined. In [18], the performance of *Naive Bayes* (NB) and *SVM* classifiers is examined to determine sentiments exploiting `PySpark`. Today, no detection for non-genuine user accounts with certainty leads to reduced levels in accuracy and reliability. A technique for fake account detections was discussed in [5] that attempted to correlate content of tweets and their initiators. Our paper is structured as follows: Sect. 2 outlines our Greek NB-model, Sect. 3 discusses the elements of our architecture. Section 4 presents our experimental results while Sect. 5 offers concluding remarks.

2   Creating a Sentiment Analysis Model for Greek

Sentiment analysis is the process of identifying non-trivial, subjective considerations extracted from a collection of textual corpora. These sources contain latent information on opinions expressed by the general public. As a process, SA has to be automated as it seeks to both analyze predominantly voluminous text-data and classify encountered opinions as positive, negative, or anything in between. The ability to extract insights from social data has enabled the creation of impactful applications and is now a widely-adopted practice followed by companies and organizations across the globe. The reach of sentiment analysis applications remains broad and powerful as they help track customer reviews, citizen opinions and survey responses. Clearly, the impact of such applications shall remain strong as they offer valuable insights and help to enhance sales, improve corporate marketing strategies, and analyze trends for political strategy planning. Moreover, sentiment analysis applications may offer clues to stock markets swings based on world news, financial reports and recorded social media sentiments [26].

In this paper, we focus on the Greek Twitter-sphere as there is much potential in harnessing the above trends and seek to develop a pertinent classification model based on Spark. In order to collect training data for our model, we used the Twitter's Streaming API in conjunction with Python3. To reveal the hidden sentiments behind the collected tweets, we used a sentiment dictionary for the Greek language [25] featuring 2, 316 entries that are evaluated for the following 6 emotions: *anger, disgust, fear, happiness, sadness*, and *surprise*. In our effort, we considered only the polarity of each word in the lexicon while refraining from taking into account gradients for every distinctive sentiment encountered. As tweets are textual snippets, we encountered several occasions in which the textual body of the message contained no lexicon word. Evidently, this shortcoming might ultimately create issues with low-coverage and diminished reliability for sentiment analysis [14,16]. To address this deficiency, we embarked on the time-consuming task of manually annotating and labeling the sentiment expressed in every of these $10K$ captured tweets while keeping in mind the lexicon polarity. In this context, we have created a training dataset consisting of 10, 000 tweets in Greek with *balanced* negative and positive polarity.

A key challenge in developing our model is the necessary processing of Greek language due to its complex morphological features including high inflection and stressing rules. For this reason, we elected to preprocess Greek tweets to create an "even" output before we could train our model. This preprocessing entails punctuation and stop-word removal as we deem them to be noise potentially blurring the final result of our model [11]. We also used a language stemmer in order to remove possibly unnecessary and confusing endings of Greek words [19]. Stemming is a *text-normalization* technique that reduces inflected/derived words to their base form. This was essential due to multiple endings words have in Greek under noun and verb tense declension. To this end, words derived from one another can be all mapped to an *equal* or *shorter form* of the word, yielding a more dense training dataset. It is equally important to indicate that our preprocessing further "cleans" tweets by removing tags, urls and hashtags.

The normalized text of every tweet has to subsequently be converted to an appropriate form of feature representation so that a ML algorithm can perform classification as such algorithms do not directly work with text. The transformation of text to vectors of numbers is accomplished through a *Term Frequency-Inverse Document Frequency* (*TF.IDF*) approach [20]. *TF.IDF* is a score that a machine can maintain to evaluate the effectiveness of each word encountered within a snippet by measuring the relative usage of the word across a number of considered documents. In this respect, *TF.IDF highlights* the importance of every word in a snippet that is part of a collection of passages. To have the examined snippets expressed as a set of *TF.IDF* numbers, each tweet has to be first split to its stem words before proceeding into model building and classification.

For our proposed system, we opted to realize a ML-model-based on *Naive-Bayes* (NB) for our sentiment classification. Although we considered a wide range of choices including *Logistic Regression* and *Decision Tree* classifiers, we opted for NB as our classification approach turns out through experimentation to be both effective and efficient. This is attributed to NB's short training phase which renders the NB-model appropriate for just-in-time predictions. Bayes theorem assumes that there is no dependency between every pair of features and stipulates that:

$$P(A|B) = \frac{P(A)P(B|A)}{P(B)}$$

where $P(A)$ is the probability of hypothesis A being true, $P(B)$ is the probability of event B being true, $P(A|B)$ is the conditional probability of hypothesis A given that B event s true, and finally, $P(B|A)$ is the conditional probability of event B given that A is true [10]. In general, tweet words are not deemed independent of each other and do not strictly comply with Naive-Bayes assumption [17]. Despite this, our suggested approach for the Greek corpora yields strong classification prediction in practice.

Provided we have fully annotated the 10,000 Greek tweet-dataset, we would like to estimate whether the incoming tweet *'Για καφεδάκι στο μπαλκόνι με θέα την θάλασσα'* can be classified as either positive or negative. A liberal translation of the tweet is *'For a short coffee at the balcony with sea view'*. Once our stemming and preprocessing occur, the tweet is transformed to: *'καφεδακ μπαλκον θε θαλασσ'* To SA-evaluate the latter, we have to compute the 2 probabilities and find the largest one:

(1) P(positive|'καφεδακ μπαλκον θε θαλασσ')
(2) P(negative|'καφεδακ μπαλκον θε θαλασσ')

As per Bayes' Theorem, *(1)* can be written as follows:
(1) $\implies$ (P('καφεδακ μπαλκον θε θαλασσ'|positive) * P(positive)) /
　　　　P('καφεδακ μπαλκον θε θαλασσ')

which based on the independence assumption becomes:
(1) $\implies$ (P('καφεδακ'|positive) * P('μπαλκον'|positive) * P('θε'|positive) *
　　　　P('θαλασσ'|positive) * P(positive)) /
　　　　(P('καφεδακ') * P('μπαλκον') * P('θε') * P('θαλασσ'))

All elements of the above expression can be readily derived from our existing dataset. We can similarly transform and compute expression *(2)*. Based on the highest probability value, we can then characterize the sentiment expressed by the incoming tweet.

There is still one more aspect requiring attention: stems that have not been detected so far will be very likely encountered with the arrival of new tweets. This in fact may change the composition of the established class of words thus far. Unless we treat them differently new stems will yield zero value probabilities

```
1 df = spark.read.csv("greekTrain10000.csv")
2
3 hashingTF=HashingTF(inputCol='text',outputCol='featTF')
4 idf=IDF(inputCol=hashingTF.getOutputCol(),outputCol='features')
5 nb=NaiveBayes()
6
7 ourpipeline=Pipeline(stages=[sanitizer,hashingTF,idf,nb])
8 derivedmodel=ourpipeline.fit(df)        #data training
9
10 predictions=derivedmodel.transform(incomingtweets)
```

Fig. 1. Building the model from the dataset in Greek

creating issues in the computation of the probabilities. To address this issue, we resort to *Laplace Smoothing* [10]. In order to avoid the problem of zero probabilities, an additional smoothing term can be added to the Bayes model. A small value (usually 1) is added in the numerator, so that the overall probability does not become zero.

To materialize our model, we used `Spark ML Pipeline`. A pipeline is envisaged as a series of data transformations that may entail diverse operations including feature extraction, normalization, dimensionality reduction, and model training. These components function in a producer-consumer paradigm using exchange datasets as their means of communication [2]. The `Spark ML Pipeline` realizes such a series of computing phases with each such stage serving as either *transformer* or *estimator*. Transformers apply a well-defined transformation on a dataset while estimators feature the additional capability of producing models by traversing the dataset. In our model, NB is an estimator, while *TF.IDF* is a transformer. Pipelines constitute a viable abstraction as ML-workflows do frequently have many phases. By representing these phases as composable elements, users can carry out changes readily, should they desire to impart modifications, improve functionalities and even search for enhanced parameter tuning while considering the entire workflow as a whole [2].

Our `Spark` pipeline of line 7 in the code segment appearing in Fig. 1, employs the *TF.IDF* computation as well as NB-classifier as defined in lines 3–5. The `ourpipeline.fit()` method is called on the original `DataFrame` that contains the "*clean* and *stemmed*" tweet snippets and labels. The `HashingTF` and `IDF` methods convert the words column into *feature vectors* in the form of a new column consisting of respective vectors for the `DataFrame` in question. As NB is an *estimator*, the `Pipeline` method invokes the NB-`fit()` to produce a Naive-Bayes `derivedmodel`. The latter features the same number of phases as the original `Pipeline` and as soon as the `transform()` method is applied, the dataset is passed through its fitted pipeline. The outcome of line 10 of the code segment are the predictions of all incoming tweets that we fetch on the fly from Twitter. It is worth pointing out that these predictions due to their reduced size can be produced rapidly to comply with our stated just-in-time classification requirement.

3 Proposed System Architecture

We aspired to realize a software architecture that carries out SA in near real-time while deploying on an aggregation of contemporary and off-the-shelve components. In this endeavor, our prime objective has been to yield highly-accurate classification of messages in the Greek Twitter-sphere while observing timely constraints. Just-in-time processing of tweets is predominantly concerned with the effective management of snippet processing within their expected-deadline [3], successfully addressing overheads ensued [4,12], and attaining low–latency via *easy-pass-through* of data frames in a pipelined data systems [24]. Spark plays a central role in our architecture for it offers the appropriate *enclosure* within which efficient handling of tweets and stemmed derivatives occurs. Figure 2 depicts the workflow that our suggested architecture handles based on data-pipelines.

Fig. 2. Overall workflow of the suggested architecture

Our tweet collection occurs the time instance messages are uploaded by users via the Twitter Streaming API. At this stage, a fundamental challenge is to ascertain whether the initiator of the snippet is a legitimate user. As in any social networking environment, Twitter does suffer from accounts that cannot be traced to real persons and so, they are deemed as fake accounts. The goal of such accounts is to manipulate public opinion about statements made or public figures, to exert influence for brands and services and in general to exercise unethical initiatives. To address this issue, we created an ML *fake detection service* with the intention to further improve the overall precision of our SA analysis. Once through the above check, snippets are directed to the ML-model we have created for Greek based on Spark's MLlib so as to achieve sentiment prediction as either positive or negative.

Figure 3 depicts the various components that our approach entails. To access tweets in real-time, we use the Python3 library tweepy[1], an open-source, gitHub-hosted project that allows for the communication with the Twitter's API. This Streaming API allows us to retrieve snippets complying with stated criteria of interest and requires a persistent *HTTP*-connection and user authentication through the OAuth protocol. The latter helps users access the platform's API without sharing their credentials. Once fetched, the tweets are directed to a RabbitMQ configuration so as we can exploit a number of benefits this system offers including: 1) persistent, deadline-designated and acknowledgement delivered queuing, 2) routing and tracing of messages using exchanges, should we

---

[1] https://github.com/tweepy/tweepy.

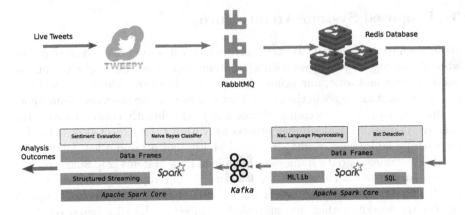

Fig. 3. Architectural elements for our SA in Greek Twitter-sphere.

want to impose different classes of snippet at the input of our architecture, and 3) easy-to-use queue monitoring and management through a versatile Web-interface. Subsequently, tweets are directed to the Redis main-memory database for storage while Spark deploys its instances and operations for bot-detection as well as pre-processing, stemming and ultimately tweet–characterization. Directly pushing tweets from the API into Redis is not a plausible choice for it could create operational issues due to flush-crowds occasionally formed. In this case, the arrival message rate to Redis is greater than its rate to absorb incoming tweets resulting into an unreliable operation for the proposed architecture. It is worth pointing out that RabbitMQ guarantees the integrity of all the messages that it handles in transition and that its dispatched tweets to Redis in the same temporal oder received. The cooperation of RabbitMQ with Redis is the basis for providing just-in-time tweet–classification and SA analysis as our architecture properly places time-outs mechanisms for any potential blocking operation along its constituent elements [24].

The Spark instantiation on the bottom right of Fig. 3 undertakes 2 distinct processing tasks for every Redis-stored message that also contains respective user-data: a) bot and fake user–account detection, and b) cleansing the text of natural language, filtering and stemming. A bot sends out automated posts often at a rate impossible to be matched by a human, with the sole purpose of alerting individuals to imminent and/or noteworthy events and actions. Although the negative contribution of botnets to the social discourse is hard to refute [6,9], botnets have been also used as alert-mechanisms in physical phenomena, emergencies and their aftermath including storms and forest-fires. Evidently, the type of SA analysis we investigate in this paper, would be biased if we also consider tweets by fake users. To address this issue, we have experimented with a Twitter bot-detection dataset from KAGGLE[2] and created and adopted a corresponding *random forest model*; we did this outside Spark's environment [5].

---

[2] https://www.kaggle.com/charvijain27/detecting-twitter-bot-data.

In this regard, our model does not in principle depend on our infrastructure to complete individual predictions. Moreover, a key advantage of training a model outside the Spark environment is that it yields lower latencies when deployed by our architecture and is well suited when fraud-detection and/or ad–bidding have to run continuously with data incoming at high-rates.

To train our bot-detection model, we used the following specific tweet features: 1) number of followers an account has, 2) number of users an account follows, 3) number of public lists a user is a member of, 4) number of tweets a user liked, 5) number of tweets including re-tweets, posted by an account, and finally, 6) whether a user has a verified account. Posts that have cleared the bot-detection module, often present unhelpful, irrelevant portions of text and they may have missing parts or noisy segments. If remain untreated, all these aspects will contribute to additional noise which might in turn yield our SA to be unreliable and likely weaker than expected. This is the motivation behind our pre-processing that involves cleansing of tweets so that useless lexemes are discarded. Stemming is also part of this phase whose outcome is the genuine messages. With the assistance of a Kafka producer clean and stematized tweets are stored in a Kafka-node in a *topic*-specific fashion. Following on the pipeline, a Kafka consumer has to subscribe to a corresponding store to be able to receive new data.

The Apache Kafka is a messaging and integration platform that offers decoupling and buffering for the Spark–Streaming. In general, Spark–Streaming uses very low level operations which are applied to individual records found in RDDs. Structured Streaming on the other hand, as depicted in the bottom-left of the Spark instantiation of Fig. 3, operates on entire Dataframes; as a processing engine, Structured Streaming is built atop the Spark-SQL. In our architecture, we opted for the use of Structured Streaming as it demonstrates clear processing advantage when real-time handling is necessary. Unlike its Spark-counterpart, Structured Streaming treats all arriving data as an *unbounded input table* in which every item in the Twitter-stream is a row appended [21]. As new rows enter the table, the ML-model gets dynamically updated [21]. In our proposal, a Kafka consumer receives cleansed tweets and organizes them in a DataFrame. All rows in this DataFrame are essentially our test-data that have to be classified using our NB approach for Greek as described in Sect. 2. Ultimately, our sentiment prediction for every encountered tweet is reported by our classifier on tty/designated file.

4   Experimental Results

We have implemented our SA architecture for streamed tweets based on Apache Spark *v2.3.4* along with Python3 API, PySpark *v2.3.4* that supports Spark's programming model. We deployed Tweepy *v3.8.0* to live access Twitter and developed our messaging system based on RabbitMQ *v3.8.3* in conjunction with the Pika-client. We used Redis v5.0.6 and its respective redis-py library to have fetched tweets get stored in main-memory while Kafka *v2.11.2* offered the pipeline to

`Spark's Structured Streaming` module. The entire system is hosted on an *Ubuntu 18.04* server with 8 cores on which `Spark` runs locally with 8 worker threads, one for each logical machine core.

In this section, we present the findings of our experimental evaluation with our system prototype. To this end, our specific goals have been to:

1. assess the quality of our Greek dataset while experimenting with a range of `Spark` ML-classifiers,
2. ascertain the overall efficiency of our architecture and gain and understanding of the processing overheads involved while results are compiled with streamed tweets, and finally,
3. investigate the effectiveness of our tweet fake-account detection component and its contribution to the overall performance of our system prototype.

■ **Assessment of SA-Model for Greek:** Although the training of any ML-mode is of key importance, the behavior of this model under new input workloads is an even more critical aspect of any ML-pipeline formed to address a specific task. In our experimentation, we initially sought to establish the accuracy of our adopted model and demonstrate that we can trust its predictions. To accomplish this, we used *cross-validation*, a technique that entails partitioning of the original observation dataset into a training and an evaluation set; the former is used to train the model and the latter to show the validity of experimental outcomes. Cross-validation technique can also be used to compare the performance of different ML-models working off the same dataset.

With the help of cross-validation, we have investigated the effectiveness of our SA-model for the Greek language under 3 different classifiers provided by `Spark-MLib`: 1) Naive–Bayes (NB), 2) Decision Tree, and 3) Logistic Regression. The dataset *ratio* for our cross-validation was set to 70:30, that is, we trained our models with 70% of the data while using the remaining 30% for testing validation.

Provided that for the dataset used in the experiment we have compiled the ground truth, we measure the performance of the above 3 classifiers in our assessment using the following metrics: a) *Accuracy*, b) *F1*-score, and c) *Area Under the ROC Curve(AUC)*. Accuracy measures how many observations, both positive and negative, were correctly classified. It is the ration of correct predictions made over all predictions made. *F1*-score is based on *Precision* and *Recall* and combines them into one metric by calculating the harmonic mean. *Precision* is the number of correct positive results divided by the total predicted positive observations. *Recall* is the number of correct positive results divided by the number of all relevant samples (total actual positives). *F1*-score yields an enhance measure of the incorrectly classified cases. *AUC* provides an aggregate measure of performance across all possible classification thresholds and is a probability curve that designates the degree or measure of *separability*. It essentially "states" how much a model is capable of distinguishing between classes. Thus, a successful model has *AUC* near 1 that means excellent separability. On the other hand, a *AUC* value near 0 reveals an unsuccessful model of poor separability.

Table 1. Measurements across the 3 classifiers.

METRICS	Naive-Bayes	Logistic regression	Decision tree
Accuracy	80.23	81.43	77.36
AUC	0.87	0.75	0.72
F1-score	0.75	0.79	0.71
Training time	1.15 s	6.23 s	14.87 s
Avg. resp. time per tweet	$1.3 \ 10^{-5}$ s	$5.8 \ 10^{-6}$ s	$4.5 \ 10^{-3}$ s

Table 1 shows all the measurements that each of the 3 models has attained while carrying out our cross validation. We also depict the total *training time* required as well as the *average response time* to process a tweet from the dataset. The *Logistic Regression* classifier shows a slightly better accuracy performance if compared with its NB-counterpart. On the other hand, `Naive-Bayes` demonstrates a more stable behavior in terms of its *AUC* score consistently for our dataset. The *Decision Tree* classifier had the poorest performance among the 3 contenders. Despite the fact that, *Logistic Regression* classifies a new tweet slightly faster than *Naive-Bayes*, we should also consider the length of the training phase needed as this is essentially a daemon-like process that occurs in `Structured Streaming`. Consequently, slower rates such as 6.23 secs and 14.87 secs do constitute significant time overheads that will ultimately create bottlenecks in the delivery of just-in-time classification. Taking also into account the achieved average response times, we have opted for the *Naive-Bayes* as the choice for our SA-model classifier.

We should note that all classifiers gave very promising results while operating on our Greek dataset. We consider this to be a strong indicator of the quality of the dataset. While generating this dataset from scratch, we had to overcome 2 challenges: 1) we encountered numerous tweets (in the thousands) that turned out to be either simply noise or simply unusable clutter (junk). This made the selection of useful tweets a tedious task as we had to ensure that the vocabulary in our dataset had to be from a wide range of topics and be equally representative to all, and 2) the Greek language necessitated due diligence due to its complex morphological features. In this respect, we had to overcome the additional "noise" imposed by the language by carefully crafting a pre-processing and stemming phase.

■ **Monitoring the Live-Feed:** We have evaluated our prototype by fetching tweets posted in Greek during the period of April 14th, 2020 to May 12th, 2020. The messages were passed through our prototype that designated every preprocessed and cleaned tweet as positive or negative. We should note that during the entire observation period Greece has been on a strict stay-at-home directive. Our goal was to monitor the behavior of our SA system in real–life condition and witness if the produced results reflected reality.

We tracked on the average 42,592 tweets per-day and our average weekly volume was 298,144. This traffic is only a small fraction of the worldwide activity reported for Twitter [23] as the number of users writing in Greek still remains modest if compared with more popular languages. From all acquired tweets, those with hashtags #covid19 and #COVID19greece displayed an interesting behavior as the timeline of Fig. 4 shows. Overall, we consistently observed that the number of negative tweets outweighs the number of positives on a daily basis.

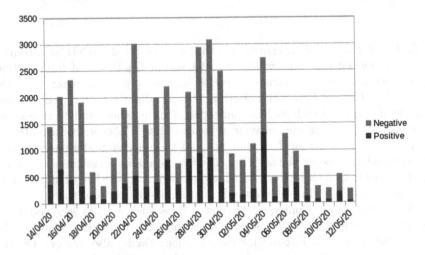

Fig. 4. tweets prediction for *#covid19, #COVID19greece*

As these tweets are related to the pandemic of the corona-virus, such a behavior was expected. Figure 4 clearly outlines a different picture on the 4th of May when the number of negative posts is about *equal* to those characterized as positives. This was the day that we noted the largest number of positive tweets linked to corona-virus, as well as the largest number of positives throughout our live experiment. We believe that this finding is directly associated to the fact that Greece entered its first phase of lifting lockdown on May 4th, after a 52–days general shelter-in-place government order.

Table 2. Detecting bot activity

METRICS	Decision tree	Naive Bayes	Random forest
Accuracy	85.27	75.35	87.17
AUC	0.87	0.75	0.93
F1-score	0.84	0.74	0.87
Training time	$3.74\ 10^{-2}$ s	$6.08\ 10^{-3}$ s	$3.42\ 10^{-2}$ s
Avg. resp. time per account	$6.67\ 10^{-7}$ s	$2.45\ 10^{-6}$ s	$3.33\ 10^{-7}$ s

■ **Effectiveness in Detecting Fake Accounts:** In order to facilitate as much as possible the just-in-time classification, we had to ensure that bot activity was detected early on so as respective processing for fake tweet-users can be avoided. To achieve this and be able to discard malicious users, we used the *Kaggle* bot detection dataset [1] to experiment with various algorithmic ML-options. Due to the limited number of datasets related to Twitter fake accounts, we tried to investigate the performance of our dataset in light of a wide range of *Sklearn*-classifiers. Among the possible examined choices, the more promising on the *Kaggle* dataset were those of *Random Forest, Naive Bayes,* and *Decision Tree.* As mentioned earlier, we used cross-validation with ratio 70:30 to ascertain the effectiveness of our choices and used scores: *Accuracy, F1*-score, and *AUC.* We also consider the training time required of every candidacy and the measured average response time required per account. Table 2 depicts our results while experimenting with the 3 more promising classifiers. Overall, *Random Forest* and *Decision Tree* yielded higher accuracy than Naive Bayes. We find also the same to be the case as far as AUC and F1-score metrics is concerned. *Random Forest* and *Decision Tree* feature a very short training phase around a fraction of millisecond. We observe similar trends in the average response time. Hence, we opted for deploying a *Random Forest* classifier for our prototype that correctly identifies 87% of all Twitter fake accounts.

5   Conclusions

We investigate the problem of classifying tweets composed in Greek. Due to its syntactic structure and complex grammar, the language presents challenges for building a highly accurate SA-model. Moreover, our intention has been to prevent non-contributing posts from ultimately being part of the discourse developed over time on specific topics. Our main objective has been to accurately classify incoming tweets, to base the foundation of our work on the use of off-the-shelf software components and to ascertain the utility of our proposed architecture. To better enable our proposed system, we have developed a *Naive-Bayes* SA-model based on a set of 10k captured tweets that we have manually classified as either positive or negative. We present various design choices in the context of ML-algorithms deployed and we are concerned with the overhead imposed so as to facilitate just-in-time handling of live tweets. Through experimentation, we establish both the effectiveness and efficiency of our prototype that is primarily based on Spark, the RabbitMQ messaging system, and the Redis database.

References

1. Bot Detection Dataset. https://www.kaggle.com/charvijain27/detecting-twitter-bot-data. Accessed 3 Apr 2020
2. Armbrust, M., et al.: Spark SQL: relational data processing in spark. In: Proceedings of ACM SIGMOD Conference, Melbourne, Australia, May–June 2015

3. Bestavros, A., Braoudakis, S.: Timeliness via speculation for real-time databases. In: Proceedings of the IEEE Real-Time Systems Symposium, San Juan, Puerto Rico, December 1994

4. Biyabani, S., Stankovic, J., Ramamritham, K.: The integration of deadline and criticalness in hard real-time scheduling. In: Proceedings of RT Symposium, Huntsville, AL, December 1988

5. Efthimion, P., Payne, S., Proferes, N.: Supervised machine learning bot detection techniques to identify social Twitter bots. SMU Data Sci. Rev. 1(2) (2018)

6. Ferrara, E., Varol, O., Davis, C., Menczer, F.: The rise of social bots. Commun. ACM 59(7), 96–104 (2016)

7. Giatsoglou, M., Vozalis, M., Diamantaras, K., Vakali, A., Sarigiannidis, G., Chatzisavvas, K.: Sentiment analysis leveraging emotions and word embeddings. Expert Syst. Appl. 69, 214–224 (2017)

8. Hardwick, J.: Top 100 Most Visited Web Sites by Search. ahrefs.com/blog/most-visited-websites. Accessed 9 May 2020

9. Howard, P.: How political campaigns weaponize social media bots. IEEE Spectr. (2018)

10. Juan, A., Ney, H.: Reversing and smoothing the multinomial Naive Bayes text classification. In: Proceedings of the 2nd International Workshop on PRIS, January 2002

11. Kalamatianos, G., Mallis, D., Symeonidis, S., Arampatzis, A.: Sentiment analysis of Greek tweets and hashtags using a sentiment lexicon. In: Proceedings of PCI Conference on Informatics, October 2015

12. Kanitkar, V., Delis, A.: Real-time processing in client-server databases. IEEE Trans. Comput. 51(3), 269–287 (2002)

13. Karageorgou, I.: Stemmed and Classified Tweet Dataset in Greek. www.github.com/ioannakarageorgou/grtweetsdataset. Accessed 9 May 2020

14. Karanasou, M., Ampla, A., Doulkeridis, C., Halkidi, M.: Scalable and real-time sentiment analysis of Twitter data. In: Proceedings of the ICDM SENTIRE Workshop, Barcelona, Spain, December 2016

15. Kellog, K.: 7 Biggest Social Media Sites in 2020. searchenginejournal.com/social-media/biggest-social-media-sites/. Accessed 9 May 2020

16. Kiritchenko, S., Zhu, X., Mohammad, S.: Sentiment analysis of short informal text. Artif. Intell. Res. 50, 723–762 (2014)

17. McCallum, A., Nigam, K.: Comparison of event models for Naive Bayes text classification. In: Proceedings of the AAAI/ICML-1998 Workshop on Learning for Text Categorization, pp. 41–48. AAAI Press (1998)

18. Nirmal, V., Amalarethinam, G.: Real-time sentiment prediction on streaming social network data using in-memory processing. In: World Congress on CCCT, Tiruchirappalli, India, June 2018

19. Papatheodorou, D.: Greek Stemmer. https://github.com/DimitrisCC/GrPolitics_Twitter_SentAnalysis/blob/5c165306f3cb00d001942013fd252589614a13f9/preprocessing.py. Accessed 3 Apr 2020

20. Rijsbergen, C.J.V.: Information Retrieval, 2nd edn. Butterworth-Heinemann, Waltham (1979)

21. Salloum, S., Dautov, R., Chen, X., Peng, P., Huang, J.: Big data analytics on apache spark. Int. J. Data Sci. Anal. 1, 145–164 (2016). https://doi.org/10.1007/s41060-016-0027-9

22. Shafahi, M., Kempers, L., Afsarmanesh, H.: Phishing through social bots on Twitter. In: Proceedings of 2016 IEEE International Conference on Big Data, Washington, DC (2016)

23. statista.com: Statista Inc. www.statista.com/statistics/970920/monetizable-daily-active-twitter-users-worldwide. Accessed 12 May 2020

24. Stonebraker, M., Cetintemel, U., Zdonik, S.: The 8 requirements of real-time stream processing. ACM SIGMOD-Rec. **34**, 42–47 (2005)

25. Tsakalidis, A., Papadopoulos, S., Voskaki, R., Boididou, C., Cristea, A., Liakata, M., Kompatsiaris, Y.: Building and evaluating resources for sentiment analysis in the Greek language. Lang. Resour. Eval. **52**, 1021–1044 (2018). https://doi.org/10.1007/s10579-018-9420-4

26. Zimbra, D., Abbasi, A., Zeng, D., Chen, H.: State-of-the-art in Twitter sentiment analysis: a review and benchmark evaluation. ACM Trans. MISs **9**(2), 1–29 (2018)

Smart Contract Satisfiability Checking for Blockchain Consistency

Salima Benbernou$^{(\boxtimes)}$ and Mourad Ouziri

Université de Paris, LIPADE, Paris, France
{salima.benbernou,mourad.ouziri}@u-paris.fr

Abstract. In a blockchain environment, smart contracts have been defined to be a way of setting up trust between parties by providing a self-executing equivalent of legal contracts. Besides, ensuring correctness and reliability of smart contracts is vital to checking trust in blockchain-based systems. In this paper, we discuss a logic-based approach in order to ensure the quality of the blockchain in terms of trustworthiness of smart contracts by considering some minors behaving as a *logical satisfiability* service. The service selection is designed as a Proof of Work of the minors.

Keywords: Blockchain · Smart contract · Proof of Work · QoS · Logic-based satisfiability

1 Introduction

Recently, a Blockchain has attracted great attention from both academia and industry [9,18]. A Blockchain is an emerging technology for decentralized and transactional data sharing across a large network of untrusted participants. It is a chain of blocks, in which each block contains many transactions and the history of all the exchanges made between its users since its creation, and is linked with the previous block by a pointer. The chain is replicated over a peer-to-peer (P2P) network, Each block is validated by the nodes of the network called the "miners". Generally speaking a Blockchain is a distributed and tamper resistant ledger that does not rely on a centralized authority to establish trust, with a core layer mechanism for decentralized trust management. The blockchain originally devised for the Bitcoin cryptocurrency [16]. A distributed consensus protocol, namely Proof-of-Work (PoW), is used to ensure that honest nodes in the network have the same ledger. The PoW was first introduced for Bitcoin blockchain, where it is considered as a piece of data which is difficult (costly, time-consuming) to produce but easy for others to verify and which satisfies certain requirements. The PoW consists in asking the miners of a blockchain to solve a complex mathematical problem requiring significant computing power. The higher the computing power controlled by a minor, the more likely he is to succeed in solving the mathematical problem in question first, and to pocket a

© Springer Nature Switzerland AG 2021
M. Aiello et al. (Eds.): Papazoglou Festschrift, LNCS 12521, pp. 264–272, 2021.
https://doi.org/10.1007/978-3-030-73203-5_20

reward for this work. Public blockchain systems, exemplified by cryptocurrencies such as Ethereum and Monero, use memory-hard proof-of-work (PoW) algorithms in consensus protocols to maintain fair participation without a trusted third party. However, PoW allows for inconsistency because the chain can have forks. These protocols handle forks by deterministically selecting one branch over the other. For example, in PoW the longest branch is selected.

Moreover, distributed applications collaborate with each other following service level agreements (SLAs) to provide different services. The SLAs can be written as self executing computer programs, called *smart contracts* [19] in the extended blockchain. A smart contract is therefore, an appealing feature of blockchain technology, it has its states stored on the blockchain, and the states are modified via transactions that invoke the contract. A smart contract is executable code that runs on top of the blockchain to facilitate, execute and enforce an agreement between untrusted parties without the involvement of a trusted third party. This process makes it possible to secure all of the data by preventing its modification or deletion afterwards. The earlier bockchain approaches proposed such extension after the PoW paradigm are Ethereum [1] and Hyperledger [2], which are enterprise oriented frameworks.

Despite recent intensive research, existing blockchain systems do not adequately address all the characteristics of distributed applications. In particular, the consistency of the blockchain. Current blockchain based systems focus on checking the smart contracts by checking the terms and conditions of its execution because it is tamper-proof. However, the semantic aspect of the contract is not at all handled. For example, a car constructor can not sell vegetables, but sells cars. In this paper, we propose a blokchain-based system managing the smart contract ensuring consistency through the network in addition to safety. To do so, in a nutshell, we consider each miner as a service and the approach will select the services according to their ability to validate a logical mathematical problem as a PoW. Once the miners are selected, the mining algorithm of miners to validate the consensus turns into logical operations mechanism.

In summary, we make the following contributions:

- A smart contract management approach to ensure the consistency of the blockchain beside the safety.
- A PoW-based service selection. A miner is considered as a service. The service selection is done according to the PoW.
- The PoW consensus is considered as a SAT solving problem: A framework based on the logical satisfiability checking to design a PoW in order to verify the QoS of minors for their selection in the contribution of consensus in order to make the blockchain consistent.

In the remainder of the paper, we present in Sect. 2 a motivation example. In Sect. 3 we discuss the related work. In Sect. 4 we provide the framework of the proposed approach, we discuss the semantic based approach to handle the blockchain consistency. We conclude the paper in Sect. 5.

2   Motivating Example

Let's consider the universities wish to manage their students in a secure/safety and consistent manner. To ensure the data safety, the universities decide to use the blockchain paradigm. The management covers the recruitment, registration and diploma award phases. In this domain, a smart contract takes the form of a student acceptation by the university, student registration to the university and student graduation from the university. That is, a smart contract is the record *(party 1, party 2, object)* where:

- *party 1* and *party 2* are the contracting parties of the smart contract, they can be a student, a university, a company or any contracting entity.
- *object* of the contract can be: admitted (on recruitment phase), registered, graduated, etc.

We show in what follows the shortcomings of existing blockchains in particular for the smart contracts and how the proposed blockchain in this paper makes it possible to meet the two quality objectives: security/unalterability/safety/reliability/integrity (non data falcification) and consistency. The universities define educational domain rules that govern the student management. These domain rules are used by the blockchain to ensure consistency.

Let's consider the following governance rules followed by the universities, namely *consistency rules* (CR):

- (CR1): Students are human. Only students can be recruited. In contrary, companies, countries and cities shouldn't.
- (CR2): Only students admitted in the recruitment phase can register.
- (CR3): Only registered students can be graduated.
- (CR4): Only higher education institution can award diploma. Companies and persons are not allowed to do it.

The blockchain depicted in Fig. 1.(a) contains smart contracts about:

- the admission of the students s1 and s2 to the university u1 (block 1) and the admission of the insurance company c1 to the university u2 (block 2),
- the registration of the students s1 and s2 to the universities u1 and u2 (blocks 2 and 3), respectively.
- the graduation of the students s1 by the university u1 (block 3).

This blockchain natively ensures safety. In fact, smart contracts are secured by hashing and linking the blocs together. Any alteration to any smart contract of a block will be easily detected as the hash of the block will not correspond to its content (smart contracts of the block) and the linking with the previous block will be broken. However, the semantic consistency of the smart contracts in the blockchain is not ensured as (1) the smart contract (s2, u2, registered) shouldn't be validated following the rule (CR2) because there is no prior admission of s2 in u2 (2) the smart contract (c1, u2, admitted) is inconsistent following the rule (CR1).

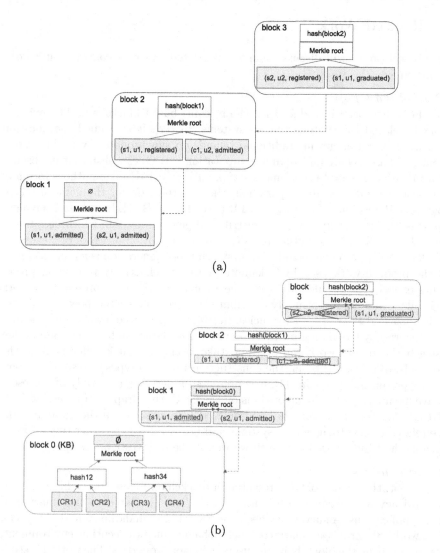

Fig. 1. An example of a blockchain with inconsistent smart contracts

We propose a logic-based blockchain to ensure the consistency of the smart contracts with respect to the above rules CR maintained in the head of the blockchain as depicted in Fig. 1.(b). The consistency of the blockchain is verified when a new contract is submitted to prevent the addition of any new contract that leads to inconsistencies in the blockchain. Rules are indexed in a Merkle tree to ensure safety (Block 0).

3   Related Work

In this section we will discuss some works related to smart contracts and PoW management.

-Proof of Work-PoW
The PoW has been introduced for the bitcoins based blockchain. The existing work is related to cryptocurrencies systems. In [12], it is studied the question of using Pow paradigm in traditional bounds on synchronous Byzantine agreement (BA) and secure multi-party computation (MPC) establish that in absence of a private correlated-randomness setup, such as a PKI. The authors formally demonstrate how the above paradigm changes the rules of the game in cryptographic definitions. The work in [14] is related to Blockchain-based payment systems here it is proposed a new distributed payment system which uses Incrementally Verifiable Computation (IVC) where the notion of Proof of Necessary Work (PoNW) has been introduced, in which proof generation is an integral part of the proof-of-work used in Nakamoto consensus,effectively producing proofs using energy that would other-wise be wasted. In [8], it is presented a work that allows miners to optimally distribute their computational power over multiple pools and PoW cryptocurrencies. In [10], it is proposed TwinsCoin, the first cryptocurrency based on a provably secure and scalable public blockchain design using both proof-of-work and proof-of-stake mechanism, it is different from the proof-of-work based Bitcoin, the construction uses two types of resources, computing power and coins. In [11], it is presented a performance study of representative memory-hard PoW algorithms on the CPU, the Graphics Processing Unit (GPU), and the Intel Knights Landing(KNL) processors. All the quoted works are related to cryptocurrencies systems and not handling the other type of PoW such as the logical based approach we would like to investigate in this work.

-Smart contracts
At present, the smart contract research in blockchain focuses on codifying, security, privacy and performance issues and the rest is related to the smart contract applications. A survey has been conducted in [5] handling smart contracts. The work [3] verifies a smart contract behavior in its execution environment, hence capturing the blockchain and users behavior properties. The work [17] studies the safety and security of smart contracts in the Azure Blockchain Workbench, an enterprise Blockchain-as-a-Service offering from Microsoft. The paper [7] discusses the runtime verification tool ContractLarva and outline its use in instrumenting monitors in smart contracts written in Solidity, for the Ethereum blockchain-based distributed computing platform. The work [4] presents syntactic verification of smart contract dedicated to automate a casino system application. It is proposed and approach an approach to verifying the smart contracts written in Solidity by automatically translating Solidity into Java and using, KeY, a deductive Java verification tool. In [15], it is discussed how to use the blockchain framework for trust management in the supply chain application. In [6] is presented CAPER, a permissioned blockchain system to support both internal and

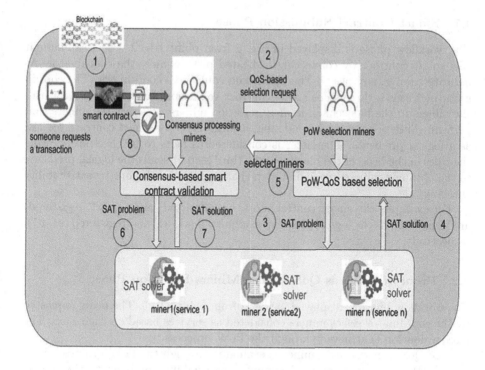

Fig. 2. Logic-based Blockchain Framework

cross-application transactions of collaborating distributed applications. All the quoted works are not handling the consistency checking of the smart contract.

4   Logic-Based Blockchain Framework

In this section, we discuss the logic-based blockchain framework. We propose to handle the consistency in addition to the safety basics of the blockchain. When someone submits a new smart contract, the validation process performs a logic reasoning to check the consistency of the smart contract upon the blockchain as depicted in Fig. 2. The process follows three main phases (i) Smart contract submission phase (ii) Proof of Work as QoS for the miners selection phase where each miner is considered as a service providing a work (iii) Logic-based consensus calculus phase. In what follow, we detail each phases.

The considered blockchain is a decentralized peer-to-peer architecture. The peers are miners which all perform the following same tasks: handling the submitted smart contracts, selecting miners, achieving tasks of the PoW and validating contracts.

4.1   Smart Contract Submission Phase

The workflow phase is displayed in Fig. 2 from point 1 to 2. Users can submit new smart contract by connecting dedicated peer, namely the coordinator. As indicated above, any peer in the blockchain could be a coordinator. The coordinator performs a three steps smart contract validation. In the first step, it asks the miners in the blockchain, namely selection miners, to select the miners that perform validation. In the second step, it formulates the smart contract request as a logical predicate. The latter is considered as facts to be checked following the rules in the head of the blocks. In the third step, it sends the logical predicate to the obtained miners in the first step that perform validation (by satisfiability checking).

For example, the smart contracts (s1, u1, admitted) and (s1, u1, registered) are formulated as the logical predicates: admitted (s1, u1) and registered (s1, u1), respectively.

4.2   Proof of Work as QoS for the Miners Selection Phase

The workflow phase is displayed in Fig. 2 from point 2 to 5. The peers requested by the coordinator select miners considered as services based on their QoS. The QoS evaluation is achieved through the PoW proccess.

The QoS provided by a miner is evaluated through the PoW proccess. That is, the "PoW selection miners" submit a satisfiability problem to the miners of the blockchain to be resolved. The miners use a SAT solver to resolve the satisfiability problem [13]. The QoS is measured based on the correctness of the returned resolution and the response time. The SAT problems are randomly generated following the two parameters: number of rules and predicates. These parameters allow to fit the complexity of the SAT problem. The miners with the required minimum QoS are selected and returned to the coordinator. The number of selected miners must respect a quorum to prevent of falsification. This is the first level of securing the validation process in our proposed logic-based approach.

4.3   Logic-Based Consensus Calculus Phase

The workflow of this phase is displayed in Fig. 2 from point 5 to 8. From point 5 each selector miner returns a set of miners that solve the logical problem of the query. The number of selection miners responding to this request must reach a minimum in order to avoid any malicious response in the blockchain.

If the coordinator does not receive the quorum, it restarts the process again. If after many attempts the quorum is still not reachable, the contract validation fails for safety. This is the second quorum of safety level.

Once the second quorum is reached, the coordinator sends the logic predicate to the selected minors to validate the contract using SAT solver. The validation responses will be sent to the coordinator (points 6–7). The validation of a new smart contract sc is achieved as the satifiability decision problem and expressed by the logical satisfiablity formula: $< \{Rules\}, \{Smarts\ contracts\} \cup sc > \not\models \bot$.

The final decision will be collectively taken by the miners using the majority voting based on the threshold percentage. This means that the smart contract is validated and then added to the blockchain if the percentage of the minors responding "SAT" (positive) is greater than a threshold δ.

For example, let's consider the blockchain starting with block 1 of Fig. 1. And let's validate the contract $(c1, u2, admitted)$. The coordinator submits the following SAT problem to the 100 selected miners:

$< \{CR1, ..., CR4\}, \{(s1, u1, admitted), (s2, u1, admitted)\} \cup (c1, u2, admitted) > \not\models \bot$. Based on the value of $\delta = 90\%$ and 95 miners respond UNSAT (negative), then the smart contract will not be validated.

5 Conclusion

In this paper, we discuss the trustworthiness of smart contracts and the consistency issues in the blockchain. We propose a logic-based blokchain system to manage the smart contract with ensuring consistency through the network in addition to safety. The safety is ensured by the traditional blockchain mechanism whereas consistency is ensured at two levels: (1) the QoS of the miners through a PoW as a SAT problem (2) the satifiability of the blockchain as a consistent logical knowledge base.

References

1. Ethereum blockchain app platform (2017). https://www.ethereum.org
2. Hyperledger (2020). https://www.hyperledger.org
3. Abdellatif, T., Brousmiche, K.: Formal verification of smart contracts based on users and blockchain behaviors models. In: 9th IFIP International Conference on New Technologies, Mobility and Security, NTMS 2018, Paris, France, 26–28 February 2018, pp. 1–5. IEEE (2018)
4. Ahrendt, W., Bubel, R., Ellul, J., Pace, G.J., Pardo, R., Rebiscoul, V., Schneider, G.: Verification of smart contract business logic. In: Hojjat, H., Massink, M. (eds.) FSEN 2019. LNCS, vol. 11761, pp. 228–243. Springer, Cham (2019). https://doi.org/10.1007/978-3-030-31517-7_16
5. Alharby, M., van Moorsel, A.: Blockchain-based smart contracts: a systematic mapping study. CoRR, abs/1710.06372 (2017)
6. Amiri, M.J., Agrawal, D., Abbadi, A.E.: CAPER: a cross-application permissioned blockchain. Proc. VLDB Endow. **12**(11), 1385–1398 (2019)
7. Azzopardi, S., Ellul, J., Pace, G.J.: Monitoring smart contracts: contractlarva and open challenges beyond. In: Colombo, C., Leucker, M. (eds.) RV 2018. LNCS, vol. 11237, pp. 113–137. Springer, Cham (2018). https://doi.org/10.1007/978-3-030-03769-7_8
8. Chatzigiannis, P., Baldimtsi, F., Griva, I., Li, J.: Diversification across mining pools: optimal mining strategies under pow. CoRR, abs/1905.04624 (2019)

9. Delgado-Mohatar, O., Fierrez, J., Tolosana, R., Vera-Rodriguez, R.: Blockchain and biometrics: a first look into opportunities and challenges. In: Prieto, J., Das, A.K., Ferretti, S., Pinto, A., Corchado, J.M. (eds.) BLOCKCHAIN 2019. AISC, vol. 1010, pp. 169–177. Springer, Cham (2020). https://doi.org/10.1007/978-3-030-23813-1_21

10. Duong, T., Chepurnoy, A., Fan, L., Zhou, H.-S.: TwinsCoin: a cryptocurrency via proof-of-work and proof-of-stake. In: Lokam, S.V., Ruj, S., Sakurai, K. (eds.) Proceedings of the 2nd ACM Workshop on Blockchains, Cryptocurrencies, and Contracts, BCC@AsiaCCS 2018, Incheon, Republic of Korea, 4 June 2018, pp. 1–13. ACM (2018)

11. Feng, Z., Luo, Q.: Evaluating memory-hard proof-of-work algorithms on three processors. Proc. VLDB Endow. 13(6), 898–911 (2020)

12. Garay, J., Kiayias, A., Ostrovsky, R.M., Panagiotakos, G., Zikas, V.: Resource-restricted cryptography: revisiting MPC bounds in the proof-of-work era. In: Canteaut, A., Ishai, Y. (eds.) EUROCRYPT 2020. LNCS, vol. 12106, pp. 129–158. Springer, Cham (2020). https://doi.org/10.1007/978-3-030-45724-2_5

13. Gomes, C.P., Kautz, H.A., Sabharwal, A., Selman, B.: Satisfiability solvers. In: van Harmelen, F., Lifschitz, V., Porter, B.W. (eds.) Handbook of Knowledge Representation, Volume 3 of Foundations of Artificial Intelligence, pp. 89–134. Elsevier (2008)

14. Kattis, A., Bonneau, J.: Proof of necessary work: succinct state verification with fairness guarantees. IACR Cryptol. ePrint Arch. 2020, 190 (2020)

15. Malik, S., Dedeoglu, V., Kanhere, S.S., Jurdak, R.: TrustChain: trust management in blockchain and IoT supported supply chains. In: IEEE International Conference on Blockchain, Blockchain 2019, Atlanta, GA, USA, 14–17 July 2019, pp. 184–193. IEEE (2019)

16. Nakamoto, S.: Bitcoin: a peer-to-peer electronic cash system (2009). http://bitcoin.org/bitcoin.pdf

17. Wang, Y., Lahiri, S.K., Chen, S., Pan, R., Dillig, I., Born, C., Naseer, I., Ferles, K.: Formal verification of workflow policies for smart contracts in Azure blockchain. In: Chakraborty, S., Navas, J.A. (eds.) VSTTE 2019. LNCS, vol. 12031, pp. 87–106. Springer, Cham (2020). https://doi.org/10.1007/978-3-030-41600-3_7

18. Zhang, Y., Zheng, Z., Dai, H.-N., Svetinovic, D.: Guest editorial: special section on "blockchain for industrial Internet of Things". IEEE Trans. Ind. Inf. 15(6), 3514–3515 (2019)

19. Zheng, Z., et al.: An overview on smart contracts: challenges, advances and platforms. Future Gener. Comput. Syst. 105, 475–491 (2020)

Author Index

Printed in the United States
by Baker & Taylor Publisher Services

Printed in the United States
by Baker & Taylor Publisher Services